An Introduction to International Migration Studies

European Perspectives

IMISCOE

International Migration, Integration and Social Cohesion in Europe

The IMISCOE Research Network unites researchers from, at present, 29 institutes specialising in studies of international migration, integration and social cohesion in Europe. What began in 2004 as a Network of Excellence sponsored by the Sixth Framework Programme of the European Commission became, as of April 2009, an independent self-funding endeavour. From the start, IMISCOE has promoted integrated, multidisciplinary and globally comparative research led by scholars from various branches of the economic and social sciences, the humanities and law. The network furthers existing studies and pioneers new scholarship on migration and migrant integration. Encouraging innovative lines of inquiry key to European policymaking and governance is also a priority.

The IMISCOE-Amsterdam University Press Series makes the network's findings and results available to researchers, policymakers and practitioners, the media and other interested stakeholders. High-quality manuscripts authored by network members and cooperating partners are evaluated by external peer reviews and the IMISCOE Editorial Committee. The committee comprises the following members:

IMISCOE Policy Briefs and more information can be found at www.imiscoe.org.

An Introduction to International Migration Studies

European Perspectives

edited by Marco Martiniello & Jan Rath

IMISCOE Textbooks

Amsterdam University Press

Cover design: Studio Jan de Boer BNO, Amsterdam
Layout: The DocWorkers, Almere

ISBN 978 90 8964 456 5
e-ISBN 978 90 4851 735 0 (pdf)
e-ISBN 978 90 4851 736 7 (ePub)
NUR 741 / 763

Contents

Chapter Abstracts

1 An Introduction to International Migration Studies: European Perspectives

Marco Martiniello and Jan Rath

No country in Europe is unaffected by migration, although its impact varies from place to place. Immigration is often associated with undermined social cohesion, urban crime, domestic insecurity and public health issues. Immigrants are increasingly regarded as a liability for the welfare state, for the educational system and for economic prosperity. But while Europe is preoccupied with immigration, isn't it once again becoming a continent of emigration? Are we not already seeing the first signs of a new European exodus as a response to the economic crisis affecting Europe at all levels? What is the situation in Europe today? What theoretical perspectives are now at the fore in international debates; and what concepts and controversies have emerged? In fact, Europe needs new immigrants to contribute to economic development and to support national welfare and pension systems. This chapter's authors consider these issues, attempting to describe, analyse, understand and explain them.

Part I: Theoretical Perspectives

2 Beyond 'Push-Pull': The Economic Approach to Modelling Migration

Dragos Radu and Thomas Straubhaar

This chapter presents recent developments in the economic analysis of migration. Its aim is to introduce students of social sciences other than economics to the application of the neoclassical research programme in migration studies. We briefly survey the main research questions addressed by economists in relation to labour migration, and present some of their methodological assumptions and limitations. Four main themes can be identified in the economic literature on migration: (i) the determinants; (ii) the economic effects of migration; (iii) the experiences of migrants; and (iv) the political economy of migration policy. Our focus lies on models that analyse migration decision-making (initiation and perpetuation of migration flows). We particularly emphasise the effort to incorporate into formal economic models concepts that have been traditionally pursued separately in economics and sociology. Can economics account for socially mediated influences on migration choices? Recent theoretical and empirical research uses non-market interactions to explain specific aspects of migrants' decisions concerning settlement, duration of stay and labour market integration, which had not been accounted for in the standard approach.

3 Historical-Structural Models of International Migration

Ewa Morawska

Historical-structural models of international migration represent a variety of approaches. However, they all share two major premises; namely, the location of the causes of international migration in the realm of historically specific macro-structural forces and the primacy of the disequalising economic forces of capitalism in explaining the directions and character of transnational population movements. This chapter first gives an overview and critical assessment of three major theories representing the historical-structural approach: segmented labour markets theory; dependency theory; and world system theory. Then the most recent structuration model of international migration is presented, which attempts to bridge the macro-micro gap in this field of study by retaining the historical-structural part of the explanation of transnational population flows and linking it with the micro-level, actors-focused mode of interpretation.

4 Social Networks and International Migration

Monica Boyd and Joanne Nowak

This chapter provides a comprehensive overview of the relationship between social networks and international migration. It begins with a detailed definition of the concept of social networks and outlines the historical relationship between social networks and migration research. Next, the different types of networks typically involved in the migration process are described, with a focus on three key networks in the migration literature – labour, personal (family) and illegal networks, as well as the costs and benefits of each of these networks to migrants. The internal and external influences shaping migrant networks are then discussed, followed by conceptual and methodological critiques of the social networks approach. In the conclusion, future areas of research to expand the field of migration and social networks are suggested.

5 Transnational Migration

Eva Østergaard-Nielsen

This chapter introduces a selection of the empirical, theoretical and methodological discussions on the meaning, scope and impact of transnational migration. This includes a review of the proliferation of the transnational perspective in migration studies over the last decade, and a critical analysis of the long-standing debates on the scope, representativity, durability and newness of the different dimensions of migrant transnationalism. These discussions include both earlier, more exploratory studies and more recent critical calls for closer scrutiny of the local and global politics of migrant transnational practices and the impact of transnational relations on migrant livelihood. The final sections present recent contributions to the ongoing methodological discussion on how to grasp the complexity of transnational migration. Throughout the chapter particular attention is paid to the politics of migrant transnationalism at the local, national and international levels.

6 *Jus Sanguinis* and *Jus Soli*: Aspects of Ethnic Migration and Immigration Policies in EU states

Eftihia Voutira

This chapter analyses and reconceptualises the two state-based principles seen from the standpoint of international law as the key determinants of nationality rights: *jus sanguinis* (the law of kinship) and *jus soli* (the law of residence). The main hypothesis is that east-west migration has been construed on the level of EU kin state policies as 'privileged return migration' (e.g. Germans, Greeks, and Finns from the FSU) in light of these ethnic groups' right to return to their respective historical homeland. The chapter also presents the debate between the different philosophies of 'membership' and state incorporation, i.e. liberal, communitarian and ethnic. Finally, it addresses the issue of the post-Soviet Russian diaspora as a case of *jus sanguinis* migration from an anthropological perspective.

7 Migration and Social Transformation

Stephen Castles

Studies of migration play a very limited role in the general social theories that seek to provide a framework for analysing contemporary society. In fact, a great deal of migration research is driven not by scientific inquiry, but by policy needs. This chapter argues for a conceptual framework for migration studies that overcomes its isolation from wider issues of global power, wealth and inequality. This proposed framework is based on a concept of social transformation deriving from the work of Karl Polyani. The accelerated social transformation processes arising from neo-liberal globalisation form a crucial context for analysing migration. The chapter argues for a broad interdisciplinary approach to migration studies and for the linking of micro-level studies of local causes and effects of migration to a broader political economy of global relationships. Linking across socio-spatial levels also means addressing the dialectics of structure and agency in every aspect of human mobility.

Part II: Types of Migration

8 Guest Worker Migration in Post-War Europe (1946-1974): An Analytical Appraisal

Ahmet Akgündüz

Guest worker migration in post-war Europe was not a new phenomenon, but the resumption of a well-established pattern. In general, migrant workers were initially recruited to primarily work in agriculture, mining, construction, and other jobs that were unattractive to native labourers. From the early 1960s on, however, migrants were attracted as a response to labour shortages, not only in agriculture, mining, construction, or in the secondary sector, but specifically in industry. In the leading labour-recruiting countries (e.g. Germany, France, Switzerland and the Netherlands) in particular, the majority of migrant workers were employed in the manufacturing industry; though mainly in low-status, low-paying jobs with inferior legal, political and social rights. The admission policy was initially 'Southern Europeans only'; however, when the volume of supply from Southern European countries became insufficient, this policy became 'Southern Europeans first'. Western Europe was very successful at tightly regulating the admission of foreign labour according to demand.

9 Skilled Migration in Europe and Beyond: Recent Developments and Theoretical Considerations

Aimee Kuvik

This chapter discusses aspects central to the theoretical understanding of and European research on skilled migration. It begins by discussing the various definitions of skilled migration, the lack of internationally comparative statistics and the relatively low numbers of skilled migrants in many European countries. It then gives an overview of recent developments, with an emphasis on the global increase in policy interest in skilled migration, such as the expansion of multinational companies and international businesses in the 1980s and the global shortage of IT workers in the 1990s. Following this overview, theoretical perspectives are discussed, drawing on general theories for labour migration, network theories and individual determinants of migration, and their application to skilled migration processes. The final section highlights new paradigms that are emerging; particularly, the global competition for talent and skilled migration as a contributor to economic and human capital development, and issues for further research in Europe.

10 Environmental Migration

François Gemenne

The topic of environmental migration has recently gained significant currency on the international agenda, and is often described as one of the most grave humanitarian consequences of climate change. Yet this issue had – until recently – been little addressed by migration studies, despite the fact that environmental changes have played a key role as migration drivers throughout history. This chapter aims to address the main theoretical debates surrounding the concept of environmental migration in order to provide an assessment of the state of research on the subject to date. The first part describes the studies that have been conducted thus far, and takes a critical look at the emergence of environmental migration as a new field in migration studies. The second part addresses the key controversial issues of current debates: definitions, estimates and models. Finally, a third part assesses what we know of the environment-migration nexus, and what have been the major advances and challenges of research.

11 Student Migration

Russell King and Allan Findlay

The international moves of students are an important but often overlooked component of global migration. Such moves can be divided into 'credit' mobility, where students move for a short period, such as a semester, and then return to their home institutions to complete their programme, and 'degree' mobility, where students complete an entire study programme abroad, such as a bachelor's or doctoral degree. Student migration/mobility is designed to acquire human capital, and may be a prelude to an international career or further migrations after graduation; issues of 'brain drain' may also arise. Theoretically, student migration may be viewed as a subset of skilled migration; as part of the globalisation of higher education, and as part of a 'youth culture' of travel and mobility. It is also a phenomenon with strong social-class implications. The final part of the chapter looks at the geography of international student migration: North America, North-West Europe and Australia are key destinations; China, India, South Korea and Japan the major sources. Different patterns, however, pertain to credit-mobility schemes such as the Erasmus exchange programme.

12 Sunset Migration

Russell King

'Sunset migration' is about the movement, around retirement age, of usually middle- and upper-class individuals, often couples, to places where climate and other environmental factors (scenery, proximity to the sea, cultural resources) are the main attractions. Within Europe, these are north-to-south migrations targeting regions such as coastal Spain, the Balearic and Canary Islands, southern France, Tuscany, Malta and Cyprus. It can be viewed as a kind of 'lifestyle migration', but it is also often linked to a prior history of mobility such as living abroad as 'expats', or visiting the retirement destination as a tourist. The chapter reviews different typologies of retirement migration, the driving forces behind it, and social and economic impacts. That last includes settlement and housing types, issues of integration or non-integration and demands placed on local health and welfare services. For the retirees, difficult decisions have to be made when faced with challenges such as physical or mental illness or the loss of a partner.

13 Undocumented Migration: An Explanatory Framework

Joanne van der Leun and Maria Ilies

In an open world, people inevitably move across borders. Forces pushing people out of their countries and pulling them towards others will not disappear. If immigrants are not allowed to come legally, they come illegally. Drawing upon the vast literature on irregular immigration, this chapter provides social science students with tools to understand the concept of irregular immigration. This concept is difficult to grasp, as immigration policies and scientific texts often do not directly define who is an irregular immigrant. Throughout the chapter, the authors look at how irregular immigration is constructed and defined, how theoretical frameworks explain the movement and integration of people, and how receiving governments manage the flows and stocks of illegal immigrants. In addition, an overview of recent estimates of the number of irregular migrants is provided.

Part III: Regulation of Migration

14 Whither EU Immigration After the Lisbon Treaty?

Elspeth Guild

The EU has gradually acquired a central role in the definition of migration and its regulation in the 27 member states of the European Union. In this process, the member states have increasingly ceased to be participants in regulating migration in their territory, instead acting as the operational branch of EU regulation – carrying out (more or less faithfully) the migration laws and regulations that have been adopted at the EU level. This move away from national competence to unilaterally determine the content of immigration law and to facilitate the execution of EU adopted law has been masked in many of the larger member states, but a discourse exists that still insists on national sovereignty in respect to border controls, immigration controls and residence of foreigners. Nonetheless, the Europeanisation of EU immigration law is well developed and likely will continue to be consolidated at the supranational level.

15 The Regulation of Undocumented Migration

Giuseppe Sciortino

The presence of sizeable numbers of undocumented foreign residents is a regular feature of contemporary economically developed societies. However, their presence is perceived as a challenge to existing notions of political statehood and societal membership. This chapter analyses the historical evolution of the notion of undocumented residents, showing how it is strictly linked to – and contingent upon – changes in the system of internal controls within the territory of modern, liberal nation-states. It is subsequently argued that such an undocumented population is highly stratified, with different degrees of visibility and deportability. In addition to ignoring them, there are three broad strategies with which democratic states may regulate their undocumented populations: increasing the risks and costs of irregular residence through tightening the control on access to housing and labour markets as well as to welfare provisions; trying to remove them either voluntarily or through deportation; or promoting an adjustment of status that brings such a population – or a segment of it – within the bounds of official life.

1 An Introduction to International Migration Studies: European Perspectives

Marco Martiniello and Jan Rath

The vast majority of the world's citizens (some 97 per cent) never move house beyond their native country's borders. Only three per cent is internationally mobile. That is one out of every 33 persons in the world today.[1] The *share* of international migrants in the world population has been very stable over the past twenty years, but the absolute number has increased considerably – from an estimated 150 million individuals in 2000 to approximately 214 million in 2010. Much of this rise is due to global population growth. While most migrants stay within their own region of origin, a relatively small number of the 'huddled masses'[2] of men and women land in Europe: an estimated 72.1 million in 2010.[3] The share of 'first generation' international migrants in Europe in relation to the region's total population rose from 6.9 per cent in 1990 to 9.5 per cent in 2010.[4] This international migration has no doubt changed the face of Europe (Castles and Miller 1999).

migrant populations

Advanced economies in the north-western part of Europe constituted the first migration catchment areas after World War II. Guest workers from Spain and Italy, and later also from other countries in the Mediterranean, gravitated to the manufacturing industries in Germany, France, the Benelux, Nordic countries and Switzerland (Martiniello 2006). Furthermore, millions of people from former colonial areas outside Europe moved to their 'motherlands' in the United Kingdom, France and the Netherlands. Those from Spanish and Portuguese colonies followed later, though at a much lower rate. At that time, Southern and Central European countries (but also countries such as Ireland) were predominantly sending countries, insofar as they were involved in international migration at all. More recently, Ireland, Spain, Portugal, Greece, Italy and a number of countries in Central Europe transformed into receiving countries and transit countries. West and north-west Europe now serves as a magnet for hundreds of thousands of newcomers from Latin America (particularly to the Iberian Peninsula), Central and Eastern Europe and beyond. In the meantime, refugees and asylum seekers from war zones all over the world have flocked to Europe hoping to find a safe haven. Today, professionals are moving to the centres of knowledge economies. These modern day 'guest workers' are known as 'expats', as are the students who enrol *en masse* in Europe's universities and other educational facilities. There are several other categories of migrants as well. There are those who used to be labelled 'spontaneous guest workers' but who today are labelled 'illegal' or 'undocumented migrants'. There are those who seek adventure, a new lifestyle, friendship or love. Europeans too are enjoying the right to free mobility. No country in Europe is unaffected by these migratory flows, although their impact varies from place to place.

categories of migrants

One question that has been ignored in the debates concerning migration in Europe is that of the impact of the global crisis and its European incarnations on migratory movements going outwards from this continent. In other words, while Europe is preoccupied with immigration, is it not once again becoming a continent of emigration? Are we not already seeing the first signs of a new European exodus in response to the economic crisis? After all, the social and political consequences of the crisis have been to increasingly deprive the European youth of employment opportunities in a very tight job market. These questions might gain prominence in the near future.

first-generation immigrants

It should be noted that, so far, we have only addressed *first-generation* immigrants. In public (and sometimes also in social scientific) discourses, 'migrants' and 'immigrants' or 'migration' and 'immigration' have become fuzzy concepts, and are used to refer to first- *and* second-generation immigrants, and occasionally even to third-generation immigrants. Here, we follow a stricter logic.

Tables 1.1, 1.2 and 1.3, as well as Figure 1.1, present numbers and shares of first-generation immigrants in Europe. To be sure, these figures refer only to those newcomers who followed a formal route; undocumented migrants are not included. Estimates of their numbers range between 2.8 and 6 million.[5] These numbers should actually be added to the official statistics. Also, these statistics only give a picture of Europe as a whole, and for specific European countries as a whole. Clearly, however, immigrants are not evenly spread throughout each country. They tend to gravitate to large cities rather than to smaller towns and rural areas, and within these cities to particular neighbourhoods. Though immigrants tend to be found in Europe's big cities rather than small villages, it is sometimes surprising to find immigrants in remote places, where they are active in agricultural jobs, such as in Southern Italy and Greece.

view of immigration

Contrary to what these impressive statistics might suggest, immigration is currently not popular among host populations (Rath 2011). There are contradictory discourses on immigration and a range of

Table 1.1 *Immigrants in Europe, 1990-2010 (thousands)*

Year	*Estimated number of international migrants at mid-year*
1990	49,401
1995	54,718
2000	57,639
2005	64,399
2010	69,819

Source: http://esa.un.org/migration/p2k0data.asp, accessed 31 October 2011

Table 1.2 *Stock of immigrants in Western and Central Europe, by destination: Top ten destinations, 2010 (thousands)*

Country	*Estimated number of international migrants at mid-year*
Germany	10,758
France	6,685
United Kingdom	6,452
Spain	6,378
Italy	4,463
Switzerland	1,763
Netherlands	1,753
Turkey	1,411
Austria	1,310
Sweden	1,206

Source: http://esa.un.org/migration/p2k0data.asp, accessed 31 October 2011

Table 1.3 *Stock of immigrants, by destination, as proportion of total population in Western and Central Europe: Top ten destinations, 2010 (%)*

Country	*Percentage of international migrants*
Luxembourg	35.2
Liechtenstein	34.6
Switzerland	23.2
Ireland	19.6
Cyprus	17.5
Croatia	15.9
Austria	15.6
Latvia	15.0
Spain	14.1
Sweden	14.1

Source: http://esa.un.org/migration/p2k0data.asp, accessed 31 October 2011

Figure 1.1 *Total population in European countries (as of 1 January 2012) and net rate of migration (2011)*

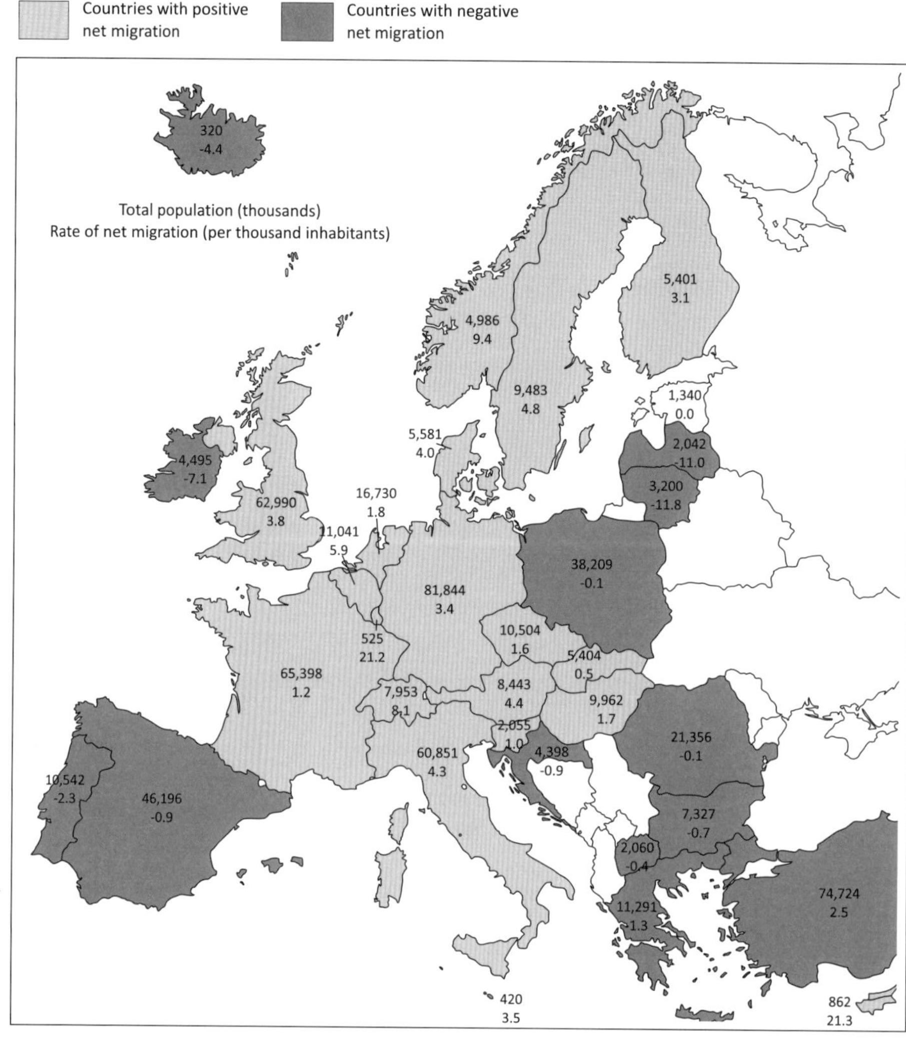

Source: Map from d-maps.com. Data from Eurostat.

attitudes towards migrants. Many Europeans consider immigration to be a historic mistake (unless, perhaps, it concerns an outstanding African or Brazilian football player), something that should have been avoided in the past and should be avoided in the future. Immigration has indeed become associated with the degradation of social cohesion, urban safety, domestic security and public health, and immigrants are increasingly regarded as a liability for the welfare state, the educational system and economic prosperity. The view of immigration as a burden for 'our society' is undoubtedly associated with the proliferation of volatile electoral and media campaigns in which savvy political and media entrepreneurs can relatively easily and successfully mobilise anti-immigration and anti-immigrant sentiments. In various countries, political movements are winning electoral support by claiming that immigration can be reduced to zero or less.

perceptions of immigration

However, not every European believes that a dramatic reduction in immigration is actually possible, or that it should even be sought after. Some take immigration and mobility as a fact of modern life and appreciate the concomitant emergence of new forms of diversity. Others take the more pragmatic view that international mobility is a prerequisite for economic prosperity and social well-being. After all, who will do both the appealing and unappealing work once the baby boomers have retired and the population is declining? To whom will they sell their houses in an otherwise shrinking housing market? Since the end of the 1990s, the European Union's official discourse on immigration has underlined the growing need for new immigrants to help European economic development in the future and to support national welfare and pension systems (Martiniello 2006). This does not mean that the EU advocates an open border policy; rather, it favours a selective approach to migration based on the principle of economic utility for the European continent.

It is clear that these discussions impact – directly and indirectly – future migratory flows. Strict immigration laws have been implemented, partly in response to the unfavourable political mood, but also in an attempt to protect the welfare state and to smooth out the integration difficulties of newcomers in their host society. Immigration rules and regulations (to some extent) take into account the dynamics of migration movements, address their root causes and interfere in the specificities of migratory trajectories in various ways (Penninx, Berger and Kraal 2006).

European body of knowledge

Social scientists have followed these processes and tried to describe, analyse, understand and explain them. In Europe, researchers found inspiration in the scholarship of their counterparts in the classic countries of immigration, such as Canada, the United States and also Australia. But as time progressed, increasing numbers of European researchers embarked on the development of a European body of knowledge. While migration to classic countries of immigration and to European countries displays many similarities, and while these similarities point to the influence of global structural processes, there remain a plethora of local and regional specificities.

theoretical perspectives

This handbook brings some of this European scholarship together; or more precisely, it brings together a sample of the scholarship that matters for Europe. The first part of the book showcases and discusses a number of theoretical perspectives on international migration. Is international migration just a matter of push and pull or demand and supply, comparable with what – according to neoclassical economists – happens in market economies? Are individuals and households driven by rational decisions? Or is migration propelled by historically specific macro-structural forces, notably the disequalising economic forces of capitalism? International migration could then be approached using a segmented labour market, dependency or world-system theory. Perhaps international migration is a network-driven phenomenon, and thus the product of social capital. Turks would then migrate to Frankfurt or Berlin rather than to Porto or Aberdeen, because they are connected to other Turks who already reside in those places. We have to consider the perseverance of transnational linkages. International mobility is not a one-off event, a single movement from A to B; instead, it is a lasting system of continual cross-border connection and mobility from A to B and vice versa, or from A to C to B, and so forth.

In the following six chapters, Dragos Radu and Thomas Straubhaar, Ewa Morawska, Monica Boyd and Joanne Nowak, Eva Østergaard-Nielsen, Eftihia Voutira and Stephen Castles present and critically discuss these different theoretical perspectives. Stephen Castles addresses the more general issues of the interrelationship of international migration and social transformation, locating migration studies within general social sciences theoretical discussions. Eftihia Voutira looks into the situation of so-called *jus sanguinis* migration, that is, the migration that is permitted or even encouraged on the basis of joint ancestry and joint ethnic, racial or religious belonging. Taken together, these chapters stress the added value of combining micro-, meso- and macro-level theorisations to understand and explain multidimensional social phenomena with respect to international migration.

types of migration

The next six chapters, forming part II of the book, address different types of migration. Clearly, the cross-border mobility of, say, guest workers involves a different category of people, occupying a different class position, engaging in different types of inter-ethnic relations and enjoying a different set of opportunities than, for example, international students or pensioners and retirees. Ahmet Akgündüz discusses guest worker migration. Aimee Kuvik explores the migration of highly-skilled professionals. François Gemenne investigates environmental migration movements. Russell King and Alan Findlay examine student migration. In a separate chapter, Russell King considers the sunset migration of pensioners and retirees. Finally, Joanne van der Leun and Maria Illies review undocumented immigrants.

The book concludes with a third part made up of two chapters, the first by Elspeth Guild and the second by Giuseppe Sciortino. These discuss the regulation of international migration, including the development of migration law in Europe and elsewhere, its effect on migration movements, the development of an informal migration system and the effect of the informal migration system on the rise of a trafficking and smuggling industry.

The editors selected, and subsequently approached, these authors on the basis of their expertise in these topics. Contributors were encouraged to provide overviews of the state-of-the art: what is the situation? What theoretical perspectives have come to the fore in international debates? What concepts and controversies have emerged? The book thus provides a thorough theoretical introduction to the field of international migration. (The field of immigrant integration will be addressed in a subsequent volume). This does not mean, however, that the editors and authors have presented a complete picture of all issues surrounding migration. Students of international migration should be aware that this is just an introduction, albeit a helpful one, for those who are interested in understanding the core features of European migration and ethnic studies.

MAIN IDEAS

There is no doubt that international migration has changed the face of Europe.

One question that has been completely ignored in the debates concerning migration in Europe is that of the impact of the global crisis and its European incarnations on migratory movements.

Official EU discourse on immigration underlines the growing need for new immigrants to contribute to European economic development and support national welfare and pension systems.

Are individuals and households driven by rational decisions? Or does migration follow historically specific macro-structural forces, notably the disequalising economic forces of capitalism?

Notes

1 http://esa.un.org/migration/p2kodata.asp, accessed 31 October 2011.
2 This term is borrowed from Ghosh (1998).
3 http://esa.un.org/migration/p2kodata.asp, accessed 31 October 2011.
4 http://esa.un.org/migration/p2kodata.asp, accessed 31 October 2011.
5 These estimates are from 2005. See additional details by Van der Leun and Ilies in chapter 13 of this volume.

References

Castles, S. and M. Miller (1999), *The Age of Migration.* 4th ed. New York: Guilford Press.

Ghosh, B. (1998), *Huddled Masses and Uncertain Shores: Insights into Irregular Migration.* Heidelberg: Springer.

IOM (2010), *The Future of Migration: Building Capacities for Change.* World Migration Report 2010. Geneva: International Organization for Migration.

Martiniello, M. (2006), 'The new migratory Europe: Towards a proactive immigration policy?', in: G. Parsons, and T. Smeeding (eds), *Immigration and the Transformation of Europe,* 298-326. Cambridge: Cambridge University Press.

Penninx, R., M. Berger and K. Kraal (eds) (2006), *The Dynamics of Migration and Settlement in Europe: A State of the Art.* IMISCOE Joint Studies. Amsterdam: Amsterdam University Press.

Rath, J. (2011), 'Debating multiculturalism: Europe's reaction in context', *Harvard International Review.* http://hir.harvard.edu/debating-multiculturalism?page=0,0. Accessed 1 November 2011.

Part I

Theoretical Perspectives

2 Beyond 'Push-Pull': The Economic Approach to Modelling Migration

Dragos Radu and Thomas Straubhaar

Introduction

Studies of labour migration currently abound in economics, both in the more theoretical branches of the discipline and in empirical research. Economists have always had an interest in analysing labour mobility and the determinants and consequences of location choices. In recent decades, labour migration has become a central feature of many macroeconomic models. It has also been studied in great detail in applied microeconomic analyses.

key themes

Traditionally, migration research in economics has centred on four key themes. First, the *determinants of migration* have been the focus of studies that analyse migration decision-making processes and secular trends and fluctuations in migration flows. The second key theme is the *economic consequences of migration* for the sending and receiving societies. These have been analysed from both a short-term welfare perspective and a long-term view regarding the economic growth effects of migration. Recent empirical studies have focused on the labour market, examining the impacts of immigration and emigration on wages and employment rates, respectively, for natives in the destination countries and for stayers in the home countries. A third theme, and one on which there is increased interest among economists, is the *experience of migrants* in their countries of destination. Research on this theme has contributed to the refining of explanations of migrants' labour market integration, the mechanisms of labour market discrimination, the economic behaviour of migrants and their intergenerational mobility, as well as choices over their duration of stay abroad. Fourth, economists have modelled changes in *migration policy* regimes using neoclassical theories of trade and factor mobility. Similarly, they have tested the predictions of economic theory with regard to public attitudes towards immigration. These four themes are interrelated, and sometimes overlap. While the specific research questions explored offer an infinitely more richly shaded mosaic, these topics provide a useful synopsis for understanding the potential and limitations of an economic approach to the study of migration.

This chapter briefly introduces these research topics and discusses some of the methodological assumptions they entail. One aim is to show how advances in both theoretical modelling and empirical implementation have managed to define the economic counterparts of concepts from other social sciences.

Economic models of migration have been criticised for their inability to account for the non-economic determinants of migration (Massey 1998: 8). This critique is partly legitimate. After all, it is logical that the economic dimension of migration choices constitutes the main interest of modelling in economics. However, as this chapter argues, there is a longer tradition in the literature that tries to loosen the exclusive focus on economic discrepancies between areas of origin and destination.

economic theories of migration

This chapter explores the argument that economic theories of migration have evolved incrementally. The simple version of the standard model has been gradually refined to incorporate social determinants of migration. Due to the particularities of the economic method, economists modelling migration decisions were often obliged to trade breadth for rigour. Therefore, migration models in economics consider many complex non-market systems and interrelations between economic, social and political institutions only in terms of abstract generality. Even though the reductionist assumptions of economic models are certainly imperfect as descriptions of real migration behaviour, refinements of the standard framework have been fruitful in enabling the economic analysis of a wide range of subtleties of migration choices.

Developments in the economic modelling of migration are reviewed in a number of prominent articles (Molho 1986; Straubhaar 1988; Shields and Shields 1989; Greenwood 1975, 1985, 1997; Greenwood et al. 1991; Ghatak et al. 1996; Cushing and Poot 2004; Gaston and Nelson 2011). Comprehensive textbook treatments of migration models are provided by Borjas (2009 ch. 8), Ehrenberg and Smith (2011 ch. 10) and Bodvarsson and Van den Berg (2009). The current chapter adds a new perspective, focusing primarily on the social spill-overs included in these models.

This chapter begins by introducing the basic methodological assumptions of migration modelling in economics. The first section reviews developments in conventional migration models, arguing that the basic human capital type models of migration have been supplemented rather than challenged by the newer models. The second section addresses approaches for conceptualising social interactions in migration behaviour from a theoretical perspective, subsequently presenting some empirical examples. The third section briefly introduces the basic mechanisms used to analyse the economic consequences of migration. It explains how the concepts of selection and self-selection have been applied in migration research. The last section of the chapter summarises outcomes of new economic research on the interaction of network effects with migration policies beyond regulation and selection mechanisms. This offers a foundation for reconsidering the possibilities and limitations of interdisciplinary linkages in migration research.

A primer on the structure of economic models of migration

There is no single, unified theoretical approach in economics that can be employed to simultaneously study all aspects of the four themes mentioned above. Existing models explore only specific aspects, and there is no consensus as to which approach is most promising. Models that focus on narrowly defined topics may even be logically inconsistent with one another (Borjas 1989).

However, methodologically there is common ground for the steady development and refinement of an economic theory of migration. This refers to the two points of departure in the economic approach to labour migration: first, the Heckscher-Ohlin theory of international trade, and second, what can be called 'the human (capital) investment revolution in economic thought' (Blaug 1980).

The immigration market

In its standard form, the Heckscher-Ohlin theory regards migration and trade as substitutes, arguing that trade, commodity price convergence and labour migration lead to an equalisation of the costs of factors of production. In this framework, if a labour abundant country exports labour intensive goods, this can be regarded as equivalent to an 'export' of labour. Therefore, the theoretical predictions of trade theory with regard to flows of goods can be applied symmetrically to migration flows (Mundel 1957; Ethier 1985).

theoretical foundations

The second theoretical foundation of migration research in economics stems from the human capital research programme, which was introduced in the early 1960s. The human capital approach is in fact the application of standard capital theory to certain economic or social phenomena. These phenomena may concern choices, for example, related to health, education, job search and migration. Whether undertaken by individuals or by social groups on behalf of their members, such choices can be viewed and modelled as investment decisions rather than as consumption. The main common feature of these phenomena is not the level (individual or social) at which decisions are taken, but the fact that the decision maker looks forward to the future to justify present action.

The standard (neoclassical) assumptions

Like other models in the field of economics, models of migration have two general features. The first is an underlying behavioural theory that describes the characteristics of the agents. The second is a model of the environment in which the actions of the agents take place. In the neoclassical tradition, the environment is represented by the market system, presupposing the functioning of all relevant institutions and also the scarcity of resources. Its counterpart in migration research is the immigration market, described above.

simple assumptions

In its starkest form, the economic approach uses two simple assumptions about individual agents: they are modelled as rational decision makers, and they are assumed to be motivated purely by self-interest. The rationality assumption itself has two components. First, agents are assumed to form correct expectations about their environment and about the choices of other agents. Second, given these expectations, agents are assumed to make choices consistent with their preferences, that is, they choose those alternatives that best satisfy their preferences. These preferences are postulated to be self-regarding, which is to say they are not affected by other agents.[1]

These strong and simplifying assumptions render a simplistic modelling of individual behaviour. Such simplification is indispensable for complex social phenomena like migration. Without it, economic models of migration would become formally intractable and their explanatory power would be lost.

Fischer, Martin and Straubhaar (1997) apply this canonical model to the immigration market. They adopt the three basic assumptions mentioned before:

1. Potential migrants have perfect information (i.e. they form correct expectations).
2. Potential migrants are unconditionally rational (i.e. they behave consistently).
3. Potential migrants are autonomous agents, with no social context (i.e. are self-regarding).

To these they add another three oversimplifying assumptions to illustrate the basic features of an immigration market:

4. Migration is cost-free.
5. Migration is risk-free.
6. Potential migrants are a homogenous group of people.

Fischer, Martin and Straubhaar (1997) discuss step-by-step how these assumptions can and have been adjusted in economic models to allow for more generality, and what can be learned from such an exercise.

This chapter uses a similar route to trace the evolution of migration modelling in economics. However, apart from relaxing some of the assumptions, it shows how the human capital approach has been used to incorporate more complexity and realism.

Determinants of migration: Human capital theory

One empirical puzzle challenging migration research in economics is the observation of labour migration patterns, which are often inconsistent with the predictions of neoclassical models. Examples of *prima facie* evidence defying the standard economic theory include, for example, the absence of migration despite persistent income gaps; or the presence of substantial migration flows even where there is little economic discrepancy between origin and destination.[2]

migration behaviour

More generally, what remains unaccounted for is the presence of large differences in migration behaviour among regions or communities without corresponding differences in economic fundamentals.

New theoretical developments in other fields of economics try to accommodate such phenomena by constructing models that integrate social interactions. The incorporation of positive social interactions implies the existence of 'social multipliers', and allows small changes in exogenous variables to transform into large changes in the endogenous variable.[3] Individual behaviour depends on the choices made by the members of a reference group, and externalities across individuals determine population-wide behaviour.

Translated to migration research, the assumption of this approach is that migration decisions are not made by an individual in isolation. Rather, they are influenced by the actual or intentional migration choices in one's peer group (endogenous effects) or by the group's specific characteristics (contextual effects). Historically, there has been little explicit modelling of these types of externalities in migration, examples of which are migrant networks, peer influences, immigrant clusters, herd behaviour and chain migration.[4] However, recent contributions show – both theoretically (see e.g. Epstein 2010) and empirically (see e.g. Bauer et al. 2007; Epstein and Gang 2006; Munshi 2003) – that social influences have a significant impact on the migrant's decisions on when and where to migrate (see also Boyd 1989 for a review).

determinants of labour migration

Most economic studies that empirically analyse the determinants of labour migration limit their sets of explanatory variables to conventional socio-economic characteristics at the micro level and to income and unemployment discrepancies at macro level. If included at all, social influences are captured by very rough measures, for example by using stocks of immigrants to specific locations as proxies for network connections.[5] The reason for this omission is twofold. First, there is a lack of adequate data that would enable micro-econometric analyses of the individual and group characteristics of migrants. Second, methodological problems in the economic analysis of social interactions have generated a rather pessimistic view of the feasibility of identifying 'endogenous social effects' (Manski 1993).

The individual perspective

In standard economic analysis, the decision to migrate is explained as the result of an individual cost-benefit calculation, whereby a forward-looking migrant seeks to maximise their expected well-being over a time horizon by means of relocation. The seminal model for analysing *labour* migration was expounded by Larry Sjaastad (1962) as a case of seeking the highest return on one's human capital. An individual rational actor decides to migrate if the expected discounted net returns from moving to an alternative international location are positive. The decision may be affected by pecuniary and non-pecuniary aspects, as well as issues such as the likelihood of unemployment (Harris and Todaro 1970).[6]

calculating returns from migration

Net returns from migration are estimated by taking the expected returns from individual skills (wage earnings)[7] in the country of origin, and subtracting them from those expected in the destination country. In this estimation, wages are multiplied by the expected probability of employment in the country of origin and at the destination, respectively. For a given time horizon from 0 to n, the streams of expected earnings differentials are summed over the time period. To obtain the present value of the income differentials, this sum has to be discounted by a factor, r, which reflects the greater utility of earnings in the present than in the future. The estimated costs of moving, C, are subtracted from this sum to obtain the expected net returns from migration.

The migration decision making of an individual is thus formalised in the following equation:

$$ER = \int_0^n [p_{\text{dest}}(t) \cdot Y_{\text{dest}}(t) - p_{\text{orig}}(t) \cdot Y_{\text{orig}}(t)] \cdot e^{rt} dt - C \qquad (1)$$

where ER is the expected net returns from migration estimated for a time horizon from 0 (time of the decision) to n (e.g. time of retirement). The time span $[0, n]$ is divided into a continuum of periods indexed by t. The probabilities of being employed at a point of time, t, in the destination and the origin country are $p_{dest}(t)$ and $p_{orig}(t)$. $Y_{dest}(t)$ and $Y_{orig}(t)$ are the earnings for period t in case of employment in the country of destination and origin. The discount rate is represented by r, and C denotes the total sum of migration costs, which are expected to accrue only in the first period of time.

Under simplifying assumptions, the rational actor will migrate if, and only if, $ER > 0$. In other words, the trade-off faced by a potential migrant is that between the future benefits of being in a different location (the first term in equation (1), i.e. the present value of income differentials summed over the time period $[0, n]$) and the present costs of moving (the second term, C, in equation 1).

Within this standard framework, aggregate migration flows between countries are the result of simply summing individual mobility decisions. Migration would not occur in the absence of differentials in labour market conditions between countries. Given differences across individuals in moving costs, the size of the flows also depends simply on the differential in expected returns from migrating: the higher the present value of expected earnings differentials net of the moving costs, the more individuals will choose to relocate.

effects of migrant networks

Within this broad framework, individual human capital characteristics decisively affect the migration decision.[8] In migration modelling, these characteristics also account for the heterogeneity of individual responses to migration stimuli. In addition to personal characteristics, social conditions and local amenities, heterogeneous preferences also enter into the migration decision process and explain the diversity in the propensity to emigrate.

The effects of migrant networks have been illustrated and tested using the simple mechanics of standard models, for example by Bauer and Zimmermann (1997) and Jewell and Molina (2004). Both augmented the human capital model by defining the migration costs and the probability of employment as functions of existing connections to migrant networks (defined as friends, the household or family members abroad) as follows: $C = C(N)$ and $p = p(N)$ in (1), where N denotes the size of the network, and is usually proxied by the number of family members or acquaintances already in the destination area. In the context of studying the migration decisions of ethnic Germans from the former Soviet Union to Germany and, respectively, of Mexicans to the United States, both studies show the network effects to be robust to the introduction of controls for human capital characteristics and local conditions.

Relative income, risk sharing and families[9]

The standard human capital model of migration can be augmented by postulating that the decision to migrate is not made by the migrant in isolation. Migration decisions are instead the result of a joint process involving the migrant and some group of non-migrants (within families or households) (Stark and Bloom 1985; Stark 1991).

joint process

Mincer (1978) was the first to examine the impact of changes in women's participation in the labour force on the migration decisions of families. Mincer shows that family ties represent negative 'personal' externalities. Increased rates of women's participation in the labour force produce a stronger interdependence of migration decisions among family members. In other words, a family will migrate only if the gains from the movement of one member compensate for the losses (opportunity costs) experienced by the other family members.

Other approaches model the migration decision as a risk-sharing behaviour of families or communities. Similar to the simple human capital model, these view international migration as an uncertain investment decision that involves large unrecoverable costs. Unlike isolated individual actors, families or groups are able to diversify the allocation of their labour resources over geographically dispersed and structurally different markets in order to minimise the risks and to loosen constraints on markets other than the labour market (e.g. credit and capital markets).

A second important feature of these models is the assumption that individuals, as well as families or groups, evaluate their income not solely in absolute terms (as implied in the standard model), but engage in interpersonal income comparisons (Stark and Taylor 1989, 1991). The relative deprivation approach considers migration by household members[10] as an important strategy to improve the household's income position relative to others in the household's reference group. Belonging to a reference group with low relative deprivation is preferable to belonging to groups with high levels of relative deprivation, even if absolute income is higher in the latter. Thus, in addition to income differentials between origin and destination, the income *distributions* in both locations will influence migration decisions.

comparison of income

The inclusion of this comparison of income distributions (at the original location and at the destination) in the migration decision model can produce substantial changes in the theoretical predictions of standard migration models. In addition to this, the newer models introduce another mechanism likely to impact the accuracy of the expected-income models' predictions. That mechanism is the effect of asymmetric information on migration (Katz and Stark 1987). Under a regime of asymmetric information, migrants have full information about their human capital, but potential employers in the destination country do not observe their true level of skill. Assuming that the employer has information only on the distribution of skills in the migrant population but not on the individual human capital (skill information is asymmetric), the employer will pay the migrants a wage equal to the average productivity of the migrant group. Pairing the assumption of asymmetric information with that of heterogeneous workers gives rise to different implications from those of the standard model. Although highly-skilled individuals have a greater incentive to migrate, information asymmetry entails that such individuals will likely be paid less than they are worth, because employers are unaware of their true level of skill and productivity. These individuals will therefore be less likely to migrate than those with below-average skills.

Models of risk-sharing and family migration also provided the first framework for explaining how intra-group interactions could explain variations in the economic behaviour of immigrants in the host labour markets. Appealing to strategic behaviour, these approaches were the first to be used for analysing migration patterns, with heavy reliance on 'network and kinship capital' (Stark and Bloom 1985; Taylor 1986).

Endogenising migration costs: The economics of cumulative causation

determinants of migration

A complementary line of research addresses the determinants of migration decision-making in a dynamic fashion. This research started in the mid-1970s with contributions that increasingly addressed the structure of information about foreign locations available to prospective migrants. Various authors (e.g. Graves and Linneman 1976; Gordon and Vickeman 1982; and McCall and McCall 1987)[11] emphasised in their models the search process by which migrants acquire information about conditions at the destination and about the costs of moving. Building on the traditional perspective of migration behaviour, these search-theoretic models combined insights from the human capital approach and random utility theory. In this framework, two types of migration are postulated to occur: 'speculative migration', in which the migrant moves in order to search for a job, and 'contracted migration', in which the migrant moves to take a job they know to be available. The sequential decision tree for contracted migration is divided into three main conditional probabilities: the probability of searching, the probability of receiving an offer and the probability of accepting the offer (Gordon and Vickerman 1982). Using the search process, models in this vein were the first to link the heterogeneity of migration flows to the structure of information networks. Following the 'friends and relatives effects' advanced by Greenwood (1969), various mechanisms were consequently proposed for the dissemination of information regarding migrants' potential destinations (which were originally specified in migrants' utility functions, i. e. essentially wages and unemployment, but also mean and variance of wages and the demand conditions). Carrington, Detragiache and Vishwanath (1996) use a dynamic model in which migration costs endogenously decline with the stock of migrants already settled at the destination. This helps explain the timing (with endogenous moving costs migration occurs gradually over time) and the patterns (flows can increase even with simultaneously narrowing income differentials) of migration flows, which could not have been explained in traditional Harris-Todaro models.

return migration

In sequential models of migration, a primary move causes search, increases the migrants' information and triggers in turn another move, either onward or to return. DaVanzo (1983) and Tunali (1996) empirically apply this sequential approach to repeat and return migration. In this context, return migration becomes consistent with an extended human capital model, particularly when considered in the framework of family decision-making. Individuals move to acquire human capital, usually in the form of experience or training, and return to make use of it in their home region (e.g. Stark 1991). Additionally, empirical studies of return and repeat migration show the selectivity implications of these types of movements.

Polachek and Horwath (1977) introduced the concept of 'the peregrinator' – an individual who gathers information in the course of migration, possibly spending time in multiple locations. This information stock is continuously replenished but decreases after each movement. However, changes in locational characteristics are exogenous and do not enter into the migration decision. This last point is treated differently due to the dynamic features of models such as those of Burda (1995). All these models take into account uncertainty about both current and future characteristics of different locations.[12]

role of migration networks

To sum up, beyond their complex dynamic features, these models basically incorporate two rather simple concepts into the economic modelling of migration decisions: that of migration networks and, more generically, that of cumulative causation. The role of migration networks is revealed in the search-theoretic framework as a mechanism for reducing the costs and risks of migration under imperfect information. The economic counterpart of cumulative causation is introduced by the dynamic character of the search process. Each step in the search process alters the motivation and information constraints of potential migrants. Realised migrations in turn modify the characteristics in the corresponding locations (for example, in terms of income, wealth, population or land distribution).

This line of modelling is often neglected in sociological accounts of migration research in economics. If they are considered at all, attempts to dynamically model migration decisions are viewed as merely concerned with path dependency, whilst only their sociological pendants manage to capture the more complex cumulative causation (Massey and Zenteno 1999: 5328). However, the literature suggests that it is precisely the refined standard economic approach[13] that provides a comprehensive framework for explaining the dynamic features of circular and cumulative causation.[14]

Social interactions in migration choices

The previous section of this chapter sketched the advancement of migration modelling in economics with a special focus on approaches that incorporate some form of social dynamics, that is, models that account for socially mediated factors influencing the initiation and perpetuation of labour flows. The simple question was how can the role of others in migration decision-making be modelled in economics. Is there an economic analogue for the 'meso-level' effects described in other social sciences? In what way does migration behaviour in one's reference group influence individual migration choices?

feedback effects

From an economics perspective, the more general point under scrutiny here is that of feedback effects on individual choices, which in turn affect the observed equilibrium outcomes. The empirical regularities mentioned in this chapter's introduction could be due to this type of feedback effects or to some type of interaction that explains why the migration choices of an individual are positively related to the prevalence of similar choices in the individual's reference group.[15]

To better understand the possibilities and limitations of applying the economic approach to the questions addressed in this chapter, this section draws on Manski's (2000) conceptualisation of social interactions. Manski identifies three possible channels through which social interactions may enter the utility functions of migrants: through constraints, through expectations and through preferences. It is useful to bear this typology in mind in the following descriptions of existing economic models.

Models with constraints

The most direct way to introduce social interactions into models of migration is through critical mass behaviour.[16] In this case, the expected utility derived by a potential migrant from a decision to move or to remain depends on how many other individuals in the reference group choose which of the two alternatives. There are two ways to conceptualise such a behaviour in the context of migration. The first is through constraints faced by migrants. The second is through threshold effects in migration decision-making, the most prominent example being the case of chain migration. In the first case, the emphasis lies on the increasing costs of relocation; the second emphasises the increasing benefits from relocation, due to the proportion of other individuals who have already made the decision to migrate.

models using constraints

The models using constraints are constructed in the tradition of Tiebout (1956) and Tullock (1971).[17] The main idea is that, all things being equal, migrants' locational decisions take into account externalities due to bundles of publicly provided goods in the origin and/or destination area. In such models a public good is usually introduced in order to define an equilibrium condition for migration flows. In his study of the joint determination of migration flows and economic growth, Braun (1993) introduces congestion costs to slow migration flows. A similar mechanism is used in Krugman (1991),[18] whereby migration declines as income differentials are reduced.

Dustmann and Preston (2001) and Dustmann et al. (2011) used an implicitly constraints-based model when analysing the dependence of migration decisions and labour market assimilation on the local concentration of ethnic minorities (which in turn determined attitudes regarding minority populations).[19] A 'thresholds perspective' is suggested in Stark's (1991: 26) overview of migration modelling, as 'new migrants are assisted by those who have migrated earlier; one good way of having a higher proportion of all trades conducted among migrants when there are few of them is to have additional migrants. The arrival of new migrants confers benefits upon the earlier migrants'.

Expectations and the option value of waiting

Most existing economic models that account for network externalities in migration incorporate social effects into migrant decisions by allowing for uncertainty or by including the direct impacts on preferences. Between these two alternatives, uncertainty is by far the most common.

uncertainty

The models described up to now include uncertainty of two potentially different types. The first type occurs when future evolution at the destination or in the origin area are unknown, and so migration is delayed in order to allow the uncertainty to be resolved. The second type refers to unobserved present conditions at the destination. This type of uncertainty may be reduced as more individuals migrate. O'Connell (1997) incorporates both types of uncertainty in a dynamic optimising model, demonstrating that in equilibrium migration behaviour is more likely to depend on uncertainty about the future ('wait and see') than on uncertainty about the current destination ('try your luck').

Preferences and the well-being of others

Socially interdependent preferences[20] enter into the migration decision-making process either in relation to the characteristics of other members of the reference group (contextual) or in relation to the migration choices of others in one's reference group (endogenous).

Economics makes more use of the first type of preference through the relative deprivation approach. The second type is applied rather implicitly in the augmented human capital models described earlier (e.g. in Jewell and Molina 2004). Exogenous factors may be used to explain, for example, the level of human capital accumulation in the context of migration (e.g. Stark 2004; or Beine et al. 2001).

relative deprivation

Drawing on Stark and Taylor (1991), in relative deprivation models the individual (absolute) income is used to compute a measure of one's relative income position with respect to a specific reference group. The relative deprivation measure for an individual is defined either as their (subjective) self-reported feeling of deprivation or as their (objective) position in the income distribution of the reference group.

Herd effects are an additional channel through which social dynamics are introduced into the preferences of potential migrants. Herds are used in the search-theoretic framework as information externalities (e.g. Epstein 2008).

Social interactions in empirical migration research

The theoretical conceptualisation of social interactions in migration models has evolved following the logic of the economic model. At the same time, however, empirical research has lagged behind the theory. Two main categories of problems hinder advances in the empirical analysis of social dynamics in migration behaviour. The first is the difficulty of finding an adequate empirical equivalent of theoretically defined interactions. The second is more fundamental and relates to the difficulty of identifying social interactions in the non-experimental data commonly available for studying migration decisions in economics.

empirical approaches

Empirical approaches in economics have imported sociological concepts such as 'social capital', 'peer influence', and 'migrant networks'. Yet the instrumentalisation of these concepts lacks precise definition. Consequently, it is often unclear exactly what type of effect is ultimately captured in estimations. Many approaches maintain little connection to any of the theoretical structures described earlier. Instead, they merely test correlations between behavioural choices and infer the existence of interactions among individual actors.

However, even after clarifying definitional problems, several difficulties arise when trying to estimate social interactions in migration choices. The common objective of such empirical research is to find out whether some form of social dynamics explains why individuals belonging to the same group tend to make similar migration choices. Why, for example, are members of communities with a high migration prevalence themselves more willing to migrate than those coming from communities with no propensity for migration, even if both communities and individuals are otherwise similar (see e.g. Winters et al. 2001)? What explains the clustering of migrants from one specific community in a specific destination, even in the absence of network ties (as in the case of so-called 'herd effects', see e.g. Bauer et al. 2007)?

The hypothesis of interest here is that, due to particular externalities, the behaviour of the reference group affects an individual's migration decision. To empirically detect such social effects, we again refer to a typology offered by Manski, who set out three propositions regarding interactions and the effects thereof (see Manski 2000: 127).

endogenous interactions

The first relates to the so-called 'endogenous interactions', meaning the influence of group behaviour on individual behaviour. The idea here is that individuals' migration choices depend on the choices made by others in their reference group. Illustrations of these endogenous effects are found in the notions of 'herd behaviour'[21] (see e.g. Bauer et al. 2007) and community ties (e.g. Winters et al. 2001). These concepts explain similar migration choices, after controlling for personal and local characteristics, based on affiliation with a particular community.

The second proposition concerns 'contextual interactions', meaning the influences of group characteristics on individual behaviour. In other words, the migration choices of an individual vary with the exogenous characteristics of the group. In the literature, this type of contextual effect is exemplified by relative deprivation models and, more generally, in the context of cumulative causation. These approaches use either income distribution or other characteristics of the group's members to provide *explanans* for migration decisions. In Jewell and Molina (2004), an improvement in the relative income position improves a household's welfare, and relative deprivation significantly affects migration decision-making.

Manski's third proposition relates to the 'correlated effects'. These capture similarities in migration behaviour due to the similar individual characteristics of the members of a reference group or due to the fact that group members face similar institutional constraints.

correlated effects

In migration models, endogenous and contextual effects describe distinct channels through which the migration choices of individuals are influenced by their 'meso-level' or social environments. Where correlated effects are observed, it is critical to control for underlying factors that influence migration choices (either individual characteristics or macro-variables including, for example, legal arrangements).

Each of these three types of interactions has a different implication. Endogenous effects emphasise the social dynamics of migration decisions. They help us to understand the role of feedback, from group to individual choices, and imply multiple equilibria for macro-behaviour. Contextual and correlated effects do not imply the existence of such feedback.

However, most of the data used for estimating migration models in economics do not allow a differentiation of endogenous, contextual, and correlated effects. The main methodological problem in distinguishing endogenous from contextual effects arises because behaviour at the group level is itself an aggregation of individual behaviours. This is the so-called reflection problem (Manski 1993). It is not possible to discern whether migration choices considered at the group level affect individual choices or are merely the aggregation of these individual choices. Group and individual behaviour are thus simultaneous, much as an object and its reflection in the mirror move simultaneously (hence the 'reflection problem').

simultaneity

Apart from this simultaneity problem, there are two other important ways in which endogeneity can arise in empirical applications. First, due to the problem of correlated unobservables and errors-in-variables, large differences in migration patterns among otherwise similar groups may be due to correlated individual characteristics which are unobserved. Second, due to endogenous membership (the problem of self-selected participation), the observed variation in migration behaviour among groups may be determined by the fact that individuals are sorted among groups rather than by social interactions.

Glaeser and Scheinkman (2001) discuss some approaches to overcome these problems. Such methods have not been widely applied in studying migration, mainly because of inadequate data. However, panel data or cross-sectional data containing retrospective information can be used to study the dynamics of migration decisions. Individual choices can be modelled as a function of both the contemporaneous and lagged behaviour of the reference group. Another option – used for the identification of migrant networks' effects by Munshi (2003) – is to instrument for the migration behaviour at the group level using exogenous location or group members' characteristics. Munshi (2003) uses variation in rainfall across communities to predict differences in prior migration, since differences in rainfall should have no direct effect on current migration, nor on labour shocks at the potential destination, thus avoiding the simultaneity bias (Munshi 2003: 551).

In general, understanding the role of social interactions in migration decisions will require richer data than those commonly used in the economic literature. Apart from the issues previously mentioned, such data must allow for the identification of the relevant reference groups. Manipulating such data will thus elicit explanations about which groups matter for individual migration choices, and uncover interesting properties of interactions.

The economic impacts of migration

Welfare implications for destination countries

Using the marginal product of labour schedule, we can examine the impact of an increase in labour supply on the earnings of workers who are assumed to be replaced by immigrants. In the basic model, migrants reduce the earnings of substitute factors and raise the earnings of complementary factors.

Figure 2.1 illustrates the basic mechanism assumed in the simplest analysis of the welfare effects of migration in the destination countries.

The workforce at destination (assumed to be fully employed) increases by the number of migrants who enter the labour market (corresponding to the amount *GH*). The vertical line through *G* is the initial supply of labour. The increase in the workforce will cause a

Figure 2.1 *Welfare effects of immigration in destination countries*

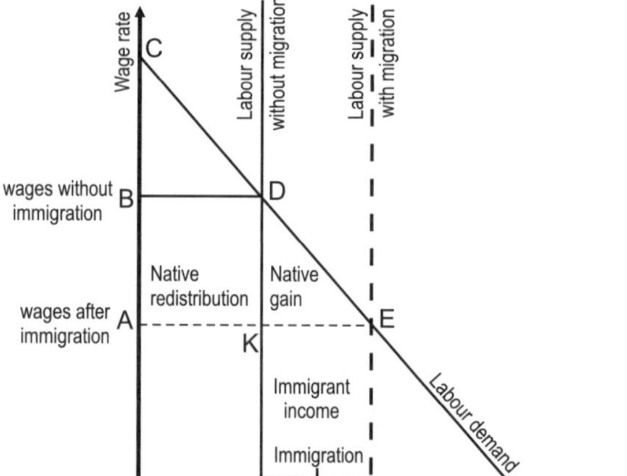

parallel shift of the labour supply curve to the right, so that the new labour supply is the dotted vertical line thorough point *H*.

We further assume that wages are perfectly flexible, both physical and human capital are fixed, and that natives and migrant workers are homogenous. The marginal product of labour in the destination country is given by the line *CA*. Labour demand is *MPL*.

labour market equilibrium

Before migration occurs, the labour market will be in equilibrium in point *D*, at the intersection of the labour demand curve and the initial labour supply curve. After migration, the new equilibrium will be at point *E*, where the new labour supply curve (with migration) intersects the labour demand curve.

By definition, the area under the marginal product of labour curve gives the total output. The total output before migration is therefore given by the trapezoid *OCDG*. After migration, the total product of labour will be equivalent to the trapezoid *OCEH*. This means an increase with the trapezoid *DGHE*. However, this area is composed of a part that is equivalent to the net gain to residents, the triangle *DKE*, and an area equivalent to the additional income earned by immigrants, the rectangle *KGHE*.

Implications for countries of origin

In economics literature on migration there is a long tradition of considering the selective emigration of the most productive workers ('brain drain') as harmful for developing countries (Gruber and Scott 1966; Bhagwati 1976; Bhagwati and Hamada 1974; Bhagwati and Rodriguez 1975). However, more recent studies emphasise that, for migrants themselves, relocation is an opportunity to improve standard of living – sometimes dramatically. Empirical studies using data about migrants, for example from Latin America (Clemens, Montenegro and Pritchett 2008), from India (De Coulon and Wadsworth 2010) and from Eastern Europe (Budnik 2009), confirm that migrants earn on average two to three times more at the destination than they would at home. From the perspective of the sending societies, the migration of the highly skilled may induce virtuous educational incentives, which may in the long run increase the overall human capital of the country of origin.

brain gain

Theoretical modelling has identified this possibility of a 'brain gain' in the past (e.g. Stark et al. 1997, 1998; Mountford 1997; Beine, Docquier and Rapoport 2001). Various studies tested this hypothesis empirically. Beine et al. (2001, 2008) use a cross-country approach to show that low emigration rates are positively correlated to average schooling levels. Using individual data, Chand and Clemens (2008) find a positive incentive effect of skilled emigration on education.

A complementary line of research looks at the positive impacts of return migration on the countries of origin. Theoretical models analysing the economic consequences of return migration for the source country have been developed (see e.g. Dustmann 1995; Mayer and Peri 2009; Dustman, Fadlon and Wiess 2011; Dustmann and Schönberg 2011). There is extensive evidence that return migrants receive an income premium for their work experience abroad Barret and Goggin 2010). Several recent studies also emphasise the importance of returnees as a source of entrepreneurship (Constant and Massey 2003; McCormick and Wahba 2001).

return migrants

Over the last two decades, return migrants have become an important and fast-growing group, for example, in labour markets throughout Central and Eastern Europe (CEE) and elsewhere. There are no precise and comparable figures as yet of the stock of East European migrants who have returned to their countries of origin. However, recent research suggests that these migrants acquire productive skills while abroad and receive a significant income premium upon return (see e.g. Co, Gang and Yun 2000 for returned woman migrants in Hungary; De Coulon and Piracha 2005 for Albanian returnees). There is also evidence that returnees in CEE have a higher proclivity for entrepreneurial activities and for self-employment than non-migrants (Kilic et al. 2009; Piracha and Vadean 2010). But at the same time they more likely not to participate in the labour market.

Overall, the economic impact of migration and return on the sending countries will crucially depend on two aspects: the magnitude of these flows and the selection of their participants. Large outflows and a large proportion of returnees will increase both the gains and losses for the sending society.

For the country of origin, a positive selection of migrants and returnees, in terms of their skills and qualifications, might represent both a challenge, due to the risk of brain drain, and an opportunity, given the incentives for learning, acquisition of qualifications and improvement of skills while abroad.

The next section briefly introduces a simple way of explaining the self-selective nature of migration flows.

The selectivity of migration

self-selection

Migrants' self-selection is one of the core topics in the economics of labour migration. The term 'self-selection' refers to the fact that migrants make rational decisions about where to locate and in which labour market to participate. In the simple version of the human capital model discussed before, this means that migrants decide whether to move or not by comparing their potential earnings in the source and in the destination country. However, as a consequence, this rational decision means that not all potential migrants will ultimately migrate, but only those who have higher expected earnings at the destination compared to their home country. The practical implication is that migrants represent not a random subsample of the population of the country of origin, but a 'self-selected' group. The economic intuition behind this argument can be illustrated using the influential Roy-model.[22] In its original version, this model analysed the way in which workers choose among various employment opportunities so that, in the end, people with specific skills and abilities sort themselves into corresponding occupations.

Figure 2.2 shows two key situations. Consider first the case of a country of origin in which there is a relatively egalitarian income distribution: the workers who have greater skills do not earn much more than the unskilled. The left panel in the figure illustrates this, by indicating a lower rate of return for skills in the home country (the flatter line plots the wages in the country of origin). We can represent this with a simple equation: $w_0 = \alpha_0 + \delta_0 \cdot s$. Here w_0 represents the wage rate in the country of origin, α_0 is a constant fixed part of the income (equivalent, e.g., to a minimum wage) and δ_0 denotes the 'return' to human capital, the way in which the labour market in the home country values skills (s). In a similar way, we can represent the expected wages at the destination as $w_1 = \alpha_1 + \delta_1 \cdot s$. Earnings at the destination consist of a fixed constant part, α_1, and a part indicating the way skills are valued in the destination country.

The slopes of the two lines in the left panel suggest that $\delta_1 > \delta_0$, which means that the distribution of wages in the destination country is more unequal than that in the country of origin. Highly skilled migrants would therefore be able to obtain a higher income premium on their human capital in the destination country than at home. This creates an incentive for migrants with above-average skill levels to leave, leading to what economists refer to as 'positive selection'.

Figure 2.2 *The selectivity of migration flows*

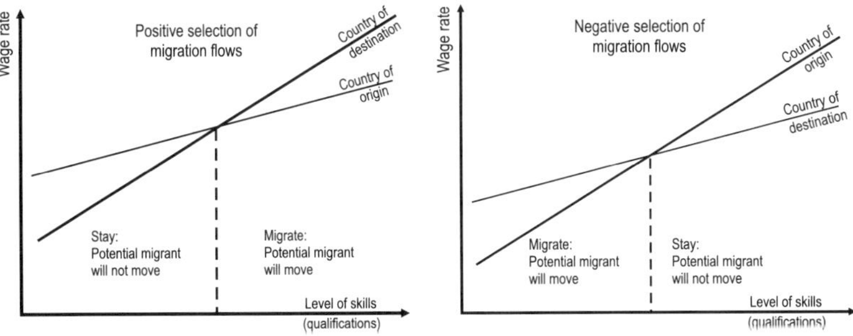

If, on the contrary, $\delta_0 > \delta_1$, meaning that the potential destination country offers a lower rate of return for human capital (e.g., if it taxes skilled workers more, while subsidising the unskilled), this country would mainly attract workers with relatively low earnings capacities. This situation is depicted in the right panel of figure 2 and illustrates the possibility of a negative self-selection of migration flows between origin and destination.

Migrant networks and migration policy: An economic perspective

In the first part of this chapter we discussed one empirical puzzle that challenges migration research in economics: the observation of large differences in migration behaviour among regions or communities in the absence of corresponding differences in economic fundamentals. Another similar puzzle addressed by economic research is the discrepancy between the modest economic impacts of migration and the strong public opposition to increased immigration that is observed in most receiving countries. In both cases, there is a substantial variation in either individual choices or individual attitudes, which remains unaccounted for in standard neoclassical models.

attitudes towards immigration policy

Economic explanations for attitudes towards immigration policy are often inconsistent with empirical findings. For example, some groups – like Hispanic and Black minority members in the United States – express relatively positive views on immigration despite predictions that they themselves will be the ones most affected by labour market competition.

New economic models apply a broader class of externalities to explain individual attitudes towards immigration policy. Recognising that immigration not only has labour market and fiscal effects but also changes the composition of the local population, Card, Dustmann and Preston (2012) look at how concerns about compositional amenities, associated with neighbourhood characteristics, affect views on immigration. They find these to be substantially more important than economic concerns.

The economic intuition behind these two puzzling relationships (small flows despite large differentials and strong attitudes despite negligible effects) helps to uncover important aspects of the interaction between migration networks and migration policy outcomes.

We argued in the first part of this chapter that network effects and social interactions were gradually incorporated into migration models, starting with the traditional Harris-Todaro framework and ending with the dynamic features of search-theoretic models. This section introduces some new research topics in economics that ask how network effects interact with migration policies beyond the regulation and selection mechanisms. How do networks impact labour market outcomes and the welfare attitudes of migrants? Do ethnic networks explain some of the observed complementarity in trade and factor flows? Are networks relevant for understanding the consequences of policies towards refugees and asylum seekers? Will the presence of migrant networks lead to different effects of enforcement?

Ethnic networks, trade and capital flow

migration and trade

Some insights with potentially important political implications for both the origin and destination countries result from the observed simultaneous growth in trade, FDI (foreign direct investment) and migration flows. The concomitant rise in goods and factor flows is in contrast to the predictions of the standard neoclassical theory. Trade theory regards migration and trade as comparable, since both contribute to factor price equalisation. Similarly, capital is expected to flow where labour is abundant, thus lowering the incentive to migrate. However, evidence suggests that migrant networks in fact facilitate bilateral economic transactions, leading to significant trade creation effects (Gould 1994; Rauch and Trindade 2002). They may also increase bilateral FDI flows from the host to the home countries of migrants (Javorcik et al. 2011). A large part of the FDI flows to China is handled by the Chinese diaspora (*The Economist* 2011). The fundamental intuition is that ethnic networks help in reducing information costs and overcoming contract enforcement difficulties in cross-border transactions. Both the trade-creation effect and the impact of migrant networks on FDI flows have been largely neglected in the debates around migration policy.

Cross-border network ties in migrant communities appear to act as entrepreneurial springboards as well, both in the destination and the home countries. Diaspora networks promote the transfer of knowledge and technology. They also boost innovation (Naghavi and Strozzi 2011; Agrawal et al. 2011) and investment (Woodruff and Zeneto 2007) in the sending countries.

Enclaves, labour market outcomes and welfare attitudes

job search networks

The role of ethnic enclaves and migrant networks for migrants' labour market outcomes, human capital accumulation, and welfare persistence in the host country are more difficult to uncover and properly identify. However, substantive evidence suggests that migrants help friends and relatives get jobs in the destination countries. Exogenously, larger networks increase the probability of employment in higher paying jobs, for example, for Mexican migrants in the United States (Munshi 2003) and for refugees in Denmark (Damm 2009). Job search networks help migrants from a particular group earn higher wages in firms with a relatively large share of employees from the same group. Such firms also display higher retention rates for migrants of similar ethnic origin compared to majority workers or workers from other groups (Dustmann et al. 2011). The race, ethnicity and immigrant status of hiring managers affects the racial composition of new employees, and separations are more frequent when workers and managers have dissimilar origins (Åslund et al. 2009, Giuliano et al. 2009).

ethnic networks

However, social interactions within ethnic networks and communities might also have adverse effects, for example, on the schooling outcomes of second-generation immigrants. Conditional on the school system, negative migrant-to-migrant peer effects explain part of the persistence of educational inequality and the considerable disadvantage of immigrants that are not due to individual heterogeneity (Entorf and Lauk 2008). These ethnic externalities – in the presence of 'good or bad' neighbourhoods – have a strong influence on the intergenerational mobility of migrants and ethnic minorities (Borjas 1992, 1995).

Similarly, social networks within ethnic minority groups can favour the emergence of 'welfare cultures' (Bertrand et al. 2000; Bratsberg et al. 2008). There are two main channels through which migrant networks can influence individual choices towards welfare: through sharing information about welfare provisions within minority language communities (information channel) and through established social norms within particular ethnic groups which in turn determine individual and group attitudes.

Networks and illegal migrants: The rational back door

Networks can also be part of a process to circumvent restrictive or highly selective migration policies. Moreover, it is highly unlikely that any restrictions can or even rationally intend (Entorf 2000; Hanson 2007) to totally prevent illegal migration. Networks play an important role for the entry and informal employment opportunities of illegal migrants. The use of informal job networks helps, for example, illegal immigrants from Mexico to better integrate into the US labour market.

smugglers

However, in many instances network ties also make a large fraction of irregular migrants more likely to use smugglers. Networks can encourage 'debt-financed migration.' Smugglers in the network are sometimes paid only after the successful passage of migrants into the host country has been achieved (Gathman 2008). However, smugglers often tax the income migrants have earned in the host country in order to recoup their 'debt-financed migration' (Friebel and Guriev 2006).

Conclusion

This chapter surveyed some of the striking changes at work within the economic modelling of migration. It focused on the channels through which formal modelling has evolved to incorporate more realistic assumptions about social ties. In particular, it asked to what extent migration models have successfully incorporated interaction-based models of behaviour. Such theoretical advancement allows further steps to be taken towards migration models that can account for heterogeneity across individuals, while incorporating the interplay between individual decisions and group behaviour.

Interaction-based models are used in many areas of economics, but systematic work with them has yet to be done in the field of migration. The reasons are empirical and methodological rather than theoretical. A survey of the literature reveals that several traditional economic approaches to explain migration choices have adopted structures reflecting social dynamics – most prominently in the search-theoretic models and human capital framework.

These developments do not refute former approaches to the modelling of migration decisions. Methodologically, they are consistent with their forerunners, while shifting perspectives and units of analysis (as in the case of the 'new economics of labour migration') and incorporating more complex dynamics (as in the search-theoretic models).

This methodological consistency of migration models in economics remains the touchstone of limitations for interdisciplinary research on migration issues. While recent economic models manage to import some fundamentally sociological concepts, this does not imply an unlimited convergence between approaches from the two disciplines. Recent developments in socio-economics have attempted to relax assumptions about rational expectations and to develop mechanisms allowing preferences to evolve. However, all economic explanations of migration behaviour will necessarily remain explicable only in terms of individuals, not of other social categories. Nonetheless, the nature of the divergence between the two disciplines is more spurious than commonly presumed in the sociological critique of economic approaches to migration behaviour. Notwithstanding dominant perceptions, most mainstream economics models incorporate social variables not attachable to particular individuals (Schumpeter 1909; Schelling 1978).

MAIN IDEAS

Economic models of migration have been criticised for their inability to account for the non-economic determinants of migration.

The economic approach uses two simple assumptions about individual agents: they are rational decision makers and they are motivated purely by self-interest.

Individual rational actors decide to migrate if their expected discounted net returns from moving to an alternative international location are positive.

The decision to migrate is not made by the migrant in isolation.

Individuals move to acquire human capital, usually in the form of experience or training; they may return to their home region to make use of it.

The migration choices of an individual vary with the characteristics of the groups of which they are part.

Interaction-based models have been used in many areas of economics, yet such systematic work has yet to be done in the field of migration.

In all of the economic theories of migration, behaviour will necessarily remain explicable only in terms of individuals, not of other social categories.

Notes

1 See also Hargreaves Heap et al. (1992) for a textbook treatment, and Camerer and Fehr (2006) for a critical discussion.
2 Migratory episodes displaying such empirical riddles for economists have been observed i.e. by Myrdal (1944) for the US and, more recently, by Fidrmuc (2001) and Hunt (2000) for East European regions.
3 See e.g. Durlauf (2001) and, for a general survey, Manski (2000).
4 Some notable exceptions are Taylor (1986), Chau (1997) and Helmenstein and Yegorov (2000). A pioneering contribution to exploring the social determinants of migration is the little-noted essay by Thadani and Todaro (1984).
5 However, this type of model reached a high level of sophistication in the attempt to identify the importance of networks in both the decision to migrate, e.g. as in Winters et al. 2001, and among immigrants at the destination, e.g. as in Munshi 2003.
6 The models discussed in this section are human capital investment models and their variants, incorporating expected income measures.

7 The use of earnings is of course a simplifying assumption. It could easily be replaced by a general utility function, which captures much more than that. However, the basic mechanics of the model would be the same.
8 This is indeed one major topic of empirical micro research on migration decision making. For surveys compare Greenwood (1975, 1985, 1997).
9 The type of models considered in this section are usually referred to as the 'new economics of migration.' Although not treated systematically, the main features of these models (see Stark and Bloom 1985 for a summary) were already considered in the economic literature years before. They extend rather than challenge the basic assumptions of the standard human capital model.
10 This approach is applicable to both individual and group models of migration decision-making.
11 Molho (1986) provides a structured review of migration models from a search-theoretic perspective.
12 McKenzie and Rapoport (2004) consider the dynamic effect of networks on migration propensities and inequality in the region of origin. They show that migrant networks – in the presence of remittances – induce migration to reduce income and wealth inequality. Jewell and Molina (2004) report similar results using an augmented Harris-Todaro model.
13 The term itself has been coined by an economist, i.e. Myrdal (1957).
14 Pioneer work in this fashion is attributed to Ira S. Lowry (e.g. 1966).
15 Often such interactions are described as social norms, peer pressure, conformity, contagion, herd effects, imitation or bandwagon.
16 Schelling (1978) and Marvell and Oliver (1993) develop a formal theory to model colective action and apply this to diverse cases of critical mass behaviour.
17 There is also a considerable bulk of empirical research in the pure Tibout-tradition on the effects of local public goods on migration decision making: Cebula (2002); Borjas (1999).
18 In an analogous manner, Lazear (1995) and Konya (2001) use diversity and assimilation costs, respectively.
19 *Negative* network externalities in Bauer, Epstein and Gang (2004); public goods in Hammond and Sempere (2004).
20 For a more general discussion of socially interdependent preferences compare Postlewaite (1998).
21 Bickhchandani et al. (1998) is a comprehensive survey about how herding and learning by observing the past behaviour of others helps explain otherwise puzzling economic phenomena.
22 The model introduced by Roy (1951) was first applied to the case of migration decisions by Borjas (1987).

References

Agrawal, A., D. Kapur, J. McHale and A. Oettl (2011), 'Brain drain or brain bank? The impact of skilled emigration on poor-country innovation', *Journal of Urban Economics* 69 (1): 43-55.

Arrow, K. J. (1994), 'Methodological individualism and social knowledge', *American Economic Review* 84 (2): 1-9.

Barrett, A and J. Goggin (2010), 'Returning to the question of a wage premium for returning migrants', *National Institute Economic Review* 213: R43-R51.

Batista, C., A. Lacuesta and P. Vicente (2010), 'Testing the "brain gain" hypothesis: Micro-evidence from Cape Verde', *Journal of Development Economics* 97 (1): 32-45.

Bauer, T. and K. Zimmermann (1997), 'Network migration of ethnic Germans', *International Migration Review* 31 (1): 143-149.

Bauer, T., G. S. Epstein and I. N. Gang (2007), 'The influence of stocks and flows on migrants' location choices', *Research in Labor Economics*, 26: 199-229.

Becker, G. (1974), 'A theory of social interactions', *Journal of Political Economy*, 82 (6): 1063-1093.

Beine, M., F. Docquier and C. Özden (2011), *Dissecting Network Externalities in International Migration*, CESifo Working Paper No. 3333. Munich: CESifo.

Beine, M., F. Docquier and H. Rapoport (2001), 'Brain drain and economic growth: Theory and evidence', *Journal of Development Economics* 64 (1): 275-289.

Beine, M., F. Docquier and H. Rapoport (2008), 'Brain drain and human capital formation in developing countries: Winners and losers', *Economic Journal* 118 (4): 631-652.

Bertrand, M., E. Luttmer and S. Mullainathan (2000), 'Network effects and welfare cultures', *Quarterly Journal of Economics* 115(3): 1019-1055.

Bhagwati, J. (1976), *The Brain-Drain and Taxation: Theory and Empirical Analysis*, New York, North Holland.

Bhagwati, J. and K. Hamada (1974), 'The brain drain, international integration of markets for professionals and unemployment: A theoretical analysis', *Journal of Development Economics* 1 (1): 19-42.

Bhagwati, J. and C. Rodriguez (1975); 'Welfare-theoretical analyses of brain brain', *Journal of Development Economics* 2 (3): 195-222.

Bikhchandani, S., D. Hirshleifer and I. Welch (1998), 'Learning from the behavior of others: Conformity, fads, and informational cascades', *Journal of Economic Perspectives* 12 (3): 151-170.

Blaug, M. (1980), *The Methodology of Economics*. Cambridge: Cambridge University Press.

Bodvarsson, O. and H. van den Berg (2009), *The Economics of Immigration: Theory and Policy*. Heidelberg: Springer.

Borjas, G. (1987), 'Self-selection and the earnings of immigrants', *American Economic Review* 77 (4): 531-53.

Borjas, G. (1992), 'Ethnic capital and intergenerational mobility', *The Quarterly Journal of Economics* 107 (1): 123-50.

Borjas, G. (1995), 'Ethnicity, neighbourhoods, and human capital externalities', *American Economic Review* 85 (3): 365-390.

Borjas, G. (1999), 'Immigration and welfare magnets', *Journal of Labor Economics* 17 (4): 607-37.

Borjas, G. (2009), *Labor Economics*, 5th edition. New York: McGraw-Hill.

Borjas, G.J. (1989), 'Economic theory and international migration', *International Migration Review*, XXIII (3): 457-485.

Boyd, M. (1989), 'Family and personal networks in international migration: Recent developments and new agendas', *International Migration Review* 23 (3): 638-670.

Bratsberg, B., O. Raaum and K. Roed (2010), 'When minority labor migrants meet the welfare state', *Journal of Labor Economics* 28 (3), 633-676.

Braun, J. (1993), 'Essays on economic growth and migration', PhD dissertation, Harvard University.

Budnik, K. B. (2009), 'Rationality of post-accession migration', *Focus on European Economic Integration* Q1/09: 57-83.

Burda, M. (1993), 'The determinants of East-West German migration: Some first results', *European Economic Review* 37: 452-461.

Burda, M. (1995), 'Migration and the option value of waiting', *The Economic and Social Review* 27(1):1-19.

Burda, M., W. Härdle, M. Müller and A. Werwatz (1998), 'Semiparametric analysis of German East-West migration intentions: Facts and theory', *Journal of Applied Econometrics* 13: 525-541.

Camerer, C. and E. Fehr (2006), 'When does "economic man" dominate social behaviour?', *Science* 311: 47-52.

Card, D., C. Dustmann and I. Preston (2012), 'Immigration, wages, and compositional amenities', *Journal of the European Economic Association* 10 (1): 78-119.

Carrington, W., E. Detragiache and T. Cishwanath (1996), 'Migration with endogenous moving costs', *American Economic Review* 86 (4): 909-30.

Cebula, R. (2002), 'Migration and the Tiebout-Tullock Hypothesis revisited', *Review of Regional Studies* Spring: 56-65.

Chand, S. and M. Clemens (2008), *Skilled Emigration and Skill Creation: A Quasi-Experiment*, CGD Working Paper 152. Washington, DC: Center for Global Development.

Chau, N. (1997), 'The pattern of migration with variable migration costs', *Journal of Regional Science* 37 (1): 35-54.

Clemens M., C. Montenegro and L. Pritchett (2008), *The Place Premium: Wage Differences for Identical Workers across the US Border*, CDG Working Paper 148. Washington, DC: Center for Global Development.

Co, C.Y., I. Gang and M. Yun (2000), 'Returns to returning', *Journal of Population Economics* 13: 57-79.

Constant, A. and D. Massey (2003), 'Self-selection, earnings, and out-migration: A longitudinal study of immigrants to Germany', *Journal of Population Economics* 16 (4): 631-653.

Cushing, B. and J. Poot (2004), 'Crossing boundaries and borders: Regional science advances in migration modelling', *Papers in Regional Science* 83: 317-338.

Damm, A. (2009), 'Ethnic enclaves and immigrant labor market outcomes: Quasi-experimental evidence', *Journal of Labor Economics* 27 (2): 281-314.

DaVanzo, J. (1981), 'Repeat migration, information costs, and location-specific capital', *Population and Environment: Behavioral and Social Issues* 4 (1): 45-73.

DaVanzo, J. (1983), 'Repeat migration in the United States: Who moves back and who moves on?', *Review of Economics and Statistics* 65: 552-559.

De Coulon, A. and J. Wadsworth (2010), 'On the relative rewards to immigration', *Review of Economics of the Household* 8 (1): 147-169.

Durlauf, S. (2001), 'A framework for the study of individual behavior and social interactions', *Sociological Methodology* 31: 47-87.

Dustmann, C. (1995), 'Savings behavior of migrant workers: A life cycle analysis', *Zeitschrift für Wirtschafts- und Sozialwissenschaften*, 4: 511-533.

Dustmann, C. and A. Glitz (2011), 'Migration and education', *Handbook of the Economics of Education*, Vol. 4, pp. 327-344. Amsterdam: Elsevier.

Dustmann, C. and I. Preston (2001) 'Attitudes to ethnic minorities, ethnic context and location decisions', *The Economic Journal* 111 (470): 353-373.

Dustmann, C., A. Glitz and U. Schönberg (2011), *Referral-based Job Search Networks*, NORFACE-Migration Discussion Paper 2011-12. London: Norface Research Programme on Migration.

Dustmann, C., F. Fabbri and I. Preston (2011), 'Racial harassment, ethnic concentration and economic conditions', *Scandinavian Journal of Economics*, 113 (3): 689-711.

Dustmann, C., I. Fadlon and Y. Weiss (2011), 'Return migration, human capital accumulation and the brain drain', *Journal of Development Economics* 95 (1): 58-67.

Ehrenberg, E. and R. Smith (2011), *Modern Labor Economics: Theory and Public Policy*. 11th ed. Saddle River (NJ): Prentice Hall.

Entorf, H. (2002), 'Rational migration policy should tolerate non-zero illegal migration flows', *International Migration* 40 (1): 27-43.

Entorf, H. and M. Lauk (2008), 'Peer effects, social multipliers and migrants at school: An international comparison', *Journal of Ethnic and Migration Studies* 34(4): 633-654.

Epstein, G. (2008), 'Herd and network effects in migration decision-making', *Journal of Ethnic and Migration Studies* 34 (4): 567-583.

Epstein, G. (2010), 'Informational cascades and the decision to migrate', in: G. S. Epstein, I. N. Gang (eds), *Migration and Culture (Frontiers of Economics and Globalization*, Vol. 8, pp. 25-44. Bingley (UK): Emerald Group Publishing.

Epstein, G. and A. Hillman (1998), *Herd Effects and Migration*, CEPR Discussion Paper 1811. London: Centre for Economic Policy Research.

Epstein, G. and I. Gang (2006), 'The influence of others on migration plans', *Review of Development Economics* 10 (4): 652-665.

Ethier, W. J. (1985), 'International Trade and Labor Migration', *American Economic Review*, 75 (4): 691-707.

Fidrmuc, J. (2004), 'Migration and regional adjustment to asymmetric shocks in transition economies', *Journal of Comparative Economics*, 32 (2): 230-247.

Fischer, P., R. Martin and T. Straubhaar (1997), 'Should I stay or should I go?' in: T. Hammar et al. (eds), *International Migration, Immobility and Development*, 49-90. Oxford/New York: Berg.

Friebel, G. and S. Guriev (2006), 'Smuggling humans: A theory of debt-financed migration', *Journal of the European Economic Association* 4 (6): 1085-1111.

Gaston, N., and Nelson, D.R. (2011), 'Bridging trade theory and labour econometrics: The effects of international migration', *Journal of Economic Surveys* , doi: 10.1111/j.1467-6419.2011.00696.x.

Gathman, C. (2008), 'Effect of enforcement on illegal markets: Evidence on migrants smuggling along the South-Western border', *Journal of Public Economics* 92: 1926-1941.

Ghatak, S., P. Levine and S. Price (1996), 'Theories and evidence: An assessment', *Journal of Economic Surveys* 10 (2): 159-198.

Giuliano, L., D. Levine and J. Leonard (2009), 'Manager race and the race of new hires', *Journal of Labor Economics* 27 (4): 589-632.

Glaeser, E. and J. Scheinkman (2001), 'Measuring social interactions', in: S. N. Durlauf and H. P. Young (eds), *Social Dynamics*, 83-131. Washington: Brooking Institute.

Gordon, I and Vickerman, R. (1982), 'Opportunity, preference and constraint: An approach to the analysis of metropolitan migration', *Urban Studies*, 19: 247-261.

Gould, D. (1994), 'Immigrant links to the home country: Empirical implications for US bilateral trade flows', *The Review of Economics and Statistics* 76 (2): 302-316.

Granovetter, M. (1978), 'Threshold models of collective behaviour', *American Journal of Sociology* 83 (6): 1420-1443.

Graves, P. and P. Linneman (1976), 'Household migration: Theoretical and empirical results', *Journal of Urban Economics* 6 (3): 383-404.

Greenwood, M. (1969), 'An analysis of the determinants of geographical labor mobility in the United States', *Review of Economics and Statistics* 51: 189-194.

Greenwood, M. (1975), 'Research on internal migration in the United States', *Journal of Economic Literature* 13: 397-433.

Greenwood, M. (1985), 'Human migration: Theory, models, and empirical studies', *Journal of Regional Science* 25: 521-544.

Greenwood, M. (1997), 'Internal Migration in Developed Countries', in M. R. Rosenzweig and O. Stark (eds), *Handbook of Population and Family Economics*, pp. 647-720. Amsterdam: Elsevier.

Greenwood, M., P. Mueser, D. Plane and A. Schlottmann (1991), 'New directions in migration research: Perspectives from some North American regional science disciplines', *Annals of Regional Science* 25 (4): 237-270.

Grubel, H. and A. Scott (1966), 'The International Flow of Human Capital', *American Economic Review* 56 (1/2): 268-274.

Hargreaves Heap, S., M. Hollis, B. Lyons, R. Sugden, and A. Weale (1992), *The Theory of Choice. A Critical Guide.* Oxford, Cambridge (Mass): Blackwell.

Hammond, P. J. and J. Sempere (2004), *Migration with Local Public Goods and the Gains from Changing Places.* Department of Economics Working Paper 05/001. Stanford: University of Stanford.

Hanson, G. (2007), *The Economic Logic of Illegal Migration*, CSR No. 26. New York: Council of Foreign Relations.

Harris, J. and M. Todaro (1970), 'Migration, unemployment, and development: A two-sector analysis', *American Economic Review* 60: 126-143.

Helmenstein C. and Y. Yegorov (2000), 'The dynamics of migration in the presence of chains', *Journal of Economic Dynamics and Control* 24 (2): 307-323.

Javorcik, B., Ç. Özden, M. Spatareanu and C. Neagu (2011), 'Migrant networks and foreign direct investment', *Journal of Development Economics* 94 (2): 231-241.

Jevell, R. and D. Molina (2004), 'Determining the determinants. Mexican migration to the US: A comparison of income and network effects', mimeo.

Katz, E. And O. Stark (1987), 'International migration under asymmetric information', *Economic Journal*, 97 (387): 718-726.

Kilic, T, C. Carletto, B. Davis and A. Zezza (2009), 'Investing back home: Return migration and business ownership in Albania', *Economics of Transition* 17 (3): 587-623.

Konya, I. (2002), 'A dynamic model of cultural assimilation', *Boston College Working Paper in Economics 546*, Chestnut Hill, MA.

Koser, K. (1997), 'Social networks and the asylum cycle: The case of Iranians in the Netherlands', *International Migration Review* 31 (3): 591-611.

Krugman, P. (1991), 'History versus expectations', *Quarterly Journal of Economics* 106 (2): 651-667.

Lazear, E. (1999), 'Culture and language', *Journal of Political Economy*, 107 (S6): S95-S126.

Lowry, I. S. (1966), *Migration and Metropolitan Growth: Two Analytical Models.* San Francisco: Chandler Publishing Company.

Manski, C. (1993), 'Identification of endogenous social effects: The reflection problem', *Review of Economic Studies* 60 (3): 531-542.

Manski, C. (2000), 'Economics analysis of social interactions', *Journal of Economic Perspectives* 14 (3): 115-136.

Marvell G., and P. Oliver P (1993), *The Critical Mass in Collective Action.* Cambridge: University Press

Massey, D., J. Arango, G. Hugo, A. Kouaouci, A. Pellegrino and J. Taylor (1993), 'Theories of international migration: A review and appraisal', *Population and Development Review* 19: 431-466.

Massey, D., J. Arango, G. Hugo, A. Kouaouci, A. Pellegrino and J. Taylor (1998), *Worlds in Motion: Understanding International Migration at the End of the Millennium.* Oxford: Oxford University Press.

Massey, D. S. and R. M. Zenteno (1999) 'The dynamics of mass migration', *Proceeding National Academy of Sciences* 96 (9): 5328-5335.

Mayer, K. and G. Peri (2009), 'Brain drain and brain return: Theory and application to Eastern-Western Europe', *Berkeley Electronic Journal of Economic Analysis & Policy* 9 (1): Article 49.

McCall, B. P. and J. J. McCall (1987), 'A sequential study of migration and job search', *Journal of Labor Economics*, 5 (4): 452-476.

McCormick B. and J. Wahba (2001), 'Overseas work experience, savings and entrepreneurship amongst return migrants to LDCs', *Scottish Journal of Political Economy* 48 (2): 164-178.

McKenzie, D. and H. Rapoport (2004), *Network Effects and the Dynamics of Migration and Inequality: Theory and Evidence from Mexico*, SCID Working Paper No 201. Stanford: Stanford University.

Mincer, J. (1978), 'Family migration decisions', *Journal of Political Economy* 86: 749-773.

Molho, I. (1986), 'Theories of migration: A review', *Scottish Journal of Political Economy* 33 (4): 396-419.

Mountford, A. (1997), 'Can a brain drain be good for growth in the source economy?' *Journal of Development Economics* 53 (2): 287-303.

Mundell, R. (1957), 'International trade and factor mobility', *American Economic Review*, 47: 321-335.

Munshi, K. (2003), 'Networks in the modern economy: Mexican migrants in the US labor market', *Quarterly Journal of Economics* 118: 549-599.

Myrdal, G. (1944), *An American Dilemma: The Negro Problem and Modern Democracy.* New York: Harper.

Myrdal, G. (1957), *Economic Theory and Under-Developed Regions.* London: Duckworth.

Naghavi, A. and C. Strozzi (2011), 'Intellectual property rights, migration, and diaspora', IZA Discussion Paper 5864. Bonn: IZA

Nakosteen, R. and M. Zimmer (1980), 'Migration and income: The question of self-selection', *Southern Economic Journal* 46: 840-851.

O'Connell, P. (1997), 'Migration under uncertainty: "Try your luck" or "Wait and see"', *Journal of Regional Science* 37 (2): 331-374.

Piracha, M. and F. Vadean (2010), 'Return migration and occupational choice: Evidence from Albania', *World Development* 38 (8): 1141-1155.

Piracha, M. and F. Vadean (2012), 'Migrant educational mismatch and the labor market', in: K. Zimmermann and A. Constant (eds), *International Handbook on the Economics of Migration.* Cheltenham: Edward Elgar Publishing.

Polackhek, S. and F. Horwath (1977), 'A life cycle approach to migration: Analysis of the perspicacious peregrinator', in: D. G. Ehrenberg (ed.), *Research in Labor Economics*, 103-149. Greenwich: JAI Press.

Postlewaite, A. (1998), 'The social basis of interdependent preferences', *European Economic Review* 42: 779-800.

Rauch, J. and V. Trindade (2002), 'Ethnic Chinese networks in international trade', *The Review of Economics and Statistics* 84 (1); 116-130.

Roy, A. D. (1951), 'Some thoughts on the distribution of earnings', *Oxford Economic Papers* 3: 135-146.

Schelling. T. (1978), *Micromotives and Macrobehavior.* New York: Norton.

Schiff, M. (2002), 'Love thy neighbor: trade, migration, and social capital', *European Journal of Political Economy* 18 (1): 87-107.

Schumpeter, J. A. (1909), 'On the Concept of Social Value', *Quarterly Journal of Economics* 23 (2): 213-232.

Shields, G. M. and M. P. Shields (1989), 'The emergence of migration theory and a suggested new direction', *Journal of Economic Surveys* 3 (4): 277-304.

Sjaastad, Larry A. (1962), 'The costs and returns of human migration', *Journal of Political Economy* 70 (October): 80-93.

Stark, O. (1991), *The Migration of Labour*, Oxford: Basil Blackwell.

Stark, O. (2003), 'Tales of migration without wage differentials: Individual, family, and community contexts', ZEF Discussion Paper Nr. 73, Bonn: Centre for Development Research.

Stark, O. (2004) 'Rethinking the brain drain', *World Development*, 32(1): 15-22.

Stark, O. and D. Bloom (1985), 'The New Economics of Labor Migration', *American Economic Review* 75:173-178.
Stark, O. and J. Taylor (1989), 'Relative deprivation and international migration', *Demography* 26: 1-14.
Stark, O. and J. Taylor (1991), 'Migration incentives, migration types: The role of relative deprivation', *Economic Journal* 101: 1163-1178.
Stark, O., C. Helmenstein and A. Prskawetz (1997), 'A Brain Gain with a Brain Drain'; *Economics Letters* 55 (2): 227-234.
Stark, O., C. Helmenstein and A. Prskawetz (1998), 'Human capital depletion, human capital formation and migration: A blessing or a "curse"?' *Economics Letters* 60 (3): 363-367.
Straubhaar, Th. (1988), *On the Economics of International Migration*, Bern: Haupt.
Taylor, J. E. (1986), 'Differential migration, networks, information, and risk', in: O. Stark (ed.), *Research in Human Capital and Development, Vol. 4. Migration, Human Capital and Development*. Greenwich: JAI Press.
Thadani, V.N. and M. P. Todaro (1984), 'Female migration: a conceptual framework', in Fawcett, J., S. Khoo and P. Smith (eds) *Women in the Cities of Asia: Migration and Urban Adaptation*. Boulder, Co: Westview Press, pp. 36-59.
The Economist (2011), 'The magic of diasporas: How migrant business networks are reshaping the world', 19 November.
Tiebout, C. (1956), 'A pure theory of local expenditures', *Journal of Political Economy* 64: 416-424.
Todaro, M. (1969), 'A model of labor migration and urban unemployment in less developed countries', *American Economic Review* 59 (March): 138-148.
Tullock, G. (1971), 'The cost of transfers', *Kyklos*, 24(4): 629-643.
Tunali, I. (1996), 'Migration and remigration of role household needs in Turkey, 1963-1973', *Economic Development and Cultural Change* 45 (1): 31-68.
Winters, P., A. de Janvry and E. Sadoulet (2001), 'Family and community networks in Mexico-US Migration', *Journal of Human Resources* 36 (1): 159-184.
Woodruff, C. and R. Zenteno (2007), 'Migration networks and microenterprises in Mexico', *Journal of Development Economics* 82 (2): 509-528.
Yap, L. (1977), 'The attraction of cities: A review of the migration literature', *Journal of Development Economics* 4: 239-264.

3 Historical-Structural Models of International Migration

Ewa Morawska

Introduction

This chapter presents and critically evaluates the major tenets of three theories of international population movements commonly referred to as 'historical-structural'. These are the segmented labour market theory, dependency theory and world-system theory. Also discussed is the gradual shift of these theories and their associated models from being exclusively economic to encompassing broader economic and political structural explanations.[1]

The historical-structural theories of international migration were first formulated in the social sciences during the 1950s and 1960s in reaction to the models of migration then predominant – the rational choice model and the classical and new economy models – which explained transnational population movements as the result of individual and small group (household) micro-level factors and within the framework of the harmoniously functioning capitalist market premised on the notion of modernisation, understood as a progressive convergent development of different parts of the world.

Although, as we shall see, the historical-structural models discussed here differ in the time and scope of the processes they cover, and in the main emphases of their arguments, they all share major premises derived from the Marxist (or Marxisant) persuasion of their advocates. These common attributes include the following: placing the causes of international migration in the realm of historically conditioned macro-structural forces; the primacy of the inherently exploitative and disequalising economic forces of global capitalism in explaining the directions and character of transnational population movements; and critical assessment of the mechanisms and effects of international migration as integrally related to the operation of the globalising capitalist market.

Segmented labour market theory of international migration

segmented labour market model

Theories of the segmented or dual labour market originally appeared in the literature of the undeveloped and underdeveloped world in the 1950s. They were first applied to advanced industrial economies in the mid-1960s to account for the enduring disadvantage of black workers in American cities. Since then, they have been extended to explain the mechanisms of the international migration of labour between less developed and more developed regions.

There are four central premises of the segmented labour market model as it applies to international migration, as specified by its most renowned advocate, Michael Piore (1979; see also Berger and Piore 1980). The first of these posits that highly-developed industrial economies are characterised by an inherently uneven distribution of capital and resources that extends to the labour force in the form of a segmented labour market structure. The labour market is divided into two distinct sectors. The primary, capital-intensive sector offers stable, skilled jobs with good remuneration and advancement opportunities. The secondary, labour-intensive sector offers low-skilled, low-paid and unstable jobs. The second premise holds a permanent demand for labour to be the logical result of the requirement for a cheap and flexible workforce, which characterises the secondary sector of employment in highly industrialised economies. The third premise rests on this second and holds international migration to be predominantly caused by the structural demand for cheap and dispensable labour rather than decisions made by individuals. The fourth, and final, premise of the segmented labour market model of international migration is that employers in highly developed countries, unwilling to raise wages in the secondary sector but unable to find native workers prepared to take such poorly paid jobs, seek migrant workers to fill the ensuing employment gap. These workers are temporary and, therefore, disposable labourers from undeveloped and underdeveloped regions of the world who view bottom-level jobs simply as a means to earn an income which by their home-country standards appears satisfactory.[2]

primary and secondary sector employment

The dual labour-market hypothesis suggests that the functioning of the labour market is best understood in terms of a model in which employment is divided into a primary and a secondary sector. Migrants are found in the low paid secondary sector. Jobs in the primary sector are largely reserved for natives, leading to a fundamental dichotomy between the jobs of migrants and the jobs of natives. The role of migrants in industrial economies is largely determined by the role and function of the secondary sector in which migrants are found and by the evolution of its labour requirements (Piore 1979: 35-36).

Two other concepts are important in the context of segmented labour markets. Although they do not explain the forces either triggering or sustaining international migration – the subject of this chapter – they are included here because they often appear in connection with the segmented labour market model in discussions of the location of immigrant and ethnic groups in receiver-country economies. These concepts are *internal colonisation* and the *cultural division of labour.*

internal colonisation thesis

Like the segmented labour market model, the internal colonisation thesis was first formulated by Latin American and African scholars to account for the uneven development of and persistent rural-urban inequalities in the undeveloped and underdeveloped regions of the world (see e.g. Casanova 1965; Stavenhagen 1970; Wolpe 1975; Walton 1975). Subsequently, the internal colonisation thesis has been extended to explain the interregional (global) disparities in economic development deriving from the enduring heritage of colonial relationships (Castells 1973; Rofman and Romero 1973). A further extension, and of concern here, has been to the situation of immigrants and racial minorities from undeveloped and underdeveloped parts of the world who are brought into the secondary sectors of highly industrialised receiver countries by the demand for cheap and subordinate labour and now subject to 'domestic' colonial exploitation, in which immigrant communities form an economic and social underclass within an otherwise wealthy nation (Casanova 1965; Carmichael and Hamilton 1970; Clark 1965).[3]

The other concept, that of a cultural division of labour, refers to enduring inequities in job status in the labour market of particular ethnic and racial groups which have been explicitly (in the nineteenth to early twentieth centuries) or implicitly (in the post-World War II era) justified in terms of group cultural superiority or inferiority due to the supposed presence or absence of innate skills and intelligence (for the most elaborate exposition of the cultural division of labour argument, see Hechter 1976, 1979).[4]

cultural division of labour

Let us now briefly evaluate the strengths and weaknesses of the segmented labour market model. In regard to strengths, three points are to be noted. First, by making the operation of the structural forces of global capitalism the focus of analysis of mechanisms that trigger cross-border population movements, the segmented labour market model has provided a new and important perspective on international migration traditionally explained in solely individualistic terms.

The second point is really a half-strength, but worth mentioning. The original formulation of the dual labour market theory presented the 'pull' structural forces of cross-border migration in purely economic terms, reflecting contradictory demands of capital and labour, with the resulting bifurcation of the labour market in industrialised receiver societies. However, subsequent developments of the model recognise the role of nation-states and politics in shaping international migration. Thus, in their 1980 book on *Dualism and Discontinuity in Industrial Societies,* Berger and Piore acknowledge that 'economic analysis does not provide a sufficient account of the origins [and operation] of dualism' (ibid.: 85). True, it is a narrow recognition, as the role of the state and politics appears only as the transmitter of capitalist interests by acting on behalf of capitalist employers to support labour-recruitment programmes. However, the statement cited here opens an avenue for bringing politics into the analysis as a more autonomous agent.

The third important strength of the segmented labour market model has been its recognition of the context-dependent and, thus, changing circumstances of industrial capitalism and its accompanying state-political arrangements. By recognising the context dependency of the examined phenomena, the model also acknowledges the historical time-specific and place-specific nature of the mechanisms responsible for international migration.

criticisms

Although migration scholars still use the segmented labour market model, criticisms of this approach have been numerous. Five of them should be noted here. First, just as the segmentation model opposed the overly individualistic emphasis of classical accounts of cross-border population movements, it has itself been criticised for its exclusive focus on the structural forces that trigger international migration. The segmentation model pays scant attention to the human agency of the migrants themselves, their motivations, preferences and decisions. Second, critics have argued that the model is difficult to prove empirically. In particular, the boundaries between labour market sectors, which the theory posits as sharply defined, are in reality much more blurred. Especially damaging to the model's premise of two separate sectors of employment has been evidence of the existence of ethnic economic enclaves in large, concentrated immigrant and ethnic communities that offer more security and advancement opportunities than do mainstream secondary economic sectors (Portes and Bach 1985). The next two assumptions of the segmented labour market model considered by critics as empirically unproven are the notions that recruitment programmes instituted by receiver-country employers constitute the main venue for bringing in migrant workers, and that the length of stay of migrant workers in the receiver country is mostly short-term and temporary. Regarding the former premise, extensive empirical research has demonstrated that, particularly in the later, sustaining phases of international migration that follow the original, triggering stage (Massey et al. 1998), it is not the recruitment programmes in the receiver countries that keep immigration flowing, but the transnational support networks of the migrants themselves. As for the temporal nature of the employment of low-skilled migrant workers in industrial economies, the history of millions of *Gastarbeiter* in Europe and of Mexican labourers imported for seasonal agriculture in the south-west United States demonstrates that short-term relocation is not always the norm. Indeed, a great many of both of these sets of migrant workers remained permanently in the receiving countries against the dialectical logic of capital and labour and the wishes of their employers.[5] The fifth criticism of the segmented labour market theory concerns its narrow focus. The theory rests on a generalised perception of capitalism that emphasises the demand for low-skilled labour migrants from undeveloped and underdeveloped regions by wealthy economies. However, it largely ignores the rapidly growing demand for highly-skilled workers – from wherever in the world – who enter the primary sector of employment with high status and top-paying jobs.

Dependency theory of international migration

dependency model

Like the segmented labour market theories were inspired by the Marxist critique of capitalism, dependency models of economic development emerged during the 1950s in response to the dominant modernisation viewpoint that represented world development as the universal, progressive evolution towards increasing urbanisation and industrialisation. Latin American scholars, especially those working at the United Nations Economic Commission for Latin America (ECLA), were among the first to point out that the world is in fact not experiencing an inexorable progression toward modernisation and development. Rather, they argued, undeveloped and underdeveloped regions of the world are trapped in enduring poverty as a direct result of their subordinate, exploitative relationship to more highly developed capitalist countries.

The dependency thesis subsequently gained a great number of diverse followers who agree on the fundamental idea of a negative relationship in economic development between powerful capitalist countries and the undeveloped and underdeveloped parts of the world. However, different proponents of the theory have varied considerably in the degree of importance they assign to political influence on barriers to development.[6]

Preoccupied with the internal relocations of rural populations to the cities, advocates of the dependency model of economic development originally had little interest in international migration. By the 1970s, however, as the so-called compass labour transfers accompanying accelerated globalisation of the capitalist economy flowed from the undeveloped and underdeveloped southern and eastern regions (S/E) of the world to the industrialised North and West (N/W), scholars working with the dependency theory were quick to incorporate this phenomenon into the model.

international migration

The main argument of the dependency theory of international migration holds that the historical process of subordinate incorporation of the undeveloped and underdeveloped parts of the world into the major capitalist economies dislocates millions of people in these poor regions from their traditional way of life and makes them prone to internal (rural to urban), as well as cross-border, migration in search of livelihoods. On the side of the highly developed receiver countries, it is the demand for labour – the cheapest possible – that constitutes the major mechanism of the transnational compass movement of people. Dependency theorists view labour-related transfers across the world as primarily caused by the structural demands of global capitalism for cheap labour and the geographic division of that labour. The political relationships of power and domination, which link the economically powerful and dependent parts of the world, are also seen as important in this context.[7]

models compared

Although they share a primary concern with the structural mechanisms of international migration deriving from the operation of modern capitalism, the dependency account of cross-border population movements differs from the segmented labour model in several important aspects. In particular, the dependency theory provides a more encompassing and coherent explanatory framework for the role of international migration in the globalising capitalist economy than does the dual labour market model.

Three more specific advantages of the dependency theory over the segmented labour market concept are worth pointing out. One of these is that a number of dependency theorists have proposed a vision of the functions of international migration that is less constrained by the principles of orthodox Marxism and more sensitive to human agency, in comparison to their segmented market colleagues. As the former view it, the significance of international migration for the operation of global capitalism lies, first and foremost, in providing a source of labour and mobile 'human capital' (in the form of skilled migrants) for capitalist enterprises. It is important to note, however, that income-seeking cross-border migrations also serve as a safety valve for the exploited masses of people who live on the periphery as they try to cope with their difficult situations.[8]

The two other advantages of dependency theory over the segmented labour market concept concern the dependency model's more accurate representation of the actual characteristics of S/E-N/W labour migrations across the contemporary world. First to note in this context is the preoccupation of dependency theorists with so-called 'brain drain' (i.e. the selective migration of highly educated and skilled people from undeveloped and underdeveloped regions to more industrialised parts of the world). Resulting from the dependency advocates' primary concern with the diminished prospect for economic development of the undeveloped and underdeveloped regions of the world associated with their relationship with powerful industrialised countries, attention to the growing demand for brain-drain (im)migrants in highly developed economies has corresponded well with actual developments characterising post-industrial transformation of global capitalism in the post-1970 era.[9]

compass migration

The second advantage of dependency theory over the assumptions of the segmented labour market model in regard to S/E-N/W labour migrations has been the explicit recognition of the permanent nature of a large part of these migrations. Dependency theorists view the long-term or permanent character of compass migrations as the product of two factors. The first is the enduring stagnation in economic development in the undeveloped and underdeveloped parts of the world due to their incorporation into global capitalism. The second cause, on the side of the receiver, the developed economies, is a continuous structural demand for labour at both ends of the skills spectrum that cannot be met by the domestic workforce.

strengths and weaknesses

All of the above-noted features of the dependency model of international migration can be assessed as strengths of this approach. Of particular value, and worth reiterating, is the dependency theory's account of transnational population movements in the context of a historical analysis of the long-term structural transformations of modern capitalism. The corresponding assessment is that problems of international migration cannot be comprehended outside of a broader theory of economic development, of which it constitutes an integral part. Closely related to this postulate, and important for students of international migration to remember, is the basic premise of the dependency theory; that is, the unequal *inter*dependence of different parts of the globalising capitalist world and its operational elements, including transnational population flows for the purpose of work.

These are the dependency model's theoretical strengths. Its other forte lies in its empirical testability. Unlike the segmented labour market theory, the dependency model allows for the formulation of specific testable propositions. The most important of these is that 'international flows of labour follow international flows of capital, but in the opposite direction' (Massey et al. 1998: 55; see also Sassen 1988).

Inevitably, dependency theorists' accounts of international migration have attracted criticism from fellow scholars. The most common complaint is the model's weak conceptualisation of the decision process at the individual level – a shared feature of all the historical-structural theories. Critics argue that it is impossible to explain individual actions purely by placing them within their larger structural environment, because there is a discontinuity between the units of analysis (i.e. systems of economic production vs. the movement of people).

The remaining points of criticism of the dependency theory, which can be equally directed against other historical-structural models derived from a Marxist tradition, concern its unjustified economic reductionism in explaining the mechanisms of international population movements. Critics appreciate the earlier-noted recognition by dependency model scholars of the defence-strategy functions performed by cross-border migration for bread-seekers from undeveloped and underdeveloped regions. However, they argue that its theoretical implications for the perception of the role of individual agents in migratory processes remain unelaborated.

The other, related, point of criticism against the dependency model concerns its overly narrow interpretation of the role of state and political factors in shaping international migration. Dependency scholars see population movements as simply serving the interests of the dominant capitalist system. Other considerations are a priori excluded by the model's premises. For instance, interests of political superiority motivated Western governments to allow thousands of refugees into their countries from Soviet-dominated Eastern Europe during the post-War era and the German government's policy of 'guilty responsibility' for the Holocaust offers immediate naturalisation to any Jews wishing to settle in that country.

Finally, also issuing from fellow scholars' unhappiness with the tendency of dependency theorists toward economic reductionism, has been a criticism of the dependency model's non-recognition of ideological, cultural and material ties between highly industrialised and undeveloped and underdeveloped countries which, related but not reducible to solely economic (e.g., colonial) ties, may also impact the direction, volume and composition of international migrations.[10]

The world-system theory of international migration

The most recent of the three approaches considered here, and one still widely used today, is the world-system theory of international migration. It evolved during the late 1970s and early 1980s from the dependency model and from historical analyses of the expansion of the global capitalist system from the sixteenth century onward by scholars such as Fernand Braudel (1981, 1982) and Immanuel Wallerstein (1974, 1980).

global interdependency

The world-system theory shares with the dependency theory a view of the world as interrelated through mutual economic dependence, but with a profound inequality in economic development and exploitation between its different parts. They also share a similar historical approach to the analysis of how these interdependencies operate. However, the world-system theory in general, and its application to international migration in particular, is more theoretically elaborated and sophisticated than its dependency predecessor. It accounts for the emergence of a global market economy through the increasingly inclusive interdependency of dominant capitalist powers concentrated in the North and West (N/W) of the world (referred to as its *core*) and the subordinate and exploited undeveloped and underdeveloped regions concentrated in the southern and eastern (S/E) parts of the world (called the *periphery* or *semi-periphery*, depending on the degree of dependence) (Wallerstein 1974, 1976).[11]

The expansion of the world capitalist market is viewed as involving the emergence of a global division of labour.

> Within and forming the world-scale division of labour [argue world-system theorists], a complex network of cross-national movements of capital, commodities, and labour takes place as the expansion of the whole proceeds on the basis of the disharmonious rates of growth among and within regional aggregates. These flows bind the peripheral populations to events and decisions in the core, just as they tie the formation of the core to the evolution of the social formations of the periphery (Petras 1981: 45).

world-system theory

International migration of labour occurs within this historically interdependent grid as a natural consequence of the incorporation of the undeveloped and underdeveloped world into the capitalist market. As such, it is an integral element of the development of the modern world economy. Migration patterns are generated by the economic command of stronger core economies over weaker, peripheral and semi-peripheral ones and by political, ideological, and material links created in the process of capitalist exchange between these increasingly connected parts. In an important departure from the more reductionist dependency approach, world-system theory, especially in its more recent reformulations, allows for these non-economic considerations to operate under specific conditions as semi-autonomous migration-inducting mechanisms. According to world-system theory, it is possible to predict the main worldwide patterns of the exchange of labour for capital by identifying economic dependency relations and, emerging from it, political and cultural connections of dominance and subordination between different parts of the world.

international migration

The international flow of labour follows international flows of goods and capital, but in the opposite direction. Capitalist investment foments changes that create an uprooted mobile population in (semi-) peripheral countries while simultaneously forging strong material and cultural links with core countries, leading to transnational movement (Massey et al. 1998: 41).

The world-system model of international migration does, however, predict more than just a simple compass direction, S/E to N/W, of cross-border labour flows. First, on the basis of an analysis of the historical origins of the capitalist world-system, it posits that transnational population flows

> are especially likely between past colonial powers and their former colonies, because cultural, linguistic, administrative, investment, transportation, and communication links were established early and were allowed to develop free from outside competition during the colonial era, leading to the formation of specific transnational markets and cultural systems (Massey et al. 1998: 41).

Global cities

Second, according to world-system scholars, a large proportion of this population movement from periphery and semi-periphery to core heads towards so-called global cities or the command centres of global capitalism with banking, finance, administration, high-tech, legal and professional services, and a corresponding collection of second- and third-layer service industries. The structural characteristics of global cities and, especially, their intensely bifurcated labour markets with a strong demand for workers at both the upper and lower ends, create a large pool of migrant labour. In the United States, global cities include New York, Chicago, Los Angeles and Miami; in Europe they are London, Paris, Frankfurt, and Milan; Tokyo, Sydney, and Singapore form the global hubs of the Pacific.[12]

world-system theory revised

Since its original formulation nearly a quarter of a century ago, the world-system theory of international migration has been revised numerous times. Scholars working in this paradigm have done this largely in response to critiques of the model's economic reductionism, its unjustified focus solely on labour migration and its overly macro-structural emphasis. This last shortcoming has led to a failure to recognise the role of micro-level factors, such as local social networks and individual human agency, in shaping international migration.

The world-system model benefits from being sufficiently flexible to modify its claims in response to criticism. Moreover, it is amenable to combination with theoretical approaches informed by other analytic priorities, which is probably its greatest strength. The many valuable revisions of world-system theory models have resulted in a pluralised and multi-dimensional approach to the study of international migration.

One particularly valuable revision was introduction of the concept of 'semi-periphery' (the original formulation of the world-system theory divided the world into only two parts: core and periphery; see Wallerstein 1974). This addition allowed further refinement of levels of dependency conditional on the particular circumstances of the examined country or region. These include the core of the semi-periphery and the semi-periphery of the core. Thus, more nuanced, context- and time-dependent analyses are permitted of the flows of international migration.

political and cultural factors

Theoretical recognition of the potential role of political factors and culture (symbolic and material) in shaping international migration has allowed scholars to elaborate on the effects of specific agents in particular historical situations. Thus, for example, political and military interventions by the governments of core countries to protect their economic interests in peripheral and semi-peripheral ones or to fend off competing political influences (such as during the Cold War) generate another kind of international migration in the form of refugee movements. Similarly, the process of state-building in the former colonies of core countries and their accompanying ethnic conflicts have been observed to generate waves of cross-border refugees, both to neighbouring countries as well as farther away to core parts of the world, particularly to former colonial powers. For receiving areas, reconstructed world-system theorists recognise the immigration policies of core country governments as being a factor affecting migration. These policies result from both their economic interests in the sender countries and more directly from political concerns, such as election campaigns.[13]

World-system theory's most felicitous feature, at least in this author's opinion, has been its compatibility with micro-level explanations of international migration that are sensitive to human agency. Supporting this claim are two theoretical approaches that offer encompassing, world-system–cum–micro-level accounts of international migration tested by empirical research. They are Douglas Massey et al.'s (1998) cumulative causation model and Ewa Morawska's (2001; 2011) structuration theory of international migration.

macro and micro explanatory approaches

The authors of *Worlds in Motion* base their synthetic model on the premise that both macro-level and micro-level explanatory approaches to international migration 'play some role in accounting for international migration in the contemporary world although different models predominate at different phases of the migration process' (Massey et al. 1998: 281). Thus, the *initiation* of international migratory flows, they argue, is best accounted for by a combination of propositions from the multi-dimensional world-system model, neoclassical economics (see chapter 2 of this volume) and the new economics of migration theories. At the global level, socio-economic and political transformations are seen as important causal factors of migration patterns. A key transformation in this respect is the incorporation of non-market or pre-market countries of the South and East into the capitalist world economy. Concomitant with this is the penetration of capitalist culture into the incorporated regions and the continued demand for immigrant workers in secondary sectors of the post-industrial receiver economies of the North and West (segmented labour market theory). Rapid advances in global transportation and communication (world-system theory) and the immigration policies of receiver governments have further stimulated this 'compass' movement from South and East to North and West of large numbers of people in search of livelihoods in the 'core' regions of the world. At the micro level, factors triggering international migrations from less developed to more developed parts of the world include wage differentials between sending and receiving countries and regions (neoclassical economics) and the calculated efforts of sending households to diversify risk by engaging in both local and international markets (new economics of migration).

cumulative causation model

A combination of specific propositions derived from the segmented labour market model and micro-level social capital theories explains, according to Massey et al. (1998), the *perpetuation* of international migratory flows. The transnational movement of people is sustained by continued inducements to immigration that are generated, in sender communities, by increased income discrepancies resulting from earlier migrations and the ensuing relative deprivation of those at the bottom of the sending community. In receiving communities, the formation of ethnic enclave economies augments demand for immigrant workers (segmented labour market theory), and the growth and expansion of migrant networks of information and assistance that stretch between the sending and receiving communities eases the actual process of relocation (social capital theory). Over time, this movement perpetuates itself, making additional migration more likely – and the attempts of receiver states to control it ineffective. Migrations are thus sustained by established transnational support networks, by increasing discrepancies in the distribution of income and material affluence in home-country communities, and by the 'culture of migration' created during continued transnational travels (theory of cumulative causation). This synthetic approach to explain international migration has been empirically applied by Massey and his team in their analyses of documented and undocumented migrations of Mexicans to the United

States (see Duran and Massey 1992; Massey et al. 1987; Massey et al. 1994).

This author (EM) has integrated the world-system approach into a theoretically more encompassing explanatory framework known as the structuration model.[14] The basic idea underlying the view of international migration as a structuration process can be summarised as follows: Whereas the long-term and immediate configurations of forces at the upper structural layers set the dynamic limits of the possible and the impossible within which people act, it is at the level of closer social surroundings that individuals and groups evaluate their situations, define purposes and undertake actions of which the consequences – both intended and unintended – in turn affect these local-level and, over time, larger-scope structures.

structures

'Structures' are conceived of as patterns of social relations (including economic and political ones) and cultural formations that are (re) constituted through everyday practice of social actors. These are plural in character (e.g. different-purpose organisations, strong and weak informal networks, various cultures and subcultures), scope (e.g. global, regional, national, local), dynamics (more or less stable), and durability (longer to shorter duration). This multiplicity imbues structures at all levels with inherent tensions and, as a result, differential capacity to enable and constrain human agency. The complexity and interrelatedness of structures and their constitutive dependence on potentially ever-innovative human agency (see below) make them also fundamentally mutable, 'dynamic [not static], as the continually evolving outcome and matrix of a process of social interaction' (Sewell 1998: 27).

human agency

Human agency is conceptualised by Emirbayer and Mische (1998: 970) as follows:

> a temporally embedded engagement by actors of different structural environments that, through the interplay of habit, imagination, and judgement, both reproduces and transforms those structures in interactive response to the problems posed by changing situations.

Human agency comprises three analytically distinguishable components (although in practice they are closely related). The *iterational* or habitual element refers to 'the selective reactivation by actors of past patterns of thoughts and action, as routinely incorporated in practical activity'. The *projective* element encompasses 'the imaginative generation by actors of possible future trajectories of action, in which received structures of thought and action may be creatively reconfigured in relation to actors' hopes, fears, and desires for the future'. Finally, the *practical-evaluative element* entails 'the capacity of actors to make practical and normative judgements among alternative possible trajectories of action, in response to the demands, dilemmas, and ambiguities of presently evolving situations'. Depending on the particular configuration of circumstances, 'one or another of these three aspects might predominate' in guiding the actions of any one individual (Emirbayer and Mische 1998: 971-972).

Each of these elements of social actors' engagement with their environment involves schemas and resources. The former are 'virtual' as an available commonly-shared 'cultural kit' or repertoire of basic guideposts, that is, general principles and strategies of action that are informed by past experience and memories adjusted to present situations and projected outcomes in the future. Schemas are actualised through their application to concrete situations. They are socially constructed in a dual sense: they are acquired in the process of in-group socialisation, and they are created and recreated through the symbolic and behavioural practice of participating in different social networks and institutions. As a matrix of generalised orientations to action, schemas are also transposable; that is, they can be applied to different and new situations.

resources

Resources, both human (i.e. knowledge, skills, positions in different social structures and the opportunities derived therefrom) and nonhuman (i.e. animate and inanimate objects), exist in time and space as specific characteristics and possessions of historical actors. It is their actualisation in people's minds, bodies, social relations, and the physical surroundings they control that makes them resources. As with schemas, resources are transposable to new and different situations encountered by actors as they pursue their purposes. They are therefore never fully unambiguous in their potential utility-defining meanings (Sewell 1998: 9-12). Because resources embody schemas as practice-orienting guideposts, and, correspondingly, schemas are enacted in resources and their material and symbolic products, they mutually imply and reconstitute each other over time.

By applying schemas (resources in their everyday pursuits), actors create and recreate different structures of social life. This reproduction, however, is never ideal. Inherent in all humans is 'the capacity to appropriate, reproduce, and, potentially, to innovate upon received cultural categories and conditions of action in accordance with their personal and collective ideals, interests, and commitments' (Emirbayer and Mische 1998: 970-972). The concrete forms and 'contents' of this reproduction are shaped by sets of particular cultural schemas and resources available in time- and place-specific environments in which people practise, and by specific configurations of iterational, projective and practical-evaluative considerations. Agency arises from actors' knowledge of schemas and (some) control of resources, which means the ability to apply these tools to new situations. New situations, in particular, enable actors to reinterpret schemas and redesign resources. As a result, as social actors innovate and devise ways to cope with the world, 'thoughts, perceptions, and actions [occur that are] inconsistent with the reproduction of existing social patterns' (Sewell 1998: 12).

(re)constitution process

Thus conceptualised, the structuration model is particularly useful for interpreting the pursuits of migrants who move into or between different environments and so confront new circumstances. Considered in this framework, the activities of migrants are neither simply the products of structures nor outcomes of their own volitions. Rather, they are results of dialectics of *power to* (act) and *power over* (things or people), as these actors (re)define and pursue their purposes, playing with or against different structures. How much power individuals can derive from their sociocultural resources is contingent upon the influence of other macro and micro structures that support particular orientations: the dynamism or stagnation of economies, the open or ethnic-ascriptive (segmented) nature of the labour market, the restrictiveness of sender and receiver state immigration policies and the 'gaps' created by their imperfections, civic-political pluralism or the exclusivity of the receiving society, and the parochialism or cosmopolitanism of the host culture. Within these intersecting frameworks, the specific configurations of individuals' orientations and, thus, their transformative potential, are further influenced by their changing over time socio-demographic characteristics, by their economic resources and by their social-cultural capital, and, in the case of contemporary migrants, by their civic-political status in the receiving country. These aspects can greatly influence individual decisions to relocate for the purposes of finding employment. Thus constituted, migrants' orientations and practices reproduce or transform, in turn, these very social structures.

cumulative causation and structuration models compared

An appealing feature of the cumulative causation approach is its advance specification of which theories, including the world-system theory, explain successive phases of international migration. In comparison, the advantage of the structuration framework is twofold. First, it integrates the structural aspects (including features of world-system theory) and agentic mechanisms of transnational population flows into a theoretically coherent account. Second, it views the mutual reconstitution of social structures and human action as context-dependent and historical, that is, as a time-bound and place-specific *process of becoming*, rather than as a permanent condition. Within this interpretative framework, empirical research faces four major challenges:

- To establish which of multiple societal structures at the macro, mezzo and micro levels impact the international migration patterns of specific groups of people;
- To determine how these structures operate;
- To demonstrate how individuals make decisions to stay where they are or migrate in search of employment; and
- To establish how cross-border travel is organised and carried out.

Conclusion

This chapter examined the major premises of three historical-structural models of international migration: the segmented labour market theory, dependency theory and world-system theory. As we have seen, all three models are informed by similar underlying ideas, derived from the Marxist orientation of their advocates: the location of the causes of international migration originate in historically conditioned macro-structural forces, and in particular, the divisive effects of the globalising capitalist market; and the 'involved' (as opposed to a neutral 'scientific') critical assessment of the mechanisms and effects of the analysed phenomena – of concern here, international migration – as integrally related to the exploitative operation of global capitalism. At the same time, we have noted differences between the three historical-structural models as well. They differ in the spatial and temporal scope of their analysis and also in their theoretical flexibility and capacity to incorporate criticisms and ideas from other analytic approaches.

The historical-structural theories have undoubtedly contributed to our understanding of the contexts and mechanisms of international migration. Their attentiveness to historical processes and to the macro-structural forces of capitalist globalisation has by now become a postulate of any satisfactory social-science account of transnational population flows. The lesson to learn from scholarly critiques of these theories, and from the earlier-noted attempts of migration scholars to improve upon them, is that while historical-structural analysis is a necessary component of the encompassing theoretical explanation of international migration, it alone is insufficient. As previously noted, micro-level societal and human agency factors also have important roles to play in international migration processes. Their inclusion within and alongside historical-structural analysis allows for a more encompassing explanation of this complex phenomenon.

MAIN IDEAS

The three historical-structural theories of international migration differ in their spatial and temporal scope of analysis.

The historical-structural models have undoubtedly contributed to our understanding of the contexts and mechanisms of international migration.

Historical-structural analysis is a necessary component of theoretical explanations of international migration; but it alone is insufficient.

In receiving countries, demand for labour constitutes the major mechanism of transnational movements of people from the South and East to the North and West.

Unlike the segmented labour market concept, the dependency model allows for the formulation of specific testable propositions.

The many valuable revisions of world-system theory models have resulted in a pluralised and multi-dimensional approach to the study of international migration.

Notes

1 The term 'historical-structural' was originally (in the 1950s) assigned to the dependency theory of international migration. Since then, however, migration specialists have come to use it to refer to all three models identified here.

2 For other representatives of the segmented labour market model, see Harris and Todaro (1970); Freedman (1976); Edwards, Reich and Gordon (1973); Tolbert, Horan, and Beck (1980); Dickens and Lang (1985).

3 However, see John Walton (1975), the major proponent of the internal colonisation thesis, for a critique of the extrapolation of this concept to highly developed societies on the grounds that the nature of class inequality in these societies is quite different from that of undeveloped and underdeveloped regions.

4 While representatives of the dominant racial and ethnoreligious groups occupy positions in the primary sector of the economy to which they are viewed as naturally predisposed, the subordinate ones, usually non-white (or perceived as such) and of ethno-religious origins viewed as culturally inferior or even threatening to the dominant position of the majority, hold low-paid, unsafe and unstable positions in the secondary economic sector.

5 It must be emphasised, however, that this criticism is valid only with hindsight. When the segmented labour market theory of international migration was formulated, thousands of *Gastarbeiters* were indeed going back and forth between their home and destination countries.

6 Paul Baran's (1957; 1973) reworkings of the ideas of Marx and Lenin in application to the emerging global capitalism of the mid-twentieth century shaped the work of these scholars. For the original formulations of this approach, see Prebisch (1964); Cardoso and Faletto (1969); Cardoso (1977); Furtado (1971). Also see Frank (1969, 1978); Amin (1974, 1976) and Abel and Lewis (1985: Section I) for different elaborations of the dependency thesis.

7 For the best-known expositions of the dependency model of international migration, see Singer (1975); Portes and Browning (1976); Munoz et al. (1977); Petras (1981); Bonacich and Hirata (1981).

8 For an elaboration of this function of international migration, see Portes (1978); Portes and Bach (1985).

9 For dependency theorist writings on brain-drain compass migrations, see Khoshkish (1966); Kannappan (1968); Adams (1969); Watanabe (1969); Walton (1976); Glaser (1978).

10 For general evaluations of the dependency model of international migration by social scientists, see Portes (1978); Portes and Walton (1981); Wood (1981); Massey et al. (1998).

11 For contemporary social scientists' representations of this approach, see Amin (1976); Petras (1981); Sklair (1990); Shannon (1996).

12 For global cities and the international migrants they attract, see Castells (1989); Sassen (1980, 1991). For the world-system model of international migration see also Kritz et al. (1981); Portes and Walton (1981); Stalker (2000).

13 For different types of international migrants within the world-system framework, see Massey et al. (1998, 2004); Zolberg (1981; 1989); Zolber and Benda (2001); Zolber, Suhrke and Aguayo (1989).

14 For its original conceptualisations, see Bourdieu (1977); Giddens (1976, 1984); and for more recent reformulations, see Sewell (1992); Mische and Emirbayer (1998); Stones (2005).

Recommended Reading

Boyd, R. et al. (1997), *International Labour and the Third World: The Making of a New Working Class.* Aldershot: Avebury.

Kritz, M. et al. (eds) (1981), *Global Trends in Migration: Theory and Research on International Population Movements.* Staten Island: Center for Migration Studies.

Massey, D. et al. (1998), *Worlds in Motion: Understanding International Migration at the End of the Millennium.* Oxford: Clarendon Press.

Piore, M. (1979), *Birds of Passage: Migrant Labor and Industrial Societies.* Cambridge: Cambridge University Press.

Sassen, S. (1980), 'The internationalization of the labor force', *Studies in Comparative International Development* 15 (4): 3-28.

Wood, C. (1981), 'Equilibrium and historical-structural perspectives on migration', *International Migration Review* 16 (2): 299-319.

References

Abel, C. and C. Lewis (eds) (1985), *Latin America, Economic Imperialism and the State: The Political Economy of the External Connection from Independence to the Present.* London: The Athlone Press.

Adams, W. (1969), *The Brain Drain*. New York: Macmillan.
Amin, S. (1976), *Unequal Development: An Essay on the Social Formations of Peripheral Capitalism*. New York: Monthly Review Press.
Amin, S. (1974), *Accumulation on a World Scale: A Critique of the Theory of Underdevelopment, Vols. I and II*. New York: Monthly Review Press.
Baran, P. (1973), 'On the political economy of backwardness', in: K. Wilber (ed.), *The Political Economy of Development and Underdevelopment*, 82-93. New York: Random House.
Baran, P. (1957), *The Political Economy of Growth*. New York: Monthly Review Press.
Berger S. and M. Piore (1980), *Dualism and Discontinuity in Industrial Societies*. Cambridge: Cambridge University Press.
Bonacich, E. (ed.) (1994), *Global Production: The Apparel Industry in the Pacific Rim*. Philadelphia: Temple University Press.
Bonacich, E. and L. Hirata (1981), 'International labor migration: A theoretical orientation', paper presented at the conference on New Directions in Theory and Methods of Immigration and Ethnic Research, Duke University, 15-17 May.
Bourdieu, P. (1977), *Outline of a Theory of Practice*. Cambridge: Cambridge University Press.
Braudel, F. (1982), *The Wheels of Commerce: Civilization and Capitalism 15th-18th Century, Vol. 2*. New York: Harper and Row.
Braudel, F. (1981), *The Structures of Everyday Life: Civilization and Capitalism 15th-18th Century, Vol. 1*. New York: Harper and Row.
Cardoso F. (1977), 'The consumption of dependency theory in the United States', *Latin American Research Review* 12 (3): 7-24.
Cardoso, F. and E. Faleto (eds) (1969), *Dependency and Development in Latin America*. Berkeley: University of California Press.
Carmichael, S. and C. Hamilton, (1970), *Black Power*. New York: Random House.
Casanova, P. (1965), 'Internal colonialism and national development', *Studies in Comparative International Development* 1 (1): 27-37.
Castells, M. (1975), 'Immigrant workers and class struggle in advanced capitalism: The Western European experience', *Politics and Society* 5 (1): 33-66.
Clark, K. (1965), *Dark Ghetto*. New York: Harper and Row.
Dickens W. and K. Lang (1985), 'A test of dual labor market theory', *American Economic Review* 75 (2): 792-805.
Duran, J. and D. Massey (1992), 'Mexican migration to the United States: A critical review', *Latin American Research Review* 27 (1): 3-42.
Edwards, R., R. Reich and D. Gordon (eds) (1973), *Labor Market Segmentation*. Lexington: D.C. Heath.
Emirbayer, M. and A. Mische (1998), 'What is agency?', *American Sociological Review* 103 (3): 962-1023.
Frank, A. (1978), *Dependent Accumulation and Underdevelopment*. London: Macmillan.
Frank, A. (1969), *Latin America: Underdevelopment or Revolution*. New York: Monthly Review Press.
Freedman, M. (1976), *Labor Markets: Segments and Shelters*. Montclair: Allanheld, Osmun.
Furtado, C. (1971), *Development and Underdevelopment: A Structural View*. Berkeley: University of California Press.
Giddens, A. (1984), *The Constitution of Society*. Berkeley: University of California Press.
Giddens, A. (1976), *New Rules of Sociological Method*. London: Hutchinson.
Glaser, W. (1978), *The Brain-drain: Emigration and Return, a UNITAR study*. Oxford: Pergamon Press.

Harris J. and M. Todaro (1970), 'Migration, unemployment and development: A two-sector analysis', *American Economic Review* 60 (5): 126-142.
Hechter, M. (1979), 'Group formation and the cultural division of labor', *American Journal of Sociology* 78 (3): 293-319.
Hechter, M. (1976), 'Ethnicity and industrialization: On the proliferation of the cultural division of labor', *Ethnicity* 5 (2): 214-224.
Kannappan, S. (1968), 'The brain drain and developing countries', *International Labour Review* 98 (3): 1-26.
Khoshkish, A. (1966), 'Intellectual migration: A sociological approach to brain drain', *Journal of World History* 10 (1): 178-197.
Kritz, M. et al. (eds) (1981), *Global Trends in Migration: Theory and Research on International Population Movements*. Staten Island: Center for Migration Studies.
Massey D. and E. Taylor (eds) (2004), *International Migration: Prospects and Policies in a Global Market*. Oxford: Oxford University Press.
Massey, D. et al. (1998), *Worlds in Motion: Understanding International Migration at the End of the Millennium*. Oxford: Clarendon Press.
Massey D. et al. (1994), 'An evaluation of international migration theory: The North American case', *Population and Development Review* 20 (1): 699-725.
Massey, D. et al. (1987), *Return to Aztlan: The Social Process of International Migration from Western Mexico*. Berkeley: University of California Press.
Morawska, E. (2011), *A Sociology of Immigration: (Re)making Multifaceted America*. Basingstoke: Palgrave Macmillan.
Morawska, E. (2001), 'Structuring migration: The case of polish income-seeking travelers to the West', *Theory and Society* 31 (4): 47-80.
Munoz, H. et al. (1977), *Migracion y desigualdad social en la ciudad de Mexico*. Mexico: Universidad Nacional Autonoma de Mexico and Colegio de Mexico.
Petras, E. (1981), 'The global labor market in the modern word-economy', in: M. Kritz et al. (eds), *Global Trends in Migration: Theory and Research on International Population Movements*, 44-63. Staten Island: The Center for Migration Studies.
Piore, M. (1979), *Birds of Passage: Migrant Labor and Industrial Societies*. Cambridge: Cambridge University Press.
Portes, A. (1978), 'Migration and underdevelopment', *Politics and Society* 8 (1): 1-49.
Portes A. and L. Bach (1985), *Latin Journey: Cuban and Mexican Immigrants in the United States*. Berkeley: University of California Press.
Portes A. and J. Walton (1981), *Labor, Class, and the International System*. New York: Academic Press.
Portes A. and H. Browning (eds) (1976), *Current Perspectives in Latin American Urban Research*. Austin: Special Publications Series of the Institute of Latin American Studies, University of Texas.
Prebisch, R. (1964), *The Economic Development of Latin America in the Post-war Period*. New York: United Nations.
Rofman, A. and L. Romero (1973), *Sistema Socioeconomico y Estructura Regional en la Argentina*. Buenos Aires: Amorrortu Editores.
Sassen, S. (1988), *The Mobility of Labour and Capital: A Study in International Investment and Labour*. Cambridge: Cambridge University Press.
Sassen, S. (1980), 'The internationalization of the labor force', *Studies in Comparative International Development* 15 (4): 3-28.
Sewell, W. (1998), 'A theory of structure: duality, agency, and transformation', *American Journal of Sociology* 98 (1): 1-29.
Shannon, T. (1996), *An Introduction to the World-system Perspective*. Boulder: Westview Press.
Singer, P. (1975), *Economia Politica de la Urbanizacion*. Mexico City: Editorial Sigolo XXI.

Sklair, L. (1990), *A Sociology of the Global System*. London: Harvester Wheatsheaf.

Stalker, P. (2000), *Workers without Frontiers: The Impact of Globalization on International Migration*. Boulder: Lynne Rienner.

Stavenhagen, R. (1970), *Agrarian Problems and Peasant Movements in Latin America*. Garden City: Doubleday.

Stones, R. (2005), *Structuration Theory*. Basingstoke: Palgrave Macmillan.

Tolbert, C., P. Horan and E. Beck (1980), 'The structure of economic segmentation: A dual economy approach', *American Journal of Sociology* 85 (3): 1095-1116.

Wallerstein, I. (1980), *The Modern World System II: Mercantilism and the Consolidation of the European World Economy, 1600-1750*. New York: Academic Press.

Wallerstein, I. (1974), *The Modern World System I: Capitalist Agriculture and the Origins of the European World Economy in the Sixteenth Century*. New York: Academic Press.

Walton, J. (1976), 'Urban hierarchies and patterns of dependence in Latin America: Theoretical bases for a new research agenda', in: A. Portes and H. Browning (eds), *Current Perspectives in Latin American Urban Research*, 43-69. Austin: Special Publications Series of the Institute of Latin America Studies, University of Texas.

Walton, J. (1975), 'Internal colonialism: Problems of definition and measurement', in: W. Cornelius and F. Trueblood (eds), *Latin American Urban Research*, 29-52. London: Sage Publications.

Watanabe, S. (1969), 'The brain drain from developing to developed countries', *International Labour Review* 99 (3): 401-433.

Wolpe, H. (1975), 'The theory of internal colonialism: The South African case', in: I. Oxaal et al. (eds), *Beyond the Sociology of Development*, 208-228. London: Routledge and Kegan Paul.

Wood, C. (1981), 'Equilibrium and historical-structural perspectives on migration', *International Migration Review* 16 (2): 299-319.

Zolberg, A. (1981), 'International migrations in political perspective', in: M. Kritz et al. (eds) *Global Trends in Migration: Theory and Research on International Population Movements*, 3-27. Staten Island: Center for Migration Studies.

Zolberg A. and P. Benda (eds) (2001), *Global Migrants, Global Refugees: Problems and Solutions*. New York: Berghahn Books.

Zolberg, A., A. Suhrke and S. Aguayo (1989), *Escape from Violence: Conflict and the Refugee Crisis in the Developing World*. New York: Oxford University Press.

4 Social Networks and International Migration

Monica Boyd and Joanne Nowak

Introduction

This chapter looks at the relationship between social networks and international migration. It defines social networks and explains the relevance of the social networks approach to international migration. After outlining the main types of social networks involved in migration today, it discusses the heterogeneity of networks based on gender, ethnicity, race and generation. The chapter also reviews the impact on these networks of external forces and characteristics, especially immigration history and policies. The final section critiques the social networks approach and makes suggestions for future research.

What are social networks?

strengths and weaknesses of social ties

Ties or connections between individuals that vary in strength, type and duration (Granovetter 1973; Wellman 1979; Williams 2006) are referred to as 'social networks'. They are often based on reciprocal exchanges or shared goals (Lomnitz 1976; Feld 1981; Gurak and Caces 1992), which can vary over time, depending on the circumstances. Several different variables are used to measure social networks. For example, in the early 1970s, Granovetter focused on the 'strength' and 'weakness' of social ties. According to the author, the strength of an interpersonal tie is based on 'the amount of time, the emotional intensity, the intimacy (mutual confiding), and the reciprocal services which characterize the tie' (Granovetter 1973: 1361). Using these criteria, one can assess whether a tie is strong, weak or absent. Other scholars have measured networks based on their density within a given area. In denser areas, the size of the network increases, and individuals have more contacts with whom to exchange information and resources. However, once networks become too dense, a 'congestion' effect arises whereby individuals have too many friends to transmit information, and this eventually reduces the efficiency of information exchange (Zenou and Wahba 2005). To summarise, the *strength* and *density* of ties are two common measures of social networks.

What is the social networks approach?

meso-level

A significant limitation of current social theories is their inability to relate micro-level interactions to macro-level phenomena. The meso-level nature of the social networks approach bridges this gap by demonstrating how interaction within small groups aggregates to large-scale patterns (Granovetter 1973). In particular, it outlines the connections and relationships among individuals, as well as between individuals and the larger community (Wellman 1979; Goldenberg and Haines 1992). Since the community is understood in terms of networks rather than a bounded physical territory, it can span geographical regions and borders.

A central aspect of the social networks approach, then, is its emphasis on the *networks that connect individuals across time and space*. This is why it is so well suited to the study of migration. Rather than analysing the individual migrant as an isolated and helpless actor, scholars can examine the active connections between migrants and individuals in both the sending and receiving countries, along with the migrant's utilisation of resources from families and communities (Wellman 1979; Massey et al. 1987; Boyd 1989; Tilly 1990; Gurak and Caces 1992; Massey et al. 1993).

How do social networks inform migration research?

Since the late 1980s and 1990s, scholars of social networks have better elaborated the multi-level relationship between social networks and migration (Granovetter 1982; Boyd 1989; Massey and España 1987; Massey et al. 1993; Portes et al. 1999). During this period, the social networks field made three key contributions to our understanding of migration.

why migration persists

The first notable contribution is the explanation of how social networks play a key role in not only developing but also *sustaining migration flows over time*. In particular, migrant networks develop their own internal momentum and eventually function independently of the original forces and actors that created them, including the policies of the host and home countries (Gurak and Caces 1992; Massey et al. 1993). The social networks approach not only addresses why individuals migrate, but also why migration persists over the long term.

As the second key contribution, a study of social networks moves the research focus beyond push-pull economic forces and the world-system inequalities shaping migration flows and highlights how migrants themselves shape migration outcomes through their use of social resources and connections (Boyd 1989; Massey et al. 1993).

Rather than individuals autonomously deciding to migrate, their entire household is often involved in choosing who migrates, based on an estimate of who has the best chance of succeeding in the host country (Boyd 1989; Stark 1991; Gurak and Caces 1992; Castles 2000). Individuals from middle-income groups are often the first to migrate, if only due to a certain level of disposable income being necessary to cover transportation and settlement costs. Once these 'pioneering' migrants settle in the host country, they frequently maintain links with their home communities, establishing flows of communication and resources to facilitate the future migration of other family members. Although the more skilled and financially able may be the first to migrate, the resources they provide reduce the costs of migration for others, making the process more accessible (Gurak and Caces 1992; Massey et al. 1993). Using a social network approach, therefore, enables researchers to better identify the resources and actors involved in the migrant's decision-making process.

understanding of 'household'

The third important contribution of the social networks approach is that it does not restrict its understanding of the 'household' to the physical structure in which individuals reside. Migrants often continue to communicate with family members and remain part of a household through transnational linkages (Boyd 1989; Piper 2005). By broadening the research scope to include meso-level and transnational networks, the social networks approach more fully considers the numerous actors and forces that influence where and why individuals choose to migrate.

What types of networks are involved in the migration process?

The three social networks most commonly involved in the migration process are labour, personal (family) and illegal migrant networks. The following section considers each type, and outlines its benefits and costs to migrants.

Labour networks

Labour networks are important to the migration process. They facilitate the transmission of information in regard to employment opportunities, necessary skills and experience, as well as labour contacts. With each successive set of labour flows crossing a border, migrant labour networks expand in size and resources (Gallo and Bailey 1996). Migrants involved in well-developed networks of this type are better able to secure employment before and/or upon arrival in their host countries. If they cannot find work due to labour shortages, or encounter difficulties having their credentials recognised, they can rely on labour networks for additional employment information, as well as social and financial assistance to start their own business (Gallo and Bailey 1996).

Not all migrants, however, depend on labour networks to find employment within their community. For example, they may find work independently (without the assistance of networks) by drawing on their own linguistic and cultural skills, as well as experience. However, they tend to rely on social networks when a prospective employer is of a different ethnicity (Sernau et al. 2002).

benefits of labour networks

The benefits of relying on labour networks continue to be debated. Networks undoubtedly assist individuals in finding employment, but it is often in the informal sector where migrants have little contact with members of the mainstream population. Consequently, opportunities may be limited to develop a wider range of networks or to learn the host language on the job. In addition, the process is not always efficient. Epstein et al. (2002) say that relying on labour networks and cumulative causation can harm migrants by encouraging 'herd behaviour' which may not match migrants' skills with the most appropriate job positions. Lastly, labour networks can lead to oppressive situations. Members of an immigrant network may recruit other immigrants for exploitative purposes, such as working for low-paying and/or dangerous employers (Anderson and Calzavara 1986).

From the employer's perspective, the benefits of migrant labour networks are similarly mixed. While labour networks may bring an influx of new employees, the reverse is also possible. For instance, if a worker moves to another company, other members of the worker's network may be encouraged to leave the company as well (Anderson and Calzavara 1986).

The importance of labour networks in the migration process exists worldwide. European research shows that informal labour networks, including family, friends and acquaintances, are key sources of information on which immigrants rely; especially those most vulnerable to unemployment, such as young and less educated immigrants (Drever and Hoffmeister 2008).[1] These networks serve as important alternatives to formal degrees and training for migrants who do not have formal credentials. However, other European studies have also highlighted the 'dark side of networks', in countries such as Italy, where immigrants can be segmented into marginal communities and economies (Caponio 2008).

formal or informal

The different returns that migrants receive from labour networks may be related to whether these networks are formal or informal. Scholars argue that formal labour networks may provide better returns to migrants, since networks based on formal organisational ties, such as schools and professional bodies, are better able to match migrants' skills with appropriate employment (Poros 2001; Vertovec 2002). Others challenge these conclusions. Duleep and Reget (1992) find that, while immigrants admitted through family reunification initially earn less than those admitted on the basis of their skills, the former have higher earnings growth (Duleep and Reget in Gallo and Bailey 1996). Moreover, relying on formal labour networks can create inequalities within immigrant groups. The reality is that not all migrants have access to formal or organisationally-based labour networks, and since employment positions advertised by formal organisations are open to public competition, belonging to such networks offers no guaranteed labour outcome to migrants (Poros 2001; Vertovec 2002). Clearly, the debate on the relative costs and benefits of these different types of networks cannot be resolved without further research.

costs and benefits of remittances

Another debate centres on the costs and benefits of remittances in labour migration. Because remittances represent the exchange of monies across borders, they can be described as financial networks (Boyd 1989). These financial networks are related to labour migration, since the flow of money/earnings across borders relies on the networks developed by labour migrants with their families and communities. Without these quasi-formal channels, sending financial resources and goods becomes more difficult (Piotrowski 2006). Several researchers express concern over the dependence of migrant households on remittances, suggesting that this may lead to reduced productivity and labour market involvement in their home communities (Hellermann 2006; Vathi and Black 2007). Others critique the growing commodification of social networks, which, over time, could reduce their strength and personal meaning (Hellermann 2006). Still others argue that remittances can contribute to growing inequalities within communities of origin by increasing the living standards of migrant families and leaving non-migrant households behind (Waddington 2003). Although the extent to which remittances provide benefits and/or costs to labour migrants remains unclear, ultimately they represent a significant aspect of labour networks, and therefore comprise an important area of research in social networks and migration.

Personal and family networks

personal networks

A second type of analysis considers the personal relations migrants have with members of their host and home communities. These personal networks have at least three types of possible benefits for migrants. First, they assist with the settlement process by providing a sense of community and familiarity, as well as a means by which migrants may sustain or modify their home culture in the host country (Castles 1990). Migrants also use these networks to maintain emotional contact with their families over long distances and to impart new ideas and practices to relatives across borders (Gupta and Ferguson 1992; Herman 2006; Piotrowski 2006). Over time, these personal networks may develop into transnational social spheres in which individuals can maintain a sense of identity and community without regular face-to-face contact (Gupta and Ferguson 1992). Longer periods of temporary migration may foster the growth of transnational families – where one or both parents live apart from their families for a given period of time (Evergeti and Zontini 2006; Landolt et al. 2008). In such cases, migrant women may arrange personal networks of care in their home communities to look after relatives left behind, or they may try to develop stable transnational networks of care to raise children across borders (Evergeti and Zontini 2006; Landolt et al. 2008).

The second benefit of personal networks is that they can also provide social support to migrants involved in protest or social justice activities. These networks can include families in the immediate area, as well as families/supporters in other cities and countries who rally around the same cause (Bakan and Stasiulis 2003; Silvey 2003). By linking migrants across borders and regions, such personal networks enhance migrants' ability to advocate for improvements in living and working conditions (Bakan and Stasiulis 2003).

Third, personal networks can be of benefit by facilitating the transformation of ideas and skills from migrants to their families back home. These socially-based migrant linkages are powerful agents of change because the ideas of the host culture are transmitted by social peers (Lindstrom and Munoz-Franco 2005). However, participation in personal networks can also have its disadvantages. Tilly (2007) argues that while strong ties or 'trust networks' provide access to benefits like social capital, they can impose significant obligations on their members. In particular, networks erect thicker and more strongly demarcated boundaries than other types of social ties. Such boundaries imply privileged benefits, but they can also lead to harsh consequences – such as exclusion – for those who do not fulfil their obligations in the network.

Given these varying results, additional research is needed to weigh the positive and negative impacts of personal networks for migrants.

Illegal migrant networks

criminal networks

Despite a keen interest in illegal migration, few sociologists and political scientists have focused on illegal migrant networks until recently.

A few notable exceptions include studies in the area of sexual trafficking and human smuggling (Portes 1978; Salt and Stein 1997; Hughes 2000), but law and criminology scholars are increasingly using the social networks framework to describe the typology of today's transnational criminal networks (Zhang and Gaylord 1996; McIllwain 1999). In their analysis of the networks involved in transnational crime, Bruinsma and Bernasco (2004) argue that the form of the network depends on the nature of the crime. For instance, hierarchical chain networks with few direct links between members characterise sexual trafficking and smuggling networks, while strong ethnically homogeneous ties predominate in the drug trafficking sector. A networks framework can also explain the seemingly irrational decisions of certain illegal migrants; Kinsella (2006) argues that for members of illicit transnational networks, the enhancement of prestige and power within the network may be more important than increasing short-term profits.

Another contribution of the research on illegal networks is the analysis of reciprocal relationships between legal status and social networks. Early in the development of the networks approach, Boyd (1989) pointed out that illegal migrants often have fewer family and friendship ties than legal migrants. As a result, they are more vulnerable to exploitation in mainstream employment sectors and illegal job markets, both in and outside their own communities. More recent research has demonstrated that a broader range of network ties facilitates obtaining legal status. In her long-term ethnographic study of Mayan immigrants in Houston, Hagan (1998) found that immigrants with a broader range of work, neighbourhood and recreational networks were better able to develop social ties with other long-term immigrants, as well as with native-born individuals. In fact, the latter provided valuable assistance to the Mayan immigrants in securing affidavits for their legalisation efforts, while those without these broad networks faced significant difficulties in settling legally.

The present flurry of government attention on the growing number of illegal immigrants signals a need for additional studies exploring the differences in the use, risks and benefits of illegal migrant networks.

What is the internal variation of networks?

Gendered networks

Historically, research on social networks was often gender-blind, assuming that men dominate social networks and that women simply follow their migrant husbands (Boyd 1989; Matthei 1996; Boyd and Grieco 2003; Piper 2005). However, since the 1980s, scholars have *gender* begun to challenge this orthodoxy, noting that migration decision-making processes and household migration strategies are shaped by gender (Boyd 1989). For instance, in social contexts where norms and mores require women's physical and emotional commitment to a family structure, familial pressure may prevent women from accessing the resources and networks needed to migrate. Hondagneu-Sotelo (1994) further demonstrates how social forces can intimately impact women and men's mobility. By drawing on her in-depth field work in Mexican migrant communities, Hondagneu-Sotelo is able to show how male migrants, as well as other family members, can limit the information and assistance provided to prospective independent female migrants as a result of patriarchal gender norms that disapprove of female emigration. Even other women within social networks can erect and reinforce barriers to female migration. Hellermann's (2006) study highlights tensions between married and single migrants, where the former assume that the latter are prostitutes.

facilitate international migration

Faced with these obstacles, prospective women migrants develop alternative routes to migration. Family members often accompany women during the migration process to satisfy gender norms and security concerns (Curran and Rivero-Fuentes 2003). Another alternative is the creation of female-only migrant networks, which circumvent the gender barriers found in mainstream male-dominated networks (Hondagneu-Sotelo 1994). While this phenomenon has been documented among Mexican female migrants, studies confirm its presence in Europe as well. Hellermann's (2006) study of female Eastern European migrants demonstrates that some women look for alternative networks outside their ethnic community as a result of the paternalistic attitudes they encounter in the more established networks. Recent quantitative work empirically tests the benefits of these gendered networks in terms of how they facilitate international migration. Curran and Rivero-Fuentes (2003) find that having access to a pre-existing female migrant network significantly facilitates international migration for women. Thus, gender-specific networks represent a key resource for female migrants, especially in the pre-migration stage.

ethnic enclaves

The benefits women receive from migrant networks in the countries of destination are more ambiguous. Ethnic enclaves provide a significant illustration of this point. Earlier research found that many ethnic women saw their economic roles as subservient to their male counterparts; they worked with the permission of their husbands and were seen as a cheap, flexible source of labour for co-ethnic male entrepreneurs, often relatives (Anthias 1983; Phizacklea 1983; Boyd 1989). Studies conducted roughly a decade later showed that little had changed. Enclave employment still provided women with low wages, few benefits and scant opportunity for mobility (Zhou and Logan

1989; Gilbertson 1995; Greenwell et al. 1997). However, Greenwell et al. (1997) make an important point regarding the interpretation of these findings. They suggest that if the community in which people are working is lower class, the returns to local networks may differ from the returns experienced by individuals participating in local ethnic networks in higher-class communities. Consequently, scholars must consider the social class composition of the community in which the networks are operating, in order to capture the intersections between gender and class in ethnic enclaves.

gendered division of labour

Moving beyond the specific context of ethnic enclaves, the general employment returns from migrant networks differ by gender. In particular, the gendered division of labour within receiving countries intimately influences the shape of these networks. As a result of segmented labour demand, female migrant networks often channel migrant women into specific feminised labour sectors (Bastia 2007). For instance, numerous studies from the 1990s highlight how personal networks used by female migrants lead to informal, low-wage employment, largely because female network members are concentrated in the domestic and care-giving sectors (Hagan 1998; Hondaganeu-Sotelo 2001). Moreover, the physical restrictions of household-based employment prevent women from forming larger networks and ties, while men have more opportunities for social interaction and networking in their more varied and often public sector workplaces (Bolumar et al. 2007). Livingston's (2006) work among Mexican immigrants confirms that women who use network-based job searches are less likely to find stable, formal sector employment than women who search for employment without help from the network. Informal workplaces can also place women in more vulnerable positions for exploitation and abuse, sexual and otherwise (Bolumar et al. 2007). The opposite is true for male Mexican immigrants, who are more likely to find formal sector employment through their network searches. Since formal sector employment is positively associated with wages and other benefits, the use of migrant networks in job searches often reduces the labour market returns for Mexican migrant women and raises them for men (Livingston 2006).

More recent research suggests that these earlier studies overlook an important interaction between education or class and gender. In particular, Ryan's (2007) study on Irish nurses in Britain reveals that foreign female workers keep the networks they have used in the pre-migration and migration stages, but expand their social circles and establish new networks over time. Thus, when female migrants work in more public spheres (nursing), they tend to increase the breadth and width of their networks.

Overall, the impact of gendered networks on the labour market integration of migrants remains complex. In some ways, using gender-specific networks can facilitate employment searches for potential migrants, since they result in at least some form of employment. However, in other ways these networks can also reinforce gendered labour markets within the host societies.

networks influence gender relations

Another avenue of research explores how networks influence gender relations and identities. During the settlement process, women tend to be more vulnerable and socially isolated, and personal networks often represent a key source of support. They can also influence gender norms and relations among female migrants. In a study of gender relations among Mexican family households in the United States and Mexico, Parrado and Flippen (2005) found that the maintenance of friendships among immigrant Mexican women was associated with a higher rate of male involvement in household tasks, as well as greater female participation in household finances. Interestingly, the impacts of social networks on gender relations were significantly greater among migrants in the United States than among their peers back home. Surprisingly, family networks had an effect opposite to that of social networks: regular contact with family members in Mexico provided women with more control and resources in their relationship, but among Mexican migrant women in the United States, contact with family networks *decreased* men's involvement in housework and wives' financial participation in the household (Parrado and Flippen 2005). While it would be simplistic to conclude that family networks do not represent an important resource for migrants, a more nuanced analysis suggests that such contacts can represent additional domestic responsibilities for migrant women and reinforce traditional family norms and values.

social bonds impacted

Social bonds and networks can be interrupted, or at the very least impacted, by the process of migration. When social and family networks are disrupted, the interdependence of husbands and wives increases. However, women are disproportionately affected by the disruptions of their established networks, since they often have less developed networks than their spouses and are faced with building new ones. Several studies show that female migrants are often left with the responsibility of building new care networks in their host societies, despite having greater time constraints due to the need to care for their family (Purkayastha 2005; Salaff and Greve 2004). At the same time, if they have left family behind in their home societies, women migrants must continue transnational 'nurturing responsibilities' (Parrenas 2005; Landolt et al. 2008). These additional emotional and time-related obligations place significant pressure on migrant women who already face the challenge of adapting to a new society. In addition, little is known about the long-term effects of transnational parenting on migrant children.

Given the significant influence of social networks on migrants' lives, additional research into the negative effects of social networks is needed. More specifically, without a gender-sensitive approach to the study of migrant networks, one can overlook why and how women make use of certain social networks over others and underestimate women migrants' social and cultural labour (Salaff and Greve 2004).

Variations in networks due to race, ethnicity and class

The ethnic composition of social networks can create markedly different integration experiences for migrant groups. In particular, Sernau et al. (2002) argue that labour networks among immigrant minorities who have lower levels of human capital may need to be interpreted differently from networks of white professional men possessing higher levels of such capital (and who represent much of the existing labour network research). In addition, scholars need to consider the possibility that labour market information can be circulated along chains of actors with both co-ethnic and non-ethnic network ties of varying strengths. The focus on ethnically homogeneous networks must be expanded to include labour networks with a variety of actors.

ethnic stereotypes

Other studies highlight how ethnic stereotypes held by members of the receiving society can result in the racist treatment of migrants (Simmons and Plaza 1998; Hellermann 2006). Faced with such treatment, migrants are more likely to rely on ethnic networks within their own community when pursuing business and social relations, as well as in deciding where to live (Castles 1990; Zhou 1997). In terms of the latter, while discrimination can partly explain immigrant residential patterns, internal group preferences can also play a role. For instance, research on Muslim immigrants in Europe suggests that members of ethnic or religious groups sometimes voluntarily choose to reside within their own communities. In the case of European Muslim immigrants, this self-segregation is related to a preference to remain near relatives, peers and Muslim institutions (Varady 2008). Thus internal group preferences, as well as ethnic stereotypes and discrimination from the larger society, must be considered in immigrant integration research.

Gender and ethnic stereotypes within the host societies can also intersect to create particular integration challenges for migrants. Ethnographic research shows that women migrants from Eastern Europe experience discriminatory treatment from host societies based on the assumption that women from this region are in the sex trade (Hellermann 2006). Clearly, the relationship between race, ethnicity and social networks requires additional nuanced and multi-faceted research.

class

One important factor influencing social networks is class. In fact, class issues come into play as soon as a social network begins. As noted earlier in the chapter, studies confirm that individuals from the middle and upper-middle classes are typically the first to migrate from a given community (Massey et al. 1993; Castles 2000). This reflects the significant financial resources needed to migrate and the social capital needed to settle in the host society. However, these class differences are neither permanent nor absolute. While many initial migratory flows consist of individuals with higher incomes, over time migratory paths expand and incorporate other strata of the sending population.

Although these initial class-based effects diminish over time, socio-economic status continues to affect social networks in other ways. Granovetter's seminal work in the 1970s and 1980s demonstrated that lower income groups are more likely to use strong ties consisting of family and close friends. Such ties result from individuals' limited social capital and access to other networks (Granovetter 1982). In contrast, higher income groups are more self-sufficient and can rely on distant networks of weak ties, composed of loosely-connected friends and acquaintances. Importantly, the weaker ties often serve as bridges to a variety of new networks and contacts that enable higher income individuals to expand their social capital and networks (Granovetter 1982). Later studies support Granovetter's findings, showing that higher-skilled occupational groups rely more on networks of professional contacts to secure employment, residence and so on, while lower-skilled occupational migrants tend to rely on kinship networks (Vertovec 2002; Salaff and Greve 2004). However, this rigid dichotomy is not the only possible outcome. Some scholars argue that ties can overlap, such as in the case of family businesses, which involve both formal and interpersonal relations (Poros 2001).

Given the intimate role of race/ethnicity, as well as class, in shaping the nature and operation of social networks, these factors must continue to be researched.

Variations in networks across generations

In addition to variations in networks along ethnic and racial lines, social networks also vary over time and across generations. Much of the literature focuses on the short-term adaptive functions of networks; relatively fewer studies discuss the effects of social networks on second-generation immigrants.

networks across generations

The literature on the second generation of migrants reveals three negative consequences of immigrant networks across generations. First, strong attachment to social networks among second-generation youth in lower-income ethnic communities can decrease social integration and reduce their long-term socio-economic mobility. This barrier to mainstream integration is largely a result of second-generation immigrants adopting 'undesirable' attitudes and characteristics from the underprivileged community into which they have been assimilated (Portes and Zhou 1993; Zhou 1997). Second, personal networks may channel new migrants and second-generation immigrants into bounded ethnic niches, which provide few economic opportunities or occupational choices (Kim 2006). This can eventually lead to a decline in their occupational mobility. Third, participation in ethnic enclaves (or neighbourhoods that have a high representation of their language group) may reduce the likelihood among immigrants of acquiring majority language skills over time (Chiswick and Miller 1992).

Other studies provide evidence of the long-term benefits of participating in migrant networks. Zhou and Portes (1993) argue that when ethnic communities emphasise the importance of education, financial success and mobility, strong ethnic community networks can increase the likelihood of economic advancement among second-generation youth. In addition, more recent statistical models challenge and complicate earlier findings, which found that living in linguistic enclaves retards majority language proficiency over time. Chiswick and Miller (1996) show that the impact of minority language concentration is reduced to statistical insignificance once other measures are included – most notably whether individuals are married to a fellow foreigner, whether a family member (other than spouse or children) is living in the country and whether they use ethnic media.

What external forces influence social networks?

rite of passage

Two external forces have a major impact on migrant social networks – immigration history and immigration policies within host and home societies. Regarding the former, scholars suggest that social norms inducing further migration emerge in communities that have experienced significant migration over time and have a large percentage of migrants abroad (Hondagneu-Sotelo 1994; Curran and Saguy 2001; Massey and Kandel 2002). For instance, studies of Mexican migrants suggest that migration is now a rite of passage for men in migrant-sending communities, influencing them to participate in migrant networks (Hondagneu-Sotelo 1994; Massey and Kandel 2002).

The immigration policies of both the home and host countries also influence the number and nature of migrant networks. Many countries play active roles in facilitating the emigration of their citizens. A notable example is the Filipino government, which has pursued a labour emigration policy since the early 1980s (Asis 2006; Parrenas 2001). In contrast to the absent or ad-hoc emigration policies of other countries, the Filipino government has created official government departments and programmes to manage its migration flows. The Philippine Overseas Employment Administration provides pre-departure orientation to migrants and ensures its emigrants have full access to information on future employment (Tyner 2000; Agunias and Ruiz 2007). In addition, in 1995 the government attempted to increase the protection of its workers abroad through the enactment of the *Migrant Workers and Overseas Filipino Act* (Asis 2005). These government activities facilitate the migration of workers via official routes, thereby reducing the need for migrants to resort to meso-level social networks for assistance.

policies of governments

The activities and policies of governments in the receiving countries are equally influential for three reasons. First, host governments can affect migrant networks through their immigration selection policies and admissibility criteria (Gurak and Caces 1992). The Canadian immigration point system, for instance, formally assesses the prospective contributions of immigrants to the Canadian economy and society based on such criteria as level of skill, knowledge of official languages and education. The majority of new immigrants are therefore highly skilled and educated (Boyd and Alboim 2012). In contrast, the US does not afford privilege to skilled migrants, and many new immigrants rely on family networks in order to enter the country (Green 2004). As a result of the different immigration policies, different migrant networks predominate in the two countries.

Second, policies of the host government with respect to the provision of social services affect the reliance of migrants on social networks (Boyd and Grieco 2003; Collyer 2005). Simply put, the extent to which migrants rely on their own contacts and support networks will vary, based on the level of services provided by the government. For instance, the US has attempted to reduce the social services provided to immigrants through several initiatives, such as Proposition 187 in California, which denies educational and other benefits to illegal immigrants (Martin 1995). When key social services are absent, local migrant networks in host communities are essential for maintaining a decent standard of living (Collyer 2005; Williams 2006).

access to citizenship

Third, social networks are influenced by migrants' access to citizenship status. An increasing number of countries permit citizens to hold dual citizenship, such as Brazil, Colombia, Costa Rica, the Dominican

Republic, El Salvador and Mexico (Levitt and De la Dehesa 2003). Such migrants are better able to maintain connections with their home communities because they can more easily return home and/or invest in home businesses. Without this option, migrants often choose to focus their efforts, loyalty and even citizenship on either the home or host country. In brief, if migrants face a difficult naturalisation process, they are more likely to rely on their own networks for information and support than on other members of their host society.

What are the main critiques of the networks approach?

Since the second half of the twentieth century, the networks approach has broken new ground in international migration research. Nonetheless, there are three main conceptual criticisms of the field and a number of methodological concerns.

narrow view

First, traditional understandings of the 'migrant network' do not permit a comprehensive study of international migration. Critics suggest that the concept of networks should be expanded to include employers, governments, labour smugglers and all other actors involved in the origin and perpetuation of migratory flows. These less traditional network actors have been largely ignored, as the 'migrant network' concept focuses on horizontal relationships between migrants and their sending communities (Krissman 2005). This narrow view does not allow for an accurate assessment of the many different types of migrant networks and actors today.

A second weakness is the limited attention given to power inequalities within migrant networks and how these influence the lives of migrants. Many scholars point out that social network members do not occupy equal positions of power. As such, migrants can be exploited by actors within their own network as a result of their gender, age, and so on (Evergeti and Zontini 2006; Hellermann 2006). More in-depth analyses of the dynamics and inequalities within networks are needed.

Finally, a third criticism addresses the limited information available on the returns migrants receive from social networks relative to the native-born. Kazemipur (2006) notes that immigrants to Canada receive fewer socioeconomic returns from their networks, mobilise fewer network resources and have less diverse social webs than their native counterparts. Moreover, the pay-offs to network members are significantly higher for immigrant men than immigrant women, and become smaller once the duration of time in Canada is taken into account. Future research might well consider migrants' use of networks, then, as well as the returns they obtain from them, in comparison to non-immigrant groups.

methodological limitations

In terms of methodological limitations, one critique centres on the methods used in networks research. Spittel (1998) argues that the 'network effect' needs empirical verification. The term 'network effects' refers to situations where networks are seen to stimulate migration; for example, when individuals live in a community or household where immigration has occurred they are more likely to migrate themselves. Spittel offers two counter-theses that challenge the empirical validity of this argument. The first, the common-cause hypothesis, argues that individuals within a network may be influenced by a set of common factors, independent from migration ties. In this case, the effect of belonging to a network on the likelihood of migrating is better explained as a spurious relationship arising from a set of common causes. The other argument, the self-selection hypothesis, posits that individuals who are more likely to migrate are also more likely to participate in networks. Interestingly, later in his article Spittel confirms that social networks explain higher rates of migration – net of common cause and self-selection. Future scholars are encouraged to follow in Spittel's footsteps by focusing on the methodological rigour of the networks field, in order to enhance the strength and precision of networks research as a whole.

Another methodological critique posits that only focusing on networks in the migration process reduces the quality of research in this area. In particular, Trappers et al. (2008) argue that if migration were *solely* dependent on social networks and chain migration, immigrants would continuously migrate to the regions where networks are already established. Given the shifting migrant destination points, this is clearly not the case. For instance, in Europe migrants do not concentrate in a few regions, but in many different ones. Rather than resulting from social networks, Trappers et al. (2008) argue that these movements are also a result of business cycle labour shortages. Notwithstanding the influence of networks in individual and household decision-making, the authors emphasise that one must consider how multiple explanatory variables, including socio-cultural and economic, interact at different levels to produce migration outcomes.

validity of criteria

A final methodological concern is whether the criteria used to evaluate the function and/or benefits of social networks are valid. Fuglerud and Engebrigsten (2006) argue that some scholars assess the benefits of social networks based on outcomes that are more favourable to the host society, such as social integration, cohesion and individual success, rather than to the migrants themselves. Scholars studying network participation often portray those who increase their ties with other networks as 'lost' to the original migrant network. Others suggest that this loss could be interpreted as the migrant network undergoing a process of expansion and evolution (Gurak and Caces 1992).

Building on this idea, changes in the location and concentration of networks merit further examination. Light (2006) demonstrates how large flows of migrants into a particular region can actually deflect rather than attract migrants over time. As migration in a given locale shifts from being stimulated by local demand to reflecting network development, poverty levels rise. Light notes that Los Angeles gradually became unattractive to migrants as a result of growing competition in a limited number of available industries and neighbourhoods, not to mention the increasing enforcement of municipal employment and housing codes in the area – the latter undertaken by political figures in response to an influx of immigrants. As a result, since the 1990s migrant flows have diffused beyond the Southwestern states to many different regions of the US as networks in destination sites communicate the changing contexts of reception (or deflection) to prospective migrants. As these emerging patterns show, future networks research must go further than merely explaining why people migrate from A to B; it must begin to analyse 'why they now go from A to C' (Light 2007: 1165).

Conclusion: Lines for future research

Scholars have long highlighted the need to examine different types of networks (Boyd 1989; Fawcett 1989). Significant work has been done to address this concern, most notably in research on the impacts of gender, race and class on networks, as well as the differences between illegal and legal networks. Nonetheless, many research questions remain unanswered.

avenue for future research

A promising avenue for future research involves moving beyond traditional understandings of networks and actors, with 'actors' taken here to mean migrants involved in personal and labour networks. Indeed, new types of networks and actors are implicated in international migration, as the phenomenon expands across regions. Abella (1992) argues that labour recruitment agencies, overseas employment promotion companies and legal contractors played a crucial role in increasing labour emigration from Asia in the late twentieth century (Lim 1992). Networks of Mexican lobby groups in the United States are becoming significant players in immigration politics due to their growing numbers, institutionalisation and coordination with other interest groups (Gimpel and Edward 1999). In certain regions (such as West Africa), commercially-based social networks are increasing their presence in migration flows, whereas in the past, ethnic-based networks were dominant (Kress 2006). What are the particular features of these more recent network actors? How do they influence the type and number of migrants crossing borders? These questions move the orthodox social networks focus beyond the migrants who physically move across borders, suggesting the need to include the growing number of actors indirectly involved in migrant networks.

Similarly, though scholars in a variety of disciplines have begun to study illegal networks, significantly more research is needed. In particular, the focus must move beyond traditional large-scale smuggling networks that operate over the long term, to more micro-scale networks. A notable example is Collyer's (2007) study of small-scale networks' facilitation of illegal migration from sub-Saharan Africa to Europe. The author highlights the tendency to overlook the role of these smaller networks, consisting of a few individuals and lasting for just a short duration of time, in smuggling in the developing world. Further research is needed to determine how the use of these small-scale illegal networks differs by region, as well as by class, race and gender.

differences within networks

In addition to examining the differences between networks, it is also useful to explore the differences within networks. Hellermann (2006) highlights the relationship between social networks and a migrant's level of human, financial and social capital. While significant work has been done on the minimum level of financial capital needed to take part in migrant networks, the same cannot be said of social and human capital. What basic levels of social and human capital are needed to access migrant networks? Does this vary by gender, ethnicity and region? Another important research question asks how the use of migrant networks differs between older and newer waves of ethnic migrant groups in a receiving country. A recent European study argues that new Polish immigrants to the United Kingdom utilise a variety of networks in their host communities. They sometimes participate in relatively established networks and institutions formed by previous immigrant generations, while at other times they use newer networks and ethnic resources. Technological advances and cheaper modes of transportation facilitate more variety in types of migrants, resulting in 'not just a single "little Poland" in exile, but a multitude of little Polands, as networks rapidly spring up and constantly evolve' (White and Ryan 2008: 1498). By increasing the choices available to migrants, the growing number of networks may reduce the inequalities identified in the less numerous and more broad-based networks of previous decades. Further research on these subtle differences would surely produce novel findings.

diverse set of tools

To explore these nuanced issues, however, scholars must deconstruct networks along various dimensions and consider a variety of networks. This calls for a more diverse set of methodological tools. Gurak and Caces (1992) suggest that increased comparative and multi-level examinations of migration networks would provide richer detail on the functioning of migrant networks and better capture the members within them. An example of such analysis, conducted by Miller-Martinez and Wallace (2007), measures the influence of individual, meso-level (cultural) and structural factors on migrant decision-making. This type of analysis offers a rich understanding of the forces influencing social networks today.

Another area of research involves examining differences in the benefits migrants receive from social networks based on citizenship status. Amuedo-Dorantes and Mundra (2007) demonstrate that access to friendship-based networks increases the wages of illegal Mexican migrants in the United States – more so than for legal migrants. However, the reverse is true of family-based networks.

Scholars are also considering the connections between age and social networks. Miller-Martinez and Wallace (2007) focus on how social networks (in terms of their dynamics and composition) vary as migrants age. Do elderly migrants participate in and develop different social networks from younger migrants?

migration and development

A final emerging area of research is the relationship between migration and development. Scholars now assess the positive and negative effects of migration on socio-economic development in the sending and receiving countries. Rather than rely on macro-level and top-down development approaches, this perspective emphasises migrants themselves as agents of development, assuming a role in development projects (such as by sending remittances to their home communities via home town associations or sending monies directly home to family). Much remains to be done, given the relatively limited number of studies available in North America and Europe (Massey et al. 1996; Castles 2000; Migration Information Source 2007). While an emphasis on migrants as agents of development is important, additional research is needed on assistance that could possibly be provided by the state in both destination and origin countries to help migrants retain ties to their home communities, in order to increase the likelihood of remittances and skill transfers. Recent European research on Kurdish-Turkish immigrants in Denmark, for instance, demonstrates the often-tense political relationship between the host and origin state. The study emphasises the integration of immigrants and the cross-border activities of immigrants engaged in transnational development projects with their home communities (Christiansen 2008). Similar research has been done on Mexican immigrants in the United States facing pressures to assimilate into the host country by severing homeland ties (Glick Schiller et al. 1995). Nonetheless, additional research within and across regions would help to develop a fuller understanding of these processes.

stimulants and impediments to migration

Another related area of research regards the effect of migrant networks in stimulating or impeding return migration. Haug's (2008) study of return migration among European migrants demonstrates that social capital aspects, that is, the number of household members who have returned, significantly influences return migration. In fact, social capital has the largest effect on return migration – more so than individual factors. Furthermore, return migration decisions are determined by social capital factors *independent* of individual characteristics such as age or employment. However, whether return migration differs as a result of the type of network (labour, personal) remains unclear. This analysis of return migration leads to a further question – under what conditions do certain networks appear, weaken and disappear while others persist? Given current concerns about skill shortages and brain-drain in sending countries, additional insights into how and why return migration occurs are both theoretically and practically useful.

Since its appearance on the academic scene, the social networks approach to the study of migration has evolved from focusing on a handful of actors to including an ever-expanding number of actors and processes stretching across multiple borders. Studies in North America, Europe and elsewhere have contributed to the growth of this research by highlighting the networks and nuances of their particular regions. It is now time to bridge these divides and create 'networks of network scholars' to synthesise findings, develop informed conclusions and suggest fruitful areas for future research. Multi-site research could provide a rich and comprehensive analysis of the function and impact of migrant networks. With increasing migration from a variety of regions, and in the continued absence of any institutionalised international migration regime (Massey 1995), the number of migrant networks is likely to expand significantly in the near future. In an interdependent and borderless world, the networks approach is a valuable conceptual, methodological and policy tool for the study of immigration and migrants.

MAIN IDEAS

The *strength* and *density* of ties are two common measures of social networks.

A limitation of current social theories is their inability to relate micro-level interactions to macro-level phenomena.

The social networks approach addresses why individuals migrate as well as why migration persists.

Networks help individuals to find employment, but often this is in jobs in the informal sector where migrants have little contact with the mainstream population.

Gender shapes migration decision-making processes and household migration strategies.

Women migrants are usually responsible for building new care networks in the host society, though they are under greater time constraints due to the need to care for their family.

Note

1 Although informal labour networks often consist of friends, family and acquaintances, they are distinct from personal networks. The main focus of informal labour networks is to facilitate labour migration flows, not family reunification.

References

Abella, M. (1992), 'Contemporary labor migration from Asia: Policies and perspectives of sending countries', in: M. Kritz, L. Lim and H. Zlotnik (eds), *International Migration Systems: A Global Approach*, 263-278. Oxford: Oxford University Press.

Agunias, D. R. and N. G. Ruiz (2007), 'Protecting overseas workers: Lessons and cautions from the Philippines', *Migration Policy Institute* September: 1-32. www.migrationpolicy.org/research/migration _development.php. Accessed 7 January 2009.

Amuedo-Dorantes, C. and K. Mundra (2007), 'Social networks and their impact on the earnings of Mexican migrants', *Demography* 44 (4): 849-863.

Anderson, G. and L. Calzavara (1986), 'Networks, education and occupational success', in: K. Lundy and B. Warme (eds), *In Work in the Canadian Context: Continuity Despite Change*, 314-327. 2nd ed. Toronto: Butterworths.

Anthias, F. (1983), 'Sexual divisions and ethnic adaptation: The case of the Greek-Cypriot women', in: A. Phizacklea (ed.), *One Way Ticket: Migration and Female Labor*, 73-94. London: Routledge.

Asis, M. (2006), 'The Philippines' culture of migration', *Migration Information Source* January. www.migrationinformation.org/Feature/display.cfm?ID=364. Accessed 9 January 2009.

Asis, M. (2005), 'Caring for the world: Filipino domestic workers gone global', in: S. Huang, B. Yeoh and N. A. Rahman (eds), *Asian Women as Transnational Domestic Workers*, 21-53. Singapore: Marshall Cavendish Association.

Bakan, A. and D. Stasiulis (2003), *Negotiating Citizenship: Migrant Women in Canada and the Global System*. New York: Palgrave Macmillan.

Bastia, T. (2007), 'From mining to garment workshops: Bolivian migrants in Buenos Aires', *Journal of Ethnic and Migration Studies* 33 (4): 655-669.

Bolumar, F., A. Laser, M. V. Zunzunegui, J. del Amo and L. Mazarrasa (2007), 'The contribution of a gender perspective to the understanding of migrants' health', *Journal of Epidemiology and Community Health* 61 (2): 4-10.

Boyd, M. (1989), 'Family and personal networks in international migration: Recent developments and new agenda', *International Migration Review* 23 (3): 638-670.

Boyd, M. and N. Alboim (2012), 'Managing international migration: The Canadian case', in: D. Rodríguez-García (ed.), *Managing Immigration and Diversity in Quebec and Canada: A Transatlantic Dialogue with Catalonia, Spain, and Europe*. Barcelona: CIB-DOB Foundation.

Boyd, M. and E. Grieco (2003), 'Women and migration: Incorporating gender into international migration theory', *Migration Information Source* March. www.migrationinformation.org/Feature/display.cfm?id=106. Accessed 26 May 2007.

Bruinsma, G. and W. Bernasco (2004), 'Criminal groups and transnational illegal markets: A more detailed examination on the basis of social network theory', *Crime, Law and Social Change* 41: 79-94.

Caponio, T. (2008), '(Im)migration research in Italy: A European comparative perspective', *The Sociological Quarterly* 49: 445-464.

Castles, S. (2000), 'International migration at the beginning of the 21st century: Global trends and issues', *International Social Science Journal* 52 (165): 269-281.

Castles, S. (1990), 'Formal and informal networks of immigrants', workshop on the adaptation of migrants. *United Nations Educational Scientific and Cultural Organization*.

Chiswick, B. and P.M. Miller (1996), 'Ethnic networks and language proficiency among immigrants', *Journal of Population Economics* 9 (1): 19-35.

Chiswick, B. and P.M. Miller (1992), 'Language in the labor market: The immigrant experience in Canada and the United States', in: Barry Chiswick (ed.), *Immigration, Language and Ethnic Issues: Canada and the United States*, 229-296. Washington, DC: American Enterprise Institute.

Christiansen, C.C. (2008), 'Hometown associations and solidarities in Kurdish transnational villages: The migration-development nexus in a European context', *The European Journal of Development Research* 20 (1): 88-103.

Collyer, M. (2007), 'In-between places: Trans-Saharan transit migrants in Morocco and the fragmented journey to Europe', *Antipode* 39 (4): 668-690.

Collyer, M. (2005), 'When do social networks fail to explain migration? Accounting for the movement of Algerian asylum-seekers to the UK', *Journal of Ethnic and Migration Studies* 31 (4): 699-718.

Curran, S. and E. Rivero-Fuentes (2003), 'Engendering migrant networks: The case of Mexican migration', *Demography* 40 (2): 289-307.

Curran, S. and A. Saguy (2001), 'Migration and cultural change: A role for gender and social networks?' *Journal of International Women's Studies* 2: 54-77.
Drever, A. and O. Hoffmeister (2008), 'Immigrants and social networks in a job-scarce environment: The case of Germany', *International Migration Review* 42 (2): 425-449.
Epstein, G., T. Bauer and I. Gang (2002), 'Herd effects or migration networks? The location choice of Mexican immigrants in the United States', *Institute for the Study of Labor.* ftp://repec.iza.org/RePEc/Discussionpaper/dp551.pdf. Accessed 28 November 2007.
Evergeti, V. and E. Zontini (2006), 'Introduction: Some critical reflections on social capital, migration and transnational families', *Ethnic and Racial Studies* 29 (6): 1025-1039.
Fawcett, J. (1989), 'Networks, linkages and migration systems', *International Migration Review* 7: 163-176.
Feld, S.L. (1981), 'The focused organization of social ties', *American Journal of Sociology* 86 (5): 1015-1035.
Fuglerud, O. and A. Engebrigtsen (2006), 'Culture, networks and social capital: Tamil and Somali', *Ethnic and Racial Studies* 29 (6): 1118-1134.
Gallo, C. and T. Bailey (1996), 'Social networks and skills-based immigration policy', in: H. Duleep and P. V. Wunnava (eds), *Immigrants and Immigration Policy: Individual Skills, Family Ties, and Group Identities,* 203-217. Greenwich: JAI Press..
Gilbertson, G. (1995), 'Women's labor and enclave employment: The case of Dominican and Colombian women in NYC', *International Migration Review* 29 (3): 657-671.
Gimpel, J. and J. Edward (1999), *The Congressional Politics of Immigration Reform.* Boston: Allyn and Bacon.
Glick Schiller, N., L. Basch and C. Szanton Blanc (1995), 'From immigrant to transmigrant: Theorizing transnational migration', *Anthropological Quarterly* 68 (1): 48-63.
Goldenberg, S. and V. Haines (1992), 'Social networks and institutional completeness: From territory to ties', *Canadian Journal of Sociology* 17 (3): 301-312.
Granovetter, M. (1982), 'Strength of weak ties: A network theory revisited', in: P. Marsden and N. Lin (eds), *Social Structure and Network Analysis,* 105-130. Beverly Hills: Sage Publishing.
Granovetter, M. (1973), 'The strength of weak ties', *American Journal of Sociology* 78 (6): 1360-1380.
Green, A. (2004), 'Beyond harmonization: How United States immigration rules would have worked in Canada', *Policy Matters* 5 (4): 1-32.
Greenwell, L., R. Burciago Valdez and J. DaVanzo (1997), 'Social ties, wages and gender in a study of Salvadoran and Filipino immigrants in Los Angeles', *Social Science Quarterly* 78 (2): 559-577.
Guarnizo, L.E. and M.P. Smith (1998), 'The locations of transnationalism', in: M.P. Smith and L.E. Guarnizo (eds), *Transnationalism From Below,* 3-34. New Brunswick: Transaction Publishers.
Gupta, A. and J. Ferguson (1992), 'Beyond "culture": Space, identity and the politics of difference', *Cultural Anthropology* 7 (1): 6-23.
Gurak, D. and F. Caces (1992), 'Migration networks and the shaping of migration systems', in: M. Kritz, L.L. Lim and H. Zlotnik (eds), *International Migration Systems: A Global Approach,* 150-176. New York: Oxford University Press.
Hagan, J.M. (1998), 'Social networks, gender, and immigrant incorporation: Resources and constraints', *American Sociological Review* 63 (1): 55-67.
Haug, S. (2008), 'Migration networks and migration decision-making', *Journal of Ethnic and Migration Studies* 34 (4): 585-605.
Hellermann, C. (2006), 'Migrating alone: Tackling social capital? Women from Eastern Europe in Portugal', *Ethnic and Racial Studies* 29 (6): 1135-1152.

Herman, E. (2006), 'Migration as a family business: The role of personal networks in the mobility phase of migration', *International Migration* 44 (4): 191-230.

Hondagneu-Sotelo, P. (2001), *Doméstica: Immigrant Workers Cleaning and Caring in the Shadows of Affluence*. Berkeley: University of California Press.

Hondagneu-Sotelo, P. (1994), *Gendered Transitions: Mexican Experiences of Immigration*. Berkeley: University of California Press.

Hughes, D. (2000), 'The Natasha trade: The transnational shadow market of trafficking in women', *Journal of International Affairs* 53 (2): 625-652.

Kandel, W. and D. Massey (2002), 'The culture of Mexican migration: A theoretical and empirical analysis', *Social Forces* 80: 981-1004.

Kazemipur, A. (2006), 'The market value of friendship: Social networks of immigrants', *Canadian Ethnic Studies* 38 (2): 46-71.

Kim, D.Y. (2006), 'Stepping-stone to intergenerational mobility? The springboard, safety net or mobility trap functions of Korean immigrant entrepreneurship for the second generation', *International Migration Review* 40(4): 927-962.

Kinsella, D. (2006), 'The black market in small arms: Examining a social network', *Contemporary Security Policy* 27 (1): 100-117.

Kress, B. (2006), 'Burkina Faso: Testing the tradition of circular migration', *Migration Information Source* May. http://www.migrationinformation.org/Profiles/display.cfm?ID=399. Accessed 16 May 2008.

Krissman, F. (2005), 'Sin coyote ni patron: Why the migrant network fails to explain international migration', *International Migration Review* 39 (1): 4-44.

Landolt, P., J. Bernhard and L. Goldring (2008), 'Transnationalizing families: Canadian immigration policy and the spatial fragmentation of care-giving among Latin American newcomers', *International Migration* 47 (2): 3-31.

Levitt, P. and R. de la Dehesa (2003), 'Transnational migration and the redefinition of the state: Variations and explanations', *Ethnic and Racial Studies* 26 (4): 587-611.

Light, I. (2007), 'Review symposium on deflecting immigration: Networks, markets, and regulations in Los Angeles', *Ethnic and Racial Studies* 30 (6): 1152-1166.

Light, I. (2006), *Deflecting Immigration: Networks, Markets and Regulation in Los Angeles*. New York: Russell Sage Foundation.

Lim, L.L. (1992), 'International labor movements: A perspective on economic exchanges and flows', in: M. Kritz, L.L. and H. Zlotnik (eds), *International Migration Systems: A Global Approach*, 133-149. Oxford: Oxford University Press.

Lindstrom, D. and E. Munoz-Franco (2005), 'Migration and the diffusion of modern contraceptive knowledge and use in rural Guatemala', *Studies in Family Planning* 36 (4): 277-288.

Livingston, G. (2006), 'Gender, job searching, and employment outcomes among Mexican immigrants', *Population Research and Policy Review* 25 (1): 43-66.

Lomnitz, L. (1976), 'Migration and networks in Latin America', in: M. Kritz, L.L. Lim and H. Zlotnik (eds), *International Migration Systems: A Global Approach*, 150-176. New York: Oxford University Press.

Martin, P. (1995), 'Proposition 187 in California', *International Migration Review* 29 (1): 255-263.

Massey, D. (1995), 'The new immigration and ethnicity in the United States', *Population and Development Review* 21 (3): 631-652.

Massey, D.S. and F. García España (1987), 'The social process of international migration', *Science* 237 (4816): 733-738.

Massey, D. and W. Kandel (2002), 'The culture of Mexican migration: A theoretical and empirical analysis', *Social Forces* 80 (3): 981-1004.

Massey, D., J. Durand, W. Kandel and E. Parrado (1996), 'International migration and development in Mexican communities', *Demography* 33 (2): 249-264.

Massey, D., J. Arango, G. Hugo, A. Kouaouci, A. Pelligrino and J.E. Taylor (1993), 'Theories of international migration: A review and appraisal', *Population and Development Review* 19 (3): 431-466.

Massey, D.S., R. Alarcón, J. Durand and H. González (1987), *Return to Aztlan: The Social Process of International Migration from Western Mexico.* Berkeley/Los Angeles: University of California Press.

Matthei, L.M. (1996), 'Gender and international labor migration: A networks approach', *Social Justice* 23: 38-53.

McIllwain, J. (1999), 'Organized crime: A social network approach', *Crime, Law and Social Change* 32: 301-323.

Migration Information Source (2007), 'Top ten migration issues of 2007 – Issue # 9 – Migration and development issues: No longer a novelty in policy discussions', December. www.migrationinformation.org/Feature/display.cfm?id=656. Accessed 16 May 2008.

Miller-Martinez, D. and S. Wallace (2007), 'Structural contexts and life-course processes in the social networks of older Mexican immigrants in the United States', in: S. Carmel, C.A. Morse and F.M. Torres-Gil (eds), *Lessons on Aging from Three Nations, Volume 1: The Art of Aging Well,* 141-154. Amityville: Baywood Publishing.

Parrado, E.A. and C. Flippen (2005), 'Migration and gender among Mexican women', *American Sociological Review* 70 (4): 606-632.

Parrenas, R.S. (2005), 'Long distance intimacy: Class, gender and intergenerational relations between mothers and children in Filipino transnational families', *Global Networks* 5 (4): 317-336.

Parrenas, R.S. (2001), 'Transgressing the nation-state: The partial citizenship and "imagined (global) community" of migrant Filipina domestic workers', *SIGNS* 26 (4): 1129-1154.

Phizacklea, A. (1983), 'In the front line', in: A. Phizacklea (ed.), *One Way Ticket: Migration and Female Labour,* 95-112. London: Routledge.

Piotrowski, M. (2006), 'The effect of social networks at origin communities on migrant remittances: Evidence from Nang Rong district', *European Journal of Population* 22 (1): 67-94.

Piper, N. (2005), 'Gender and migration', paper prepared for the Policy Analysis and Research Programme of the Global Commission on International Migration', *Asia Research Institute National University of Singapore.* http://72.14.205.104/search?q=cache:ssJvPhA2Gm4J:www.gcim.org/attachements/TP10.pdf+Gender+and+Migration:+A+paper+prepared+for+the+Policy+Analysis+and+Research+Programme+of+the+Global+Commission+on+International+Migration,+nicola+piper&hl=en&ct=clnk&cd=1&gl=ca. Accessed 25 May 2008.

Poros, M. (2001), 'The role of migrant networks in linking local labor markets: The case of Asian Indian migration to New York and London', *Global Networks* 1 (3): 243-259.

Portes, A. (1978), 'Introduction: Toward a structural analysis of illegal (undocumented) migration', *International Migration Review* 12 (4): 469-484.

Portes, A., L.E. Guarnizo and P. Landolt (1999), 'The study of transnationalism: Pitfalls and promise of an emergent research field', *Ethnic and Racial Studies* 22 (2): 217-237.

Portes, A. and M. Zhou (1993), 'The new second generation: Segmented assimilation and its variants', *Annals of the American Academy of Political and Social Science* 530 (1): 74-98.

Purkayastha, B. (2005), 'Skilled migration and cumulative disadvantage: The case of highly qualified Asian Indian immigrant women in the US', *Geoforum* 36 (2): 181-196.

Ryan, L. (2007), 'Migrant women, social networks and motherhood: The experiences of Irish nurses in Britain', *Sociology* 41 (2): 295-312.

Salaff, J. and A. Greve (2004), 'Can women's social networks migrate?' *Women's Studies International Forum* 27: 149-162.

Salt, J. and J. Stein (1997), 'Migration as business: The case of trafficking', *International Migration* 35 (4): 467-491.

Sernau, S., V. Nee and J. Sanders (2002), 'Asian immigrants' reliance on social ties in a Multiethnic labor market', *Social Forces* 81 (1): 281-314.

Silvey, R. (2003), 'Spaces of protest: Gendered migration, social networks, and labor activism in West Java', *Political Geography* 22: 129-155.

Simmons, A. and D. Plaza (1998), 'Breaking through the glass ceiling: The pursuit of university training among African-Caribbean migrants and their children in Toronto', *Canadian Ethnic Studies* 30 (3): 99.

Spittel, M. (1998). 'Testing network theory through an analysis of migration from Mexico to the United States', Center for Demography and Ecology, University of Wisconsin-Madison. Working Paper No. 99-01. www.ssc.wisc.edu/cde/cdewp/99-01.pdf. Accessed 10 January 2009.

Stark, O. (1991), *The Migration of Labor.* Cambridge: Basil Blackwell.

Tilly, C. (2007). 'Trust networks in transnational migration', *Sociological Forum* 22 (1): 3-24.

Tilly, C. (1990), 'Transplanted networks', in: V. Yans-McLaughlin (ed.), *Immigration Reconsidered: History, Sociology and Politics*, 79-95. New York: Oxford University Press.

Trappers, A., M. Hooghe, B. Meuleman and T. Reeskens (2008), 'Migration to European countries: A structural explanation of patterns, 1980-2004', *International Migration Review* 42 (2): 476-504.

Tyner, J. (2000), 'Migrant labor and the politics of scale: Gendering the Philippine state', *Asia Pacific Viewpoint* 41 (2): 131-154.

Varady, D. (2008), 'Muslim residential clustering and political radicalism', *Housing Studies* 23 (1): 45-66.

Vathi, Z. and R. Black (2007), 'Migration and poverty reduction in Kosovo', Working Paper Series. *Development Research Centre on Migration, Globalization and Poverty*, Sussex University. http://www.migrationdrc.org/publications/working_papers.html. Accessed 29 November 2007.

Vertovec, S. (2002), 'Transnational networks and skilled labor migration', *Working Paper WPTC-02-02.* Presented at the conference Ladenburger Diskurs 'Migration', Gottlieb Daimler-und Karl Benz-Stiftung. Ladenburg. 14-15 February. www.transcomm.ox.ac.uk/working%20papers/WPTC-02-02%20Vertovec.pdf. Accessed 7 January 2009.

Waddington, C. (2003), 'Livelihood outcomes of migration for poor people', *Working Paper Series. Development Research Centre on Migration, Globalization and Poverty*, Sussex University. www.migrationdrc.org/publications/working_papers/WP-T1.pdf. Accessed 29 November 2007.

Wellman, B. (1979), 'The community question: The intimate networks of East Yorkers', *American Journal of Sociology* 84 (5): 1201-1231.

White, A. and L. Ryan (2008), 'Polish "temporary" migration: The formation and significance of social networks', *Europe-Asia Studies* 60 (9): 1467-1502.

Williams, L. (2006), 'Social networks of refugees in the United Kingdom: Tradition, tactics and new community', *Journal of Ethnic and Migration Studies* 32 (5): 865-879.

Zenou, Y. and J. Wahba (2005), 'Density, social networks and job search methods: Theory and application to Egypt', *Journal of Development Economics* 78 (2): 443-473.

Zhang, S. and M. Gaylord (1996), 'Bound for the golden mountain: The social organization of Chinese alien smuggling', *Crime, Law and Social Change* 25: 1-16.

Zhou, M. (1997), 'Segmented assimilation: Issues, controversies and recent research on the new second generation', *International Migration Review* 31 (4): 975-1008.

Zhou, M. and J. Logan (1989), 'Returns on human capital in ethnic enclaves: New York City's Chinatown', *American Sociological Review* 54: 809-820.

5 Transnational Migration

Eva Østergaard-Nielsen

Introduction

The transnational perspective has gained a remarkable foothold in migration studies. A wealth of studies have documented that migrants do not necessarily cut their ties with their country of origin. Instead, migrants may live their lives travelling back and forth across state borders (their papers permitting) and form sustained transnational relations with their country of origin. These activities and the current and potential impact of them have attracted growing attention from academics and policymakers alike.

This chapter introduces some of the key empirical, theoretical and methodological discussions in research on migrant transnationalism. Its objective is not to establish the extent to which the transnational optic explains why people move from point A to point B (or beyond).[1] Indeed, cross-border mobility is not the only defining feature of migrant transnationalism, because migrants can be transnational through their networks and practices without physically crossing a state border. Instead, this chapter focuses on the contribution of the transnational perspective, which breaks with the idea of migration and migrant incorporation as a unilinear process. States and societies are not bounded units, according to the analytical framework of the transnational perspective. The perspective invites scholars to view migratory dynamics as embedded in a multi-level transnational field spanning more than one locality. In this way, the transnational optic helps to overcome the dichotomy between countries of origin and those of reception, bridging studies of migration and migrant incorporation (Faist 2004).

migrants as actors

A further contribution of the transnational perspective is the focus on migrants as actors in economic, social and political transnational spaces. Understanding migration through an analysis of the agency of the migrants themselves is not unique to studies of migrant transnationalism. Yet, the focus on the role and impact of various types of migrant transnational activities not only gives voice to migrants' perceptions and practices, but also emphasises that migrant activities are informed by and challenge other actors and policies in transnational spaces. As the transnational perspective underlines, migrant transnationalism draws on and feeds into contemporary processes of globalisation and localisation of identities and agency.

This chapter first discusses the proliferation of the transnational perspective in migration studies. Next it reviews the debates on the scope, degree of representation, durability and newness of migrant transnationalism. Some concepts and theoretical approaches are reviewed that seek to classify and explain transnational migration and its implications. Where relevant, the discussions include both earlier, more exploratory studies and more recent critical calls for closer scrutiny of the local and global politics of migrant transnationalism and the impact of transnational relations on migrant livelihood. The final sections present key dimensions of the ongoing methodological discussion on the complexity of transnational migration and their implications for migration research. Throughout the chapter, particular attention is paid to the politics of migrant transnationalism. This focus highlights the fact that transnational migration and various forms of transnational relations do not take place in an institutional vacuum. Rather, they are linked with state and non-state actors, policies and institutions at the local, national and international levels.[2]

Enter the transnational optic in migration studies

transnational turn

The understanding that migration entails continuous and regular border-crossing practices is not new to migration studies (Portes et al. 1999). However, the emphasis placed on the 'transnational turn' (Vertovec 2009) has become more prominent during the past two decades. Calls for more attention to the meaning of migrant transnationalism have come particularly from anthropology and sociology. Notably, the work of Glick Schiller and her collaborators defined migrant transnationalism as 'the process by which trans-migrants, through their daily activities, forge and sustain multi-stranded social, economic and political relations that link together their societies of origin and settlement, and through which they create transnational social fields that cross national borders' (Basch et al. 1994: 6). Studies by Portes and his collaborators emphasised the regularity of migrant transnational practices as a defining criterion, and attempted to systematically categorise the various forms of transnational action (Portes et al. 1999). The Economic and Social Research Council (ESRC) Transnational Communities Programme, based at Oxford University, launched a multi-disciplinary research programme, which served as a valuable platform for projects, conferences and networks both within Europe and across the Atlantic.[3] These efforts, and many more, illustrate the tendency to place the transnational dynamic itself at the centre of the analysis of actors, processes and practices.

the term 'transnational'

The term 'transnational' is by no means only related to migration studies, but has a long-standing place in the social sciences, where it has been assigned different meanings and given different weights in theoretical debates across disciplines (Levitt and Khagram 2007). In international relations, for example, the term transnational has played a role in the discussion of the importance of state actors versus other types of actors in the analysis of international politics (Keohane and Nye 1971; Josselin and Wallace 2001). Here 'transnational' is distinguished from 'international' (relations between states) by referring to the cross-border relations or actions of non-state actors, such as NGOs, multinational companies or religious organisations. Along these lines, Risse-Kappen (1995) defines transnational relations as 'regular interactions across national boundaries when at least one actor is a non-state agent or does not operate on behalf of a national government or an intergovernmental organization' (Risse-Kappen 1995: 3). In this vein, studies of transnational networks and practices of NGOs, civil societies or religious organisations use the term transnational to understand how the cross-border dimension links the local with the global and influences state policy (Keck and Sikkink 1998; Khagram and Alvord 2006).

international and supranational

Similarly, with the entry of 'transnational' into the migration studies vocabulary, a number of studies have distinguished the transnational from the international, the supranational (i.e. government structures at the international level, such as the EU) and the global (Portes 2001; Bauböck 2003; Faist 2004). The international and supranational are largely identified by the types and levels of political actors and institutions. However, the emphasis on migrant cross-border flows, practices and processes necessitates clarification of the difference between the transnational and the global. One suggestion is a differentiation based on scale. Whereas global processes span the entire planet, the transnational is more 'anchored' across specific state borders (Glick Schiller et al. 1992; Glick Schiller 2005).

diasporas

A final antecedent, or perhaps rather an accompanying, field of study is on diasporas, a subject that has experienced a boom since the 1980s. Transnational identification and contact with the homeland is a defining feature of diasporas. Originally a concept that refers primarily to the dispersal and exile of the Greek or Jewish populations, the term diaspora has become interchangeable with all types of migrants and refugees (Cohen 1997; Dufoix 2008). This expansion sparked an academic debate on how inclusive the concept should be. Efforts were made to set up criteria to determine the defining characteristics of a diaspora (Sheffer 1986; Safran 1991). Yet, a later development has seen the definition of diaspora take a constructivist turn, by emphasising diaspora as a category of practice, and focusing on the conditions and processes through which migrant or refugee groups define themselves as a diaspora – or are ascribed this label by other actors in the country of origin or residence (Brubaker 2005; Dufoix 2008). The use of the term diaspora then becomes synonymous not with the state of dispersal, but with the emerging sense of a collective identity related to a common point of origin, and the creation of a long-distance relationship between emigrants and their homeland. In the current broader definition of diaspora, the concept overlaps with that of migrant transnational practices, and the two concepts are often used synonymously in both academic and policy-making circles.

Key debates, the delimitation of migrant transnationalism

defining migrant transnationalism

The transnational optic in migration studies is continuously being debated. In the first round of literature on migrant transnationalism, the scope and significance of migrant cross-border ties were emphasised (Portes 2001; Vertovec 2004b; Levitt and Jaworsky 2007). Consequently, and in parallel with reflections on the meaning of the term diaspora and the broad use of the term 'migrant transnationalism', there have been attempts to come up with more precise definitions and classifications. As pointed out by Portes (2001), 'a concept that seeks to cover an excessive range of empirical phenomena ends up by applying to none in particular, thereby losing its heuristic value' (Portes 2001: 182). The key points of the debate between critics and advocates of the transnational optic on migration include the distinctiveness, scope and durability of contemporary migrant transnationalism.[4] A pressing question concerns defining the main determinants of migrant transnationalism. This question is often answered by 'it depends', as different migration trajectories, migration cycles, processes of migrant incorporation, gender, politics and institutional contexts all play a role.

One of the most frequent criticisms is that migrant transnationalism is a case of 'old wine in new bottles'. A re-reading of the literature on European migration to the United States at the turn of the twentieth century shows how migrants used migration and transnational ties as a strategy to improve their livelihood in both their country of immigration and their country of origin (Foner 1997; Gabaccia 2000; Gjerde 2001). The main reply to this criticism is that while transnational migration is not new, the transnational perspective on migration is. Portes (2001), among others, has argued that only with the recognition of the significance and newness of migrant transnationalism have scholars begun to identify antecedents and parallels between cases whose interrelationship was not clear until the arrival of a 'coined and refined' concept of migrant transnationalism (Portes 2001).

new technology

Moreover, although there is no reason to reify transnationalism as a completely new phenomenon, something *is* new about contemporary migrant transnationalism, including its scale and intensity, as well as the politicisation and institutionalisation of the phenomenon. Modern communication technology, the Internet, affordable air travel and the globalisation of media have facilitated the ways in which migrants stay in touch with their country of origin. The communication industry's targeting of 'ethnic markets' (Vertovec 2004a) is an interesting illustration of migrants' use of modern communication technology; migrants and refugees can now retain or develop links with their country of origin with greater intensity than before. New technology makes a difference in the ways and depth to which migrants can keep abreast of and participate in social, economic or political affairs in both their country of origin and country of settlement (Smith 1997). It is this intensity that makes migrant transnationalism more interesting for other state and non-state actors in both countries, as these actors have launched a range of policies to tap into migrant transnational resources (Smith 1997; Østergaard-Nielsen 2003b).

generations

However, highlighting the historical precedence of contemporary migrant transnationalism does not necessarily mean that this phenomenon is durable in the sense of extending beyond each first generation of migrants. Do transnational practices or identification with the country of origin decline over generations? Are the children and grandchildren of migrants simply less connected or less interested in their homeland than their parents? Or are there other differences over time and between generations that we need to consider when framing and carrying out research on migrant transnational orientation, mobility and activity (Smith 2006)? The relatively few quantitative studies that have investigated the durability of migrant transnationalism in Europe have related it to the integration process in the migrants' country of residence, and have confirmed that local and trans-national orientation are not mutually exclusive (Snel et al. 2006; Morales and Jorba 2010). Meanwhile, qualitative studies indicate that, in addition to trying to look at quantitative changes in transnational experiences over time and between generations, it is as important to explore the qualitative differences in how migrants relate to their country of origin over time (Levitt 2002; Smith 2006; Østergaard-Nielsen 2009a). Increasing connectedness between localities and global economic and political developments facilitate the redefinition of cross-border transactions and identification for both non-migrants and migrants alike. The transnational dimension of the activities of migrant descendants may take on new and more complex forms, which render the dyadic homeland-host-country framework analysis inadequate. For instance, second-generation migrants may primarily identify with wider regional or religious issues and less with their parents' country of origin (Østergaard-Nielsen 2009a).

representative of experience

A further concern regards whether studies of migrant transnationalism are representative of the wider migrant experience. In part, this concern is ascribed to the predominance of in-depth case studies that 'sample on the dependent variable', by studying migrant transnationalism when it is manifest, and not studying it when it is not (Portes 2001). Studies at the level of individual migrants operated with a distinction between 'narrow' or 'core' (i.e. regular and intense transnational practices) and 'wide' or 'broad' (i.e. more *ad hoc* or irregular migrant transnationalism) (Itzigsohn et al. 1999; Guarnizo et al. 2003; Waldinger 2008). These studies have found that only a small proportion of migrants engage in regular migrant transnationalism, although there are important discrepancies between the economic, social and political spheres.

Mapping migrant transnationalism

Parallel to the debate regarding the newness, scope and durability of migrant transnationalism, there has been a process of categorising and conceptualising the practices, networks and arenas of migrant transnationalism. Concepts such as transnational social spaces (Faist 2000; Pries 2001), transnational social fields (Glick Schiller 2005) or transnational social formations (Guarnizo 1998) seek to capture the multi-layered cross-border sites, structures and institutions of migrant transnationalism (Levitt and Jaworsky 2007).

mapping exercises

In terms of categories, a number of mapping exercises have divided migrant transnational practices according to theme, intensity, type of actor and network or relationship with state institutions and public policy. With regard to themes, the distinction between economic, social and political migrant transnationalism presents a more nuanced analysis of the field (Portes et al. 1999). Some types of practices fit neatly into these categories, whereas others overlap. Other practices warrant additional categories, as in the case of transnational religious networks of migrants (Levitt 2007).

remittances

Among the main practices analysed within *migrant economic transnationalism* are the remittances that migrants send back to their families, the foreign direct investment of migrants and diasporas and the cross-border business networks involving migrants (Portes et al. 2002). While remittances are usually analysed in terms of migrants and their homelands, migrant business networks may have a wider regional or even global span, as in the case of the Fujianese (Chinese) migrants (Pieke et al. 2004). The total sum of what are often very small individual contributions ranks as a top source of foreign income for a range of emigration countries such as Mexico, Morocco and India.[5] The subject of collective remittances, such as joint contributions by hometown associations (HTAs), is another important area that has been widely examined, particularly in terms of Latin American migrant collectives in the USA (Waldinger et al. 2007, Portes et al. 2007). In Europe it has been noted that Turkish, Ecuadorian and Moroccan migrant associations contribute to local development in their countries of origin (Caglar 2005; Lacroix 2005; Østergaard-Nielsen 2009b; Boccagni Forthcoming-b).

politics

The category of *political migrant transnationalism* includes cross-border voting by migrants in local or national homeland elections and support for political parties or other political actors in the homeland. Migrants may also engage indirectly in the politics of their countries of origin via the institutions of the country of residence. This engagement can be in the form of 'block-voting' on homeland political issues or various types of campaigns on behalf of or against the homeland political regime. One way of mapping migrant political transnationalism is in terms of the subject of mobilisation, such as *emigrant politics* (when migrants lobby their country of origin for external citizenship rights or for support for problems of discrimination abroad); *homeland* or *diaspora politics* (activities to support or criticise political processes and actors in the country of origin); and *trans-local politics* (local-to-local engagement in the country of origin) (Østergaard-Nielsen 2003c). The last category also includes migrants' collective contributions to development projects, because these can challenge local power hierarchies (Portes 1999). Studies of migrant political transnationalism have paid some attention to refugees and asylum seekers and their mobilisation around conflicts or post-conflict reconstruction in their countries of origin (Al-Ali et al. 2001; Orjuela 2007; Kleist 2008; Turner 2008). Political practices and networks of migrants constitute a dimension of migrant transnationalism that is more directly related to state concerns with issues regarding dual loyalties or security threats. There is also a wider concern about how patterns of temporary migration in particular combine with citizenship and political representation in both the countries of residence and of origin (Bauböck 2007; Martinello and Lafleur 2008).

social and cultural commitment

Finally, the category of *socio-cultural migrant transnationalism* includes a wide variety of practices related to migrants' social and cultural commitment to their country of origin. This category is very broad and in this context I will primarily mention migrants' transnational organisation of family life. Studies on socio-cultural migrant transnationalism demonstrate that not just migration, but also the linkages between migrants and their home community, may impact social and cultural hierarchies in either place. Studies of transnational family life (Sørensen 2007) have analysed how families function across borders when the family has pooled resources to send an older child abroad, or when the parents migrate and leave the children behind with other members of the family. Such studies tell the complex story of how transnational parenthood can be facilitated through modern means of communication, while at the same time, migration and migrant transnationalism may reinforce or change gender or generational roles within the family (Salih 2003; Sørensen and Guarnizo 2007). Although gender is also a highly relevant variable in the understanding of migrant economic and political practices (Itzigsohn and Giorguli-Saucedo 2005), it is particularly present in studies of socio-cultural migrant transnationalism. This focus has been reinforced by the feminisation of migration, where women migrate alone and find jobs, especially in the domestic service sector. This raises the question of how the feminisation of migration translates into new and distinct transnational family relationships (Sørensen and Guarnizo 2007).

Policies and politics of migrant transnationalism

overlapping transnational spaces

Migrant transnationalism, as with other types of transnational social formations, rethinks the idea of congruence between nation-state borders and social, economic and political action. It focuses on overlapping transnational spaces and processes as part and parcel of migration and migrant agency. However, migrant cross-border practices are embedded within bordered political processes and institutions. Policies and politics in the countries of origin and of residence both influence and are influenced by migrant transnationalism.

With regard to migrant integration policies, the environment of high levels of politicisation of migration and migrant integration processes in the global North has fed into the growing interest in migrant transnationalism in both academic and policy-making circles. First, a range of migration policies aimed at managing migration, such as seasonal worker recruitment schemes and migrant return programmes, intersect with migrant cross-border movement and with economic and social transnational networks and practices. Notably, the frequently contested issue of migrants' right to family reunification throughout Europe underscores the tension between the migrants' wish to regroup in the country of residence and restricted migration policies (which may be among the reasons for the transnationalisation of families in the first place). Second, migrant transnationalism inspires debates regarding how migrants' relations with their country of origin are compatible with their process of integration. Third, migrant transnationalism is central to the re-emergence of the agenda for migration and development, positing migrants as important actors in processes of development and democratisation in their countries of origin. Co-development policies are based on the notion that migrants feel a continued responsibility for their families, and sometimes also the wider local community in their country of origin (Østergaard-Nielsen 2009b).

role of the state

Migrant transnationalism has often been analysed in relation to the role and interest of the state. The concepts of transnationalism from 'above' vs. 'below' seek to capture the dynamics between 'state-led' and 'migrant-led' transnationalism (Guarnizo and Smith 1998; Goldring 2002), and there has been a focus on the role of the state of origin in transnational spaces of migrant transnationalism (Guarnizo and Smith 1998; Itzigsohn 2000; Mahler 2000; Brand 2002; Levitt and Dehesa 2003; Østergaard-Nielsen 2003a; Vilhena 2006; Gamlen 2008). Smith (1997) distinguishes between 'homeland policies', where sending states create institutions aimed at orienting migrants towards a later return, and 'global nation policies', where sending states seek to encourage emigrants to stay in touch. A growing number of emigration countries have shifted from the former set of policies to the latter. For instance, in Mexico, Morocco, Turkey and China, emigrants whose plight was ignored for years have been addressed in celebratory rhetoric elevating them as valuable citizens who are making an important economic contribution to their homeland. This has been accompanied by policies and administrative measures aimed at strengthening transnational relations with emigrants. A key example includes policies vying for the continued loyalty of expatriates, such as the extension of dual citizenship to emigrant populations that would otherwise have to renounce their citizenship upon naturalisation in their countries of residence (Faist 2007). There is also a growing tendency to grant external voting rights to expatriates, as illustrated by the recent overview by IDEA (2006); at least 115 countries allow their expatriates to continue voting in their homeland (IDEA 2006; Bauböck 2007). Another set of policies is directed at maximising migrants' economic contribution to their homelands. This includes channelling remittances via national banks, encouraging emigrants to holiday and spend money in the homeland, or setting up favourable schemes for homeland investment for overseas nationals. Policy programmes to attract emigrant contributions to local and regional development include the 3 for 1 scheme in Mexico, where the regional and federal government match emigrant economic contributions to government-approved development activities (Goldring 2002; Fitzgerald 2008; Smith 2008). Taken together, these policies illustrate how emigrant countries not only tap into the economic resources of citizens abroad but also reincorporate them into their domestic and foreign policy, and appeal to their love for and sense of duty towards their country of origin.

common interests

Parallels in the political measures of countries of origin are explained by their common interests. These interests are usually identified as economic (to secure the continuous inflow of remittances and direct foreign investment) and political (to mobilise political support and to control subversive political dissidence). To explain differences in the policies that are reaching out to emigrants, comparative political analyses of sending countries include the domestic and international structural and historical factors that make some sending states more interested in their overseas nationals than others (Sheffer 1986; Guarnizo 1998; Itzigsohn 2000; Levitt 2001; Østergaard-Nielsen 2003a). The outreach policies have been explained with reference to processes of democratisation in the countries of origin, the size and political clout of emigrant organisations, bilateral relations between the two countries and the impact of global rights regimes (Levitt and Dehesa 2003). The common conclusion is that migration provides the governments of peripherally-positioned sending countries in particular with new options for reconfiguring their reach through transnational economic, social and political ties with nationals abroad. However, it is important not to gloss over the somewhat ambiguous relationship between emigrants and their country of origin. Emigrant collectives may remain sceptical of the political elite in their country of origin, whom they blame for having made it impossible to stay home in the first place. Official policies to reach out to emigrants may lack credibility because it is not easy to convince an overseas community of the sincerity of official interest after years of neglect. Indeed, Mexico, Turkey and India show that relations with the expatriate population do not change overnight (Lall 2003; Martínez-Saldaña 2003; Østergaard-Nielsen 2003a).

Governments and political parties in the countries of origin have been heralded as central political actors in studies of migrant transnationalism. Yet, receiving states also play a central role, by defining the boundaries for inclusion and exclusion of migrants. Although neither US-based nor European-based research on migrant transnationalism constitute homogeneous blocks, it could be argued that the emphasis on the receiving state has been more prominent in European-based research. US-based comparative research designs favour studying several migrant groups in one receiving country (the US), rendering the different countries of origin a central explanatory variable. European-based research includes more studies of one migrant group in several receiving countries, with a focus on how transnationalism relates to the social, economic and political context of their countries of residence. Migrant relations with the sending country are by default transnational in the sense of taking place across state borders. In contrast, migrant relations with the receiving state are not transnational as such, but migrants' ties to their country of origin can feature in debates on the role and meaning of migrant transnationalism in relations between states and migrants within the same territory.

settlement

There are several lines of analysis on how migrant transnationalism is located in the context of countries of settlement. First, there is the issue of how the very process of settlement influences migrant transnationalism. Studies on both sides of the Atlantic have analysed how migrant transnational practices and engagement enter into the equation of their process of settlement or integration (Østergaard-Nielsen 2001; Levitt 2002; Guarnizo et al. 2003). The studies find that integration and transnationalism are not opposites, in the sense that local and transnational attachments are not a zero-sum game. Migrants' transnational orientation does not necessarily go away with time, to be replaced with exclusive incorporation into the country of residence.

politics of migrant transnationalism

Second, there is the issue of the politics of migrant transnationalism, including to what extent receiving countries tolerate migrant cross-border activities and to what extent that explains variance in migrant transnationalism. For instance, comparative research on migrant transnational political practices have investigated incorporation regimes and the scope and forms of migrant transnationalism (Koopmans and Statham 2003). The discursive political environment for migrant transnationalism varies across countries and depends on the kind of migrant transnationalism. Receiving countries with a more assimilatory regime, such as Denmark, have been known to perceive migrants' sustained transnational relations with their country of origin as largely incompatible with integration. Such perceptions may be reflected in the lack of tolerance for dual citizenship or in the withdrawal of funding for migrant associations oriented towards the homeland (Østergaard-Nielsen 2009a). In contrast, the Spanish emerging policy field of co-development includes support for migrant transnational engagement in development projects in their country of origin and draws on migrant transnationalism as a resource for improving synergies between policies on migration and development and dynamics of migrant incorporation (Østergaard-Nielsen 2011). In sum, the conclusion that migrant transnationalism has 'come out of the closet', in terms of being more accepted in receiving-country contexts (Joppke and Morawska 2003), cannot be applied to all states and all types and experiences of migrant transnationalism (Østergaard-Nielsen 2009a).

multi-layered political field

The focus on the actors, politics and policies in both the states of origin and those of residence are important elements in the analysis of migrant transnational spaces. Yet, a framework of analysis that goes beyond state institutions and actors is also important. Migrant cross-border practices take place in a multi-layered and multi-sited political field with a strong interplay between the local and the global. For instance, migrant or refugee transnational political action may be directed at local or national governments or at supranational European institutions, while drawing on global human rights norms and involving other local transnational actors or state representatives. While migrant transnational practices need to be located within their political context in both the country of origin and of residence, it is increasingly clear that transnational spaces are more complex than is suggested in the initial triadic framework of host-country, homeland and migrant collective.

Migrant transnationalism and change

migrant contribution

A complex and debated dimension of migrant transnationalism surrounds the transformative potential of migrants' cross-border economic, political and social activities. The focus shifts from the 'why', 'what' and 'how' of migrant transnationalism to the 'then what'. Inherent in the term 'remittances' is the notion that migrants are contributing to their context of origin – be it money or social, cultural or political values and ideas (Levitt 2001). An underlying premise is the understanding of the migrant as an individual or collective actor whose resources, and thus contribution, can be channelled and even enhanced in the transnational field. Migrant transnationalism 'from below' has been argued to have the potential to challenge power hierarchies in the country of origin and at the same time potentially empower and emancipate the migrants abroad (Portes et al. 1999).

Yet, from the outset, research has questioned whether economic, social and political remittances or contributions have any wider impact in terms of provoking social and political change in the country of origin, and whether the transnational responsibilities drain the resources needed to overcome hardships in their country of residence. In the same vein, the -ism of migrant transnationalism has been criticised for resembling an ideology or a normative optic, which overlooks the fact that migrant transnationalism is not as a default a counter-hegemonic project (Waldinger and Fitzgerald 2004). Still, research findings point both to the independence and transformative potential of migrant transnationalism from below and to how state institutions seek to co-opt or are at least involved in channelling migrants' transnational practices (Guarnizo and Smith 1998; Mahler 1998; Faist 2000; Østergaard-Nielsen 2003c; Smith 2003; Portes et al. 2007; Lyons and Mandaville, forthcoming).

economic impact of remittances

Academic research paints a complex picture of the economic, political and social impact of migrant transnationalism. The *economic impact of remittances* is the subject of a long-standing debate among migration and development experts. The question is whether remittances serve to improve the lives of families left behind and stimulate longstanding local and national economic development, or if they stifle the economy, create patterns of 'unproductive consumption' and ultimately create dependency (Nyberg-Sørensen et al. 2003; de Haas 2005). There is evidence for both the positive and the negative economic impact of remittances. This evidence makes it difficult to generalise about the impact of migrant transnational economic practices and spaces without employing a differentiated and contextualised understanding of the types of migration and economic flows in question (Guarnizo 2003; Sørensen 2007).

political change

In terms of *political change*, studies have probed to what extent migrants go through a process of 'democratic apprenticeship' abroad (Pedraza 2002). This process may include appropriating or reinforcing ideas of respect for human rights, liberal democracy and linking the failure of development to undemocratic rule. In turn, migrants can remit these ideas to their country of origin, through their actual return or via their transnational engagement from afar. In the latter case they may have access to less biased information and exert an influence in the politics of their homeland that would be unobtainable if they had not left. Research and recent political events have shown that migrant political transnationalism can weigh in on political processes in the country of origin, in the form of block-voting for certain candidates, challenging local power hierarchies through co-development projects, or lobbying for international support or assistance in homelands torn by conflict (Lyons and Mandaville, forthcoming). Yet, some have questioned whether migrants are default agents for democratisation. Diasporas and migrant groups may pursue a particularist, nationalist or religiously fundamentalist agenda (Kaldor et al. 2003; Waldinger and Fitzgerald 2004). This criticism has been elegantly summed up by Anderson (1992), depicting the migrant as a long-distance nationalist who supports political factionalism from afar, without having to suffer the consequences (Anderson 1992). Thus, we should not generalise about migrant civil society, which can include both counter-hegemonic and less counter-hegemonic mobilisation.

socio-cultural change

Finally, *in terms of socio-cultural change and migrant livelihood*, studies of migrant transnationalism have indicated the emancipatory impact of migrant transnational resources, which could 'act as an effective antidote to the tendency towards downward assimilation' (Portes 1999: 471). Yet, the impact of migrant transnationalism on socio-economic processes of change in both the country of origin and of residence has also been seen as ambiguous (Glick Schiller and Fouron 1999). Migrants have been perceived both as a support for social and political change, and as responsible for increased individualism and materialism in their countries of origin (Levitt 2001). Studies of cross-border family life balance narratives of how transnational households verge towards more egalitarian positions of women in the household, with criticism of how global care chains lead to a care drain in the country of origin, or how social mobility within transnational spaces can lead to a breakdown of transnational households (Ehrenreich and Hochschild 2003). There is a need to critically examine the social and political discourses that particularly vilify the migration of mothers as responsible for socio-economic problems that were perhaps the cause of, rather than the result of, transnational migration (Pedone 2006; Sørensen and Guarnizo 2007). Finally, as pointed out by Carling (2008), the 'asymmetries in transnational migration' – differentiated social mobility among migrants and non-migrant members of the same family – can be a source of frustration on both sides. Families 'back home' may have an unrealistic image of the hardships endured by their migrant family members, demanding more remittances and ignoring the sacrifices that migrants make abroad (Carling 2008). Feeling equally at home in both countries is perhaps too ambitious a way of describing the experience of separation from your loved ones (Boccagni Forthcoming-a).

transformations

The transnational perspective places the study of migration in the centre of debates on issues of globalisation and transnationalisation (Held et al. 1999). According to the transformationalist perspective within globalisation studies, the state is transforming into a political organisation, which involves collective identities and social orders that borders can no longer contain (Beck 2002; Vertovec 2009). Vertovec (2004) suggests that migrant transnationalism, rather than jump-starting substantial social and political transformations, 'may contribute significantly to broadening, deepening or intensifying conjoined processes of transformations that are already ongoing' (Vertovec 2004b: 972). In this vein, the transnational optic increasingly goes beyond an analytical dichotomy between migrants and states, and countries of residence and of origin, and instead embraces the complexities of the role of migrants in transnational processes.

Methodological challenges of migrant transnationalism

methodological nationalism

One of the most interesting dimensions of studies on migrant transnationalism has been the debate on how the transnational optic challenges social science methodology. The core argument is that the focus on transnational dynamics implies a departure from migratory phenomena as a bounded national or local issue. As stated by Levitt (2007), it is necessary to 'trade in a national lens for a transnational one' to pick up on transnationalism (Levitt 2007: 21). One of the most-cited concepts is that of methodological nationalism (Beck 2002; Wimmer and Glick Schiller 2002). The concept refers to 'the assumption that the nation/state/society is the natural social and political form of the modern world' (Wimmer and Glick Schiller 2002: 302). As a result, our capacity to see and understand transnational processes has been impaired. The methodological nationalism argument points to important issues, but what is the alternative to repeating traditional research designs in the study of transnational migration?

The transnational perspective on migration was initially heralded as a breakaway from methodological nationalism. However, the nation-state continues to be dominant in comparative studies of migrant transnationalism, looking at different migrant groups in one receiving state, or the same migrant group in different receiving states. Moreover, migrant transnational studies have been criticised for looking through an 'ethnic lens' – focusing on a particular migrant group and presuming the maintenance of ethnic community boundaries over time. In so doing, researchers lose sight of the complex dynamics of interaction with the wider social environment (Glick Schiller and Caglar 2009).

unit and level of analysis

The question of units and levels of analysis continues to be discussed among scholars of transnational studies. They are faced with the challenge of researching activities and relations across several sites, actors and institutions. Among the suggestions is that studies of migrant transnationalism may benefit from a comparative scalar perspective, in which particular localities are analysed as embedded in wider horizontal and vertical (scalar) economic, political and social structures (Glick Schiller and Caglar 2009). Caglar (2005) analyses Kurdish migrants' local-to-local transnational networks and activities between Berlin and Southeast Turkey, in relation to the changing geographical organisation of state intervention (Caglar 2005). Another interesting contribution is Mazzucato's study of a multi-nodal network of Ghanaian migrants in the Netherlands. The nodes of the network are studied on-site over time to evaluate the experiences of migrants and non-migrant individuals and the households involved. In this way, studies of migrant transnationalism take the simultaneity in migrant transnational networks seriously and avoid reproducing dichotomies between 'here' and 'there'. This approach captures the two-way flow of resources in migrant transnational networks, through examples of how migrants support their families and how the families can be an important transnational resource for the migrants (Mazzucato 2010).

qualitative vs. quantitative

A final point regards qualitative vs. quantitative research designs. As mentioned, studies of migrant transnationalism have been dominated by qualitative studies with a low number of cases; often just one. Qualitative approaches seem immediately better geared to the study of migrant transnationalism if the goal is 'a thick and empirically rich mapping of how global, macro-level processes interact with local lived experiences' (Levitt and Jaworsky 2007: 143). For other scholars more quantitative studies are needed, because the field otherwise fails to establish the scope of migrant transnationalism and link it with the more quantitative methodology-oriented part of the social sciences.

Conclusion

The transnational perspective on migration has come to stay. However, instead of providing a fixed theoretical framework, it offers an ongoing discussion of the meaning, scope and impact of migrants' cross-border relations. These topics point to many important inroads for further empirical studies and theoretical considerations. Regarding the scope and durability of the transnational practices of migrants, studies are still needed on whether migrant transnationalism is largely a first-generation phenomenon; or, if not, on how transnational identification, networks and practices differ across generations of migrants. Another important theme relevant to the study of migrant political transnationalism is to move beyond the nation-state as both the level and unit of analysis. More systematic comparison is needed of the dynamics of migrant transnationalism at the local and the supranational level, in order to explore the interrelationships of the multi-level discursive and political structures for migrant transnational agency. A more nuanced understanding of the dynamics of exclusion and inclusion could be obtained with further research on the patterns of collaboration between migrants and other transnational actors, such as NGOs, social movements and religious institutions. On these themes, more critical studies are needed of the social, economic and political power hierarchies in which migrant transnationalism is embedded and which some migrant transnational practices seek to challenge (Glick Schiller 2005). A closer view of these would seem relevant to provide a clearer picture of why and how migrants go transnational and with what consequences.

Discussions on the scope, *raison d'etre*, novelty, ontology and methodology of the transnational perspective have benefited from several trends in migration studies. On the one hand, there are suggestions to anchor studies more firmly in both mono-disciplinary and interdisciplinary reflections on the challenges to key social science concepts posed by an unbounded understanding of state, nation and society (Faist 2004; Glick Schiller 2007). On the other hand, there are calls to include migrant transnationalism in wider studies of the various types of transnational actors, networks and processes (Levitt and Khagram 2007), while exploring the potential for cross-fertilisation. Comparing migrant transnationalism with other types of transnationalisms across actors, arenas and time may allow us to identify shared patterns and driving forces and to improve methodological tools. In any case, although the analytical implications of transnational migration continue to be debated, this dialogue provides a welcome perspective on the complexity of cross-border migration and migrant identities, networks and agency in the context of globalisation. *ongoing debate*

MAIN IDEAS

Migrants may repeatedly travel back and forth across state borders (their papers permitting) and form sustained transnational relations with their country of origin.

Migrants can be transnational through their networks and practices without physically crossing a state border.

Transnational migration is not new, yet modern communication technology, the Internet, affordable air travel and the globalisation of media enable migrants to stay in touch with their country of origin.

Policies and politics in both countries of origin and residence of migrants influence and are influenced by transnational migration and the linkages between migrants and home communities.

Transnational migration and the transnational linkages and practices of migrants may impact political, economic and socio-cultural hierarchies in both countries of origin and residence.

Transnational migration has provoked efforts to rethink concepts and research tools that can capture the scope and complexity of migrant cross-border practices.

Notes

1 For an interesting incorporation of the transnational perspective in a structuration model for understanding international migration, see Morawska (2000).

2 Given the extension and growth of this field of literature, it is not possible to do justice to the entire scholarship. This essay reflects my background in political science and anthropology and mainly concentrates on English-language, European and US-based publications, although it is important to emphasise the richness of scholarship undertaken elsewhere and published in other languages. In particular, the dimensions of refugees and forced migration have largely been left out, but for an interesting analysis of these dimensions, see Al-Ali et al. (2001). For a recent and very comprehensive overview of articles and books, see Levitt and Jaworsky (2007) and Vertovec (2009), among others. I am grateful to Paolo Boccagni, Mihaela Vancea, Irina Ciornei and the editors for useful comments and suggestions.

3 See www.transcomm.ox.ac.uk.

4 For a comprehensive summary of these debates see Vertovec (2004b).

5 http://www.migrationinformation.org/dataHub/remittances/All_profiles.pdf.

Recommended literature

Basch, L.G., N. Glick Schiller, et al. (1994), *Nations Unbound: Transnational Projects, Postcolonial Predicaments and Deterritorialized Nation-states.* Langhorne: Gordon and Breach.

Levitt, P. and B.N. Jaworsky (2007), 'Transnational migration studies: Past developments and future trends', *Annual Review of Sociology* 33: 129-156.

Portes, A., L.E. Guarnizo, et al. (eds) (1999), Special issue of *Ethnic and Racial Studies* 22 (2).

Portes A., S. Vertovec, P. Levitt and J. de Wind (2003), Special issue of *International Migration Review* 37 (3).

Vertovec, S. (2009), *Transnationalism: Key ideas.* London, Routledge.

Waldinger, R. and D. Fitzgerald (2004), 'Transnationalism in question', *American Journal of Sociology* 109: 1177-1195.

Wimmer, A. and N. Glick-Schiller (2002), 'Methodological nationalism and beyond: Nation-state building, migration and the social sciences', *Global Networks, A Journal of Transnational Relations* 2 (4): 301-334.

References

Al-Ali, N., R. Black, et al. (2001), 'Refugees and transnationalism: The experience of Bosnians and Eritreans in Europe', *Journal of Ethnic and Migration Studies* 27 (4): 615-634.

Anderson, B. (1992), 'The new world disorder', *New Left Review* 32 (193): 3-13.

Basch, L.G., N. Glick Schiller, et al. (1994), *Nations Unbound: Transnational Projects, Postcolonial Predicaments and Deterritorialized Nation-states.* Langhorne: Gordon and Breach.

Bauböck, R. (2007), 'Stakeholder citizenship and transnational political participation: A normative evaluation of external voting', *Fordham Law Review* 75 (5): 2393-2447.

Bauböck, R. (2003), 'Towards a political theory of migrant transnationalism', *International Migration Review* 37 (3): 700-723.

Beck, U. (2002), 'The cosmopolitan society and its enemies', *Theory, Culture and Society* 17 (1-2): 17-44.

Boccagni, P. (Forthcoming-a), 'Private, public or both? On the scope and impact of transnationalism in immigrants' everyday lives', in T. Faist and R. Bauböck (eds), *Diaspora and Transnationalism: Concepts, Theories and Methods*. Amsterdam: Amsterdam University Press.

Boccagni, P. (Forthcoming-b). '"Whom should we help first?" Transnational helping practices in Ecuadorian migration', *International Migration*.

Brand, L. (2002), 'States and Their Expatriates: Explaining the Development of Tunisian and Moroccan Emigration-Related Institutions', working paper no. 52. San Diego: The Center for Comparative Immigration Studies, University of California.

Brubaker, R. (2005), 'The "diaspora" diaspora', *Ethnic and Racial Studies* 28 (1): 1-19.

Caglar, A. (2005), 'Hometown associations, the rescaling of state spatiality and migrant grassroot transnationalism', *Global Networks, A Journal of Transnational Relations* 6 (1): 1-22.

Carling, J. (2008), 'The human dynamics of migrant transnationalism', *Ethnic and Racial Studies* 31 (8): 1452-1477.

Cohen, R. (1997), *Global Diasporas*. London, UCL Press.

De Haas, H. (2005), 'Migration, remittances and regional development: The case of the Todgha Oasis, Southern Morocco', paper presented at Ceres Summer School 2005. The Hague, Netherlands.

Dufoix, S. (2008), *Diasporas*. Berkeley: University of California Press.

Ehrenreich, B. and A.R. Hochschild (eds) (2003), *Global Women: Nannies, Maids, and Sex Workers in the New Economy*. New York: Metropolitan Books.

Faist, T. (2007), 'Introduction: The shifting boundaries of the political', in T. Faist and P. Kivisto (eds), *Dual Citizenship in Global Perspective: From Unitary to Multiple Citizenship*, 1-23. Basingstoke: Palgrave Macmillan.

Faist, T. (2004), 'Towards a political sociology of transnationalization. The state of the art in the migration research', *Archives Europeennes de Sociologie* 45 (3): 331-368.

Faist, T. (2000), *The Volume and Dynamics of International Migration and Transnational Social Spaces*. Oxford: Oxford University Press.

Fitzgerald, D. (2008), *A Nation of Emigrants: How Mexico Manages its Migration*. Berkeley: University of California Press.

Foner, N. (1997), 'What's new about transnationalism? New York immigrants today and at the turn of the century', *Diaspora* 6 (3): 355-375.

Gabaccia, D.R. (2000), *Italy's Many Diasporas*. London: UCL Press.

Gamlen, A. (2008), 'The emigration state and the modern geopolitical imagination', *Political Geography* 27: 840-856.

Gjerde, J. (2001), 'Transatlantic linkages: The interaction between the Norwegian American and Norwegian "nations" during the century of migration, 1825-1920', *Immigrants and Minorities* 20 (1): 19-35.

Glick Schiller, N. (2007), 'Beyond the nation-state and its units of analysis: Towards a new research agenda for migration studies', working paper. Bielefeld: COMCAD.

Glick Schiller, N. (2005), 'Transnational social fields and imperialism', *Anthropological Theory* 4 (4): 439-461.

Glick Schiller, N., L. Basch, et al. (1992), 'Towards a transnational perspective on migration', *Annals of the New York Academy of Sciences* 645: 1-24.

Glick Schiller, N. and A. Caglar (2009), 'Towards a comparative theory of locality in migration studies: Migrant incorporation and city scale', *Journal of Ethnic and Migration Studies* 35 (2): 177-202.

Glick Schiller, N. and G.E. Fouron (1999), 'Terrains of blood and nation: Haitian transnational social fields', *Ethnic and Racial Studies* 22 (2): 340-366.

Goldring, L. (2002), 'The Mexican state and transmigrant organizations: Negotiating the boundaries of membership and participation', *Latin American Research Review* 37 (3): 55-99.

Guarnizo, L.E. (2003), 'The economics of transnational living', *International Migration Review* 37 (3): 666-699.

Guarnizo, L.E. (1998), 'The rise of transnational social formations: Mexican and Dominican state responses to transnational migration', *Political Power and Social Theory* 12: 45-94.

Guarnizo, L.E., A. Portes, et al. (2003), 'Assimilation and Transnationalism: Determinants of Transnational Political Action among Contemporary Migrants', *American Journal of Sociology* 108 (6): 1211-1248.

Guarnizo, L.E. and M.P. Smith (1998), 'The locations of transnationalism', in M.P. Smith and L.E. Guarnizo, *Transnationalism from Below*, 3-34. New Brunswick: Transaction Publishers.

Held, D., A. McGrew, et al. (1999), *Global Transformations: Politics, Economics and Culture*. Stanford: Stanford University Press.

IDEA (Institute for Democracy and Electoral Assistance) (2006), *Voting from Abroad: The International IDEA Handbook*. Stockholm: International Institute for Democracy and Electoral Assistance.

Itzigsohn, J. (2000), 'Immigration and the Boundaries of Citizenship', *International Migration Review* 34 (4): 1126-1154.

Itzigsohn, J., C.D. Cabral, et al. (1999), 'Mapping Dominican transnationalism: Narrow and broad transnational practices', *International Migration Review* 34: 316-339.

Itzigsohn, J. and S. Giorguli-Saucedo (2005), 'Incorporation, transnationalism, and gender: Immigrant incorporation and transnational participation as gendered processes', *International Migration Review* 39 (4): 895-920.

Joppke, C. and E. Morawska (2003), 'Integrating immigrants in liberal nation-states', in C. Joppke and E. Morawska, *Toward Assimilation and Citizenship: Immigrants in Liberal Nation-States*, 1-36. Basingstoke: Palgrave MacMillan.

Josselin, D. and W. Wallace (2001), 'Non-state actors in world politics: The lessons', in D. Josselin and W. Wallace, *Non-State Actors in World Politics*, 251-260. Basingstoke: Palgrave MacMillan.

Kaldor, M., H. Anheier, et al. (2003), 'Global civil society in an era of regressive globalisation', in H. Anheier, M. Glasius and M. Kaldor, *Global Civil Society 2003*. Oxford: Oxford University Press.

Keck, M.E. and K. Sikkink (1998), *Activists beyond Borders: Advocacy Networks in International Politics*. Ithaca: Cornell University Press.

Keohane, R. and J. Nye (eds) (1971), *Transnational Relations and World Politics*. Cambridge: Harvard University Press.

Khagram, S. and S. Alvord (2006), 'The rise of civic transnationalism', in S. Batliwala and L.D. Brown, *Transnational Civil Society*, 65-81. Bloomfield: Kumarian Press.

Kleist, N. (2008), 'Mobilising "the diaspora": Somali transnational political engagement', *Journal of Ethnic and Migration Studies* 34 (2): 307-323.

Koopmans, R. and P. Statham (2003), 'How national citizenship shapes transnationalism: Migrant and minority claims-making in Germany, Great Britain and the Netherlands', in C. Joppke and E. Morawska (eds), *Toward Assimilation and Citizenship: Immigrants in Liberal Nation-states*, 195-238. Basingstoke: Palgrave MacMillan.

Lacroix, T. (2005), *Les Réseaux Marocains du Développement: Géographie du Transnational et Politiques du Territorial*. Paris: Presses de la Fondation Nationale des Sciences Politiques.

Lall, M. (2003), 'Mother India's forgotten children', in E. Østergaard-Nielsen (ed.), *International Migration and Sending Countries: Perceptions, Policies and Transnational Relations*, 121-139. Basingstoke: Palgrave MacMillan.

Levitt, P. (2007), *God Needs No Passport*. New York: The New Press.

Levitt, P. (2002), 'Keeping feet in both worlds: Transnational practices and immigrant incorporation', in C. Joppke and E. Morawska (eds), *Integrating Immigrants in Liberal Nation-states: From Postnational to Transnational*. London: Macmillan-Palgrave.

Levitt, P. (2001), 'Transnational migration: Taking stock and future directions', *Global Networks* 1 (3): 195-216.

Levitt, P. and R. de la Dehesa (2003), 'Transnational migration and the redefinition of the state: Variations and explanations', *Ethnic and Racial Studies* 26 (4): 587-611.

Levitt, P. and B.N. Jaworsky (2007), 'Transnational migration studies: Past developments and future trends', *Annual Review of Sociology* 33: 129-156.

Levitt, P. and S. Khagram (2007), *Constructing Transnational Studies: The Transnational Studies Reader*. New York: Routledge.

Lyons, T. and P. Mandaville (forthcoming), 'Think locally, act globally: Towards a transnational comparative politics', *International Political Sociology*.

Mahler, S.J. (2000) 'Constructing International Relations: The Role of Transnational Migrants and other Non-State Actors', *Identities* 7 (2): 197-232.

Mahler, S.J. (1998), 'Theoretical and empirical contributions toward a research agenda for transnationalism', in M.P. Smith and L.E. Guarnizo (eds), *Transnationalism from Below*, 64-100. New Brunswick: Transaction Publishers.

Martinello, M. and J.-M. Lafleur (2008), 'Towards a transatlantic dialogue in the study of immigrant political transnationalism', *Ethnic and Racial Studies* 31 (4): 645-663.

Martínez-Saldaña, J. (2003), 'Los Olvidados become heroes: The evolution of Mexico's policies towards citizens abroad', in E. Østergaard-Nielsen (ed.), *International Migration and Sending Countries*, 33-56. New York: Palgrave MacMillan.

Mazzucato, V. (2010), 'Operationalising transnational migrant networks through a simultaneous matched sample methodology', in R. Bauböck and T. Faist (eds), *Diaspora and Transnationalism: Concepts, Theories and Methods*, 134-148. Amsterdam: Amsterdam University Press.

Morales, L. and L. Jorba (2010), 'The transantional links and practices of migrants' organisations in Spain', in R. Bauböck and T. Faist (eds), *Diaspora and Transnationalism: Concepts, Theories and Methods*, 180-199. Amsterdam: Amsterdam University Press.

Morawska, E. (2000), 'Structuring migration: The case of Polish income-seeking travelers to the West', *Theory and Society* 30: 47-80.

Nyberg-Sørensen, N., N.V. Hear, et al. (2003), 'The migration-development nexus: evidence and policy options', *International Migration* 40 (5): 49-73.

Orjuela, C. (2007), 'War, peace and the Sri Lankan diaspora: Complications and implications for policy', in A. Swain (ed.), *Diasporas, Armed Conflicts and Peacebuilding in their Homelands*. Uppsala: Department of Peace and Conflict Studies, University of Uppsala.

Østergaard-Nielsen, E. (2011), 'Codevelopment and citizenship: The nexus between policies on local migrant incorporation and migrant transnational practices in Spain', *Ethnic and Racial Studies*, 34 (1): 20-39.

Østergaard-Nielsen, E. (2009a), 'The end of closet transnationalism? The role of homeland politics in the political incorporation of Turks and Kurds in Europe', in J. Mollenkopf and J. Hochschild (eds), *Immigrant Political Incorporation in the United States and Europe*. Ithaca: Cornell University Press.

Østergaard-Nielsen, E. (2009b), 'Mobilizing the Moroccans: Policies and perceptions of transnational civic engagement among Moroccan migrants in Catalonia', *Journal of Ethnic and Migration Studies* 35 (10): 1623-1641.

Østergaard-Nielsen, E. (2003a), 'International migration and sending countries: Key issues and themes', in E. Østergaard-Nielsen (ed.) *International Migration and Sending Countries: Perceptions, Policies and Transnational Relations.* Basingstoke: Palgrave MacMillan.

Østergaard-Nielsen, E. (ed.) (2003b), *International Migration and Sending Countries: Perceptions, Policies and Transnational Relations.* Basingstoke: Palgrave MacMillan.

Østergaard-Nielsen, E. (2003c), 'The politics of migrants' transnational practices', *International Migration Review* 37 (3): 665-690.

Østergaard-Nielsen, E. (2001), 'Transnational political practices and the receiving state: Turks and Kurds in Germany and the Netherlands', *Global Networks: A Journal of Transnational Affairs* 1 (3): 261-282.

Pedone, C. (2006), 'Los cambios familiares y educativos en los actuales contextos migratoris ecuatorianos: Una perspectiva transatlántica', *Athenea Digital* 10: 154-171.

Pedraza, S. (2002), 'Democratization and migration: Cuba's exodus and the development of civil society – hindrance or help?', *Cuba in Transition* 12: 247-261.

Pieke, F.N., P. Nyíri, et al. (2004), *Transnational Chinese: Fujianese Migrants in Europe.* Stanford: Stanford University Press.

Portes, A. (2001), 'Introduction: The debates and significance of immigrant transnationalism', *Global Networks* 1 (3): 181-193.

Portes, A. (1999), 'Conclusion: Towards a new world – the origins and effects of transnational activities', *Ethnic and Racial Studies* 22 (2): 463-77.

Portes, A., L.E. Guarnizo, et al. (2002), 'Transnational entrepreneurs: An alternative form of immigrant economic adaptation', *American Sociological Review* 67: 278-298.

Portes, A., L.E. Guarnizo, et al. (1999), 'The study of transnationalism: Pitfalls and promises of an emergent research field', *Ethnic and Racial Studies* 22 (2): 217-237.

Portes, A. and C. Escobar, et al. (2007), 'Immigrant transnational organizations and development: A comparative study', *International Migration Review,* 41 (1): 242-281

Pries, L. (ed.) (2001), *New transnational spaces.* London: Routledge.

Risse-Kappen, T. (1995), *Bringing transnational relations back in.* Cambridge: Cambridge University Press.

Safran, W. (1991), 'Diasporas in modern societies: Myths of homeland and return', *Diaspora* 1 (1): 83-99.

Salih, R. (2003), *Gender in Transnationalism: Home, Longing and Belonging Among Moroccan Migrant Women.* London/New York: Routledge.

Sheffer, G. (ed.) (1986), *Modern Diasporas in International Politics.* Kent: Croom Helm.

Smith, M.P. (2003), 'Transnationalism, the state, and the extraterritorial citizen', *Politics and Society* 31 (4): 467-502.

Smith, R.C. (2008), 'Contradicitons of diasporic institutionalization in Mexican politics: The 2006 migrant vote and other forms of inclusion and control', *Ethnic and Racial Studies* 31 (4): 708-741.

Smith, R.C. (2006), *Mexican New York: Transnational Lives of New Immigrants.* Berkeley: University of California Press.

Smith, R.C. (1997), 'Reflections on migration, the state and the construction, durability and newness of transnational life', *Soziale Welt.* Sonderband 12.

Snel, E., G. Engberson, et al. (2006), 'Transnational involvement and social integration', *Global Networks* 6 (3): 285-308.

Sørensen, N.N. (2007), *Living Across Worlds.* Geneva: International Migration Organization.

Sørensen, N.N. and L.E. Guarnizo (2007), 'Transnational family life across the Atlantic: The experience of Colombian and Dominican Migrants in Europe', in N.N. Sørensen (ed.), *Living Across Worlds: Diaspora, Development and Transnational Engagement*, 151-176. Geneva: International Organization for Migration.

Turner, S. (2008), 'The waxing and waning of the political field in Burundi and its diaspora', *Ethnic and Racial Studies* 31 (4): 742-765.

Van Hear, N. (1998), *New Diasporas: The Mass Exodus, Dispersal and Regrouping of Migrant Communities*. London: UCL Press.

Vertovec, S. (2009), *Transnationalism: Key ideas*. London: Routledge.

Vertovec, S. (2004a), 'Cheap calls: The social glue of migrant transnationalism', *Global Networks* 4 (2): 219-224.

Vertovec, S. (2004b), 'Migrant transnationalism and modes of transformation', *International Migration Review* 38 (3): 970-1001.

Vilhena, D.V. d. (2006), *Vinculación de los Emigrados Latinoamericanos y Caribeños con su País de Origen: Transnationalism y Políticas Públicas*. Población y Desarrollo. Santiago de Chile: CEPAL.

Waldinger, R. (2008), 'Between "here" and "there": Immigrant cross-border activities and loyalties', *International Migration Review* 42 (1): 3-29.

Waldinger, R. and D. Fitzgerald (2004), 'Transnationalism in question', *American Journal of Sociology* 109: 1177-1195.

Waldinger, R., E. Popkin, et al. (2007), 'Conflict and contestation in the cross-border community: Hometown associations reassessed', *Ethnic and Racial Studies* 31: 843-870.

Wimmer, A. and N. Glick Schiller (2002), 'Methodological nationalism and beyond: Nation-state building, migration and the social sciences', *Global Networks, A Journal of Transnational Relations* 2 (4): 301-334.

6 *Jus Sanguinis* and *Jus Soli*: Aspects of Ethnic Migration and Immigration Policies in EU States

Eftihia Voutira

Theoretical framework

This chapter presents, analyses and re-conceptualises two state-based principles traditionally identified in international law as the determinants of nationality rights. The first is *jus sanguinis,* meaning 'right of blood' or kinship, whereby nationality is transmitted by birth via the matrilineal or patrilineal side or both. The second is *jus soli,* or 'right of soil', which associates the right to citizenship with birth within the territory of a given state. Both concepts have Latin ancestry; they denote the manner by which citizenship is allocated within a state. A third variant of acquiring citizenship is *jus domicili,* or 'right of residence'. Unlike the other two principles of acquiring citizenship at birth, the right of residence 'binds the acquisition of citizenship to permanent residents on a state territory, usually by way of naturalization. *Jus domicili,* as well as naturalization by way of marriage, amends pure *jus sanguinis*' (Ohliger 2005: 344).

citizenship allocation principles

These citizenship allocation principles are not directly related to migration as a social phenomenon. They are *mediated* by distinct state practices and philosophies of immigration as they evolve over time and in differing historical circumstances. Citizenship based on *jus sanguinis* specifies that a body of citizens will be a community of descent. Thus, it denies the children of immigrants born in their parents' country of immigration the right to automatically acquire citizenship of their country of birth. This was the case for second-generation Turks born in Germany before the 1999 Constitutional Reforms on Nationality (e.g. Bade 1997: 1-39; Morris 2000). At the core of such state practices is the concept of membership and belonging that defines the state's own identity. To borrow Michael Walzer's famous phrase within normative political theory, 'the primary good we distribute to each other is membership [...] men and women without membership anywhere are stateless persons' (1983: 31).

It can be argued that these two principles constitute the basic norm of membership as regulated by societies, and in this respect they relate to the regulation of migration issues from the standpoint of *emigration* (who leaves or is allowed to go) and *immigration* (who enters and is allowed to do so). Implicit in the idea of 'membership' is the concept of 'community', which suggests a bounded world within which the distribution and redistribution of membership takes place among individuals sharing mutual rights and responsibilities; a society organised according to the principles of justice as 'fair' distribution, as described by the political philosopher John Rawls (2001).[1]

political membership

The association of political membership with migration as a situation in which some people are seen as having less than equal membership is lucidly discussed in Sheila Benhabib's *Rights of Others* (2004: 4). That volume opens with the following definition: '[by] political membership, I mean the principles and practices for incorporating aliens and strangers, immigrants and newcomers, refugees and asylum seekers, into existing polities'. This crucially important topic receives excellent treatment in Benhabib's book and in other recent works. Yet, as an analytical issue, to frame the question of political membership in this way is to omit an important element. It is not enough to focus only on the situation of those who do not belong, leaving untouched the basis for entitlement of those who 'naturally' belong. For those on the 'inside', the question is to what extent is membership acquired and maintained in the absence of migration? Furthermore, how is membership distributed evenly within the state and between its stakeholders? On what basis is the coveted entitlement to citizenship conferred upon some, while being denied to others? Who benefits and who loses when birthright principles are entrenched in citizenship laws?

These fundamental questions are addressed by political philosophy and constitutional law, but they have come under scrutiny on epistemological grounds as well. After all, many contemporary debates in the context of migration raise issues of the relation and subordination of human rights law to multilevel political membership (e.g. Miller 2008; Marchetti 2008; Joppke 2006).

This chapter starts by looking at the evolution and historical background of these two entrenched principles as the bases for belonging in a nation-state. Three philosophical models of membership and state incorporation are then considered: liberal, communitarian and the ethnic or national. The core of empirical data is provided by historical diasporas from Eastern Europe returning to the West. Problems faced by newcomers in reintegration and adaptation to their putative historical homelands involve issues similar to those faced by foreign migrants. The main difference is that their political integration affords them privileged status vis-à-vis the acquisition of state membership, and in this they have a preferred standing in comparison with other migrants.

The evolution and historical background of the two principles in international context

Full membership in a state and its associated rights and duties are exemplified by the institution of 'citizenship'. The basic modes by which individuals acquire citizenship are by birth, by naturalisation and by marriage, as articulated in the three principles outlined above. Generationally viewed over time, the acquisition of citizenship by second-generation immigrants is the result of the particular legal norm a country follows. In *jus soli* countries, an immigrant's child is automatically a citizen, though the parents may lack this entitlement. In *jus sanguinis* countries, the child inherits the nationality of the parents, independent of place of birth. Within comparative traditions of international law, citizenship regimes associated with *jus soli* are seen as being more inclusive towards newcomers, while regimes based on *jus sanguinis* are seen as more exclusive, given the priority placed on the ethnic character of nationality transmission (Ohlinger 2005: 344-5; Bertocchi and Strozzi 2005).

citizenship

Historians and commentators agree that the particular system of values defining the relations between Homeric communities and their members was a product of the grim and unstable conditions in which they existed. In James Redfield's (1975: 99) eloquent summary:

Homeric communities

> Whatever details of Minoan or Mycenean culture may persist in the poems, the Homeric picture of society generally belongs to the dark age and the early age of recovery. Homer shows us people living in small groups, dependent on one another for their mutual security against a hostile world. When the background condition of life is a condition of war, men must place great trust in those close to them. Thus combat generates a tight-knit community. A Homeric community consists in effect of those who are ready to die for one another; the perimeter of each community is a potential battlefield.

Under these precarious conditions of survival, the extension of the communal boundaries to include the stranger as a friend rather than a foe can also be seen as a buffer against uncertainty, and as a powerful mechanism of networks functioning as safety nets against future security risks. The norms of hospitality, which are based on reciprocity and the obligation to return the favour, may be seen as a mechanism for encouraging migrants and travellers to move along putative 'friendship' lines in a system of norms that imposes the social obligation to receive and accept the stranger as a guest. Unlike the modern existentialist hero represented in Camus' *The Stranger* (*L'etranger*), who dreams of a life free from social attachments, in the Homeric world, life outside the community is seen as equivalent to death. Homer calls a man without a community 'a wanderer, a man of misfortune' (Iliad II 667).

city-states

The main historical development that accounts for the transformation of this system of values in antiquity is the establishment of the Greek city-states in the sixth century BC, which allowed for the redefinition of what constituted a Homeric community in political and institutional terms. As discussed in Fustel de Coulanges' seminal work *Ancient City* (1864), this particular type of socio-political formation entailed a radically different and unique form of consciousness that emerged in that context; a civic one. The blurred boundaries of communities, which were considered as potential battlefields in the Homeric world, now become explicitly defined in terms of the laws of the city-states. As legitimised in the new constitutions of Athens and Sparta, the main criterion of membership and belonging is that of citizenship, understood as the closest form of association between the individual and the state. This association is defined in terms of active participation in and contribution to public life. In Aristotle's celebrated definition, 'a citizen is the one who shares in administration of justice and the holding of office' (Aristotle, *Politics*, Book 3, ch.1). Though inclusion in the social, economic and cultural life of the city-state is possible, those who come and go or those who resettle within the ancient city – including Aristotle himself – are excluded from sharing in the administration of justice. The salient distinction within the city-state becomes that of the citizen as opposed to the non-citizen; a birthright that defines those who can, and therefore ought to, participate in public affairs and those who cannot, such as women, foreigners and slaves.

exclusive citizenship

There is little doubt that from its inception, citizenship was an exclusionary category, implying a coercive rule of favouring members over strangers, and one that possibly remains, 'the most common form of tyranny in human history' (Walzer 1989). The rationale for the ancient exclusive principle of citizenship was based on another implicit societal norm, which assumed a rigid separation between private and public spheres. Participation in the public sphere involves taking part in the making of its laws in terms of who rules and who is being ruled, and this is open only to free, adult males, born in the territory of the Athenian state. The latter category presupposes the basic societal distinction between natives, free men and slaves. At the same time, as a result of the Persian Wars, another distinction was introduced to increase the cultural distance of the 'other' as a foreigner, that between a Greek and a barbarian. In Herodotus' words, being Greek meant 'being of the same stock, sharing a common language with common shrines of the Gods and rituals, with similar customs and the whole way of life we understand and share together' (*Histories* VIII 144). The two distinctions (citizens/slaves and Greeks/barbarians) reinforced each other until, as a result of many intra-Greek wars, Greeks ended up being slaves to other Greeks – thus one distinction undercutting the other.

birthright

For the most part, in Roman times citizenship and membership continued to be defined in exclusive terms as a birthright that conferred access to political participation and public life, but under the codification of Roman law it became progressively redefined in juridical terms. In the work of the Roman jurist Gaius, 'citizenship' under Roman law became a legal term defining the rights and immunities available to the subjects of a complex multi-ethnic empire, made up of culturally diverse communities across vast territories governed by the same judicial system. The status of citizenship became progressively dissociated from its sole earlier identification with access to 'political' life, in the sense of having the right to rule and be ruled in an Aristotelian polis. Being a 'citizen' evolved to denote a privileged legal status based on a system of jurisprudence that defined the rights and responsibilities of all members of a community who shared laws, which is not necessarily identical to a territorial community. A Roman citizen by birth, like St. Paul, who had never seen Rome and lived under the jurisdiction of the local governor in his native region of Tarsus, was privileged over other subjects in the empire in that he enjoyed imperial protection, together with the local and municipal privileges of his territorial community. Access to imperial protection in this famous case entailed the right to appeal to Caesar directly, which meant having access to a legal procedure that granted him privileges and immunities not available to those who were only municipal subjects of the empire (Pocock 1995: 36-39). Thus, the differentiation between a Roman citizen and a Roman subject was largely a legal one, determining the relative status of membership within the state. 'Otherness' was then defined in terms of what falls outside Roman law and imperial jurisdiction. During the *pax romana*, the barbarians were those who existed outside the borders of the empire; 'civilisation' was perceived in terms of the boundaries of political sovereignty and the empire's image of itself.

world religions

The emergence of world religions, such as Judaism, Christianity, Buddhism and Islam, introduced other non-secular criteria for membership and belonging, which legitimised the inclusion and assistance of strangers on religious grounds. Often, these co-existed in parallel with customary or tribal practices. For example, in Southeast Asia, 'outsiders' were regularly integrated into the local community through rituals of feeding, helping and entertaining one's neighbours in a 'disinterested' fashion, as in the Buddhist tradition of the Sherpas in Nepal (Ortner 1978). Norms of hospitality in southern African societies allowed western survivors of shipwrecks to be welcomed into local communities, even as chiefs or benefactors of these societies (Wilson 1979: 54-8; Shack and Skinner 1979: 8-14). Similarly, among Afghan refugees, tribal codes of honour in the Koranic tradition ensured temporary shelter among kin, or the obligation of asylum to the *mojajer* – the refugee – as practised by Islamic cultures (Centlivres and Centlivres-Dumont 1988; El Madmad 1993).

Seen from the unilinear standpoint of Western political traditions, the evolution from Roman concepts of statehood to feudal ones included the recognition of both descent and territorial elements, since serfs lived in an inherited state of dependency on the land-owning lords and/or clergy. In continental Europe, the introduction of *jus sanguinis* during the enlightenment became identified with the progressive dissolution of the feudal order and the emergence of the modern state.

comparative view

A longitudinal and comparative view of these two principles shows that the *jus sanguinis* principle, which was being used in continental Europe, was exported to Japan in the nineteenth century, while the British *jus soli* tradition was adopted by its colonies, including the US and Canada, where it was encoded into their constitutions.[2] Another distinction that helps to classify the presence of these principles is the concept of 'emigration' and 'immigration' countries: traditional countries of immigration, such as the US, Canada and Australia, opt for *jus soli*, while countries of emigration rely on *jus sanguinis* to maintain links with their diasporas abroad (Weil 2001: 17-35). It is difficult to generalise in terms of ideal types of citizenship norms without reference to the particular socio-historical conditions of individual countries. For example, France, the modern nation-state par excellence, created its own variant of *jus soli* for the large numbers of people born on French soil, regardless of their ancestry, with the expectation that they would become incorporated into the French social fabric, mainly through the national educational system (Schnapper 1991).

After the fall of the Berlin Wall and the establishment of new post-Soviet states, a *convergence* of the two types of citizenship laws has become the norm in most of these new states, which have sought ways to manage the multiple types of new members in their territories (Flynn 2004; Humphrey 2002: 21-39).

Three philosophies of immigration

liberal model

Seen from the perspective of political theory, one can identify three distinct philosophical models of membership and state incorporation: the liberal, the communitarian and the ethnic (Parekh 1994). According to the liberal state model, the state exists in order to provide the conditions whereby autonomous and self-determining members can freely pursue their chosen activities. The role of the state is perceived as a civil association, voluntary in its nature, and held together by a common agreement/consensus on how its collective affairs are to be conducted. The decisions made by the state are binding for all its members. Membership in a liberal state involves acknowledgment of the established authority structure, assumes obedience to its laws and encourages participation in the spirit of civility and 'liberal conversation'. These are the basic criteria of membership, and as such they are necessary to secure the basic conditions of civil life for each individual; these criteria are also seen as sufficient, since any more requirements would compromise individual moral autonomy. Theoretically, no other criteria, such as religion, race, ethnicity, political beliefs or even acceptability to/by the rest of the citizens, should enter into consideration. However, this minimal definition of the liberal view has in some instances been interpreted differently. Over the last twenty years, a large body of liberal political theory has tried to identify additional conditions that would prove, for example, the inability of migrants to respect the laws of their adopted lands. Due to the post-September 11th anti-terrorism campaign and the victimisation of 'Muslim fundamentalism', a number of issues have been raised, in both the UK and the US, by liberal democratic theorists (e.g. A. Dummett 1986; M. Dummett 2001; Rawls 2001). The issue concerns what constitutes 'grounds for exclusion', given that liberal democracy is the paradigmatic model of 'inclusion' by virtue of its appeal as a government of the people, by the people and for the people. The debate centres around the paradoxes of democracy and the degree to which people's sovereignty includes sub-groups and minorities who see themselves as oppressed not despite, but *because of*, majority rule, which maintains sub-groups in a marginal position (Taylor 1998).

communitarian model

The communitarian model considers the state as a group of people united by shared understanding, vision, interests, values, loyalties and a collective pride. As Walzer has put it, in the communitarian model people share 'some special commitment and some special sense of common life'. Qualifying the last concept, Alistair McIntyre uses the concept of 'collective traditions' (McIntyre 1998; see Taylor 1994). One of the important components in this conception involves the illusive idea of a *common past*, collective memories, shared ceremonies and rituals. The term 'communitarian' is borrowed by the underlined emphasis on a single community that recognises itself and is seen by others as being different. As Parekh (1994: 95) puts it:

> In the communitarian model, people have a strong sense of collective 'we', such that 'we' is not a plural of 'I', but rather that 'I' is a singular of 'we'. It is a political expression and articulation of the collective identity of the community and neither is nor ever can be like a club or a voluntary association.

Walzer's variant argument in favour of the communitarian approach is that 'admission and exclusion are at the core of the communal independence' (Walzer 1997). Thus, outsiders cannot be admitted indiscriminately. The question of membership is of the essence, but the criteria remain elusive. Seen from the perspective of immigration policy, this model would give preference to those who are already their 'kith and kin'. This state model, theoretically at least, signals a predilection for returning diasporas on the basis of family unification.

As one vocal proponent argues, 'liberalism' and 'communitarianism' are in many ways complementary:

> Where liberalism emphasizes rights, communitarianism stresses relations. Where liberal theorists appeal to universal and impersonal principles, communitarians have argued for the importance for particular rights and particular groups and individuals. Where liberal theorists have characteristically held that it is for each individual to arrive at their own good, communitarians have been anxious to stress the existence of the irreducibility of social goods and to argue that a failure to achieve such goods will result in a defective social order [...] communitarianism is a diagnosis of certain weaknesses of liberalism, not a rejection of it (McIntyre 1998: 244).

ethnic model

The third model of the state is the nationalist/ethnic one, which identifies membership in terms of kinship ties; a view that is often advocated by the New Right. Unlike the communitarian view, the ethnic view traces kinship ties and defines national belonging in terms of those who have access as kin to the state. It creates a set of obligations vis-à-vis members of a family or group, not in terms of racial characteristics, but often those of religion and/or ethnicity. In states that allow the acquisition of citizenship through a 'right to return' as an entitlement to citizenship on the basis of ancestry, there is an implicit link between the existing members of the polity and the larger diaspora community outside the state. The best-known example is that of

Israeli citizenship that is allocated on the basis of religious grounds to those who can prove affinity to the group. For instance, in the amended 1970 definition of the 'law of return', which establishes entitlement to Israeli citizenship, this right may be conferred upon 'a person who was born of a Jewish mother or has converted to Judaism and is not a member of another religion'. This expansive definition allowed for the resettlement to Israel of almost one million immigrants from the former Soviet Union in the 1990s. These immigrants had full and immediate access to Israeli citizenship according to the law of return. Approximately 40 per cent of those who arrived at later stages were non-Jews. The right to return to Israel and establish citizenship there is based on the definition of family membership – to the third generation – as encoded in Section 4A of the law of return (Shachar 1999). Such ethnocultural constructions of membership have also been relevant in the definition of citizenship in post-communist East-central European countries, for example, Hungary, Croatia, Belarus and Lithuania, which have all included similar ethnic membership provisions in their citizenship laws.

Types of states and types of immigration policies

The preceding discussion of the three models of state – liberal, communitarian and national – would suggest that there is an appropriate immigration theory that goes with each, which would be the case if immigration were a normative theory. However, immigration is a policy, and as such it involves an understanding of its practices over time, and a conceptualisation of those practices according to the principles of what Foucault has called 'governmentality'; this includes practices that develop in opposition to and despite the stated aims of a political authority (Wright and Shore 1997: 3-12).

communitarianism

'Communitarianism', at least as articulated in theory by Michael Walzer, suggests a dual view of migration: on the one hand, it is ultimately the citizen's right to emigrate; on the other hand, the implications of brain drain and selling one's scarce skills abroad for better remuneration may be viewed as an act of communal disloyalty, which, while it does not entail any kind of direct barrier to emigration, does imply a sense of personal shame. With regard to immigration, Walzer considers the availability of space as one determinant in deciding national immigration policy. The problem, nevertheless, remains and is articulated as one of asymmetry. As Agnes Heller (1993) more succinctly put it, 'migration involves a system of household rules. A guest is free to go whenever they please, but the household should consider how they will stay.' Heller's metaphorical allusion to the state as a family shows the difficulty of demarcating the difference between the 'communitarian' and the 'ethnic/national' view of the state. One of the theoretical difficulties identified by the critics of 'communitarianism' is that the focus on cultural/ethnic citizenship would entail a less egalitarian society, which 'communitarianism' could lead to, since non-ethnic citizens would effectively be reduced to second-class status and denied an equal right to share in the collective life of the community.

The same criticism is valid for the ethnic national view of the state. It is possible to imagine that such liberal models of immigration that are predicated on a common value system, as suggested by communitarianism, were at play during the Cold War period, when the division between the 'free world' and the rest of the population was clearly demarcated along ideological lines. Such a possibility is not tenable any more. Therefore, it is no accident that a series of liberal and libertarian political theories have turned to 'liberalism' in order to defend a more elaborate model of what is called 'migratory cosmopolitanism' (i.e. an open-door policy that allows for different 'bundles of rights' to be extended to non-citizens or denizens). The object of this liberal migration model has been identified as 'a type of universal right to free passage that takes into account the circumstances of migratory justice' (Marchetti 2008: 487). Although this recent formulation sounds promising, the plan for a worldwide regulatory system for migration and its admission criteria, developed under a universal membership regime that would grant civil, social and political rights to all migrants, does not appear to be feasible. Nevertheless, the positive elements brought about by this and other such proposals (Sassen 1999; Miller 2008) must be stressed, given their focus on immigration policy as a means of enriching cultural diversity in a country. Similarly, the humanitarian admission of asylum seekers and refugees is well defended in this model as an integral part of the moral culture of the receiving country.

East-West migration as *jus sanguinis* migration: The return of historic diasporas from Eastern Europe

dissolution of the Soviet Union

After the fall of the Berlin Wall and the dissolution of the former Soviet Union (FSU), one of the biggest emigration flows came from members of 'foreign nationalities', who according to Soviet nationality criteria could claim the right to emigrate to their historical homelands (De Tinguy 2003: 112-127; Voutira 2004). One of the paradoxes that emerged after the dissolution of the Soviet Union concerns both the migration of *people over borders* and the migration of *borders over people.* More to the point, questions of nationality and membership in the new post-Soviet states had to be rethought and reconfigured on the basis of new priorities. The Western European states receiving migrants included Germany, Poland, Finland, Greece and Bulgaria.

The case of the privileged return migrants

One of the basic paradoxes that emerged as a result of the dissolution of the former Soviet order was the transformation of the so-called 'foreign nationalities' (e.g. Germans, Finns, Poles, Turks, Bulgarians and Greeks). Those with foreign nationality status, according to Soviet nationality criteria (Martin 2001), were transformed from the least privileged – given their likelihood for exile and internal displacement throughout the Soviet era – to most privileged, after the dissolution of the FSU, given the recognition of their right to return to their European historical homelands. An anthropological approach to the study of this type of *jus sanguinis* would entail the mapping and documentation of their lives during and after their emigration from the Soviet Union (e.g. Markowitz 1995: 129-130; Kaurinkoski 2003; Voutira 2006). Focusing primarily on micro-level analysis and documentation of household adaptation strategies upon arrival in their new/historical homelands, anthropological research has documented specific patterns of cultural adaptation. Over the past 30 years, the anthropological approaches to the study of migration have evolved, starting from more traditional community-based approaches to post-structuralist accounts that have adopted a transnational perspective where migrants are no longer uprooted but move freely back and forth across international borders and between cultures and social systems. Most of these approaches assume the theoretical perspective articulated by the Appadurai (1996) model of understanding 'modernity at large'.

privileged migrants

Turning the anthropological lens, that is, ethnographic field research, on the new privileged migrants has produced a series of studies that compare newcomers and hosts from the standpoint of the relative privilege of nationality status (Kleinknecht-Strähle 1998; Voutira 2003; Mandel 2006). One such study in Germany involves comparing German repatriates from the FSU (*Aussiedler*) with Turkish migrants in Germany (*Ausslåndler*) and the local German population. The collective perception is that the newcomers from the Soviet Union remain more privileged, both with respect to state benefits in comparison to the locals, and in relation to the Turkish migrant population that still lacks basic political rights despite their long presence in the country (see Mandell 2006). An interesting issue remains the comparison between the *emic* (i.e. their own notion of adaptation) and the *etic* (i.e. from the analyst's/official point of view) when it comes to describing their incorporation as a process of moving from being an 'outsider' to being an 'insider'. Because anthropologists generally place transnational processes within the lives of individuals and their families (Brettell 2000: 106), the social networks described tend to be focused on family- and friendship-orientated social networks:

> Network/mediated chain migration does not necessarily mean that prospective migrants or migrant families are given only one or a few options as to where they go. Migrants [...] seek work first one place, then another, where they have kin and friends. In retrospect, this can appear as a step migration pattern to an ultimate destination to which a migrant recurrently returns or where he/she finally settles in with or without the family (Brettell 2000: 117).

language barriers

The socio-cultural management of the contemporary repatriation from the FSU concerns the fact that repatriates arrive with the prospect of full political, social and cultural rights, yet their incorporation remains uncertain, given that they are still *visible* in terms of their values and behaviour. There are also language barriers. This lack of communication between newcomers and their hosts is not merely a linguistic one in the literal sense – it is mediated by their mutual perceptions and is related to the level of expectations entertained both by the newcomers and by the society into which they are received.

efficiency

Although the efficiency levels by which the diverse organisations that have been set up to assist in the integration process of the different co-ethnic newcomers from the FSU to their historical European homelands differ according to the receiving state's policies, they all operate within a general compensatory framework. For example, while services in Greece do not have the efficiency or organisational structure of the Ministry of Immigrant Absorption in Israel, which has a long history of integrating its diaspora members, nor the social services departments like those in the Federal Republic of Germany for dealing with their *Aussiedler*, still their philosophy of integration is that of receiving members of the 'nation' (Shepherd 1993; Markowitz 1995). A common feature in such voluntary ethnic migration/repatriation situations is the declassing and deskilling experience that accompanies the process of immigration and resettlement. In this respect, the co-ethnic newcomers, unlike other immigrants, receive special state-funded assistance (De Tinguy 2003).

Shepherd (1993) qualifies the immigration picture, commenting from the inside on Israel's long history of immigration and distinguishing the particular ways that Soviet Jews have arrived in Israel in the decades since the 1960s:

> The main difference between the Russians who came in the seventies and those arriving now, is the quality of their 'human material' (a nasty but familiar expression which jarred with the concern expressed for the immigrants). There is no ideological motive behind the current immigration. They came for social and economic reasons. In the seventies, immigrants could cope with cultural shock better because they were motivated. They thought they were coming to a desert, that they were prepared for material difficulties. The new immigrants see the new prosperity, and want their share immediately. Israel in the 1990's is very highly developed technologically and that is where the Russians skill could be much better used. Instead the politicians either leave them to the National Insurance Institute, or talk about 'relief works' as if we were still in the sixties and could send people out to plant bushes and sweep streets. What we are seeing now, is a glorified state of state charity, a corruption of the welfare state. On the one hand the state cannot direct the immigrants to work which fits their skills, and on the other, it provides hand-outs. The immigration chiefs are still thinking in terms of the mass immigration of the 1960's which brought very new skills with them, artisans and labourers (Shepherd 1993: 33-34).

differentiation between waves

This general differentiation between the different waves of immigrants and the patterns of their entry and reception is also a standard theme in the criticism that is launched both by state and non-governmental organisational agencies in Greece vis-à-vis the post-1989 ex-Soviet Greek immigrants. This first wave of ex-Soviet immigrants to Greece commonly say, 'Those who come now, are not real Greeks suffering under the Soviet regime; they are capitalists. They only come to Greece to trade and make a better living' (Voutira 1994: 539). The argument in support of such statements is the additional proviso that the majority of people arriving come on 'tourist visas' then seek to extend their stay indefinitely, thus often having to live and work illegally.[3]

A second paradox has to do with the analysis of the East-West migration phenomenon, which includes the movement of borders *across* people, not just the movement of people *through* borders. Borders are social constructs whose objective is the regulation, both multi-directional (of capital, goods and people) and bi-directional (of arrivals and departures), of the permeability that connects a system with the exterior. Migratory policies are a part of this configuration of borders that define the territorial boundaries of states (e.g. Malkki 1997; Borneman 1997). When dealing with migration, national boundaries appear as part of a series of intermediate obstacles to the mobility of people between places of origin and places of destination.[4]

classification

Similarly, the Greek state employs a classification based on country of origin. This is evident in the study undertaken by the General Secretariat of Repatriated Greeks of the Ministry of Macedonia-Thrace entitled 'The identity of co-ethnic repatriates from the former USSR' (2000). This collective work uses the criterion of country of origin as the main axis for classifying repatriates. In terms of demographic representation, the breakdown of repatriates is 52 per cent from Georgia, 20 per cent from Kazakhstan, 15 per cent from Russia, 6 per cent from Armenia, 3 per cent from Ukraine and 2 per cent from the rest of the countries of the former USSR.[5]

The case of returning ethnic Germans

ethnic Germans

The German term 'Aussiedler' literally means 'outsettlers' or 'emigrants', and refers to ethnic Germans from Eastern and South-Eastern Europe, who migrated to the Federal Republic of Germany (FRG) between 1950 and 1992. From the standpoint of the receiving state, their status is similar to those of the ethnic Germans expelled in the immediate post-war years ('Vertriebene') and Germans who came from the German Democratic Republic (GDR) during the Cold War. The reception policies that applied to these ethnic Germans included: access to FRG territory, citizenship and specific privileges, such as access to welfare, the pension system, housing benefits, language courses and compensation for property left behind (Bade 1997; Wolff 2001). In the late 1980s, their privileged status became restricted and was supplanted by the new *Spätaussiedler* (late out-settler, late emigrant). Until German reunification, the FRG pursued the policy of actively encouraging *Aussiedler* immigration through policies such as per capita payments for *Aussiedler* from Romania and an exchange of financial loans to Poland. This preferential treatment was due to an implicit West German policy of recruitment in opposition to the GDR aiming to show that the FRG was the sole legitimate state for the German people (Kleinknecht-Strähehle 1998). At approximately 38,000 per year, the migration flow was manageable until the late 1980s (Green 2000: 122; 2004). The fall of the Berlin Wall, the challenges of reunification and the exodus of Soviet Germans to Germany increased that number to almost 400,000 per year in the 1990s. While previous migration movements involved ethnic Germans with good German language skills, the post-1990s *Aussiedler* had poor German language competence and their integration proved problematic. The introduction of the new *Spätaussiedler* status involved the progressive diminution of privileges with a view to making immigration less attractive to potential *Aussiedler*. It not only reduced migrant benefits, it also instituted an application procedure in the country of origin that required German language proficiency as a condition for immigration. The 1992 Act on the Consequences of the War replaced the *Aussiedler* with *Spätaussiedler* status and imposed an annual quota for *Spätaussiedler* immigration (220,000 per year in 1993 and 100,000 per year from 2000-2010). The logic of this new amendment was based on the recognition that there is no longer a need to emigrate from the FSU. Similarly, in order to enter Germany after 1992, Germans in other East European countries had to provide proof of discrimination on ethnic grounds by state authorities. Given the backlog of undecided cases and the possibility of family reunification, it was assumed that *Aussiedler* migration would continue until 2010 (Bade and Oltmer 1999: 29-31). The underlying rationale of the ethnic German immigration policy, known as the '*Aussiedler* policy', is related to the fact that post-war Germany, born out of the collapse of the Third Reich, adopted a compensatory attitude towards ethnic Germans – both refugees and those who were expelled. Following 1993, the shift in policy favours support of the ethnic Germans or German diaspora *in* their country of residence.

The case of returning ethnic Greeks from the former Soviet Union and Eastern Europe

Greek repatriates

Despite having a long history of emigration to Eastern Europe since WWII, particularly at the end of the Greek Civil War (1946-1949), after 1989 Greece, like Israel and Germany, began receiving large waves of repatriates or co-ethnic migrants. As in other *jus sanguinis* countries, it gives privileged status to its homogeneous co-ethnics in its immigration/naturalisation process, compared to its treatment of foreign nationals, including refugees (Voutira 2003: 61-68). This practice derives from the fundamentally nationalist ideology by which membership in the state presupposes membership in the nation. Like Germany, which is a better-known example, Greece includes the diaspora in the FSU among members of the nation and gives them axiomatic right of entry.[6] In the language of Benedict Anderson (1991), these diasporas belong to the 'imagined community' that makes up the nation. Both the citizens of the homeland and their ethnic co-nationals in the FSU are presumed to belong to the same community, sharing a collective identity independent of any actual collective experience. One of the particularities of the Soviet Greek diaspora (Voutira 2006) is their internal dispersal – or diasporisation – within former Soviet space, as a result of a long history of forced migrations and deportations under the Soviet regime. Demographically, the current situation of the Greek East-West repatriation relates to the legal status of those approximately 200,000 ex-Soviet citizens of Greek descent, who since 2000 have arrived in Greece with their new post-Soviet national identities. The overall picture of the repatriates, as it emerges from a twelve-year census study (1989-2000) conducted by the General Secretariat of Repatriated Greeks of the Ministry of Macedonia-Thrace (2000; 2001), reveals that most are adults, the vast majority are settled in Northern Greece (74 per cent), most speak Russian and hail from former Soviet republics such as Georgia (52 per cent), Kazakhstan (20 per cent), Russia (15 per cent), Armenia (6 per cent), Ukraine (3 per cent), Uzbekistan (2 per cent) and other nations formerly belonging to the USSR (2 per cent) (M. M-T 2000: 50-51).

three main phases

Seen in the context of a 15-year period (1990-2005), the Greek immigration and naturalisation policy vis-à-vis its co-ethnics may be divided into three main phases. In *Phase A* (1990-1995), the state adopted a crisis-management and rural settlements approach, channelling EU and state funds for the settlement of the newcomers in the ethnologically sensitive region of Thrace (30 per cent Muslim minority including Pomaks, Roma and Turks), in order to improve the demographic balance of the Greek Christian population. However, only 10 per cent of the total of 120,000 Soviet Greeks were willing to remain in the region. The majority opted for self-settlement in urban areas such as Athens and Thessaloniki. *Phase B* (1995-2000) involved a targeted rural-urban self-settlement approach supported by special-interest loans. One significant difference in state policy after 1999 is that the settlers' Greek descent is certified after their arrival in Greece. *Phase C* (2000-2005) was marked by new legislation providing for the possibility of dual nationality (i.e. Greek-Georgian, Greek-Russian). This led to the emergence of a new migratory pattern that includes movement between two homelands; a type of adaptation that allows post-Soviet citizens to maintain their ethnic networks on both sides of the East-West migration route.

privileged foreigners

This development of including the option of dual citizenship typically characterises this group as being 'privileged foreigners'. The notion of 'privilege' presupposes an implicit comparison: who are the privileged being compared with? The ethnic Greeks from the FSU are privileged with respect to other aliens, such as undocumented migrants and refugees, in terms of social, political and economic rights and inclusion of access to full citizenship status. By comparison, to native Greek citizens, they are also seen as privileged, since the recent economic incentives for self-settlement in both rural and urban areas are viewed as a type of favouritism not available to natives. What remains significant is the fact that for those ex-Soviet citizens willing to maintain a transient (transnational) existence between two homelands, access to both systems is not excluded; and this lack of exclusion is also a privilege.

The case of post-Soviet nations: Jus sanguinis *and* jus soli *migration as a transition issue in post-Soviet societies*

Changes in sovereignty over a territory necessarily result in changes to the nationality of the inhabitants. The formal requirement of citizenship and nationality laws follows from the fact that states define themselves politically through asserting legal authority, geographically through defending territorial boundaries and demographically by determining who has the right to live within, enter and exit these borders.[7] The new Russian nationality laws – whose function is to determine the degree of state sovereignty and control over the people living in its territory – were introduced one month before the final dissolution of the Soviet Union at the end of 1992 and were implemented the following year.

Russian Citizenship law

The Russian Citizenship law grants access to Russian nationality by the principles of both *jus sanguinis*, covering those who can establish Russian descent, and of *jus soli*, allowing residents of the Russian Federation (RF) to have access to Russian nationality.[8] Article 18 of the law goes further by granting access to any former Soviet citizen who is residing in any of the other successor states, but who is not a national of that state, if they had registered as a Russian national within three years of the law's adoption. Because Russian nationality may be provided to *any* former Soviet citizen in a successor state who cannot or would not acquire the nationality of that state, Russian nationality functions as a default access to citizenship; no former Soviet national need be stateless.

As the United Nations High Commissioner for Refugees (UNHCR) itself has observed, all of this makes for a 'liberal nationality regime', at least in the formal legal sense. However, as was the case with the Soviet constitution, there is a yawning gap between the codified principles and their implementation. In addition, all these provisions deal with those who find themselves within former Soviet borders. As the new terms in Russia have it, there is the 'near abroad' (former Soviet states) and the 'far abroad' (everywhere else). Anybody who is not in the 'near abroad' can obtain Russian citizenship only if they have a resident spouse or direct ascendant residing in the RF. Otherwise it is necessary to apply using the standard procedures for the acquisition of Russian nationality. As the three-year time limit has now elapsed, many of those in the 'near abroad' have learned of their options too late.[9]

'Russianness'

No matter how precise and inclusive Russian nationality law might be, at the popular level 'Russianness' remains both ambiguous and exclusive. Set in the context of local perceptions and social relations, the construction of 'Russianness' takes many forms and includes a variety of terms, connotations and implicit meanings. They include local press references to the 'Russophone migrants' (*russkoyazychnie pereselentsy*), negative connotations assigned by 'local Russians' (*mestnii Russkii*) to the term Russian (*ruskii*), understood as being any migrant forced to speak Russian. Others are normally seen as 'foreigners' (*inostrantsy*) or 'new-comers' (*priezhayushchie*), and social attitudes tend to be based on whether they are seen as bringing economic benefit or representing an additional burden. Significantly, the imperial view of Mother Russia as encompassing everyone who was within the FSU and has access to Russian citizenship (*rossiyanin*), as embedded in the nationality laws, is not part of daily life and is seldom used as self or other ascription (Pilkington 1995). As such, the case of the new citizens of the Russian Federation constitutes an interesting case study of the post-Soviet politics of identity and the manner in which new migration patterns and novel nationality laws interact in order to create patterns of national incorporation among post-Soviet citizens in the new states. For example, David Laitin has shown through comparative research among four former republics of the Soviet Union – Latvia, Estonia, Ukraine and Kazakhstan – that there are 'strong assimilationist incentives in the Baltics and weak ones in Kazakhstan. In Ukraine, a tip in either direction remains possible' (1998: 105). Thus the identity in formation is that of a 'Russian-speaking population' rather than simply ethnic Russian or Russian-Ukrainian, or even Estonian or Latvian. Furthermore, 'Russian-speaking population' is a new category of identity, used increasingly by Russians to identify themselves, and also one used by the natives in each of the four former republics to identify the Russians. In these four cases, a new identity is in the process of formation, and one that can be the model for understanding the prospects of assimilation for the new post-Soviet Russian diaspora in the former USSR.

Conclusion

jus sanguinis

This chapter discussed the use of the concepts of *jus sanguinis* and *jus soli* to allocate state membership, or citizenship, in different migration contexts, from the time of Homer to the present. Also, three philosophical models of membership and state incorporation were considered: liberal, communitarian and the ethnic or national. Given the focus of this chapter on *jus sanguinis* migration in the EU states, most of its empirical data were drawn from the case of historical diasporas from Eastern Europe returning to the West. The problems that newcomers face in reintegrating and adapting to their putative historical homelands are similar to those faced by foreign migrants. The main difference is that their political integration affords them privileged status vis-à-vis the acquisition of state membership. This entitles them to a preferred standing in comparison with other migrants.

Policy in most states in recent years has included variants of both *jus sanguinis* and *jus soli*, to accommodate returning diasporas and to improve upon immigrant practices. The heuristic rather than normative value of these principles rests on their adaptation to the new era of migration. The presentation of a broad historical evolutionary view of the development of citizenship regimes illustrated the manner in which different social worlds define and promote a sense of membership within specific value systems.

voluntary return migration

This chapter discussed the different forms of East-West voluntary return migration as practised by the Germans, Greeks and Jews. Looking at immigration policies that have emerged over the last fifteen years with a view to settling their respective diasporas from the FSU, these groups have been referred to as 'privileged foreigners'. The notion of 'privilege' supposes an implicit comparison: who are the less privileged? Both Greeks and Germans are privileged with respect to other aliens (e.g. undocumented migrants and refugees) in terms of social, political and economic rights and access to full citizenship status. In comparison with native populations, they are also perceived as privileged, since the recent economic incentives for self-settlement in both rural and urban areas are viewed as favouritism and unavailable to natives. What remains significant is the fact that for those ex-Soviet citizens willing to maintain a transient (transnational) existence between two homelands, access to both systems is not excluded; and this lack of exclusion is also a privilege.

One of the challenges of globalisation remains its undermining of the notion of distinct social worlds and what contemporary social theory has termed *hybridity*. This hybridity has impacted the way *jus sanguinis* and *jus soli* migration are conceptualised. There are no pure *jus sanguinis* and *jus soli* citizenship regimes in Europe. Most countries adopt measures compatible with both in order to accommodate their moral obligation towards current citizens and their legal obligations in regard to newcomers.

MAIN IDEAS

States have used the concepts of *jus sanguinis* and *jus soli* to allocate membership or citizenship in different migration contexts, from the time of Homer to the present.

The problems newcomers face in reintegrating and adapting to their putative historical homelands are similar to those confronted by foreign migrants.

The notion of 'privilege' presupposes an implicit comparison: who are the less privileged?

Citizenship regimes associated with *jus soli* are seen as more inclusive towards newcomers, while regimes based on *jus sanguinis* are viewed as more exclusive.

Notes

1 The discussion here intentionally differs from the standard accounts of political membership, which focus almost exclusively on the situation of non-citizens: specifically, those who reside in the state but who do not enjoy full membership. In today's world, one's place of birth and one's parentage are – by law – relevant to, and often constitutive of, one's access to membership in a particular political community, hence, the prioritisation over other forms of membership and belonging.

2 One hypothesis concerning the evolution of these two principles was that *jus soli* was related to the eighteenth century feudal tradition that tied individuals to the lord who owned the land where they were born. It was the French Revolution and the Civil Code of 1804 that reintroduced the Roman custom of *jus sanguinis.*

3 This has created the need for a new government agency dealing with the problem of visas. The majority of people who arrive via the tourist visa option either cannot afford to go to Moscow or are unable to obtain their documents to submit for repatriation. The new repatriation assistance service operating in Greece since 1994 is mediating in facilitating this bureaucratic process.

4 It is evident that since 1991 the wider category of former Soviet Greeks has been technically incorrect, since it refers to a now-defunct state authority, and therefore, to the need to incorporate the Greek minority into the corresponding post-Soviet Republic on a political and social level. Despite the use of old Soviet passports by most repatriates, they are now required to bear passports issued by the former USSR state in question.

5 It is perhaps noteworthy that in this case, the former intra-group appellations, such as 'Uzbek', 'Georgian' or 'Kazakh', as used by the migrants themselves, based on 'inter-subjective' criteria such as accent, differences in behaviour, cuisine and dietary preferences (for instance, the habit of putting milk in one's tea is peculiar to Central Asians), acquire a bureaucratic dimension and are legitimised by repatriates' classification in the records of the Ministry of Public Order by 'country of origin'.

6 Greek Albanians are also given a preferential status as 'people without Greek citizenship but with Greek nationality'. However, they receive fewer benefits, allocated on a discretionary basis by local authorities, than the ethnic Greeks from the FSU. The idea of a 'hierarchy of Greekness' is an apt way of describing the varieties of criteria used to determine social inclusion and exclusion practices vis-à-vis migrants in contemporary Greece.

7 See, for instance, Satvinders 1993.

8 The law of descent is accommodated by the designation 'Russian' under the nationality entry of the old Soviet passports, known as the fifth point because the 'nationality' immediately followed one's name, sex, date and place of birth. The law of descent is important for non-Russian residents of the Soviet Federation and the Russian diaspora in the 'far abroad', for whom access to Russian citizenship depends on the 'fourth point', i.e. place of birth in conjunction with their 'nationality'.

9 In an interview with members of the British Refugee Legal Service, I was informed that the majority of cases of Russians seeking asylum in the UK involves 'statelessness', which is the result of invalid, out-of-date passports related to lack of information concerning the procedures and application deadlines for the acquisition of Russian citizenship.

References

Appadurai, A. (1996), *Modernity at Large: Cultural Dimensions of Globalisation*. Minneapolis: University of Minnesota Press.

Aristotle, *Politics*, Book 3, ch.1.

Bade, K. and J. Oltmer (eds) (1999), *Aussiedler: Deutsche Einwanderer aus Osteuropa*. Universitätsverlag Osnabrück.

Bade, K. (1997), 'From emigration to immigration: The German experience in the nineteenth and twentieth centuries', in: K. Bade and M. Weiner (eds), *Migration Past Migration Future: Germany and the United States*, 1-39. Oxford: Berghahn Books.

Benhahib, S. (2004), *The Rights of Others: Aliens, Residents and Citizens*. Cambridge: Cambridge University Press.

Bertocchi G. and C. Strozzi (2005), 'Citizenship laws and international migration in historical perspective', Fondazione EniEnrico Mattei Working Papers: 71. http://ideas.repec.org/p/fem/femwpa/2005.71.html.

Bertocchi G. and C. Strozzi (2008), 'International migration and the role of institutions', *Public Choice* 137: 81-102.

Berry, J. (1992), 'Acculturation and adaptation in a new society', *International Migration*, 30: 69-85.

Borneman, J. (1997), 'State, territory and national identity formation in the two Berlins, 1945-1995', in: A. Gupta and J. Ferguson (eds), *Culture, Power, Place-Explorations in Critical Anthropology*. London: Duke University Press.

Brettell, C. (2000), 'Theorizing migration in anthropology: The social construction of networks, identities, communities and globalscapes', in: C.B. Brettel and J.F. Hollifield, *Migration Theory: Talking Across Disciplines*, 97-136. New York/London: Routledge.

Camus, A. (1988), *The Stranger*. New York: Random House.

Centlivres, P. and Centlivres-Dumont, M. (1988), 'The Afghan refugee in Pakistan: An ambiguous identity', *Journal of Refugee Studies* 1 (2): 141-152.

Dummett, A. (ed.) (1986), *Towards a Just Immigration Policy*. London: Cobden Trust.

Dummett, M. (2001), *On Immigration and Refugees*. London: Routledge.

De Coulanges, F. (1864), *La Cite Antique*. Paris: Plon.

De Tinguy, A. (2003), 'Ethnic migrations of the 1990s from and to the successor states of the former Soviet Union: "Repatriation' or Privileged Migration?"', in: R. Munz and R. Ohliger (eds), *Diasporas and Ethnic Migrants, Germany, Israel and Post-Soviet Successor States in Comparative Perspective*, 112-127. London: Frank Cass.

El Madmad, K. (1993), *L'asile dans les pays afro-arabes avec une référence spéciale au Soudan*. PhD thesis. Casablanca: University Hassan II.

Faist, T. (2006), 'The migration-security nexus: International migration and security before and after 9/11', in: M. Bodemann and G. Yurdakul (eds), *Migration, Citizenship, Ethnos*, 103-120. New York: Palgrave Macmillan.

Faist, T. (2000), *The Volume and Dynamics of International Migration and Transnational Social Spaces*. Oxford: Oxford University Press.

Flynn, M. (2004), *Migrant Resettlement in the Russian Federation: Restructuring Homes and Homelands*. Anthem Press.

Green, S. (2000), 'Beyond ethnoculturalism? German citizenship in the new millennium', *German Politics* 9 (3): 105-124.

Green, S. (2004), *The Politics of Exclusion: Institutions and Migration Policy in Contemporary Germany*. Manchester: Manchester University Press.

Gupta, A. and J. Fergusson (eds) (1997), *Culture, Power, Place-Explorations in Critical Anthropology*. London: Duke University Press.

Heller, A. (1993), 'The limits to natural law and the paradox of evil', in: S. Shute and S. Hurley (eds), *On Human Rights*. The Oxford Amnesty Lectures 1993. New York: Basic Books.

Herodotus, *Histories*, Chapter 8: 144.

Humphrey, C. (2002), *The Unmaking of Soviet Life: Everyday Economies after Socialism*. Ithaca/London: Cornell University Press.

Joppke, C. (2006), 'Citizenship between de- and re-ethnicization', in: M. Bodemann and G. Yurdakul (eds), *Migration, Citizenship, Ethnos*, 63-94. New York: Palgrave Macmillan.

Kaurinkoski, K. (2003), 'Les Grecs de Mariupol (Ukraine): Réflexions sur une identité en diaspora', *Revue Européenne des Migrations Internationales* 19 (1): 125-149.

Kleinknecht-Strähle, U. (1998), *Three Phases of Post-World-War II Russian German Migration from the Former Soviet Union to Germany*. Thesis. University of Oxford.

Laitin, D. (1998), *Identity in Formation: Russian Speaking Populations in the Near Abroad*. Ithaca: Cornell University Press.

MacIntyre, A. (1998), *The MacIntyre Reader*. Indiana: University of Notre Dame Press.

Malkki, L. (1997), 'National geographic: The routing of peoples and the territorialisation of national identity among scholars and refugees', in: A. Gupta and J. Ferguson (eds), *Culture, Power, Place-Explorations in Critical Anthropology*. London: Duke University Press.

Mandell, R. (2006), 'Being German and Jewish in Kazakhstan and Germany', in: M. Bodemann and G. Yurdakul (eds), *Migration, Citizenship, Ethnos*. New York: Palgrave Macmillan.

Markowitz, F. (1995), *Community In Spite of Itself*. Washington/London: Smithsonian Institution Press.

Marchetti, R. (2008), 'Toward a world migratory regime', *Indiana Journal of Global Legal Studies* 15 (2): 471-487.

Martin, T. (2001), *The Affirmative Action Empire: Nations and Nationalism in the Soviet Union 1923-1939*. Ithaca: Cornell University Press.

Meyer, B. and J. Geschiere (2003), *Globalisation and Identity: Dialectics of Flow and Closure*. Oxford: Blackwell Publishing.

Miller, D. (2008), 'Immigrants, nations and citizenship', *The Journal of Political Philosophy* 16 (4): 371-390.
Ministry of Macedonia and Thrace – General Secretariat of Repatriated Greeks (2000), *The Identity of the Repatriating Greeks from the Former Soviet Union*. Thessaloniki.
Ministry of Macedonia and Thrace – General Secretariat of Repatriated Greeks (2001), *The Major Characteristics of the Repatriating Greeks from the Countries of the Former Soviet Union in the Most Demographically Dense Regions of Greece*. Thessaloniki.
Morris, L. (2000), 'Rights and controls in the management of migration: The case of Germany', *Sociological Review* 48 (2): 224-240.
Ohliger, R. (2005), 'Jus Sanguinis, Migration and Naturalisation', in: M.J. Gibney and R. Hansen (eds), *Immigration and Asylum: From 1900 to the Present*, Volume 1: 344. Santa Barbara: ABC CLIO.
Ortner, S. (1978), *Sherpas through their Rituals*, Cambridge: Cambridge University Press.
Parekh, B. (1994), 'Three theories of immigration', in: S. Spencer (ed.), *Strangers and Citizens*. London: IPPR Rivers Oram Press.
Pilkington, H. (1995), 'The "other" Russians: Migration, displacement and national identity in post-Soviet Russia', paper presented to the CREES Annual Conference, Windsor Park, 23-25 June.
Pocock, J. (1995), 'The ideal of citizenship since classical times', in: R. Beiner (ed.), *Theorizing Citizenship*, 29-52. Albany: State University of New York Press.
Rawls, J. (2001), *Justice as Fairness: A Restatement*. Cambridge: Belknap Press.
Redfield, J. (1975), *Nature and Culture in the Iliad: The Tragedy of Hector*. Chicago: University of Chicago Press.
Sassen, S. (2006a), 'Repositioning of citizenship and alienage: Emergent subjects and spaces for politics', in: M. Bodemann and G. Yurdakul (eds), *Migration, Citizenship, Ethnos*, 13-33, New York: Palgrave Macmillan.
Sassen, S. (2006b), *Territory, Authority, Rights: From Medieval to Global Assemblages*. Princeton: Princeton University Press.
Sassen, S. (1999), *Guests and Aliens*. New York: New Press.
Satvinders, S.J. (1993), *Immigration, Nationality and Citizenship*. London: Mansell.
Schnapper, D. (1991), *La France de l'integration, Sociologie de la Nation en 1990*. Paris: Gallimard.
Shachar, A. (1999), 'Whose republic? Citizenship and membership in the Israeli polity', *Georgetown Immigration Law Journal* 13 (2): 233-272.
Shack, A. and Skinner E. (eds) (1979), *Strangers in African Societies*. Berkeley: University of California Press.
Shepherd, N. (1993), *The Russians in Israel: The Ordeal of Freedom*. London: Simon and Schuster.
Soysal, J. (1994), *The Limits of Citizenship: Migrants and Post-national Membership in Europe*. Chicago: University of Chicago Press.
Taylor, C. (1994), *Multiculturalism: Examining the Politics of Recognition*, Princeton: Princeton University Press.
Taylor, C. (1998) 'The Dynamics of Democratic Exclusion', *Journal of Democracy* 9 (4): 145-156.
Terry, M. (2001), *The Affirmative Action Empire: Nations and Nationalism in the Soviet Union, 1923-1939*. Ithaca: Cornell University Press.
Voutira, E. (2006), 'Post-Soviet diaspora politics: The case of the Soviet Greeks', *Journal of Modern Greek Studies* 24: 379-414.
Voutira, E. (2004), 'Ethnic Greeks from the former Soviet Union as "Privileged Return Migrants"', *Espace Populations Sociétés* 3: 533-544.

Voutira, E. (2003), 'Refugees: Whose term is it anyway? Emic and Etic constructions of "refugees" in Modern Greek', in: J. Van Selm et al. (eds), *The Refugee Convention at Fifty: A View from Forced Migration Studies*, 65-80. Lanham: Lexington Books.

Walzer, M. (1997), *On Toleration*. New Haven: Yale University Press.

Walzer, M. (1989), 'Citizenship', in: T. Ball and J. Farr (eds), *Citizenship in Political Innovation and Conceptual Change*, 211-219. Cambridge: Cambridge University Press.

Walzer, M. (1983), *Spheres of Justice: A Defense of Pluralism and Equality*. New York: Basic Books.

Weil, P. (2001), 'Access to citizenship: A comparison of twenty five nationality laws', in: A.T. Aleinikoff and D. Klusmeyer (eds), *Citizenship Today: Global Perspectives and Practices*, 17-35. Washington: Carnegie Endowment for International Peace.

Wilson, M. (1979), 'Strangers in Africa: Reflections on Nyakyusa, Nguni and Sotho evidence', in: A. Shack and E. Skinner (eds), *Strangers in African Societies*, 51-66. Berkley: University of California Press.

Wolff, S. (2001), *German Minorities in Europe: Ethnic Identity and Cultural Belonging*, Oxford: Berghahn Books.

Wright, S. and C. Shore (1997), *Anthropology of Policy: Critical Perspectives on Governments and Power*. London: Routledge.

7 Migration and Social Transformation

Stephen Castles

Introduction

The movement of people is a key aspect of social change in the contemporary world. Yet studies of migration still play a limited role in the general social theories that seek to provide a framework for analysing contemporary society. Much migration research today is driven not by scientific inquiry but by policy needs. In other words, research is initiated by policymakers and aimed at answering short-term administrative questions. A vicious circle is then perpetuated, in which social theorists see migration research as a second-rate and narrow field, which reduces their willingness to afford spatial mobility an important place in their analyses of social change. Migration researchers, for their part, become even more bound by research questions and methodologies generated by bureaucratic agendas for the management of migration and integration processes. This reinforces 'methodological nationalism' in migration research (Wimmer and Glick Schiller 2003) – that is, the use of conceptual frameworks that correspond to entrenched national assumptions about how to deal with migration and minorities. Despite the growth of transnational approaches (e.g. Levitt and Glick Schiller 2004; Portes et al. 1999), much migration research remains oriented to models of 'container societies' (Faist 2000) while critical social theory is moving away from its earlier preoccupation with borders (Beck 2007).

This chapter argues the importance of developing a conceptual framework for migration studies that overcomes its isolation from wider issues of global power, wealth and inequality. The proposed framework is based on a concept of social transformation that stems from the work of Karl Polanyi (2001). A number of social scientists, such as Stiglitz (2002), have re-worked Polanyi's theory of the nineteenth-century 'great transformation' to analyse recent economic globalisation and the rise of neo-liberalism. Here, the argument is presented that these accelerated processes of social transformation form a crucial context in which to analyse migration. Studying migration separately from this context is likely to lead to mistaken ideas about the controllability of mobility and of cultural diversity in societies affected *social transformation* by migration. In contrast, viewing migration as a key aspect of broader social transformations can enrich both migration studies and the social sciences as a whole.

processes

This chapter begins with a discussion of the processes of social transformation and what these have meant for the economies, societies, political systems and cultures of areas involved in migration. Interlocking processes of social transformation affect the areas of origin, transit and destination of migrants – keeping in mind that many areas are all of these at once. This leads to a rejection of the still-prevalent 'push-pull' theories of migration, which postulate migration as split between repelling factors in origin areas (generally in the 'South') and attracting factors in destination areas (mostly in the 'North'). In contrast, this chapter contends that the factors that drive migration are connected through complex patterns of interdependence and feedback mechanisms. It encourages a broad interdisciplinary approach to migration studies, in particular for the linking of micro-level studies of local causes and effects of migration to a broader political economy of global relationships. Linking across socio-spatial levels also means addressing the dialectics of structure and agency in every aspect of human mobility.

Social transformation, globalisation and migration[1]

shifts

The idea of *social transformation* implies a fundamental change in the way society is organised that goes beyond the continual processes of social change that are always at work (see Polanyi 2001, first published in 1944) and which arises when there are major shifts in dominant power relationships. The massive shifts in global economic, political and military affairs since the 1970s represent this type of fundamental change. The effects of globalisation are uneven, involving a process of inclusion in world capitalist market relations for particular regions and social groups, while excluding others from this market (Castells 1996). The penetration of Southern economies by Northern investors and multi-national corporations leads to economic restructuring, through which some groups of producers are included in the new economy, while other groups find their workplaces destroyed and their qualifications devalued. Thus, economic globalisation leads to the profound transformation of societies in all regions. The neglect of this connection on the part of the International Monetary Fund (IMF) and other international financial institutions (IFIs) has led to failures that 'have set back the development agenda, by unnecessarily corroding the very fabric of society' (Stiglitz 2002: 76-77).

The rapid growth in inequality between the so-called 'advanced countries' and 'the rest of the world' is often referred to as *North-South inequality.* However, by using such general terms some important differences may be missed. First, many areas do not fit this dichotomy: both the 'transitional economies' of the former Soviet bloc countries and the 'new industrial economies' of some regions of the Gulf, Asia and Latin America have an intermediate position. Second, growing inequality may also be found within each of the Northern and Southern regions, with new elites in the South gaining from their role in the transnational circuits of capital accumulation, while workers in former northern industrial centres lose their livelihoods. In Europe, this change is expressed in the decline of welfare states and the rise of racism against minorities (Schierup et al. 2006). Overall, globalisation has led not only to a growing gulf between North and South, but also to increased inequality within each region. Therefore, 'South' and 'North' should be understood more as mutable social locations than fixed geographical ones.

Green Revolution

Social transformation often begins in the realm of agriculture. The 'Green Revolution' from the 1960s to the early 1980s involved the introduction of new strains of rice and other crops that promised higher yields, but in return required large investments in fertilisers, insecticides and mechanisation. The result was higher productivity (at least for a while – sometimes this declined as the soil became depleted), but also a greater concentration of ownership in the hands of wealthier farmers; poorer farmers lost their livelihoods and often had to leave the land. That process continues today with the introduction of genetically modified seed stock. The pressure on farmers in poor regions is increased by farm subsidies in rich countries – especially US cotton subsidies and the EU Common Agricultural Policy (Oxfam 2002) – which depress world market prices.

growth in inequality

The economic advances of emerging industrial powers such as China, India and Brazil are based on a rapid growth in inequality between urban and rural incomes (Milanovic 2007: 35-39), causing displaced farmers to migrate into burgeoning cities like Sao Paolo, Shanghai, Calcutta and Jakarta. The population of Southern cities is growing at a rate of approximately 70 million a year. In 2005, approximately one billion people were estimated to be living in slum areas, such as the shanty towns of southern Africa or the *favelas* of Brazil; this number is expected to double by 2030 (New Internationalist 2006). Urban employment growth cannot keep pace, and there are few jobs for the millions of newcomers. Many earn a subsistence living through irregular and insecure work in the informal sector. Standards of housing, health and education are very low, while crime, violence and human rights violations are rife. Such conditions are powerful motivations to seek better livelihoods elsewhere, either in growth areas within the region or in the North. However, international migration is selective: only those with the financial capital to cover the high costs of mobility and the social capital to connect with opportunities abroad can make the move.

Clearly, the social transformations inherent in globalisation not only affect economic well-being, they also lead to increased violence and a lack of human security in less-developed countries. Growing numbers of people are being forced to flee their homes as refugees or internally displaced persons (IDPs). In the 1960s struggles over decolonisation and state formation often evolved into proxy wars in the East-West confrontation, with the superpowers providing modern weapons to their protégés. Such conflicts escalated, starting in the 1980s, with the proliferation of internal wars related to ethnic divisions, problems of state formation and competition for economic assets. Ninety per cent of those killed in these conflicts are civilians, and the 'new wars' have led to an upsurge in forced migration (Kaldor 2001). The great majority of those affected by violence are displaced within their own countries or seek refuge in other – often equally poor – countries in the region. However, some try to obtain asylum in the wealthier states of the North, where they hope to find more security and freedom – as well as better livelihoods. This is the reality behind the observation of the Global Commission on International Migration (GCIM), which states that international migration is driven by 'development, demography and democracy' (GCIM 2005: 12).

new technologies

Globalisation helps to create the new technologies that facilitate mobility: air travel has become cheaper and more readily available, and electronic media spread images of first-world prosperity to even the most remote villages. Globalisation also creates the cultural capital needed for mobility: electronic communications facilitate the spread of knowledge of migration routes and work opportunities. Many of the world's excluded perceive that mobility brings an opportunity for prosperity, and are desperate to migrate. Globalisation also creates the necessary social capital: informal networks facilitate migration even when official policies try to prevent it, while the 'migration industry' is one of the fastest growing forms of international business. Migration networks help to reconnect South and North, at a time when many areas of the South have become economically irrelevant to the globalised economy (Duffield 2001).

migration as transformation

Clearly, migration is not just a result of social transformation, but is also a form of social transformation that impacts the societies involved. The flows and networks that constitute globalisation take on specific forms at different spatial levels: the regional, the national and the local. These should be understood as not being in opposition to each other, but rather as elements of complex and dynamic relationships, in which global forces have varying impacts according to differing structural and cultural factors and responses at other levels (see Held et al. 1999: 14-16). Historical experiences, cultural values, religious beliefs, institutions and social structures all channel and shape the effects of external forces, leading to forms of change and resistance that bring about very different outcomes in specific communities and societies.

impact on local communities

For most people, the pre-eminent level on which they experience migration and its effects is *the local*. This applies especially where social transformations make it necessary for people to leave their communities and move elsewhere: for instance, due to environmental change and the extreme weather events it causes; changes in agricultural practices or land tenure; reconfiguration of production by multinational corporations; or development projects (such as dams, airports or factories) that physically displace people. The departure of young active people, gender imbalances and financial and social remittances all transform conditions in the local community. Similarly, the impact of immigration in host areas is felt in the way it affects economic restructuring and social relations in local communities.

Nor should the *national* dimension be neglected: despite globalist claims about the erosion of the nation-state, the number of nation-states in the UN has grown from 50, when the world body was established in 1945, to 193 in 2012. Nation-states remain important and will continue to be so for the foreseeable future. They are the nexus of policy-making on cross-border movements, citizenship, public order, social welfare, health services and education. Nation-states retain considerable political significance and have important symbolic and cultural functions. However, it is no longer possible to ignore cross-border factors in decision-making and planning. One result of this is the growing importance of *regional* cooperation through entities like the European Union (EU), the North American Free Trade Agreement (NAFTA) and the Economic Community of West African States (ECOWAS).

inequalities from globalisation

The inequalities arising from globalisation and social transformation are particularly evident with regard to migration. The governments of rich countries have developed migration regimes that encourage the highly skilled to be mobile, while low-skilled workers and people fleeing persecution are excluded. As Bauman has argued, in the globalised world, 'mobility has become the most powerful and most coveted stratifying factor'. 'The riches are global, the misery is local' (Bauman 1998: 9 and 74). Control of migration and the differential treatment of various categories of migrants have become the basis for a new type of transnational class structure.

Barriers to theoretical advancement

Migration researchers often ignore the context of global social transformation and focus their work narrowly on specific migratory phenomena. Migration studies commonly focus on specific, short-term, local dimensions of migration, especially in destination countries (where research institutes and funding tend to be concentrated). Why is this?

obstacles to advancement

There are formidable obstacles to theoretical advancement in migration studies, including the difficulties of working across disciplinary boundaries, the fragmentation of migration research into poorly-connected sub-fields, methodological nationalism, the close links of migration research with political and bureaucratic agendas and the domination of migration studies by scholars in migrant-destination countries (especially North America and Europe). All these topics have been dealt with extensively in the literature (Arango 2000; Brettell and Hollifield 2007; Castles 2000, 2007; Massey et al. 1998; Portes 1997, 1999; Portes and DeWind 2004; Schuerkens 2005; Wimmer and Glick Schiller 2003), so two other key issues will be discussed: the disconnection between migration studies and social theory, and the problems of theorising highly complex and diverse migratory experiences.

Migration scholars have often found themselves marginalised within the social sciences because many leading social theorists tend to see migration as an unimportant area of investigation. This goes back to the nineteenth- and early twentieth-century origins of social theory in the task of consolidating nation-states (Connell 1997) and national industrial societies (Wieviorka 1994). Since migrants and ethnic minorities were seen at best as extraneous, and at worst as harmful to the creation of nation-states, they were either ignored (Noiriel 1988) or – in the influential variant of the Chicago School – treated as people who needed to be 'resocialised' and assimilated in a great 'melting pot' of cultures (Park 1950).

prejudice against interdisciplinary study

The neglect of migration and cultural diversity in 'methodological nationalism' (Wimmer and Glick Schiller 2003) has been criticised and partially corrected in recent years, only to be replaced by a new barrier: the recent trend away from taking an interdisciplinary approach. Migration studies must cut across social-scientific boundaries because the migratory experience affects all dimensions of social belonging; however, this is one reason why it has attracted comparatively little interest in increasingly compartmentalised university departments. As a result, migration research often takes place in contexts outside of core social science research, usually in dedicated research centres that are heavily dependent on external funding. This forces migration researchers to take on policy-driven consultancy work, which in turn confirms the prejudice against interdisciplinary study on the part of mainstream social scientists.

To understand this fully would require a detailed study of the institutional and intellectual characteristics of the social sciences in various countries. In Britain, for instance, the initial response to the New Commonwealth immigration of the 1950s and 1960s was the reworking of the Chicago School's sociological theories of assimilation and acculturation. However, by the 1970s, issues of racism, culture identity, class and gender – influenced considerably by black, feminist and Marxist scholars – began to play an important role. Such approaches have become part of the accepted body of social analysis, but have not always advanced to embrace the newer complex forms of global mobility affecting the UK. In recent years, the problem of disciplinary barriers has become worse in the UK due to the Research Assessment Exercise (RAE), which puts such a premium on publication in disciplinary journals that young academics fear the consequences of publishing in migration journals.

Globalisation theory is now at the centre of international social science debates, and the mobility of people is a crucial form of globalisation. Nevertheless, many of the seminal works on globalisation, like those of Castells (1996, 1997, 1998), Albrow (1996) and Beck (1997), pay scant attention to the mobility of people. There are contrasting examples, as will be discussed below, yet the analysis of migration as a central element of global social change is still the exception. The social scientists who specialise in such themes – in Europe at least – tend to be located in migration research centres rather than in sociology departments.

complexity of migration

A further major obstacle to theorisation is the complexity and diversity of migration experiences, which has posed particular problems for economists. The methodological principle is to start with simple models, and then use quantitative data to test and refine them. The Harris-Todaro model, which underpins the neoclassical approach to migration, assumes that movement is motivated by the desire for the maximisation of individual income, based on rational comparison of the relative costs and benefits of remaining at home or moving. According to this model, the mere existence of economic disparities between various areas should be sufficient to generate migrant flows. In the long run, such flows should help to equalise wages and conditions in underdeveloped and developed regions, leading towards economic equilibrium (Massey et al. 1998: ch 2). This model was developed to analyse internal movements in developing countries, but is seen as applicable to international migration too, provided consideration is given to constraints arising from the role of states and their uneven power.

narrow focus of neoclassical model

The problem is that the neoclassical model has not proven very useful for analysing and explaining actual migration experiences. Its narrow focus on income maximisation and its assumption of rational economic decision-making based on full information has little to do with the reality of most migration flows. The theorists embracing the 'new economics of labour migration' (Stark 1991; Taylor 1999) have criticised the methodological individualism of the Harris-Todaro approach and shifted the focus to family strategies for income maximisation and risk diversification, but the emphasis on rational economic decision-making remains. Such theories fail to take into account the many non-economic factors that shape migration. As Collinson (2009), citing Gold (2005), points out:

> New approaches have challenged any attempt to understand migration on the basis of a single level of analysis or discrete factor such as income differentials or labour demand. They emphasise instead the inter-linkages between different migration streams; the importance of agency, autonomy, perceptions, cultural and historical factors and institutional constraints; the complex multi-level and trans-national nature of migration; and the importance of social groups and relationships – including migration networks – for shaping migration dynamics and migration experiences, straddling migration 'sending', 'receiving' and 'transit' locations, and a range of actors within them.

This list indicates the great *complexity* of migratory processes and the existence of multi-level linkages and feedback mechanisms. In other words, migratory processes cannot be explained purely by exogenous factors (such as economic forces) but also develop their own inner dynamics. Economic factors are important, but hardly sufficient to fully understand any specific experience. This is not just an issue for economics: this discipline has been the focus so far because economic data and models are so popular with policy-makers. However, any mono-causal explanation of migration is equally problematic because it cannot do justice to the complexity of migration.

diversity of migration

Complexity also implies *diversity*: with so many factors at work, the possible combinations become infinite. There is no such thing as a 'typical migratory process', which demonstrates the crucial role of *context* – the links between migration and all the other economic, social, political and cultural relationships at work in particular places at a particular historical juncture. A historical understanding of societies and the relationships between them is crucial. For instance, no analysis of migration to Britain could be complete without a thorough understanding of the history of British colonialism and racism, no analysis of Mexican migration to the USA could be valid without consideration of the historical expansion of the USA and its past labour recruitment policies, and so on.

A social transformation framework for migration studies

Awareness of complexity, diversity and context in migration might lead to the idea that theory formation is pointless, since each case appears specific. This could support the post-modern idea of the 'end of grand narratives' – that is, the fragmentation of knowledge, based on the principle that everything is specific and that there are no broad social trends or institutional patterns. Yet such a perspective ignores the reality of today's globalisation processes that lead to higher and more pervasive levels of economic, political, social and cultural integration than ever before. Contemporary social relations do display great diversity, but it is diversity within increasingly universal relationships of power and inequality. Thus, migration theory needs to provide a framework for understanding the multi-level dynamics of international migration and incorporation in a situation of rapid and complex transformation (see King 2002). Such a framework should connect with key contemporary trends, which means taking the current processes of global social transformation as a starting point.

Requirements of a conceptual framework for migration studies

conceptual framework

The key objective of theory formation in the international migration field should be the elaboration of a *conceptual framework* designed to provide theoretical and methodological orientation to social science researchers examining migratory processes of all kinds. This framework should be the following:

- *Comprehensive*. The framework needs to include all factors likely to influence migratory processes, as well as the linkages between them and the contexts that shape them.
- *Holistic*. The framework should cover entire migratory processes as they develop across space and time, starting with the migration decision-making process in the place of origin, examining experiences at all stages during the actual process of movement, and finally analysing processes of incorporation and return (where applicable) that may affect the destination and origin countries over long periods of time.
- *Capable of contextualising specific migration experiences*. The comprehensive and holistic nature of the conceptual framework does not imply that every researcher needs to analyse whole migratory

processes, but rather that in any study of a specific event, group or stage, the researcher needs to be aware of the dynamics and context of the entire process.
- *Suitable for analysing relationships between various socio-spatial levels: global, local, national and regional* (see Pries 2007). Global factors that shape migration have different local effects in various regions, due to the presence of mediating historical experiences and cultural patterns. This principle also underpins the need for an interdisciplinary approach, since the various disciplines often address different socio-spatial levels.
- *Able to incorporate both structure* and *agency*. Structure includes *macro-social* structures (e.g. states, corporations, international agencies), *micro-social* structures (e.g. families, groups, social networks, local communities) and *meso-social* structures (e.g. intermediate networks or collectivities such as the migration industry or transnational communities). Agency refers to individual and group action, which helps people to survive and cope in specific situations of change or crisis.
- *Historical*. The framework should not claim to present a universally valid theory of migration, but rather serve as an analytical tool appropriate to the current epoch of globalisation and social transformation.
- *Dynamic*. No conceptual framework in the social sciences is ever final, but is merely a distillation of the current state of understanding, to be tested and modified through further empirical work.

four stages of theory formation

On this basis, the process of theory formation in migration studies may be summarised as consisting of four stages:
1. Empirical studies of specific migration experiences, for instance, a particular form of migrant labour recruitment or a certain pattern of refugee migration and settlement.
2. The construction of middle-range theories[2] of migratory processes linking specific countries of origin, transit and destination, within the context of the wider social relations of globalisation and social transformation.
3. Building a broader conceptual framework by drawing out key lessons of middle-range theories in order to provide theoretical and methodological orientation for future migration research.
4. Using the conceptual framework as a basis for developing the themes, research questions and methods for the next round of empirical research.

However, this seemingly grounded theory approach is in fact cyclical, and we are not starting with a *tabula rasa*. Social scientists can already build on many years of migration research to start their work at any of these stages. The great expansion of empirical research on migration in recent years provides the basis for comparative analysis and theory formation. The third stage – building a conceptual framework – is increasingly urgent, but because theory is always valid only as long as it provides useful guidance for on-the-ground research, the fourth stage – testing the conceptual framework through new empirical work – must be closely linked.

Re-embedding migration in social transformation

social transformation processes

Analysis of the *processes of social transformation* could provide the basis for this conceptual framework by providing a new understanding of the links between human mobility and global change. As mentioned above, Karl Polanyi's (2001) work on the 'great transformation' of European societies following the Industrial Revolution is a useful starting point for the analysis of contemporary processes. According to Polanyi, the market liberalism of the nineteenth century ignored the *embeddedness* of the economy in society (i.e. its role in achieving social goals laid down by politics, religion and social custom). The liberal attempt to *disembed* the market was a 'stark utopia' leading to a 'double movement' – a protective countermovement to re-subordinate the economy to society. Unfortunately, in the early twentieth century this countermovement led inexorably to fascism and a world war (Block and Polanyi 2003; Polanyi 2001).

The closely-linked processes of accelerated economic globalisation and the reshaping of political and military power relationships since the end of the Cold War represent a contemporary change in society – a new 'great transformation'. These fundamental economic and political shifts are closely interwoven with a transformation of social relationships. The concept of *embeddedness* can play an important part in understanding globalisation and its consequences for human mobility. Just as nineteenth-century liberals portrayed economic affairs as something separate from the rest of society, neo-liberals today portray globalisation as a predominantly economic phenomenon. The emergence of a new economy is depicted as being the result of growing levels of foreign direct investment, the deregulation of cross-border flows of capital, technology and services, and the creation of a global production system (Petras and Veltmayer 2000: 2). The key actors in this new economic world are the multinational corporations (MNCs) and the global financial and commodity markets. The basic premise of globalisation is 'the leadership of civilization by economics' (Saul 2006: xi). This ideology is summed up in the 'Washington consensus' on the importance of market liberalisation, privatisation and deregulation (Stiglitz 2002: 67).

disembedding

Disembedding economic globalisation from its societal context is in fact deeply political, because it makes global change appear as something objective and inevitable. Clearly globalisation is not just about economics: it is also a *political process*, conceived in normative and ideological terms:

> For the theorists of this process and its many advocates these flows [...], together with the resulting economic integration and social transformation, have created a new world order with its own institutions and configurations of power that have replaced the previous structures associated with the nation-state, and that have created new conditions of peoples' lives all over the world (Petras and Veltmayer 2000: 2).

Radical proponents of globalisation regard the nation-state as obsolete – to be replaced by the power of markets and consumer choice (Ohmae 1995). This view is linked to the neo-liberal principles of a 'small state', the privatisation of utilities and services, economic deregulation and the opening of markets – especially those of developing countries – to global competition. The global economic crisis that started in 2007 has undermined public confidence in this model, so it is important to ask how the crisis has affected the global labour market and international migration.

Since the start of the economic crisis, on average in Western Europe (the EU15), the unemployment rate for the foreign-born has increased twice as much as for the native-born. In the USA, the unemployment rate for immigrants more than doubled from 4.3 per cent to 9.7 per cent. The crisis has been marked by sharp declines in construction, manufacturing, the financial sector, and wholesale and retail trade. Immigrants are over-represented in these sectors, and therefore have been most affected. Yet foreign employment in European OECD countries actually increased by 5 per cent from early 2008 to the third quarter of 2010, while employment of native-born persons declined by 2.2 per cent (OECD 2011: 74-75). This was the result of demographic shifts leading to a decline in the entry of young people into the labour force and social shifts like better education opportunities for locals. In other words, both migrant unemployment and employment increased during the crisis.

Migrant men have been worse affected by unemployment than migrant women. This happened mainly because migrant men tend to be employed in the sectors hardest hit by the downturn, while migrant women are more concentrated in less-affected sectors, notably social services, care work and domestic work. At the same time, the global economic crisis has reinforced the trend towards part-time, temporary and casual employment, and women are more likely than men to have such jobs (OECD 2011: 78-81). So the trend has not meant an improved situation for migrant women. Rather, they are often pushed into precarious jobs and forced to work even longer hours than before. Another disturbing effect of the global economic crisis in Europe has been very high rates of youth unemployment for migrants. Long-term unemployment has also been a major problem: over half of all unemployed migrants had been jobless for over a year in Germany, while the figure in most other countries was 30 per cent or more (OECD 2011: 85). Unemployment rates varied by area of origin, with Africans worst affected.

On the whole, the global economic crisis has affected old industrial economies more than emerging ones in Asia and Latin America (Phillips 2011). As new economic powers arise, patterns of work and migration seem to be changing. Despite the hesitant return to growth in the USA in 2010-2011, inflows of lower skilled migrants remained stagnant, and Mexican immigration showed no sign of recovery (Passel and Cohn 2011). Emigration to Spain from Ecuador and other Latin American countries, and to Japan from Brazil and Peru has fallen, and there has been significant return migration. However, uneven economic growth and the emergence of new migration poles (such as Brazil, Chile and Argentina) within Latin America have led to more mobility within the continent. In 2009, the recession led to declines in Asian migration, but such patterns were short-lived. Migrant departures from Bangladesh grew by 37 per cent in the first three quarters of 2011. Outflows of migrant workers from the Philippines grew by 20 per cent from 2008 to 2010, and by a further 7 per cent in the first three quarters of 2011 (Mohapatra et al. 2011). High labour demand in the oil-producing countries was a major factor stimulating migration, with large flows of labour to the Gulf oil states and Russia.

An important emerging effect of the global economic crisis is the growth of migration from the worst-hit areas of Europe to places that still offer jobs and opportunities. In early 2012 there were reports of Greeks, Italians and Irish moving to Australia, Portuguese seeking their fortunes in Brazil and Angola, and Spaniards, Italians and Britons trying their luck in Argentina. Such migrants tread paths established 50 or even 100 years ago, but with the difference that today many are highly qualified young people moving from depressed economies to seek opportunities in emerging economic centres.

Overall, the patterns of labour market disadvantage and differentiation established in earlier years have had profound effects during the global economic crisis. Migrants have been particularly hard hit by unemployment and declines in earnings. Yet the most important lesson of the global economic crisis has been that migrant workers are essential to the economies of industrial countries, especially in Europe and some Asian countries, where demographic change is leading to a declining local labour force. Overall, migrant stocks have not fallen, and new migratory patterns are emerging in response to major changes in the structure of the world economy.

globalisation paradigm

A historical perspective shows that the globalisation paradigm that emerged in the context of political strategies – initiated in the 1980s by the Reagan administration in the USA and the Thatcher government in the UK – was designed to roll back the welfare state and the relatively high wage levels of the post-war boom period. The opening of markets, the weakening of trade unions and the removal of protection of organised labour led to massive social changes. Though even a neo-liberal world economy needs control mechanisms, these were to be provided not by national governments (which, in some cases at least, are democratically elected), but by international institutions, especially the IMF, the World Bank and the World Trade Organisation (WTO). Their task was not to protect weak economies or vulnerable social groups, but rather to ensure that all economies and societies were opened up to the cold winds of competition – primarily through the mechanism of 'structural adjustment programmes'. These institutions have close links with the US Treasury, and their policies are strongly influenced by US and European interests (Stiglitz 2002).

A theory of global change in which the economy is seen as being disembedded from society, with its political and social consequences treated as inevitable 'externalities' (as economists put it), leads to a disembedded understanding of migration. In a narrow economistic view, this means seeking the determinants of migration in a range of rational choices based on economic interests. The essential link is absent that connects massive changes in global economic and political power to the resulting social transformation processes.

societal context

An alternative approach is to see migration not merely as either a result or a cause of social transformation, but as an integral and essential part of the social transformation process, meaning that theories of migration should be embedded in broader social theory. Research on any specific migration phenomenon must always include research on the societal context in which it takes place. Because awareness of change usually starts on a local level, it is important to link local-level experiences of migration (whether in the origin or receiving areas) with other socio-spatial levels – and particularly with global processes.

rapid social changes

A social transformation approach to analysing the relationship between migration and social change implies that migration itself should *not* generally be seen as the primary cause of a major change in society. For instance, US society is currently undergoing rapid change, and at the same time is experiencing large-scale immigration from

Latin America and Asia. However, the fact that these changes are occurring at the same time does not prove causality. Major current economic changes include the decline of older manufacturing industries, the shift offshore of many forms of production and the emergence of a service-based economy. These patterns are linked to rapid social changes: the decline of the blue-collar working-class and their trade unions; the decay of once prosperous industrial towns; and the emergence of new forms of work based on hierarchies of ethnicity, race, gender, origin and legal status (Ness 2005). While these changes are not *caused* by migration, migration is a *crucial component*. The USA – like other northern industrial societies – is being transformed by the economic and social consequences of globalisation. In turn, migration arises through global social transformation: it is integral to the transformation of the sending, transit and receiving societies. Non-migration factors are crucial for understanding migration and its consequences, but migration reinforces other changes linked to globalisation.

Linking socio-spatial levels

In order to develop a new approach to understanding transformation-migration relationships, it is possible to draw upon emerging ideas from a range of disciplines. As previously discussed, since the macro-level forces of global change are generally experienced at the micro- or local level, it is essential to adopt theories and methodologies that make it possible to understand the relationships between socio-spatial levels, and the dialectics of structure and agency.

double movement

At the macro-level, critical approaches in economics are a useful starting point. Stiglitz provides a critique of neo-liberal economic globalisation, derived from Polanyi's concept of transformation (Stiglitz 1998, 2002). For him, 'double movement' is represented by anti-globalisation activism (see Stiglitz's foreword to Polanyi 2001). Milanovic shows that the neo-liberal claim of improving economic outcomes for poor countries has masked a vast increase in inequality (Milanovic 2007). In political economy, the neo-liberal model is criticised as a new utopia for a self-regulating world economy (Freeman and Kagarlitsky 2004; Petras and Veltmayer 2000; Weiss 1998). While such ideas echo Polanyi's critique of attempts to disembed the economy from society, they remain essentially top-down critiques, which fail to analyse the local effects of global economic and political forces. In order to overcome this problem, it is necessary to apply the concepts and methodologies suggested by sociologists, geographers and anthropologists.

The International Sociological Association (ISA) Research Committee on 'Social Transformation and Sociology of Development' (Schuerkens 2004) uses the concept of 'glocalisation' to analyse links between global forces and local experiences, and has applied this approach to the study of migration and ethnicity (Berking 2003; Binder and Tosic 2005; Schuerkens 2005). Other sociologists show how movements to preserve cultural identity arise in reaction to globalisation (Castells 1997). Social geographers have developed new ways of understanding the changing meaning of 'territory' and the relationships between spatial levels (Lussault 2007; Sassen 2006). Social anthropology has moved away from older ideals of authenticity and singularity to study individual and group reactions to globalising forces (Levitt and Glick Schiller 2004). This implies analysing 'a simultaneous dialectic of indigenisation [...] and cosmopolitanisation' (Friedman 2004). Concepts and methods of ethnographic work on globally-dispersed communities are discussed by Hage (2005), while Hogan (2004) and Wise and Velayutham (2008) represent recent examples of studies on local mediation of global change.

new economics of labour migration

Such trends in social theory have already had considerable influence on migration studies. As already mentioned, economists have become increasingly critical of the emphasis on individual rational choice within neoclassical theory, and are investigating the role of families, communities and other social actors in migratory processes. The 'new economics of labour migration' may maintain assumptions about economic rationality, but seeks to overcome the methodological individualism of the neoclassical approach by using qualitative studies and household surveys to understand the complexity of migration decisions and their relationship to other factors (Stark 1991; Taylor 1999). In political economy a new approach designed to correct the traditional top-down macro bias uses 'relational political economy' to study livelihoods and commodity chains in conflict areas, and to explore their connections with national and global economies (Collinson 2003).

The dialectics of structure and agency

One of the most widely accepted innovations in migration theory since the 1980s has been the adoption of network theories, which focus on the collective agency of migrants and communities in organising processes of migration and incorporation (Boyd 1989; Portes and Bach 1985).[3] Informal networks provide vital resources for individuals and groups in easing the move to a new country, for instance, by providing help with work, housing and other needs on arrival. This applies not only to economic migrants, but also to refugees and asylum seekers, whose choice of route and destination is strongly influenced by existing connections (Koser 1997). Networks also provide resources for adaptation and community formation. Migrant groups develop their own social and economic infrastructure, such as places of worship, associations, shops, cafés, lawyers and doctors. In the context of the sending countries, informal networks are often analysed as being transmission mechanisms for *cultural capital*, such as knowledge about opportunities in potential destination countries and information on travel routes. In the context of migrant incorporation into receiving societies, the emphasis is more on *social capital* (Bourdieu and Wacquant 1992: 119), which includes personal relationships, family and household patterns, friendship and community ties and mutual help in economic and social matters.

migrant agency

Informal networks, cultural capital and social capital are all expressions of *migrant agency*: migrants are not simply isolated individuals who react to market stimuli and bureaucratic rules, but social beings who seek to achieve better outcomes for themselves, their families and their communities by actively shaping the migratory process. Migratory movements, once started, become self-sustaining social processes with their own inner dynamics, or as Massey et al. explains, migration is shaped by processes of *cumulative causation* (Massey et al. 1998: 45-50). It is vital to add this sociological and anthropological insight to the structural and institutional models provided by economists, political scientists and legal specialists. The social dynamics of migratory processes take a variety of forms, each of which is relevant to understanding the dialectics of structure and agency. Following are a few examples.

family and community

The family and community are crucial to migration. Research on Asian migration has shown that migration decisions are usually made not by individuals but by families. In situations of rapid change, a family may decide to send one or more of its members to work in another region or country, in order to maximise income and chances of survival (Hugo 1994). Family linkages often provide both the financial and the cultural capital (the knowledge of opportunities and means of mobility), which make migration possible.

life-cycle

Position within the life-cycle. In economic migration, the primary migrant is usually a young man or woman in search of temporary work, often intending to return home once certain savings targets have been reached. The difficulty in achieving such targets leads to a prolonged stay, which in turn encourages family reunion. People start to see their life from the perspective of their experiences in the new country. This process is particularly linked to the situation of migrants' children: once they go to school in the new country, learn the language, form peer group relationships and develop bicultural or transcultural identities, it becomes increasingly difficult for the parents to return to their homelands.

migration industry

The migration industry is a development of migration networks. Once a migration gets under way, needs arise for a variety of special services. The migration industry includes travel agents, lawyers, bankers, labour recruiters, brokers, interpreters and housing agents. The agents have an interest in migration continuing, and may go on organising it even when governments try to restrict movements, though the form may change (for example, from legal worker recruitment to asylum migration or undocumented entry). Facilitating migration is a major, and largely legal, international business (Salt and Clarke 2000: 327). Recently, governments have drawn attention to the illegal side of the migration industry – human smuggling and trafficking – and have attempted to control it through international legal and law enforcement measures.

opportunity structures

Policies as opportunity structures. People lucky enough to enjoy a middle-class position in developed countries tend to have a fairly positive view of the state and the law. This does not necessarily apply to the majority of the world's population, who live in inefficient, corrupt and violent states. Most people have to learn to endure *despite* the state, not because of it. From this perspective, migration rules become just another barrier to be overcome in order to survive. Potential migrants do not cancel migration just because the receiving state says they are not welcome – especially if the labour market tells a different story. Policies become opportunity structures to be compared and negotiated.

transnational communities

Transnational communities. Globalisation leads to changes in the way immigrants are incorporated into society. In the past, most migrants were treated either as permanent settlers, who were to be assimilated, or as temporary sojourners, who were to be kept separate from the host population through special (and often discriminatory) legal regimes. The experience of community formation and ethnic mobilisation led to the rise of a third approach in the 1970s – multiculturalism. But all these approaches were premised on the idea that people would focus their social existence on just one society at a time, and would therefore owe their allegiance to just one nation-state. The new ease of movement and improvement in communication has made it possible for many people to live their lives across borders. Transnational communities may be defined as groups based in two or more countries, which engage in recurrent, enduring and significant cross-border activities, which may be economic, political, social or cultural (Portes et al. 1999). If mobility across borders is a part of a group's economic, social, cultural and political life, this provides a powerful motivation to overcome state-imposed barriers.

Conclusion

implications

Adopting a social transformation framework for the study of migration has implications for the work of researchers. A social transformation approach excludes the possibility of having a unique body of migration theory separate from more general theories of contemporary society and social change. As part of broader social theory, migration is understood not as a *result* of social transformation or as a *consequence* of it, but as *an integral part of the social transformation processes* that affect all societies in the context of accelerated globalisation. This approach requires migration researchers to contextualise migration studies within an understanding of broader processes. Equally, it requires other social scientists to pay due attention to human mobility in their research and theory formation. An awareness of the place of migration in social transformation leads to a requirement for interdisciplinarity. Migration, as a process that affects all dimensions of human existence, cannot be understood through a mono-disciplinary lens. However, this applies to other processes of social change as well.

methodology

As for *methodology* – understood here not as specific techniques of investigation but as the underlying epistemological principles of research and analysis – a social transformation approach means going beyond simple accumulation of data through a proliferation of empirical studies. Research needs to be guided by new questions and approaches, based on a broad theoretical understanding. Moreover, it should use methods of information collection that correct exclusionary practices based on class, gender and race. Top-down approaches tend to focus on the experiences of powerful institutions and privileged groups at both the global and local levels. They may be blind to the actual situations of disempowered groups. Research concerned with sustainability, equality and human rights requires approaches that are sensitive to the needs, interests and values of all groups involved in processes of change. Such methods – known as *participatory approaches* – imply reduced reliance on official data sets and standard questionnaires in favour of techniques that allow disadvantaged groups to help define the issues and take closer part in research processes (Chambers 1997).

organisation of research

A social transformation approach to migration studies has implications for the *organisation of the research process*. The theoretical principles mentioned above imply the need for interdisciplinary research teams. Additionally, migration research should be seen as a joint venture of scholars from the areas of migrant origin, transit and destination. International networks of researchers could help to overcome the nationalist and colonialist legacy of the social sciences. Instead of Northern social scientists conducting studies of Southern peoples, research would become a collaborative process of equals. Researchers from each country would apply their understanding of local social structures and cultural practices to migration studies. Western values and methods would cease to be the yardstick and instead become approaches for study and critique.

the research–policy relationship

A social transformation approach requires redefining the *research–policy relationship*. Much social scientific research is *policy-relevant*. That is, it provides knowledge necessary to help meet social goals. But all too often, social research is *policy-driven*: its research themes and questions (and sometimes even its findings) are dictated by the short-term policy aims of governments and bureaucracies, which also control funding. Migration studies have been particularly affected by these problems. But research is not a politically neutral activity, and researchers can make conscious choices about goals. We all need funding for our research, but we can limit our participation in bureaucratic exercises. There is nothing wrong in helping to improve the evidence base for government policies. However, research must also insist on providing information and analysis to organisations that support exploited or disadvantaged groups. Working with migrants and their associations, as well as with civil society organisations, could be an important counterweight to the power of policymakers and funding bodies.

All this may sound ambitious and difficult for migration scholars (especially those early in their careers). It is understandable that scholars may wish to simply explore a specific migratory situation or to understand the decision-making processes of a particular group. Yet a social transformation approach does *not* mean that every piece of research must analyse global processes and look at the dynamics of mediation between the various socio-spatial levels. It does mean that every researcher, however specific the research topic, should be *aware* of the wider change processes in which study topics are embedded. They should understand the importance of diversity, complexity and context on any research subject. A social transformation framework provides a different analytical lens, one that can help overcome fragmentation and isolation in migration studies. It thus provides a way to incorporate the growing number of empirical studies of migration into a much better understanding of migratory processes and their place in contemporary social change.

MAIN IDEAS

A social transformation approach excludes the possibility of having a unique body of migration theory, separate from more general theories of contemporary society and social change.

Migration, as a process that affects all dimensions of human existence, cannot be understood through a mono-disciplinary lens.

Top-down approaches tend to focus on the experiences of powerful institutions and privileged groups at both the global and local levels; they may be blind to the realities of disempowered groups.

Research concerned with sustainability, equality and human rights requires approaches that are sensitive to the needs, interests and values of all groups involved in change processes.

There is nothing wrong in helping to improve the evidence base for government policies, but we can also insist on providing information and analyses to organisations that support exploited and disadvantaged groups.

Notes

1 The themes of this and the next section are dealt with in more detail in Castles and Miller 2009, chapters 2 and 3.

2 Sociologist Robert K. Merton has elaborated upon the concept of 'theories of the middle-range'. These are 'special theories applicable to limited ranges of data – theories for example of class dynamics, of conflicting group pressures, of the flow of power and the exercise of interpersonal influence...' (Merton 1957: 9). Merton saw middle-range theories as more realistic and useful than attempts (such as those of Talcott Parsons) to put forward general theories of social action or of society (see Portes 1999).

3 In fact, network theories were suggested much earlier by theories of chain migration (Price 1963).

References

Albrow, M. (1996), *The Global Age*. Cambridge: Polity.

Arango, J. (2000), 'Explaining migration: A critical view', *International Social Science Journal* 165: 283-296.

Bauman, Z. (1998), *Globalization: The Human Consequences*. Cambridge: Polity.

Beck, U. (1997), *Was ist Globalisierung?* Frankfurt: Suhrkamp.

Beck, U. (2007), 'Beyond class and nation: Reframing social inequalities in a globalizing world', *British Journal of Sociology* 58 (4): 679-705.

Berking, H. (2003), '"Ethnicity is everywhere": On globalization and the transformation of cultural identity', *Current Sociology* 51 (3-4): 248-64.

Binder, S. and J. Tosic (2005), 'Refugees as a particular form of transnational migrations and social transformations: Socioanthropological and gender aspects', *Current Sociology* 53 (4): 607-624.

Block, F. and K. Polanyi (2003), 'Karl Polanyi and the writing of "The Great Transformation"', *Theory and Society* 32 (3): 275-306.

Bourdieu, P. and L. Wacquant (1992), *An Invitation to Reflexive Sociology.* Chicago: University of Chicago Press.

Boyd, M. (1989), 'Family and personal networks in migration', *International Migration Review* 23 (3): 638-70.

Brettell, C.B. and J.F. Hollifield (eds) (2007), *Migration Theory: Talking Across Disciplines.* 2nd ed. New York/London: Routledge.

Castells, M. (1996), *The Rise of the Network Society.* Oxford: Blackwell.

Castells, M. (1997), *The Power of Identity.* Oxford: Blackwell.

Castells, M. (1998), *End of Millenium.* Oxford: Blackwell.

Castles, S. (2000), 'Thirty years of research on migration and multicultural societies', in: S. Castles (ed.), *Globalization and Ethnicity: From Migrant Worker to Transnational Citizen*, 1-25. London: Sage.

Castles, S. (2007), 'Twenty-first century migration as a challenge to sociology', *Journal of Ethnic and Migration Studies* 33.

Castles, S. and M.J. Miller (2009), *The Age of Migration: International Population Movements in the Modern World.* 4th ed. Basingstoke/New York: Palgrave-Macmillan and Guilford.

Chambers, R. (1997), *Whose Reality Counts? Putting the First Last.* London: Intermediate Technology Publications.

Collinson, S. (2009), 'The Political Economy of Migration Processes: An Agenda for Migration Research and Analysis', IMI Working Papers IMI Working Papers 12-2009, Oxford: International Migration Institute, Oxford University. http://www.imi.ox.ac.uk/publications/working_papers.

Collinson, S. (ed.) (2003), 'Power, livelihoods and conflict: Case studies in political economy analysis for humanitarian action', Humanitarian Policy Group Report 13. London: Overseas Development Institute.

Connell, R.W. (1997), 'Why is classical theory classical?' *American Journal of Sociology* 102 (6): 1511-57.

Duffield, M. (2001), *Global Governance and the New Wars: The Merging of Development and Security.* London/New York: Zed Books.

Faist, T. (2000), *The Volume and Dynamics of International Migration and Transnational Social Spaces.* Oxford: Oxford University Press.

Freeman, A. and B. Kagarlitsky (eds) (2004), *The Politics of Empire: Globalisation in Crisis.* London/Ann Arbor: Pluto Press.

Friedman, J. (2004), 'Globalization, transnationalization and migration: Ideologies and realities of global transformation' in: J. Friedman and S. Randeria (eds), *Worlds on the Move: Globalization, Migration and Cultural Security* 63-88. London/New York: I.B. Tauris.

GCIM (2005), '*Migration in an Interconnected World: New Directions for Action*', report of the Global Commission on International Migration. Geneva. http://www.gcim.org/en/finalreport.html.

Gold, S.J. (2005), 'Migrant networks: A summary and critique of relational approaches to international migration', in: M. Romero and E. Margolis (eds), *The Blackwell Companion to Social Inequalities*. Malden: Blackwells.

Hage, G. (2005), 'A not so multi-sited ethnography of a not so imagined community', *Anthropological Theory* 5 (4): 463-75.

Held, D., A. McGrew, D. Goldblatt and J. Perraton (1999), *Global Transformations: Politics, Economics and Culture*. Cambridge: Polity.

Hogan, J. (2004), 'Constructing the global in two rural communities in Australia and Japan', *Journal of Sociology* 40 (1): 21-40.

Hugo, G. (1994), 'Migration and the Family', Occasional Papers Series for the International Year of the Family, no. 12. Vienna: United Nations.

King, R. (2002), 'Towards a new map of European migration', *International Journal of Population Geography* 8 (2): 89-106.

Koser, K. (1997), 'Social networks and the asylum cycle: The case of Iranians in the Netherlands', *International Migration Review* 31 (3): 591-611.

Levitt, P. and N. Glick Schiller (2004), 'Conceptualising simultaneity: A transnational social field perspective on society', *International Migration Review* 38 (3): 1002-39.

Lussault, M. (2007), *L'Homme spatiale: La Construction sociale de l'être humain*. Paris: Seuil.

Massey, D.S., J. Arango, G. Hugo, A. Kouaouci, A. Pellegrino and J.E. Taylor (1998), *Worlds in Motion, Understanding International Migration at the End of the Millenium*. Oxford: Clarendon Press.

Merton, R.K. (1957), *Social Theory and Social Structure*. Glencoe: Free Press.

Milanovic, B. (2007), 'Globalization and inequality', in: D. Held and A. Kaya (eds), *Global Inequality: Patterns and Explanations*. Cambridge/Malden: Polity.

Mohapatra, S., D. Ratha and A. Silwal (2011), *Outlook for Remittance Flows 2012-14* Migration and Remittances Unit Migration and Development Brief. Washington, DC: World Bank. http://siteresources.worldbank.org/INTPROSPECTS/Resources/334934-1110315015165/MigrationandDevelopmentBrief17.pdf.

Ness, I. (2005), *Immigrants, Unions and the New US Labor Market*. Philadelphia: Temple University Press.

New Internationalist (2006), 'Urban explosion: The facts', *New Internationalist* 386: 18-19.

Noiriel, G. (1988), *Le creuset français: Histoire de l'immigration XIXe-XXe siècles*. Paris: Seuil.

OECD (2011), *International Migration Outlook: SOPEMI 2011*. Paris: Organisation for Economic Co-operation and Development.

Ohmae, K. (1995), *The End of the Nation-State: The Rise of Regional Economies*. New York: Harper Collins.

Oxfam (2002), *Rigged Rules and Double Standards: Trade, Globalisation, and the Fight Against Poverty*. Oxford: Oxfam.

Park, R.E. (1950), *Race and Culture*. Glencoe: The Free Press.

Passel, J.S. and D.V. Cohn (2011), *Unauthorized Immigrant Population: National and State Trends 2010*. Washington, DC: Pew Hispanic Center.

Petras, J. and H. Veltmayer (2000) 'Globalisation or imperialism?', *Cambridge Review of International Affairs* 14 (1): 1-15.

Phillips, N. (2011), 'Migration and the global economic crisis' in: N. Phillips (ed.), *Migration in the Global Political Economy*. Boulder: Lynne Rienner.

Polanyi, K. (2001), *The Great Transformation*. Boston: Beacon Press.

Portes, A. (1997), 'Immigration theory for a new century: Some problems and opportunities', *International Migration Review* 31 (4): 799-825.

Portes, A. (1999), 'The hidden abode: Sociology as analysis of the unexpected', Presidential Address to the American Sociological Association. *American Sociological Review* 651-718.

Portes, A. and R.L. Bach (1985), *Latin Journey: Cuban and Mexican Immigrants in the United States*. Berkeley: University of California Press.

Portes, A. and J. DeWind (eds) (2004), 'Conceptual and Methodological Developments in the Study of International Migration', *International Migration Review: Special Issue* 38 (3).

Portes, A., L.E. Guarnizo and P. Landolt (1999), 'The study of transnationalism: Pitfalls and promise of an emergent research field', *Ethnic and Racial Studies* 22 (2): 217-237.

Price, C. (1963), *Southern Europeans in Australia*. Melbourne: Oxford University Press.

Pries, L. (2007), *Die Transnationalisierung der sozialen Welt*. Frankfurt am Main: Suhrkamp.

Salt, J. and J. Clarke (2000), 'International migration in the UNECE region: Patterns, trends, policies', *International Social Science Journal* 165: 313-28.

Sassen, S. (2006), *Territory, Authority, Rights: From Medieval to Global Assemblages*. Princeton: Princeton University Press.

Saul, J.R. (2006), *The Collapse of Globalism and the Reinvention of the World*. London: Atlantic Books.

Schierup, C.-U., P. Hansen and S. Castles (2006), *Migration, Citizenship and the European Welfare State: A European Dilemma*. Oxford: Oxford University Press.

Schuerkens, U. (2005), 'Transnational migrations and social transformations: A theoretical perspective', *Current Sociology* 53 (4) 535-553.

Schuerkens, U. (ed.) (2004), *Global Forces and Local Life-Worlds: Social Transformations*. Thousand Oaks: Sage.

Stark, O. (1991), *The Migration of Labour*. Oxford: Blackwell.

Stiglitz, J.E. (1998), 'Towards a new paradigm for development: Strategies, policies and processes', Prebisch Lecture. Geneva: UNCTAD.

Stiglitz, J.E. (2002), *Globalization and its Discontents*. London: Penguin.

Taylor, J.E. (1999), 'The new economics of labour migration and the role of remittances in the migration process', *International Migration* 37 (1): 63-88.

Weiss, L. (1998), *The Myth of the Powerless State: Governing the Economy in a Global Era*. Cambridge: Polity Press.

Wieviorka, M. (1994), 'Introduction', in: M. Wieviorka, P. Bataille, K. Couper, D. Martuccelli, and A. Peralva (eds), *Racisme et Xénophobie en Europe: Une Comparaison Internationale*, 7-25. Paris: La Découverte.

Wimmer, A. and N. Glick Schiller (2003), 'Methodological nationalism, the social sciences and the study of migration', *International Migration Review* 37 (3): 576-610.

Wise, A. and S. Velayutham (2008), 'Second-generation Tamils and cross-cultural marriage: Managing the translocal village in a moment of cultural rupture', *Journal of Ethnic and Migration Studies* 34 (1): 113-31.

Part II

Types of Migration

8 Guest Worker Migration in Post-War Europe (1946-1974): An Analytical Appraisal

Ahmet Akgündüz

Introduction

This chapter examines the migration of labourers in post-war Europe, both officially recruited labourers and those who arrived on their own. Following the Second World War, Western European countries began the reconstruction of their economies. For sectors where labour was in short supply, they recruited foreign workers from Southern Europe, primarily Italians. However, what began as recruitment on a small scale soon burgeoned into a new international labour migration that would last more than a quarter of a century. With some shrinkage in times of recession, this movement grew consistently in volume and came to include labourers from North Africa and, for the first time, Turkey as well. By the time recruitment ended in 1973-1974, more than 5.7 million migrant workers were employed in seven countries alone: Austria, Belgium, France, Germany, the Netherlands, Sweden and Switzerland (Lohrmann 1976: 230-232; Böhning 1979: 401; Werner 1986: 544). Estimates suggest that between 1945 and 1974, the number of foreign workers and their dependants who entered Western Europe was 'something like 30 million' (Castles 1984: 1), returnees included. This was one of the largest movements of its kind in modern history, contributing to irrevocable changes in the ethnic, cultural and religious composition of Western European populations. *migrant labour*

This chapter first considers the historical background of guest worker migration in Europe and the context within which it was resumed in the aftermath of the Second World War. It then looks at receiving countries' policies for the recruitment of foreign labour. Why and how did the labour supply from Southern Europe become insufficient in relation to demand from the North? Why was recruitment extended to Turkey and to North African countries such as Morocco, Algeria and Tunisia? The chapter also addresses the major components of the guest worker system and its limits. Finally, it examines demand-supply relations in the labour market of each of the receiving countries and sectors of employment for migrant workers, critically evaluating some assessments of prior studies.

Historical background and the period up to 1960

The Western European practice of recruiting large numbers of foreign workers did not begin with post-war guest worker migrations. From the 1880s, the core countries, especially England, France, Germany (from the 1890s onwards) and Switzerland, employed foreign labourers in substantial numbers, particularly from their immediate peripheries, such as colonial Ireland and Central, Eastern and Southern Europe (Hoerder 1996, 2000; Olsson 1996).[1] For example, as early as 1886 in France, the number of foreign residents was more than 1.1 million, reflecting mainly migrant workers and their family members (Cross 1977: 10, 22, 24). Germany hosted some 1.3 million foreigners in 1910 (Herbert 1990: 20-23), and a considerable proportion of them were Poles recruited in the eastern parts of the German domain, Russian Poland and Austria-Hungary. In Switzerland, migrants made up 14.7 per cent of the population by the same year (Power 1979: 12).

In the early twentieth century, the major receiving countries such as France and Germany became dependent on the import of labour, as well as Austria-Hungary, to a varying extent; Denmark, Russia, the Netherlands and Sweden needed to recruit migrant workers, particularly seasonal ones. Other buyers of labour on the European labour market included the newly emerged industrial cities in labour-exporting areas, like Budapest and Lodz (Hoerder 2000), as well as European companies in the Ottoman Balkans and Anatolia (Quataert 1983: 72-93; Adanır 1994: 31; Akgündüz 2008: 13). Furthermore, in the early twentieth century, the Americas – particularly the United States – attracted migrants mainly from Central, Eastern and Southern Europe, because the number of arrivals from Northern and Western Europe had diminished considerably (Hourwich 1912; Hoerder 1985, 1996, 2000; Moch 1992; Olsson 1996; Bade 1997).[2] As a result, the leading European labour importers were in competition with each other for migrant labour (Cross 1977: 28-31; Herbert 1990: 93; Olsson 1996). Olsson argues that bilateral and multilateral relations among major European states during the years preceding the First World War were heavily affected by their need for foreign labour. Accordingly, the emergence of international competition for migrant labour is a crucial factor in understanding France's conflict with Germany, the rising tension between Germans and Poles and Austria's annexation of Bosnia-Herzegovina. Olsson suggests that in the war, 'Germany sought to fortify its position in Europe [...] primarily as a buyer of labour on the international labour market' (Olsson 1996: 897).

before the end of the Second World War

Having been heavily disrupted, labour migration from the periphery to the core countries of Western Europe recommenced following the end of the First World War. However, there was perceptible variation in the volume of each country's demand for labour. For example, due to economic stagnation, Germany employed relatively few foreign workers until the Nazis took power: 174,000 in 1924 and a mere 108,000 in 1932 (Herbert 1990: 121, 126). During the Nazi regime, the number of foreigners brought to work – often forcibly – soared quickly and dramatically; there were over 7.6 million foreign workers in August 1944. Of that total, 5.7 million were 'registered foreign civilian workers' and more than 1.9 million were prisoners of war (Herbert 1990: 127-181, 1997: 296-299).[3]

France, meanwhile, needed large numbers of foreign workers just after the First World War, and put a prime example of a guest worker system into practice. It signed bilateral labour recruitment agreements with several Southern, Central and Eastern European countries between 1919 and 1930,[4] and brought nearly two million migrants to work through official channels. In principle, nationals of the frontier countries were exempt from official recruitment procedures, and their migrations remained largely spontaneous. Labourers from Belgium, Luxembourg and Switzerland did not even need passports to enter France (Cross 1977: 222). However, when the economic crisis of the early 1930s made guest workers redundant, France sent them back.

Between the two world wars, other relatively small Western European countries, such as Switzerland, the Netherlands and Belgium, in addition to attracting workers from neighbouring countries, continued to admit workers in varying numbers from the countries of Southern, Central and Eastern Europe.[5]

two new migration movements supplying labour

After the Second World War, Western Europe not only resumed the admission of guest workers, but also saw at least two new migration movements that supplied labour. First was the recruitment of prisoners of war and displaced persons as labourers with the option of permanent settlement, which began with the cessation of hostilities in 1945. Britain, for example, by offering both a work contract and the right to permanent settlement, received approximately 217,000 people by December 1950, representing the largest admission in this regard. To specify, some 25,000 prisoners of war who had primarily been employed in agriculture and approximately 115,000 Poles and their dependants, many of whom had been members of the disbanded Polish armed forces, accepted work contracts and settlement offered by the British government at the end of the Second World War. When it became apparent that these admissions were insufficient in relation to labour demand, Britain recruited some 77,000 displaced persons, or 'European volunteer workers as they came to be known', living in refugee camps in the British occupied zones of Germany and Austria between October 1946 and December 1950 (Kay and Miles 1992: 33-35, 42-94).

In varying but significant numbers, Belgium, France and the Netherlands all admitted prisoners of war and displaced persons. Belgium first employed approximately 50,000 German prisoners of war in its coalmines from the end of the war until their release (Groenendijk and Hampsink 1995: 9), and recruited more than 22,000 displaced persons living in refugee camps in Germany (Kay and Miles 1992: 62). France recruited 27,000 displaced persons from its own zone of Germany and some 31,000 Germans (McDonald 1969: 119). The Netherlands recruited some 10,000 displaced persons, of whom 2,000 were former Polish soldiers (Lucassen 2001; Lange 2007: 23).

The more important movement was colonial migration. Before the Second World War, the labour-receiving countries of Western Europe, including colonial ones, had avoided recruiting non-European workers on principle, colonial labourers being brought to work temporarily and only for exceptional cases. For example, when France mobilised more than seven million citizens during the First World War (20 per cent of the total population) (Cross 1977: 42) – further exacerbating pre-war labour shortages – the French government recruited labourers in the colonies of North Africa and Indochina, and Chinese labourers by using commercial labour contractors.[6] However, when the war ended and the situation improved in the labour market, France deported the vast majority of them – by force if necessary – as was the case with North Africans.[7] In 1919, the French authorities 'rejected any further experimentation with non-European labour', and racialised the recruitment of foreign workers by making a list of the nationals they preferred.[8] Nevertheless, during the economic expansion of 1922-1924, 'when French and European immigrants could not be found for the worst jobs', 'the North Africans were hired'; but the bulk of them were again repatriated by 1931 (Cross 1983: 124-125). Similarly, Britain recruited 'several thousand coloured labourers from the colonies' during the First World War due to the acute shortage of labour, and after the war repatriated nearly all of them (Castles and Kosack 1973: 22).

However, after 1945, as a by-product of the decolonisation process, colonial migrations were not only in full swing but also mainly permanent in nature. In Britain, for example, there were 924,200 'coloured immigrants' in 1966 (Freeman 1979: 21).[9] France provided Algerians with free entry until their country became independent in 1962. The 'net balance of admission in France of Algerian migrant workers' was 400,200 between 1947 and 1963 (International Migration Digest 1965: 101), not to mention the number of immigrants who came from the former French protectorates (e.g. Morocco and Tunisia), excolonies in Africa (e.g. Mali, Mauritania and Senegal) and other colonies. The Netherlands admitted 501,736 people from the former colony of Indonesia (and partly from other colonies) between 1946 and 1960 (Nederlandse Emigratiedienst 1965: 120-121). In Germany there was no colonial immigration since the country had no colonies; immigrants were refugees and/or expellees from Eastern Europe and what was then East Germany. Accordingly, Germany received 7.9 million ethnic Germans from Poland, Czechoslovakia, Hungary and the Soviet Union by 1950 (Münz and Ulrich 1998: 27) and some 3.8 million Germans from East Germany before the Berlin Wall was built in 1961 (Fassmann and Münz 1994: 529).

freedom of movement

Another new development that Western Europe saw after the Second World War was the gradual steps being taken in the direction of the free circulation of labourers through bilateral and multilateral agreements.[10] International organisations like the International Labour Organisation (ILO), the Organisation for Economic Co-operation and Development (OECD) and the Council of Europe guided and encouraged this direction from very early on,[11] thus stimulating intra-European migration. More importantly, as part of and parallel to an economic, social and political integration process, the 1957 Treaty of Rome, which was the founding treaty of the European Economic Community (EEC, the forerunner of the EU), gave nationals of the member countries the right to take up employment in any other member state. This right was to develop into complete freedom of movement in 1968, allowing the economies of the member countries to absorb available reserve labourers within the boundaries of the Community more easily than ever.

initial labour recruitment agreements

Belgium, Britain and France were the first to recommence the employment of migrant workers in post-war Europe; each signed a bilateral labour recruitment agreement with Italy in 1946, followed by the Netherlands and Switzerland in 1948. France renewed its earlier agreement in 1951, and Germany concluded a bilateral labour recruitment agreement with Italy in 1955. However, until roughly 1960 – except in the case of France, Switzerland and, to a certain extent, Belgium[12] – the demand for migrant labour, and thus the number of recruited workers, was remarkably modest, if not negligible, in the receiving countries.[13] Italy was the main, if not the only, supply country. Only Belgium signed additional bilateral agreements with Greece and Spain,[14] and France only with Greece.[15]

Apart from France, before 1960, the receiving countries' intention in signing a bilateral labour recruitment agreement with Italy and some other countries, in so far as agreements were made, was both to initiate the entry of a limited number of workers while also restricting them to clearly specified sectors; thus, protecting the domestic labour market against a possible influx of migrants. For example, the Dutch-Italian agreement was a sector-tied one, indicating that a particular number of Italians would be recruited to work only in the coal industry. Similarly, the Belgian-Italian agreement aimed at recruiting workers only for the coalmines, and 'any occupational mobility' outside the 'sector was legally prohibited' (Martiniello 2010: 247). Even France, in the first agreement, insisted that Italians should move to specific regions and occupations (Kubat 1993: 165).

As compared to both colonial immigration and overseas emigration,[16] guest-worker migration was a relatively small movement in post-war Europe until approximately 1960. It was also smaller than intra-Western European labour migration, which was facilitated by the new regulations and political climate. For example, Belgium, Germany and the Netherlands each employed a much higher number of workers from other Western European countries, especially from their adjacent ones, than workers from Southern Europe.

The management of recruitment in years of high labour demand

changes in admission

With the completion of the absorption of prisoners of war, displaced persons and colonial immigrants into employment by the late 1950s, Western European economies entered into a trend of remarkably high and stable growth until late 1973 and early 1974 that was called 'Europe's amazing economic performance', notwithstanding a slight contraction during the recession years of 1967 and 1968. From 1960 on, not only larger economies like Germany and France and relatively smaller countries like Belgium, the Netherlands and Switzerland demanded labour in ever-increasing numbers, but also some new buyers, such as Austria, Sweden and Denmark, queued up to recruit workers from the same sources. As early as 1961, the number of migrant workers, including seasonal ones admitted by six countries (Germany, France, Belgium, the Netherlands, Switzerland and Britain) was 980,500; the following year the figure rose to about 1.1 million (International Migration Digest 1964: 223). Except for the recession years, the annual number of workers entering Western Europe remained remarkably high throughout the period, though migration was not a one-way movement; the annual return rate was also high.

In connection with a sharp increase in the demand for labour, the implementation of the guest worker system showed significant changes after 1960. During this period, the policy began to attract workers as rapidly and in as large numbers as possible from more easily accepted Southern European countries, in terms of both cultural characteristics and political position in relation to the Cold War; that is, Italy, Spain, Greece and Portugal. The demand countries, France and Germany being primary, were in a hurry to continue signing agreements with the

Southern European countries with which they had not yet signed. The countries that already had a restrictive recruitment agreement with Italy replaced the earlier agreements with new ones.[17]

Furthermore, Italian, Greek, Spanish, Portuguese and Yugoslav labourers were also given free access to sectors that were in need of labour.[18] After entering France and other labour-demanding countries on tourist passports, Southern European workers could work and simultaneously or subsequently regularise their status. For example, in 1961, 32 per cent of Italians and 57 per cent of Greeks and Spaniards entered Germany in ways other than through official recruitment (Bendix 1990: 35). Spontaneous migration of workers became an accepted form of recruitment and thus a part of the European guest worker system.[19] By and large, this applied to workers from the second group of official supply countries (Turkey, Morocco and Tunisia and Algeria) until at least the 1967-1968 recession years or even the end of the recruitment period, notwithstanding the existence to a varying degree of curbs on their free entry, especially in the later years. However, due to data limitation, it is difficult to establish whether or not and to what extent spontaneous migrants from the second group of countries received the same treatment as Southern Europeans in the regularisation of their status. For example, unlike the other receiving countries, Germany was against the regularisation of spontaneous Turkish migrants, which was documented in the 1964 German-Turkish protocol (Akgündüz 2008: 120-121).

rationale

After 1960, the rationale behind bilateral labour recruitment also changed; that is, agreements were made if the dimension of labour demand was substantial. As long as the number of spontaneously available migrants from one country was seen as adequate in relation to labour demand, the receiving side, in general, refrained from entering into a labour recruitment agreement with the supply country. For instance, because spontaneous entry of workers from the countries in the Mediterranean basin was sufficient in relation to labour demand, Britain did not make any recruitment agreements with the supply countries. This was the case with the other demand countries as well. Sweden, for example, after receiving limited numbers of Turkish workers through spontaneous entry from the early 1960s on, signed a bilateral labour recruitment agreement with Turkey in 1967, but realising that the volume of labour demand from Turkey would not be large, Sweden did not put the agreement into practice. Thus, just as in the pre-agreement years, Turkish migration to Sweden continued to consist of only those who organised their migration on their own, usually due to personal links with earlier migrants.

Unlike the previous period, after 1960, bilateral recruitment agreements aimed at accelerating and regularising the migration movements already established. This was vividly evident in the case of France's agreement with Spain, Portugal and North African countries, as well as most of Germany's agreements (e.g. with Italy, Spain, Greece, Turkey and Yugoslavia). Germany had already recruited workers from Yugoslavia through unofficial channels in modestly increasing numbers since the late 1950s, and the number of Yugoslav workers employed in 1967 was approximately 91,000. Following the 1968 German-Yugoslav labour recruitment agreement, Germany admitted 508,000 workers through the official channels in just three years' time (1969-1971) (BfA 1974: 114).

inadequate supply of Southern European labour

A rather unexpected development that each of the industrialised Western European states experienced in the early 1960s was the inadequacy of the volume of supply from Southern Europe that required them to look beyond Southern Europe for labourers (McDonald 1969: 117; Castles 1984: 13; Miles 1987: 142-152). For example, France, unlike other Western European states, explicitly recognised immigration as being vital to secure economic and demographic recovery at the end of the war and set up an administrative structure in 1945, the *Office National d'Immigration* (ONI), to plan and organise the inflow of foreign people (Mayer 1975; Freeman 1979; Miles 1986; Ogden 1991). Government advisors put the minimum number of immigrants required at over 5 million (Freeman 1979: 69-71; Cohen 1987: 125). In the beginning, the intention was to recruit 'assimilable groups' (i.e. so-called 'culturally compatible' Catholic Southern European nationals) for permanent settlement, particularly Italians (McDonald 1969; Ogden 1991; Seifert 1997). Nevertheless, the number of Italians entering France began to decrease drastically from the late 1950s onwards.[20] With the signing of a recruitment agreement with Spain in 1961, the entry of Spanish workers first increased but soon declined, partly due to the emergence of Germany as another strong buyer on the labour market. The total number of Greek workers admitted did not even reach a mentionable figure, in spite of the fact that the French-Greek labour recruitment agreement was signed in the mid-1950s. When immigration from the preferred countries proceeded more slowly than planned during the period from 1945 to the late 1950s, the French authorities put aside the idea of having permanent settlers and placed emphasis on temporary labour recruitment, and implemented *laissez-faire* principles with regard to labour migration until 1968 (Castles 1986; Freeman 1989; Husbands 1991; Ogden 1991). Government spokespersons defended this policy by pointing to the shortage of workers (Freeman 1989: 165).

Germany had the upper hand in the competition with its European contenders and was able to attract quite a high proportion of Italian, Spanish and Greek labourers,[21] notwithstanding the fact that

Switzerland was usually the largest recipient of Italians. Nevertheless, the numbers received were still not sufficient, particularly in view of the trend of a constant increase in labour demand. In the early 1960s, German employers and the Ministry of Labour were concerned with finding proper sources of labour (Bendix 1990: 31-33; Herbert 1990: 210-214),[22] as well as the difficulty of retaining recruited guest workers. In 1963, for instance, 40 per cent of all foreign workers stayed less than a year (Bendix 1990: 31). The situation not only caused additional recruitment costs for employers, but also concern about finding workers. Because Germany experienced no self-initiated colonial labour inflows, and the erection of the Berlin Wall effectively stopped entry from East Germany, the country had to make active and vigorous efforts to recruit foreign workers. Germany put 400 recruitment offices into operation throughout the Mediterranean basin (i.e. in all the countries with which recruitment agreements had been signed) (Bauer et al. 2005: 206) to attract workers, and showed its appreciation for their inflow with ostentatious ceremonies from time to time (Akgündüz 2008: 102-103).

The Netherlands turned to Spanish workers when it became evident that Italians were not coming in sufficient numbers. The initial plan was to exclusively admit unmarried skilled migrants. However, because finding workers with the required characteristics was rather difficult, this plan was soon put aside, and even the first cohort of Spaniards consisted mostly of married unskilled workers; to find skilled workers was exceptional (Tinnemans 1994: 33; Schuster 1999: 170; Akgündüz 2008). As an official document from 1964 reveals, the Netherlands acknowledged the supremacy of strong buyers, particularly Germany, on the labour market of Southern Europe and Turkey, and arranged its recruitment policy accordingly.[23] Belgium had difficulty finding and retaining Southern European labour in the 1960s. When the representatives of the Belgian coal industry approached Turkey to sign a labour recruitment agreement, they honestly told their counterparts that Southern Europeans, namely Italians and Spaniards, were no longer available, and they were ready to accept any able-bodied person who could work in the pits (Akgündüz 2008: 107).

reasons for insufficient supply of Southern European labour

The insufficiency of the labour inflow from Southern Europe was not simply due to an increase in the volume of labour demand. Two other important factors have to be taken into account as well. First, Western European countries had to compete for Southern European workers not only with each other but also with overseas countries. When Western European countries re-entered the international labour market as buyers after the war, overseas countries – especially the USA, Australia and Canada – had already been gravitational centres for Southern Europeans, and were still in need of immigrants. For example, due to the shortage of labour, Canada developed a contract-based migrant worker scheme with the Caribbean region for its fruit and vegetable industry in the mid-1960s (Satzewich 1991: 38). Australia experienced difficulty attracting 'Southern European workers, and many were returning to their homelands. The result was a series of measures to attract and retain migrants', including recruitment in Latin America and 'some relaxation of the White Australia Policy' (Castles 1992: 551). Overseas countries were successful in taking a considerable proportion of the Southern European emigration during the 1960s and 1970s,[24] thanks to the beckoning opportunities they offered and the dynamics of the previously established migration, particularly the role of social networks.

The second important factor was the relatively high economic performance and gradual dissipation of labour reserves in Southern European countries. Although several earlier studies in the description of push factors on guest worker migration in post-war Europe characterised the sending countries as having 'widespread unemployment and slow economic growth' (Salt 1976: 83); 'unemployment', 'slow pace of economic development', 'the disparity between population and economic growth' (Salt and Clout 1976: 127-128); and 'unemployment, poverty, and underdevelopment' (Castles and Kosack 1973: 28), the actual situation was rather different, as OECD data indicates. With the exception of Yugoslavia, most Southern European countries were in fact in the process of impressive economic growth[25] (notwithstanding the existence of unemployment, underemployment and various economic hardships for the labouring population as well as the rural and urban lower middle classes). This growth was particularly visible in the case of Italy. In the late 1950s, the Italian economy was beginning to boom, 'and it was not unknown for a trainload of southern emigrants, bound for France or Germany, to be "stolen" at Milan by labour-short Piedmontese industries' (McDonald 1969: 120).

Also, Southern European countries experienced such remarkably high emigration rates, both in absolute and proportional terms, that from the late 1960s, on their capacities to release labour became limited, and some of them even began to suffer labour shortages. Mayer (1965: 13), in referring to the Italian Statistical Institute, states that the number of Italians who went abroad was more than 4.6 million during the 1946-1961 period alone. He adds that 'these statistics underestimate the number of persons migrating to European countries'. However, according to Del Boca and Venturini (2003), the number of people who emigrated from Italy between 1946 and 1965 was 3.6 million. Greece observed the emigration of some 1.2 million people from 1955 to 1973 (Lianos 1975: 120), and the number of Spaniards who moved to Western Europe between 1956 and 1971 was estimated at about 1,500,000; this did not include the seasonal migrant workers who were mostly under 21 or over 40, of peasant origin and who travelled to France each year to work in the grape and beet harvests (Del Campo 1979: 158-159). The actual figure was likely to be even higher, since the official Spanish data for emigration 'are widely agreed to underrepresent the level of migration' (Bover and Velilla 2005: 391). Given that in 1970 Spain had an economically active population of 12.7 million (Paine 1974: 59), this rate of migration was quite significant. Portugal saw the departure of more than two million people between 1945 and 1974, constituting nearly a quarter of the total population, excluding its colonies in Africa (Cohen 1987: 114). In the period 1965-1974 alone, 1,218,000 people went abroad; of these, 63 per cent headed to France (Baganha et al. 2005: 420). Yugoslavia, following the government's legalisation of labour migration abroad, acquired the second highest emigration rate in Europe, after Portugal (Schierup 1990: 106-109).

Due to its high level of emigration, by 1973 Greece had imported 20,000 foreign workers, mostly from North Africa (Paine 1974: 59), and tried to recall some of its workers from Germany. Yugoslavia lost more than 10 per cent of its population of 20- to 30-year-olds and as much as 34 per cent of its skilled and highly skilled metalworkers by the beginning of 1971 (Schierup 1990: 106-109). The emigration of skilled workers became such a great problem for the Yugoslav economy (Baucic 1972; Kayser 1972; Schierup 1990) that in 1972, the government introduced legislation to restrict emigration of the highly trained (Booth 1992: 118).

alternative sources of labour supply

Where could the countries in need of labour go to recruit more workers?[26] A drastic shrinkage in the geography of labour supply in Europe following the end of the Second World War began to be felt by the late 1950s. Central and Eastern European countries – which had been important sources of labour supply to Western Europe, especially to Germany and France, as well as to the USA – were now under socialist regimes that effectively banned labour migration to the West due to the political-ideological significance of their being what they called 'a regime of proletariat and labouring population'. The only exception was a small trickle of refugees, particularly after the suppression of the 1956 uprising in Hungary and the 1968 Prague Spring in Czechoslovakia. With the exception of Yugoslavia, the socialist countries of the Balkans also banned emigration.[27] (The former Soviet Union had already started to do the same in the early 1920s, when the Bolsheviks consolidated their grip on power.) Likewise, China, which had been another major supply country of international labour migration from the mid-nineteenth century onward (Zolberg 1997), stopped releasing labour as a result of the 1949 revolution.

This new situation in post-war Europe, and the fact that the management of the guest worker system necessarily required a relative geographical proximity to sources of labour supply, caused those countries realising that the inflow of Southern European labour was insufficient to turn to a second group of countries: Algeria, Morocco, Tunisia, Turkey and Yugoslavia. There were no other alternatives within the same geographical range.[28]

Table 8.1 *Number of foreign workers (excluding undocumented ones) in selected countries (in thousands)*

Year	*Austria*	*Belgium*	*Germany*	*France*	*Netherlands*	*Sweden*	*Switzerland*
1960	*	169.7	458.7	1,092.7	46.5	94.5	424.0
1970	*	246.7	1,870.1	1,268.3	134.3	176.2	657.1
1974	218.0	278.0	2,360.0	1,900.0**	193.4	200.0	593.0

Source: Werner 1986; *no figure is given; ** for 1973

Yugoslav labourers

Yugoslavia was in the second group of sending countries only due to the timing of its official recruitment agreements, and for political-ideological reasons. Yugoslav labourers had already been employed in Western Europe from the late nineteenth century onward, but between the end of the Second World War and the early 1960s their presence was not in as high numbers as it may have been and not under the coverage of bilateral agreements. An important reason for this was that for a long time Yugoslavia, as a socialist country, found it difficult to approve and regulate the economic migration of labourers to capitalist countries, since it could be viewed as a failure of its responsibilities towards its people. However, in 1961, the Yugoslav government 'eased its restrictions on migrants working abroad' (Shonick 2009) by liberalising its policy of issuing passports, and became more open to signing labour recruitment agreements. On the other hand, the receiving countries could have their own reasons for being hesitant to make an official agreement with Yugoslavia. For example, West Germany long saw Yugoslavia's official relations with East Germany as an obstacle to concluding a bilateral recruitment agreement (Shonick 2009). The change in West Germany's stance made an agreement between the two countries possible in 1968.

North African (Algerian, Moroccan and Tunisian) labourers had been a permanent part of the French labour force even before the Second World War ended; however, the labour markets of the other demand countries were not yet familiar with them. Turkey, among all the labour-sending countries of the post-war period, was the only one that would be participating in migration to Western Europe for the first time.

Southern Europeans first

With the necessary extension of bilateral labour recruitment agreements to the second group of countries, the admission policy of Western Europe transformed from 'Southern Europeans only' into 'Southern Europeans first'. For the most part, the recruitment of workers from the second group of countries took place to the extent that the first group (Italy, Greece, Spain and Portugal) failed to meet demand. Following the removal of restrictions on Yugoslav labour migration, Yugoslavia also became a part of the first group.

The treatment of Turkey as a member of the second group was not what the rulers of Turkey wanted, as the country wished to be seen as having the same economic system, defence system and political values as the West. One of the arguments that Turkey employed to justify sending workers to Western Europe in the early 1960s was to advance the integration of the country into the European political and economic community. What is more, the founders of the Republic of Turkey ideologically represented the West as the model and ideal to aim for in development. Turkey was a founding member of the Council of Europe, a member of NATO, the IMF and the OECD, and in 1963 an associate of the EEC.

North African workers

France had the highest number of North African workers; however, Algerians were only the third largest foreign group there in the 1962 and 1968 censuses, after Italians and Spaniards. In 1968, the number of Algerians, Moroccans and Tunisians in France combined was less than half that of Italians, Spaniards and Portuguese combined (Brenner 1979: 47). The number of Algerian workers in other labour-receiving countries, including Belgium (which, except France, was the only country that had signed a recruitment agreement with Algeria), was very small, if not negligible. In the early 1970s, Italians were in first place by a large margin as being the largest foreign labour contingent in Belgium, followed by Spaniards and Moroccans. Moroccans were in third place in the Netherlands as well by the end of 1972, after Spaniards and Turks. In Germany, the number of workers from Morocco and Tunisia combined constituted only a small fraction of the foreign labour contingent, despite earlier recruitment agreements with these countries.

Turkish labour

Turkish workers' migration to Germany and their eventual presence there as the largest foreign labour contingent were often ascribed in the relevant literature to Germany's preferential treatment of Turks due to foreign policy reasons and historical ties between the two countries. Portes, for example, places the Turkish labour migration to Germany in the same category as the post-war colonial migration to the former colonial or dominant countries, claiming that between Germany and Turkey 'there is a history of client relations and geopolitical collaboration dating at least to World War I'. In this case, 'the dominant power not only finds it easier to recruit labour within its sphere of influence, but also acquires certain obligations toward this dependent population' (Portes 2000: 160-161). However, this characterisation of the labour migration from Turkey to Germany may not be entirely accurate. As available evidence indicates, neither did Germany give Turks preferential treatment for foreign policy reasons, nor is there 'a history of client relations' between the two countries (Akgündüz 2008: 117-126). Germany first refused Turkey's request to sign a bilateral labour recruitment agreement with the argument that 'Turkey is only partly a European country' and that there were several African and Asian countries willing to sign recruitment agreements with Germany. If Germany said 'yes' to Turkey then 'it would be very difficult to say no to these countries. Otherwise they could harm German foreign policy interests by recognising the German Democratic Republic' (Jamin 1998).

However, following the signing of the German-Greek labour recruitment agreement, the Turkish diplomatic mission in Bonn gave a note to the German Ministry of Foreign Affairs on 13 December 1960, stating that if Germany still refused to sign a bilateral agreement with Turkey, Turkey would consider it to be neglecting a NATO member in favour of Greece. The German Ministry of Foreign Affairs responded to the Turkish Embassy in Bonn by indicating that Germany was also willing to sign a labour recruitment agreement with Turkey. The recruitment agreement between the two countries in October 1961 was, at least in terms of the social rights of migrant workers, a 'second class' agreement as contrasted with the kind made with Southern European countries (Akgündüz 2008: 117-123). Although Germany began attracting Turkish labour before the bilateral labour recruitment agreement, and the percentage of skilled Turkish migrants was higher than that of guest workers among other nationals, the volume of Turkish migration to Germany remained limited, and smaller than Greek, Italian or Spanish migration until the end of 1967. The attraction of Turkish workers gained pace just after 1969, when Southern European labour sources largely dried up and Germany's demand for labour enlarged significantly. Between 1969 and 1973, Germany recruited more than 4.4 million workers, though in these years the volume of return migration was also high, at more than 2.3 million workers (Bauer et al. 2005: 201). In addition, according to the German Federal Labour Office (*Bundesanstalt für Arbeit*, BfA), Germany officially recruited more skilled workers from Turkey than it did from Greece, Italy, Portugal and Spain combined. In the last two years of the recruitment period (1972-1973), Turkish workers became the largest foreign labour contingent by a rather small margin, in which a higher return rate among Southern European workers was a factor.[29]

By the end of 1972, Turkish workers were the second largest foreign labour contingent in the Netherlands, after Spaniards, and the fourth largest group in Belgium. Although the Turkish-French labour recruitment agreement was signed in 1965, France only started to actively recruit workers in 1970, coinciding with a relatively rapid rise in registered job vacancies (Table 8.2), though the total number of workers recruited from Turkey by July 1974 constituted only a small fraction of the number of post-war migrants in France. In the other labour-receiving countries (e.g. Denmark, Sweden and Switzerland) the number of Turkish workers was also rather small.

Limits of the guest worker system

migrant contracts

The main components of the recruitment agreements were identical. When a demand country wanted to recruit migrants through its recruitment bureau or representative office in a supply country, it had to submit an application to the supply side. The application had to contain information about the characteristics of the workers requested, their wage, type of work, the place of work, working hours, the place of boarding and boarding expenses, and how much would be paid toward the cost of their return home. The receiving side usually signed a one-year contract with selected candidates before their departure. The contract wages depended upon whether they were recruited, as skilled or unskilled. Migrant workers' wages, as a rule, were to be identical to those for native workers doing the same work. The receiving country handled the transportation of workers to the destination country, and the costs incurred. From the perspective of workers' interests, entering Western Europe through official channels was much better, both in terms of the financial and physical costs of migration.

However, even in this most formal form of recruitment, migrants could be confronted with a breach of the basic principles right from the start. As some cases suggest (Castles and Kosack 1973: 152-175; Eryılmaz 1998; Akgündüz 2008: 64), the contract wage might be lower than that of native workers; employers could put the contracts of skilled workers aside and ask them to sign contracts for unskilled work instead; or the conditions of job and accommodation might be lower than promised. In Germany, for example, the proportion of skilled migrant workers at work was less than that specified during the recruitment by the receiving country itself.[30]

Employers quite often used nominative requests (i.e. demanding specific names given by migrant workers already working) as a form of official recruitment. For migrant workers to be able to organise a nominative request for a family member or a friend at home, the existence of vacancies in their workplace was not enough; they had to at the same time win the confidence of their employers. In this practice, the violation of the rules relating to wages, accommodation and jobs might perhaps be less visible but more frequent. The situation might be the same in the practice of large factories directly recruiting workers on their own. Needless to say, for undocumented migrant workers the likelihood was greater of facing lower wages than that of native workers doing the same work, in addition to enduring substandard working and living conditions.

tacit approval of undocumented workers

The guest worker system included a tacit approval of the employment of undocumented workers. Spontaneous migrants, in principle, could regularise their status after finding a job; however, there were always significant numbers of irregular (also called 'undocumented' or, in the popular term of the early 1970s, 'tourist') workers, though it is difficult to document their exact number per year. This was also valid for France, where an easy and almost free access to the regularisation process for spontaneous migrants existed (Kubat 1993). Germany exhibited quite an interesting example in relation to undocumented Turkish migrant workers. At Turkey's request, during the official visit of the Turkish president to Germany in 1972, the regularisation of undocumented Turkish workers was discussed at the highest level. Although the solution found was rather bureaucratic, and from the perspective of 'tourist' workers risky, according to the Turkish Ministry of Foreign Affairs, only two *länder* – Hessen and Rheiland-Pfalz – abided by the agreement, and some 8,000 'tourist' workers regularised their status, with the consent of their employers. The rest of the *länder* ignored the agreement and refused to do the same (see Akgündüz 2008: 81, 121).

limited legal rights

In terms of basic legal rights on the labour market, migrant workers were separated from native workers and placed in an inferior position. Migrants were not able to sell their labour to the highest bidder. For example, during the initial contract period, employers could fire migrants at any time, but the migrants could not quit without the consent of their employers. Employers enjoyed the freedom of easily hiring and firing migrants. Furthermore, migrant workers were permitted to change occupation only after working some years at their initial jobs (see Castles and Kosack 1973: 98-112, 125-132). These restrictions were underpinned by the regulation of residence and work permits, and the fact that migrants were often unaware of their rights and feared deportation. A similar separation of migrant workers from native ones existed in the area of trade union rights. Migrants were eligible to be members of trade unions, but were not eligible to be candidates for the election of works council or staff representatives, or to take administrative or executive posts in a trade union. In the course of time, however, this situation was modified, as it was in 1972 in France (Brenner 1979: 19). In Germany, some trade unions ignored the law and permitted their migrant members to participate in works council elections much earlier.

Labour market and sectors of employment

Despite a constant inflow of migrant workers and open door policies, for Southern Europeans at least, the situation in the Western European labour market that emerged in the years post-1960 was previously unknown and unique. OECD data permit us to comparatively view demand-supply relations in the labour market of each of the receiving countries (Table 8.2). Somehow a largely ignored fact is that, with the exception of recession years, the number of job vacancies was either higher (e.g. in Germany, Switzerland, Sweden, the Netherlands until 1972 and Austria from 1971 on), or just slightly lower than that of the registered unemployed (e.g. in Belgium, France and Austria before 1971). In the latter case, the number of unemployed was negligible even in absolute terms, putting aside the question of whether or not and to what extent their qualifications met the requirements of demand (Table 8.2).

labour shortages across sectors

As OECD data reveal, migrant workers were attracted not simply to take 'jobs that the native labour force refuses to accept' – as widely held belief or Piore's dual labour market thesis suggests[31] – but as a response to labour shortages. Furthermore, the jobs for which labour shortages existed and thus guest workers were recruited were not only in the secondary sector or in 'agriculture, construction, and mining', as Moch believes.[32] It is true that in the initial years, with the exception of France, in the receiving countries (e.g. Britain, Belgium, Germany, the Netherlands and Switzerland), guest workers were recruited to work mainly in agriculture, mining, construction, and some other jobs (including seasonal ones) that were unattractive to native labourers. However, from roughly 1963 onward the situation was significantly changed. Not only did the demand for migrant workers rise very quickly but also, especially in the leading receiving countries, industry became their main field of employment; agriculture, construction and mining, which were likely to be the most unattractive sectors for the native labour force, embraced only a small proportion of migrants.

It is apparent from the *Bundesanstalt für Arbeit* (BfA) statistics that more than half of migrant workers[33] were recruited to fill jobs in the country's two most important sectors: iron and metal production and processing (*Eisen- und Metallerzeugung und -verarbeitung*); and the

Table 8.2 *Number of registered unemployed and job vacancies in migrant-labour recruiting countries, 1960-1974 (in thousands)*

Year	Austria		Belgium		France		Germany		Netherlands		Sweden		Switzerland	
	a	*b*	*a*	*b*	*a*	*b*	*a*	*b*	*a*	*b*	*a*	*b*	*a*	*b*
1960	83	30	114	8	130	25	271	465	29	92	19	*	1	7
1961	64	38	89	13	111	38	181	552	21	119	17	*	0.6	6
1962	66	38	71	16	98	56	155	574	21	122	19	38	0.6	6
1963	72	37	59	18	97	54	186	555	24	122	20	42	0.8	6
1964	66	40	50	13	98	45	169	609	21	131	17	47	0.3	7
1965	66	42	55	9	132	30	147	649	25	129	17	54	0.3	5
1966	61	46	62	8	142	38	161	540	36	115	22	45	0.3	5
1967	65	32	85	5	192	32	460	302	75	68	29	33	0.3	4
1968	71	28	103	5	255	36	324	488	68	77	33	36	0.3	4
1969	67	34	85	12	223	78	179	747	53	106	30	60	0.2	4
1970	58	45	71	24	262	93	149	795	46	127	30	62	0.1	5
1971	52	56	71	14	337	123	185	648	62	107	45	36	0.1	4
1972	49	62	87	9	380	167	246	546	108	63	48	32	0.1	5
1973	41	66	92	14	394	252	274	572	110	67	45	35	0.1	4
1974	41	58	105	14	498	205	583	315	136	69	39	50	0.2	3

Source: OECD 1970, 1973, 1984, 1993
a: registered unemployed; *b*: jobs vacant; *no figure given

processing industry, iron and metal excluded (*Verarbeitende Gewerbe, ohne Eisen- und Metallverarbeting*) (BfA 1972, 1974a). Thus, more than half of the foreign workers were, in fact, a vital part of the labour force in key industries. Böhning indicates that the employment of foreign workers by economic sector in Switzerland was similar to that in Germany.[34] In France, too, 'foreign workers [were] heavily concentrated in the industrial sector' (Brenner 1979: 38). According to Dutch statistics, the vast majority of workers from all the recruitment countries who entered the Netherlands per year were employed in 'factories and workshops' (*arbeiders fabriek, werkplaats*). The metal production and processing industry took the highest share of migrant workers, while agriculture-horticulture, mining and construction embraced only a small fraction. However, in Belgium, the situation remained somewhat unchanged; mining continued to be an important sector of employment for migrants.

skill level

Relevant studies usually defined the jobs migrant workers took up in post-war Western Europe as either 'unskilled' or 'unskilled and semi-skilled' (see Piore 1979: 3-26; Satzewich 1991: 16; Kay and Miles 1992: 189; Moch 1992: 188). It is a fact that migrants were mainly employed as unskilled and semi-skilled workers. Workplaces showed a clear segmentation between native workers who usually occupied high-status and better-paying jobs, and migrants who usually occupied low-status, low-paying ones, and were faced with various forms of discrimination and difficulty in promotion. Nevertheless, it should not be overlooked that especially in the largest labour-receiving countries (i.e. Germany and France), a mentionable proportion of male guest workers occupied skilled positions; this was despite the fact that the receiving countries could and did employ skilled migrants as unskilled or semi-skilled workers. For example, in Germany in 1966, 28 per cent of all foreign males were employed as skilled labourers (Herbert and Hunn 2001: 199). The BfA's survey in 1968 indicated that 55 per cent of male Yugoslav workers occupied skilled positions (including master and foreman); this percentage was 16 for Turks, 15 for Spaniards, 13 for Italians, 12 for Portuguese and 7 for Greeks. The 1972 survey of the same institution yielded almost the same results for male migrants, except for Yugoslavia, whose level of skilled workers dropped to 41 per cent. However, both surveys indicated that female migrant workers were employed only as unskilled and semi-skilled workers (BfA 1973: 67). A comprehensive Dutch survey conducted in 1970, which covered 261 mostly industrial firms, showed that 17 per cent of Italians, 13 per cent of Turks, 11 per cent of Spaniards and 4 per cent of Moroccans were skilled workers (Akgündüz 2008: 161).

Conclusion

not a new phenomenon

Guest worker migration in post-war Europe was not a new phenomenon in 1945. Rather, it was the resumption of a well-established pattern starting from as early as the 1880s. After the Second World War up to the 1960s, guest worker migratory movements to Western Europe were comparatively smaller than emigration, colonial immigration and even intra-Western European labour migration. Afterwards, however, guest worker migration increased remarkably. In Germany, for example, migrant workers came to constitute more than 10 per cent of the total labour force in 1973.

With the exception of France, in every receiving country migrant workers were initially recruited mainly to work in agriculture, mining, construction and other jobs that were unattractive to native labourers (including seasonal jobs). From the early 1960s, however, migrants came in response to labour shortages principally in industry. Particularly in the leading labour-recruiting countries (e.g. Germany, France, Switzerland and the Netherlands), the vast majority of migrant workers were employed in manufacturing. It was rather unusual that despite a constant inflow of migrants and open door policies, at least for Southern Europeans, including Yugoslavs, demand-supply relations in the labour market of each receiving country remained spectacularly in favour of labour. The number of unfilled vacancies was either higher or only slightly lower (mainly in Belgium and France) than that of the unemployed until recruitment was officially halted in 1973-1974. Thus, Western Europe was very successful at tightly regulating the admission of foreign labour according to demand.

Though the admission policy was initially 'Southern Europeans only', when the demand for foreign labour further increased and the volume of supply from Southern Europe became insufficient, the admission policy was transformed into 'Southern Europeans first'. The recruitment of workers from the second group of supply countries was limited to cases where the first group failed to meet demand.

guest worker system

From the perspective of official migrants, the guest worker system represented ease and security in reaching the country of work. It offered regulated wages and working conditions, accommodation and certain social rights. This aspect of the system was a clear improvement over the situation of 'undocumented' migrant workers. Yet in the host countries, the guest worker system created a hierarchy within the working class along ethno-cultural lines. Not only were migrants usually unskilled and semi-skilled workers mainly employed in low-status, low-paying jobs, their position was also inferior to that of native labourers in legal, political and social domains and housing. Although they paid taxes and premiums, they demanded little, if anything, of the social expenditures of the state (e.g. in terms of subsidised housing, education and welfare). Furthermore, they left their paid premiums behind when they returned home, especially in the early years. Perpetuated longer than a quarter of a century, this exclusionary system was justified, sometimes only ideologically, as was the case in Germany, where the authorities long claimed that 'Germany is not an immigration country'. The legacy of the guest worker system was the creation of a range of difficulties for the acceptance and inclusion of especially ethnically and culturally more distinct segments of the migrant worker population, who went on to become permanent settlers.

MAIN IDEAS

Guest worker migration in post-war Europe was not a new phenomenon, but a resumption of an established pattern.

Before 1960, apart from France, the receiving countries' intention in signing a bilateral labour recruitment agreement was to initiate the entry of a limited number of workers while also restricting them to clearly specified sectors.

In connection with a sharp increase in the demand for labour, the policy became to attract workers as rapidly and in as large numbers as possible from Southern European countries; that is, Italy, Spain, Greece, Portugal and later Yugoslavia.

Unlike the previous period, after 1960, bilateral recruitment agreements aimed at accelerating and regularising the migration movements already established. Agreements were made if the dimension of labour demand was substantial.

The recruitment of workers from Turkey and North African countries (Algeria, Morocco and Tunisia) took place to the extent that Southern Europe failed to meet demand.

The number of unfilled vacancies was either higher or only slightly lower than the numbers of unemployed until recruitment was officially halted in 1973-1974. The volume of migration was determined by the demand for labour; this was despite the acceptance or easiness of spontaneous migration of labourers.

Particularly in the leading labour-recruiting countries, such as Germany, France, Switzerland and the Netherlands, the vast majority of migrant workers were employed in manufacturing after the early 1960s. Especially in the first three countries, migrant workers constituted a considerable proportion of the labour force, even in key industries.

Migrants were mainly employed as unskilled and semi-skilled workers in low-status, low-paying jobs; they also held inferior positions in legal, political and social domains.

Employment of undocumented workers was tacitly approved or tolerated.

Notes

1 Hoerder (2000: 45) suggests that these intra-European labour migrations were 'part of two larger migration systems of intercontinental dimension, a North Atlantic system reaching from the small towns of the Jewish Pale of Settlement in Russia to North America, and a Russo-Siberian system extending from the Russian ethnic territories to the Pacific'. Lucassen and Lucassen (2009) provide a useful and comparative analysis of migrations in Europe from 1500 to 1900.

2 Although somehow largely unnoticed, Hourwich's book presents a comprehensive analysis of how the main source of immigration to the US shifted from Northern and Western Europe to Southern and Eastern Europe, and relations between the US labour market and immigration (including return migration).

3 Herbert (1997) gives a detailed account of the living and working conditions of foreign workers – including prisoners of war – their sectors of employment and the racist hierarchy in which they were placed under the Nazi regime.

4 France established labour recruitment agreements with the following countries: Poland (1919), Italy (1919), Czechoslovakia (1920), Hungary (1924) and Yugoslavia, Romania and Austria (1929 and 1930) (Cross 1977: 89-90, 119, 123, 318).

5 In the Netherlands, there were some 54,000 foreign labourers with work permits in 1936 (Eijl 2005), the majority of whom were Germans and Belgians. The remaining workers were largely Italians, Poles, Czechs and Yugoslavs (Ellemers, 1987; Langeweg 2008). For the case of Belgium, see Caestecker (2008); Delbroek (2008).

6 For the numbers, wages and the sector of employment of these colonial and Chinese workers, see Cross 1977: 43-49.

7 Cross (1977: 224) states that 'the Colonial Ministry imported 132,421 North Africans throughout the war'. After the war the police 'summarily deported North Africans through periodic raids on their neighborhoods in Paris and Marseilles, probably only about 6,000 remained by the end of 1920'.

8 'Preferences by nationality were as follows: 1) Italians, 2) Poles, 3) Czech, 4) Portuguese, 5) Spanish, 6) Greeks, 7) Russian, 8) Germans, Austro-Hungarians, and Bulgarians' (Cross 1977: 85-6).

9 Castles and Kosack (1973: 30-31) report that net 'immigration from India, Pakistan, and the West Indies totalled 669,640 between 1955 and 1968'.

10 Such as the agreement between France and the Netherlands in 1948, and the agreement between Belgium, the Netherlands and Luxembourg in 1953 (Lange 2007).

11 For example, the recommendation of the ILO in 1949, the recommendation of the OECD in 1955 (Lange 2007: 29-33) and the Council of Europe's European Convention on Establishment in 1955 (Groenendijk 2006).

12 France admitted 315,000 Italian workers between 1946 and 1958 (McDonald 1969: 120). In Switzerland the number of Italian nationals with Swiss work permits was 242,806 in 1959 (Mayer 1965: 7-8), and Belgium employed 57,626 Italian workers in 1947 (Desle 1995: 545).

13 The number of Italian workers who arrived in Britain between 1947 and 1948 was only 440, despite the fact that the 1946 agreement aimed to recruit 2,800 workers (Kay and Miles 1992: 38). In the Netherlands, the number of Italian workers was 1,984 by the end of 1959 (Wentholt 1967: 215), and the number of Italians working in Germany was just 9,691 in 1958 (BfA *1962*: 26-27).

14 Belgium made a bilateral labour recruitment agreement with Spain in 1956 and with Greece in 1957 (Martiniello and Jamin 2000); though in 1961, the number of

Spanish workers was about ten times smaller (7,191), and that of Greek workers was over 19 times smaller (3,573), than the number of Italian workers (Desle 1995: 545).

15 France signed a bilateral labour recruitment agreement with Greece in 1954 (Freeman 1989: 74), but Greek labour migration to France remained negligible until the end of the official recruitment period (Lianos 1975).

16 Europe experienced mass emigration to overseas regions in the decade after the war ended. In the Netherlands, for example, emigration remained larger than immigration until 1960 (Nederlandse Emigratiedienst 1965: 120-125), and Britain's situation was the same until 1958. Total European (including Southern and Eastern European) emigration to overseas countries for the period 1946-1973 is estimated at more than 12.6 million (Lohrman 1976: 229).

17 Belgium lifted the limitation on the sector of employment of Italian workers as early as 1958. This took place following 'the accident at the Marcinelle mine when 136 Italian miners lost their lives' (Martiniello 2010: 247). The 1948 Dutch-Italian recruitment agreement was replaced with a new one in 1960. In 1964, with the initiative of the Italian government, which took advantage of the competition for migrant labour, a new labour recruitment agreement was made between Switzerland and Italy, giving more rights to Italians living in Switzerland (Liebig 2004: 163-164).

18 It became a legal right in 1968 for Italian nationals to take a job in the other member countries of the EEC.

19 For example, in a report dated 14 January 1970 and presented to the Dutch parliament, the Dutch Minister of Social Affairs and Public Health stated that the phenomenon of spontaneous migration was a veiled form of recruitment, and quite attractive due to the situation in the labour market, notwithstanding the existence of certain risks like the spread of infectious diseases and the oversupply of labour (*Brief van de Minister van Sociale zaken en Volksgezondheid* 1970: 4).

20 The number of Italian workers coming to France dropped to around 13,000 per year in 1963 and dropped a further four to six thousand per year from 1969 onwards (BfA 1974b: 101).

21 Germany recruited more than 107,000 workers from Italy in 1961 through its recruitment agencies (*Bundesanstalt fur Arbeit* 1963: 11), which was almost five times higher than that the number admitted by France in the same year. Likewise, Germany got the lion's share of total annual Greek emigration: approximately 53 per cent in 1961 and 69 per cent in 1965 (Lianos 1975).

22 In 1960, Chinese refugees encamped in Hong Kong were considered for recruitment; however, due to the high transportation costs, racial reasons and discomfort with the possibility of permanent settlers, the plan was not implemented (Bendix 1990: 33).

23 The report of an official Dutch delegation's visit to Greece, Turkey, Italy and Malta, dated 10-31 January 1964 (Archive of the Dutch Recruitment Bureau in Ankara, in the archive titled 'Human Rights and Oppositional Movements in Turkey' at the International Institute of Social History in Amsterdam).

24 Between 21 per cent and 61 per cent of Greeks migrated annually to Australia, Canada and the USA during the period 1955-1973 (Lianos 1975: 120-21). The total share of overseas regions in the Italian migration from 1960 to 1969 was similar (International Migration 1967, 1970). More than 80 per cent of Portuguese migrants went to the Americas, with Brazil accounting for the majority, until 1960; this percentage was 25 between 1960 and 1974 (Baganha 2003). Some 25 per cent of Yugoslav migration was directed to Canada, the USA, New Zealand and Australia after 1960 (Baucic 1972: 1-3).

25 For the annual real growth rate of GDP (gross domestic product) in Greece, Italy, Portugal, Spain and Turkey from 1960 to the mid-1970s, see OECD 1977: 124. Though Turkey was less developed than the other Southern European countries, it still had a high economic and industrial growth rate in the 1950s and during the migration years.

26 Aside from the insufficiency of labour from Southern Europe, there was another factor in finding additional supply countries. The receiving countries needed to diversify the composition of the labour force to avoid becoming dependent on particular groups of workers in order to ease the management of labour and to reduce the risk of industrial disputes.

27 The only exception was that the socialist regime in Bulgaria allowed emigration of large numbers of Turkish minorities to Turkey.

28 Germany, after the agreement with Italy, made recruitment agreements with Spain and Greece (1960), Turkey (1961), Morocco (1963), Portugal (1964), Tunisia (1965) and the former Yugoslavia (1968) (Bauer et al. 2005). Following the first agreement with Italy, France concluded bilateral recruitment agreements with Spain (1961), Morocco, Tunisia, Portugal (1963), Yugoslavia and Turkey (1965). After independence in 1962, France signed three consecutive agreements with Algeria in 1964, 1968 and 1971 in order to regulate Algerian migration according to labour demand, and similar agreements were made with Mali, Mauritania (1963) and Senegal (1964) (Brenner 1979: 22-3). Belgium's bilateral agreement with Italy was followed by agreements with Spain (1956), Greece (1957), Turkey, Morocco (1964), Tunisia (1969), Algeria and Yugoslavia (1970). The Netherlands' agreements, after that with Italy, were with Portugal (1963), Turkey (1964), Greece (1966), Morocco (1969), Yugoslavia and Tunisia (1970).

29 For a detailed study of the case, see Akgündüz 2008: 115-126.

30 For instance, on average 33 per cent to 34 per cent of the workers annually recruited from Turkey by Germany were skilled according to the standard of the recruiter, but this percentage was at least halved when workers took up work in Germany. For more on this issue, see Dohse 1982.

31 Piore (1979: 1-49; 1980: 13-22) suggests that the hypothesis of seeing labour migration as a response to labour shortages does not provide an adequate explanation. Instead, he offers his dual-labour market hypothesis. Accordingly, the market is divided into a primary and a secondary sector, and migrants come 'to take a distinct set of jobs, jobs that the native labour force refuse to accept'.

32 Moch (1997: 54) writes: 'Foreign workers and their families arrived in unprecedented numbers in the 1960s [...] In terms of their occupations and home conditions, these foreign labourers resembled historical migrants. Like nineteenth-century immigrants, they worked in agriculture, construction, and mining'.

33 From 1965 onward, this meant more than 60 per cent of Turkish migrants.

34 Böhning (1972: 47) states, 'the proportion of foreigners employed in low-productivity, low-paying jobs in Switzerland has been halved over the last 15 years, while a larger and larger share of immigrant labour has found employment in the metal and machinery industry, for example'. For more information on the sectors of employment of foreign workers in Switzerland, see Böhning and Maillat 1974: 124-165.

References

Adanır, F. (1994), 'The national question and the genesis and development of socialism in the Ottoman Empire: The case of Macedonia', in: M. Tunçay and E.J. Zürcher (eds), *Socialism and Nationalism in the Ottoman Empire, 1876-1923*. London: British Academic Press.

Akgündüz, A. (2008), *Labour Migration from Turkey to Western Europe, 1960-1974: A Multidisciplinary Analysis*. Aldershot: Ashgate.

Bade, K.J. (1997), 'From emigration to immigration: The German experience in the nineteenth and twentieth centuries', in: K.J. Bade and M. Weiner (eds), *Migration Past, Migration Future*. Providence: Berghahn Books.

Baganha, M.I.B. (2003), 'From closed to open doors: Portuguese emigration under the corporatist regime', *e-Journal of Portuguese History* 1 (1). http://www.brown.edu/Departments/Portuguese_Brazilian_Studies/ejph/html/Summer03.html.

Baganha, M.I.B., P. Gois and P. Pereira (2005), 'International migration from and to Portugal: What do we know and where are we going?', in: K.Z. Zimmermann (ed.), *European Migration: What Do We Know?* Oxford: Oxford University Press.

Baucic, I. (1972), *The Effects of Emigration from Yugoslavia and the Problems of Returning Emigrant Workers*. The Hague: Martinus Nijhoff.

Bauer, T., B. Dietz, K.F. Zimmermann and E. Zwintz (2005), 'German migration: Development, assimilation, and labour market effects', in: K.Z. Zimmermann (ed.), *European Migration: What Do We Know?* Oxford: Oxford University Press.

Bendix, J. (1990), *Importing Foreign Workers: A Comparison of German and American Policy*. New York: Peter Lang.

Besse, F. (1965), 'European workers: Mediterranean countries, reservoirs of manpower', *International Migration Digest* 2 (1): 14-17.

Booth, H. (1992), *The Migration Process in Britain and West Germany*. Aldershot: Avebury.

Bover, O. and P. Velilla (2005), 'Migrations in Spain: Historical background and current trends', in: K.Z. Zimmermann (ed.), *European Migration: What Do We Know?* Oxford: Oxford University Press.

Böhning, W.R. (1979), 'International migration in Western Europe: Reflections on the past five years', *International Labour Review* 118 (4).

Böhning W. R. and D. Maillat (1974), *The Effects of the Employment of Foreign Workers*. Paris: OECD.

Böhning, W.R. (1972), *The Migration of Workers in the United Kingdom and the European Community*. London: Oxford University Press.

Brenner, C.K. (1979), *Foreign Workers and Immigration Policy: The Case of France*. Paris: OECD.

Brief van de Minister van Sociale zaken en Volksgezondheid (1970), *Nota Buitenlandse Werknemers, Zitting 1969-1970*. The Hague.

BfA (1974a), *Ausländische Arbeitnehmer: Beschäftigung, Anwerbung, Vermittlung: Erfahrungsbericht 1972/73*. Nürnberg: Bundesanstalt für Arbeit.

BfA (1974b), *Wanderarbeitnehmer in Deutschland, Frankreich und Grossbritannien*. Nurnberg: Bundesanstalt für Arbeit.

BfA (1973), *Repräsentativ-untersuchung 1972: Beschäftigung Ausländischer Arbeitnehmer*. Nürnberg: Bundesanstalt für Arbeit.

BfA (1972), *Ausländische Arbeitnehmer: Beschäftigung, Anwerbung, Vermittlung: Erfahrungsbericht 1971*. Nürnberg: Bundesanstalt für Arbeit.

BfA (1963), *Ausländischer Arbeitnehmer: Erfahrungsbericht 1962*. Nürnberg: Bundesanstalt für Arbeit.

BfA (1962), *Ausländischer Arbeitnehmer: Erfahrungsbericht 1961*. Nürnberg: Bundesanstalt für Arbeit.

Caestecker, F. (2008) 'Arbeidsmarktstrategieën in de Belgische mijnindustrie tot 1940', *Tijdschrift voor Sociale en Economische Geschiedenis* 5 (3): 30-52.

Castles, S. and G. Kosack (1973), *Immigrant Workers in Western Europe and Class Structure*. London: Oxford University Press.

Castles, S. (1992) 'The Australian model of immigration and multiculturalism: Is it applicable to Europe?', *International Migration Review* 26 (2): 549-67.

Castles, S. (1986), 'The guest worker in Western Europe: An obituary', *International Migration Review* 20 (4): 761-78.

Castles, S. (1984), *Here for Good*. London: Pluto Press.

Cohen, R. (1987), *The New Helots: Migrants in the International Division of Labour*. Hants: Gower.

Cross, G.S. (1983), *Immigrant Workers in Industrial France: The Making of a New Laboring Class*. Philadelphia: Temple University Press.

Cross, G.S. (1977), *The Structure of Labor Immigration into France between the Wars*. Unpublished PhD dissertation. Madison: University of Wisconsin.

Del Boca, D. and A. Venturini (2003), *Italian Migration*. Bonn: Institute for the Study of Labor. http://ftp.iza.org/dp938.pdf.

Del Campo, S. (1979), 'Spain', in: R.E. Krane (ed.), *International Labor Migration in Europe*. New York: Praeger Publishers.

Delbroek, B (2008), 'Op zoek naar koolputters: Buitenlandse mijnwerkers in Belgisch-Limburg in de twintigste eeuw', *Tijdschrift voor Sociale en Economische Geschiedenis* 5 (3): 80-103.

Desle, E. (1995), 'Racism and the "foreign labour system": An exploration of their mutual relationship based on the experience of Belgium in the immediate post-war period', in: M. van der Linden and J. Lucassen (eds), *Racism and Labour Market*. Bern: Peter Lang.

Dohse, K. (1982), *Foreign Workers in the Federal Republic of Germany: Governmental Policy and Discrimination in Employment*. Berlin: Wissenschaftzentrum.

Ellemers, J.E. (1987), 'Migratie van en naar Nederland in historisch perspectief: Een beknopt overzicht', *Tijdschrift voor Geschiedenis* 100 (3): 322-30.

Eryılmaz, A. (1998), 'Interview mit Fuat Bultan' (Fuat Bultan ile söylesi)', in: M. Jamin and A. Eryılmaz (eds), *Eine Geschicte der Einwanderung aus der Turkei (Türkiye'den Almanya'ya Göçün Tarihi)*. Essen: Klartext Verlag.

Fassman, H. and R. Münz (1994), 'European East-West migration, 1945-1992', *International Migration Review* 28 (3): 520-38.

Freeman, G.P. (1989) 'Immigrant labour and racial conflict: The role of the state', in: P. E. Ogden and P.E. White (eds), *Migrants in Modern France*. London: Unwin Hyman.

Freeman, G.P. (1979), *Immigrant Labor and Racial Conflict in Industrial Societies*. Princeton: Princeton University Press.

Groenendijk, K. (2006), 'The legal integration of potential citizens: Denizens in the EU in the final years before the implementation of the 2003 Directive on long-term resident third country nationals', in: R. Bauböck, E. Ersbøll, K. Groenendijk, H. Waldrauch (eds), *Acquisition and Loss of Nationality, Volume 1: Comparative Analyses, Policies and Trends in 15 European Countries*. IMISCOE Research. Amsterdam: Amsterdam University Press.

Groenendijk, K. and R. Hampsink (1995), *Temporary Employment of Migrants in Europe*. Nijmegen: Katholieke Universiteit, Faculteit Rechtsgeleerdheid.

Herbert, U. (1997), *Hitler's Foreign Workers in Germany: Enforced Foreign Labor in Germany under the Third Reich*. Cambridge: Cambridge University Press.

Herbert, U. (1990), *A History of Foreign Labor in Germany, 1880-1980*. Ann Arbor: University of Michigan Press.

Herbert, U. and K. Hunn (2001), 'Guest workers and policy on guest workers in the Federal Republic: From the beginning of recruitment in 1955 until its halt in 1973', in: H. Schissler (ed.), *The Miracle Years: A Cultural History of West Germany, 1949-1968*. Princeton: Princeton University Press.

Hoerder, D. (2000), 'Metropolitan migration in the past: Labour markets, commerce, and cultural interaction in Europe, 1600-1914', *Journal of International Migration and Integration* 1 (1): 39-58.

Hoerder, D. (1996), 'Migration in the Atlantic economies: Regional European origins and worldwide expansion', in: D. Hoerder and L.P. Moch (eds), *European Migrants: Global and Local Perspectives.* Boston: Northeastern University Press.

Hoerder, D. (1985), 'An introduction to labor migration in the Atlantic economies, 1815-1914', in: D. Hoerder (ed.), *Labor Migration in the Atlantic Economies.* Westport: Greenwood Press.

Hourwich, I.A. (1912), *Immigration and Labor: The Economic Aspects of European Immigration to the United States.* New York: Putnam.

Husbands, T.C. (1991), 'The support for the *Front National*: Analyses and findings', *Ethnic and Racial Studies* 14 (3): 382-416.

International Migration (1970) 'Italian emigration', *International Migration* 8 (3): 117-20.

International Migration (1967), 'Italian emigration', *International Migration* 5 (3): 213-15.

International Migration Digest (1965), 'African migrant workers in Europe', *International Migration Digest* 2 (1): 97-102.

International Migration Digest (1964), 'European migrant workers in Western Europe, 1961-1963', *International Migration Digest* 1 (2): 221-227.

Jamin, M. (1998), 'Die deutsch-türkische Anwerbevereinbarung von 1961 und 1964 (1961-1964 Almanya-Türkiye Isgücü Anlasmaları)', in: M. Jamin and A. Eryılmaz (eds), *Eine Geschicte der Einwanderung aus der Turkei (Türkiye'den Almanya'ya Göçün Tarihi).* Essen: Klartext Verlag.

Kay, D. and R. Miles (1992), *Refugees or Migrant Workers? European Volunteer Workers in Britain, 1946-1951.* London: Routledge.

Kayser, B. (1972), *Cyclically Determined Homeward Flows of Migrant Workers.* Paris: OECD.

Kleindorfer, P.R. and A. Kudat (1974), *Economic and Managerial Aspects of Foreign Labor in West Germany.* Berlin: International Institute of Management.

Kubat, D. (1993), 'France: Balancing demographic and cultural nationalism', in: D. Kubat (ed.), *The Politics of Migration Policies.* New York: Center for Migration Studies.

Lange, T. de (2007), *Staat, Markt en Migrant: De Regulering van Arbeidsmigratie naar Nederland, 1945-2006.* Amsterdam: Boom.

Langeweg, S. (2008), 'Bekende buren en verre vreemden: Buitenlandse arbeiders in de Nederlandse steenkolenmijnen,1900-1974', *Tijdschrift voor Sociale en Economische Geschiedenis* 5 (3): 53-79.

Lianos, T.P. (1975), 'Flows of Greek out-migration and return migration', *International Migration* 13 (3): 119-133.

Liebig, T. (2004), 'Recruitment of foreign labour in Germany and Switzerland', in: OECD (ed.), *Migration for Employment: Bilateral Agreements at a Crossroads.* Paris: OECD.

Lohrmann, R. (1976), 'European migration: Recent developments and future prospects', *International Migration* 14 (3).

Lucassen, L. (2001), 'Sekse en nationaliteit als ordenend principe: De uitsluiting van vrouwen en vreemdelingen op de Nederlandse arbeidsmarkt (1900-1995)', in: C. van Eijl, L.H. van Vos and P. de Rooy (eds), *Sociaal Nederland.* Amsterdam: Aksant.

Lucassen, J. and L. Lucassen (2009), 'The mobility transition revisited, 1500-1900: What the case of Europe can offer to global history', *Journal of Global History* 4: 347-377.

Martiniello, M. (2010), 'Ethnic leadership, ethnic communities' political powerlessness and the state in Belgium', in: M. Martiniello and J. Rath (eds), *Selected Studies in International Migration and Immigrant Incorporation.* IMISCOE Textbook 1. Amsterdam: Amsterdam University Press.

Martiniello, M. and J. Jamin (2000) 'Towards an emerging ethnic class in Belgium?', in: A. Haynes et al. (eds), *Towards Emerging Ethnic Classes in Europe?* Weinheim: Freundenberg Stiftung.

Mayer, K.B. (1975) 'Intra-European migration during the past twenty years', *International Migration Review* 9 (4): 441-7.

Mayer, K.B. (1965), 'Post-war migration from Italy to Switzerland', *International Migration Digest* 2 (1): 5-13.

McDonald (1969), 'Labor immigration in France, 1946-1965', *Annals of the Association of American Geographers* 59 (1): 116-134.

Miles, R. (1987), *Capitalism and Unfree Labour.* London: Tavistock Publications.

Miles, R. (1986), 'Labour migration, racism and capital accumulation in Western Europe since 1945: An overview', *Capital and Class* 28: 49-86.

Moch, L.P. (1997), 'Dividing time: An analytical framework for migration history periodization', in: J. Lucassen and L. Lucassen (eds), *Migration, Migration History, History.* Bern: Peter Lang.

Moch, L.P. (1992), *Moving Europeans: Migration in Western Europe since 1650.* Bloomington: Indiana University Press.

Münz, R. and R. Ulrich (1998), 'Germany and its immigrants: A socio-demographic analysis', *Journal of Ethnic and Migration Studies* 24 (1).

Nederlandse Emigratiedienst (1965), *Emigratie 1964.* The Hague: Nederlandse Emigratiedienst.

OECD (1993), *Main Economic Indicators: Historical Statistics: Price, Labour and Wages, 1962-1991,* Paris: Organisation for Economic Co-operation and Development.

OECD (1984), *Labour Force Statistics, 1962-1984.* Paris: Organisation for Economic Co-operation and Development.

OECD (1977), *Economic Outlook* 22. Paris: Organisation for Economic Co-operation and Development.

OECD (1973), *Labour Force Statistics, 1960-1971.* Paris: Organisation for Economic Co-operation and Development.

OECD (1970), Main Economic Indicators: Historical Statistics 1959-1969. Paris: Organisation for Economic Co-operation and Development.

Ogden, E.P. (1991), 'Immigration to France since 1945: Myth and reality', *Ethnic and Racial Studies* 14 (3): 294-318.

Olsson, L. (1996), 'Labor Migration as a Prelude to World War I', *International Migration Review* 30 (4): 875-900.

Paine, S. (1974), *Exporting Workers: The Turkish Case.* Cambridge: Cambridge University Press.

Piore, M.J. (1980) 'An economic approach', in: S. Berger and M.J. Piore, *Dualism and Discontinuity in Industrial Societies.* Cambridge: Cambridge University Press.

Piore, M.J. (1979), *Birds of Passage.* Cambridge: Cambridge University Press.

Portes, A. (2000), 'Immigration and the metropolis: Reflections on urban history', *Journal of International Migration and Integration* 1 (2): 153-75.

Power, J. (1979), *Migrant Workers in Western Europe and the United States.* Oxford: Pergamon Press.

Quataert, D. (1983), *Social Disintegration and Popular Resistance in the Ottoman Empire, 1881-1908: Reactions to European Economic Penetration.* New York: New York University Press.

Salt, J. (1976), 'International labour migration: The geographical pattern of demand', in: J. Salt and H. Clout (eds), *Migration in Post-war Europe.* London: Oxford University Press.

Salt, J. and H. Clout (1976), 'International labour migration: The sources of supply', in: J. Salt and H. Clout (eds), *Migration in Post-war Europe*. London: Oxford University Press.

Satzewich, V. (1991), *Racism and Incorporation of Foreign Labour.* London: Routledge.

Schierup, C.-U. (1990), *Migration, Socialism and the International Division of Labour.* Aldershot: Avebury.

Schuster, J. (1999), *Poortwachters over Immigranten: Het Debat Over Immigratie in het Naoorlogse Groot-Brittannië en Nederland.* Amsterdam: Het Spinhuis.

Seifert, W. (1997), 'Admission policy, patterns of migration and integration: The German and French case compared', *New Community* 23 (4): 441-60.

Shonick, K. (2009), 'Politics culture and economics: Reassessing the West German guest worker agreement with Yugoslavia', *Journal of Contemporary History* 44 (4): 719-736.

Tinnemans, W. (1994), *Een Gouden Armband: Een Geschiedenis van Mediterrane Immigranten in Nederland (1945-1990).* Utrecht: NCB.

Van Eijl C. (2005), *Al te Goed is Buurmans Gek: Het Nederlandse vreemdelingenbeleid 1840-1940.* Amsterdam: Aksant.

Wentholt, R. (1967), *Buitenlandse Arbeiders in Nederland.* Leiden: Spruyt, Van Mantgem and De Does.

Werner, H. (1986), 'Post-war migration in Western Europe: An overview', *International Migration* 24 (3): 543-57.

Zolberg, A.R. (1997), 'The Great Wall against China: Responses to the first immigration crisis, 1885-1925', in: J. Lucassen and L. Lucassen (eds), *Migration, Migration History, History.* Bern: Peter Lang.

9 Skilled Migration in Europe and Beyond: Recent Developments and Theoretical Considerations

Aimee Kuvik

Introduction

Corporate and industrial globalisation, alongside the transition to service economies in the West, has encouraged the movement of skilled migrants. Skilled migration is often assumed to be a win-win situation with economic benefits for both migrant and receiving country. Negative impacts have been discussed, but these pertain mainly to the risks of 'brain drain' in the sending society. Nonetheless, due to the current lack of data on skilled migration flows, we have an incomplete picture of the impacts of skilled migration on the receiving country.

This chapter discusses aspects central to the academic understanding of skilled migration in the European context. It begins with the main definitions of skilled migration. It then reviews recent developments, discussing the increasing flows in recent decades and the background of policy concerns. Following this overview, the chapter introduces several theories that apply to skilled migration, primarily drawing on general theories of labour migration. The final section discusses new paradigms that are emerging to explain skilled labour migration. Particularly important is 'the global competition for talent' notion and the idea of skilled labour migration as a contributor to human capital and international development.

Skilled migration: Definitions, statistics, and typologies

definition of 'highly skilled'

As with most categories of immigration, there is no strict international definition of a 'highly skilled' migrant; it depends on local economic, social and demographic contexts and local concerns and policies. In the migration literature, skilled migrants are often defined as individuals with a tertiary degree or higher. Additionally, skilled migration may be defined on the basis of the policies currently in place, and thus the types of visas and permits issued.[1] However, policy-based definitions seldom look at the sector of employment or give any indication of employment among skilled individuals. For instance, 'deskilling' may occur, when highly qualified refugees work below their qualifications. An example is university graduates from the new EU member states in Central and Eastern Europe working temporarily in low-skilled jobs in Northern and Western Europe. This situation is increasingly common, particularly in the United Kingdom. This means there can be a mismatch between academic discussions of 'skilled' migration and the official statistics. Another way to look at skilled migrants is in terms of occupation. This can be done broadly in terms of 'professionals', or in terms of 'talent' – a word popular at the moment (e.g. Kuptsch and Pang 2006; Shachar 2006; Zalatel 2006). Solimano (2008: 4) defines three main types of 'talent' important to international migration:

1. Directly productive talent. This includes the mobility of entrepreneurs, engineers and other technical talent, technology innovators, and business creators. These are people who are engaged directly in activities that lead to the actual production of goods and services.
2. Academic talent. This includes the mobility of scientists, scholars, and international students. These are the individuals that often work or study in universities, research centres, and think tanks and are devoted to the production and/or acquisition of scientific and scholarly knowledge that may be eventually translated into commercially valuable products and inputs.
3. Talent in social and cultural sectors. This talent is engaged directly in the provision of critical service such as health. In turn, 'cultural workers' – such as writers, painters, musicians, etc. – are engaged in artistic and cultural creative activities that have a value of aesthetic enjoyment and personal development.

occupations of interest

Solimano (2008: 22) further states that within these main classifications, a few specific occupations of interest emerge: 'technical talent, scientists and academics, professionals in the health sector – medical doctors and nurses, entrepreneurs and managers, professionals in international organizations; and cultural talent'. While entrepreneurs and students are also often included in discussions of skilled migrants, because they are covered in other chapters of this volume, this chapter focuses particularly on skilled labour migration.

Definitions of 'skilled' migration change across *time* and *place*. In other words, 'skilled' is a relative term, dependent on the demographics and qualifications of the greater society, and on the skills that are currently in demand. Presently, there seems to be a shift away from defining 'skilled' in terms of educational qualifications, and a move towards focusing on occupation (e.g. managers, healthcare workers, scientists and other workers for the knowledge economy). This is because the main immigration policies that support skilled migration in Europe tend to focus on labour market demands. The most standardised definition pertains to human resources in science and technology (HRST), which is applied uniformly in EU and Eurostat statistics (OECD 2001: 8). However, there are other occupations that have also been of interest in the development of skilled migration as defined above. In general, statistics for these other classifications have not been harmonised. For instance, although the mobility of healthcare workers has long been a topic of global concern, Dumont and Zurn (2007: 164) report:

> Discussions on the international mobility of health professionals are severely hampered by data limitations, including ambiguity in data sources and definitions of health worker migrants, or excessive reliance on indirect quotations. These limitations are particularly acute when one seeks to make international comparisons. To a certain extent, this has contributed to confuse the debate on international mobility of health workers.

sector data

Where data on skilled migration as a whole are collected, they often do not indicate in which sector an individual is employed. However, efforts have been made to improve data on this topic, for instance through the Organisation for Economic Co-operation and Development's (OECD) Database on Immigrants and Expatriates. This is the first comparative database on this topic, and has been operational since 2005, using data collected for the year 2000.[2] Internationally comparative longitudinal statistics on highly skilled migration are still not available, and few countries have this information collected in their national statistics. Tables 9.1 and 9.2 therefore only contain a small subset of data for Europe within the international context, with a slightly different set of countries for each table, due to both national policy and data collection differences. They are arranged to show some of the changes in skilled migration patterns – or the lack thereof. Table 9.3 shows the relative levels of highly skilled immigration in 2006 across the countries of the European Union, based on the Labour Force Survey results. To conceptualise skilled migration broadly and in a lasting framework, there is a need to extend beyond the technicalities and nuances of categorical definitions to see broader patterns and implications.

Flows of skilled migration in Europe as compared to classic immigration countries

While a detailed overview of the classifications of skilled migration in various countries is outside the scope of this chapter, it is important to understand how skilled migration has progressed in Europe, in order to highlight where important shifts have occurred.

skilled migration in Europe

Skilled migration has only recently become a topic of interest to policymakers and academics in Europe. Although skilled migration is not new, it has increased in recent years, as seen both in statistics (see Tables 9.1, 9.2 and 9.3) and in the increasing variety of countries and types of policies that support skilled migration. In reviewing the literature, a few notable trends can be seen in skilled migration policies, processes and paradigms. Much of the currently available research on skilled migration is based on the extremes; one side focuses on studies from the 'immigration countries' (i.e. the United States, Canada, Australia and New Zealand), which have longer histories of receiving immigrants, as well as earlier adoption of specific skilled migration policies and programmes; and the other side focuses on countries seen to be suffering from an acute 'brain drain' or on those that are benefiting from a 'brain circulation' (Kapur and McHale 2005; Wickramasekara 2003), with China and India drawing a substantial amount of attention. While these cases are important to understanding the most prevalent forms and effects of skilled migration, they also present only a partial picture of the 'global' element in the competition for talent. The situation in many European welfare states, which have

Table 9.1 *Admission of skilled immigrants in selected countries, 1991, 1999, 2001*

Country	*Number (thousands)*			*Share of all immigrants (%)*		
	1991	*1999*	*2001*[a]	*1991*	*1999*	*2001*
Australia[b]	41	35	54	37	42	60
Canada[c]	41	81	137	18	47	55
New Zealand[d]	na	13	36	na	47	68
US	12	57	175	18	22	17
Sweden	0	3	4	6	8	10
UK	4	32	40	7	33	32

Source: Abella (2006: 14) cites source as Table II.1.2 in UN Department of Economic and Social Affairs, *World Economic and Social Survey 2004. International Migration*, New York

[a] Data for US refer to 2002

[b] Skilled category, including family members with certain tested professional qualifications and linguistic aptitudes

[c] Skilled workers category including assisted relatives who are not points tested

[d] Employment-based preference category including family members of skilled workers

more cautious approaches to immigration, is less studied and understood.

turning points

In tracing the development of skilled migration and related policies, a few turning points can be discerned that link to current thinking on skilled migration. The first is the movement of scientists to the US following the World Wars and the development of military technologies (said to have been an important influence on the US's current strength in the IT sector) during the Cold War. This development spawned the initial discussion of 'brain drain', which remains important in discussions of skilled migration. A second development is linked with the internationalisation of business, including the increase of foreign direct investment, particularly in the 1980s. The migration of business professionals in the 1970s appears to have been quite low (Salt 1983). However, as companies began setting up affiliated branches in other places, it became more common for managers to move abroad as part of moving up the career ladder. Skilled migration gained force in the 1980s and seems to have been largely linked with either intra-corporate movements or with free trade agreements (for example the North American Free Trade Agreement (NAFTA) or the European Economic Community); therefore, the flows were predominantly between advanced economies. Global business operations underwent several shifts between the mid-1980s and early 1990s that impacted policies, including the growth of business services, the expansion of multinational corporations and their subcontracting of work in other countries. In 1986, the General Agreement on Trade in Services (GATS) discussion began under the auspices of the World Trade Organization (WTO) to advance trade in services, which further facilitated global legislation to allow short-term business stays. Potentially, this also helped to broaden skilled migration from being primarily for managers to including less senior professionals, more job types and all sizes of firms, although few studies seem to record this aspect.[3] In the early 1990s, a marked shift in policies occurred in the 'immigration countries' to further facilitate the movement of skilled professionals and with the recognition of a growing trade in highly skilled services. One of the most important developments was the US's expansion of the quota of the H1B (temporary) visa for specialty occupations (largely for IT and other knowledge-based jobs) from 65,000 to 115,000 between the fiscal years 1999 and 2000 (Kapur and McHale, 2005: 55). In 2000, the quota was raised again, to 195,000 per year for the fiscal years 2001, 2002, and 2003, within a law called the American Competitiveness in the Twenty-first Century Act of 2000.[4] While the name of this act is often not cited, it seems to be an important indicator of the changing rhetoric related to skilled migration and competitiveness. The quota increases were the direct result of IT industry lobbying (Rodrik 2001; Freeman and Hill 2006). Additionally, the rising quota not only placed more emphasis on the political agenda in the US, but by the mid-1990s, other countries such as Australia, New Zealand, and the UK were also attracting more skilled immigrants on a temporary basis, although at lower levels, as shown in Table 9.2.

skilled migration growth

Table 9.2 *Temporary workers admitted under skill-based categories Selected countries, 1992-2000*

Country	Number (thousands)				
	1992	1997	1998	1999	2000
Australia	41	82	93	100	116
Canada	70	75	80	85	94
New Zealand		27	30	39	48
US*	143		343	423	505
France	5	5	4	6	8
UK	54	80	89	98	124

Source: Abella (2006: 15) cites table II.12 in UN's *World Economic and Social Survey 2004 International Migration*
* Number of admissions under H1-B visas, not number of persons

paradigm shift

The mid-1990s was an important period because of the IT boom, which associated productivity growth and the resulting policy focus on the knowledge economy. This period can be seen as the beginning of a paradigm shift, as skilled migration increasingly became associated with economic competitiveness and the subsequent discussions of a 'global competition for talent' in the literature (e.g. Kuptsch and Pang 2006; Shachar 2006; Zalatel 2006), in the media (see Bauder 2008 for a discussion of skilled immigration in the media in Germany), and in policy documents. Great interest has been generated by the example of Silicon Valley, California's leading IT area, particularly building on the research of Saxenian (2002). However, this research in all likelihood is not directly comparable due to policy differences and particularities of the area and/or industry, which allowed for extremely high levels of immigrant involvement – 32 per cent of the science and engineering workforce (Saxenian 1999: viii) and 25 per cent of the entrepreneurs by 1999 (Saxenian 1999: 20). Furthermore, as Freeman and Hill (2006: 7) argue, the changes in the US were not made with the global situation in mind:

> National politics, rather than global economic pressures, drive the twists and turns of U.S. immigration policies, with key roles being played by high tech employers, professional associations, pro and anti-immigrant organizations, and even associations of

immigration lawyers. There appears to be little space in their accounts for the kind of global legal/institutional influences signaled by WTO reforms or by the importance of global multinationals.

knowledge economy

The bursting of the IT bubble and the claims of a labour surplus in many areas did not seem to limit the associations between immigration and competitiveness, at least not on an international level. Rather, it seems to have led to a new period in which immigration became seen as a contributor to the broader 'knowledge economy' (and therefore to a set of occupations that are ever-changing in the skills required) and for specific 'new' sectors, for which governments across the advanced world were offering policy support. The OECD (2009: 161) reports that 'virtually all OECD countries expect that there will be a need for highly skilled migrants, especially in scientific and technological occupations, in coming years'. However, to date, immigration to the EU is predominantly low-skilled, and it is reported that 'the EU still tends to attract mainly less-skilled migrants: 48% of recent working-age migrants are low-skilled and only one in five is high-skilled' (European Commission 2008: 15).

policy changes

A generally restrictive approach to labour migration had been in place in most European countries following the 1973 oil crisis, the economic recession in the early 1980s and high stay rates and continuing unemployment among the low-skilled guest workers hired for post-World War reconstruction. However, despite the still-negative perceptions of guest workers lingering in Europe, new programmes for highly skilled immigration are being introduced, particularly since the mid-2000s. As mentioned previously, internationally comparative data on skilled migration have been scant since the OECD's initiative in 2001, despite evidence of growing support for skilled migration in parts of Europe. However, the European Labour Force Survey (Table 9.3) provides some indication of the magnitude of the growth of professional and skilled occupations among immigrants in Europe. As is also seen in the comparative data shown in Tables 9.1 and 9.2, the growth is uneven across countries. The largest growth rates in the number of new immigrant professionals within the EU for the ten-year period ending in 2006 are largely found where new skilled migration policies had already been adopted by the early 2000s,[5] and show evidence of how policy change can lead to changes in employment composition. These policies are outside of the scope of theoretical understandings. However, interested readers can find more information in policy-based discussions on skilled migration such as Cerna (2010), Chaloff and Lemaître (2009) and European Migration Network (2007).

Table 9.3 *Contribution of recent immigration to employment in highly skilled occupations, 2006*

	Persons in employment		*Persons in high-skilled jobs*		*Professionals*	
	Employed immigrants as a percentage of totals employment	*Employed immigrants having arrived in previous ten years as new entrants*[1]	*Immigrants in high-skill jobs*[2] *as a percentage of all persons in high-skill jobs*	*Immigrants in high-skill jobs having arrived in previous ten years as a percentage of new entrants*[1] *in high-skill jobs*	*Immigrant professionals*[3] *as a percentage of all professionals in employment*	*Immigrant professionals having arrived in previous ten years as a percentage of new entrant*[1] *professionals*
Austria	15.4	17.1	11.2	12.6	14.7	18.0
Belgium	11.1	12.0	9.8	10.6	9.5	10.4
Switzerland	24.4	32.1	20.9	30.4	23.4	35.9
Czech Republic	1.8	3.0	1.5	2.4	2.1	4.3
Germany	13.3	12.7	9.0	7.6	9.4	9.4
Denmark	5.8	8.7	5.0	6.0	6.5	8.1
Spain	14.6	30.2	7.3	9.8	7.7	10.0
Finland	2.8	3.9	2.4	2.8	3.1	4.3
France	11.2	8.1	9.4	5.9	11.1	7.7
Greece	8.3	13.0	2.5	1.8	2.4	1.5
Hungary	1.8	1.8	2.1	1.7	2.9	2.9
Ireland	13.7	26.0	13.7	23.5	14.6	25.6
Italy	8.5	13.2	3.9	3.5	4.2	3.6

Table 9.3 *Continued*

	Persons in employment		*Persons in high-skilled jobs*		*Professionals*	
	Employed immigrants as a percentage of totals employment	*Employed immigrants having arrived in previous ten years as new entrants*[1]	*Immigrants in high-skill jobs*[2] *as a percentage of all persons in high-skill jobs*	*Immigrants in high-skill jobs having arrived in previous ten years as a percentage of new entrants*[1] *in high-skill jobs*	*Immigrant professionals*[3] *as a percentage of all professionals in employment*	*Immigrant professionals having arrived in previous ten years as a percentage of new entrant*[1] *professionals*
Luxembourg	43.8	54.3	42.9	59.0	48.2	62.6
Netherlands	10.3	8.7	8.2	5.7	8.5	6.8
Norway	7.4	11.6	6.4	6.2	8.2	8.0
Poland	0.3	0.5	0.5	0.8	0.5	0.8
Portugal	7.8	9.8	9.6	4.4	10.0	4.5
Sweden	12.5	11.1	9.7	8.0	11.0	10.2
Slovak Republic	0.7	0.2	0.9	0.3	1.2	0.2
United Kingdom	11.0	18.9	11.8	17.0	14.2	22.1
United States	15.8	22.8	12.5	14.5	18.0	23.5
Average	11.0	14.5	9.1	10.6	10.5	12.7

Notes: 1. New entrants consist of immigrants having arrived in the previous ten years plus native-born persons having completed their education over the last ten years, proxied by native-born persons aged 30-39. 2. Persons in high-skill jobs include managers (except managers of small enterprises), professionals and associate professionals. These are ISCO codes 11, 12, 2 and 3. 3. Professional occupations refer to ISCO code 2.

Sources: European Community Labour Force Survey for European countries; Current Population Survey for the United States. Chaloff and Lemaître (2009: 16)

Academic literature: Skilled migration to Europe

migration literature

The skilled migration literature in Europe follows similar trends. There was little attention to the topic before the mid-1990s, with a few exceptions focused on managers and international corporations (Findlay 1990; Salt 1983, 1992). By the late 1990s and early 2000s, the topic of skilled migration in Europe was gaining attention, primarily maintaining a focus on international corporations, expatriates and managers (e.g. Koser and Salt 1997; Mahroum 1999, 2001; Beaverstock 1990, 1991; Beaverstock and Smith 1996). This focus was because few explicit policies were yet in place for attracting skilled migrants to European countries, other than internal corporate recruitment mechanisms. The UK led Europe in terms of adopting the first large-scale skilled migration programme in 2002,[6] and thus has the most literature available on skilled migration and its impact. Other research looks at comparisons – particularly between the US and Europe – for attracting skilled migrants (Peri 2005; Cervantes and Goldstein 2008), or examines the general policy setting in Europe (Zimmermann 2005). More recently, emerging research in Europe has included scientific mobility (e.g. Ackers 2005), employment of immigrants in the IT industry (Leung 2001), highly-skilled employment of new member state nationals after EU enlargement (Ferro 2004; Csedo 2008; Guth and Gill 2008; Liversage 2009) and topics related to the return migration of skilled migrants (Williams and Baláž 2005).

Migration theory and approaches relevant to assessing skilled migration

Migration theory and highly skilled migrants: Problematic assumptions

Skilled labour migration represents largely uncharted territory in modern migration theory (for a theoretical discussion of approaches relevant to professional movements, see Koser and Salt 1997). Given the relative 'novelty' of skilled migration research, theoretical discussions largely borrow from the interdisciplinary theoretical perspectives used for other forms of migration, mainly low skilled. There is no single, primary theory that has been developed and adopted for skilled migration itself, although various typologies are being formed (e.g. Iredale 2001; Mahroum 2001; Abella 2006).

migration difficult to theorise

Migration, with its multiplicity of actors, motives, and time and place contexts, has been difficult to theorise. Theory must assume a possibility of continuity and consistency. In other words, theoretical models should be applicable across a wide range of situations, and hold certain assumptions as relatively constant. Yet, migration processes are contingent on the macro-economic, political and legal environments determining who is allowed to go, to where, when, and why, and therefore in some ways bind the theories to the here-and-now. Quotas for either nationality or other criteria often control the types of migrants who are allowed in. Policies towards highly skilled migration are no exception. Countries with fairly open systems, such as the US, Australia and Canada, all set quotas on various forms of visas for skilled workers. These quotas are often revised to meet the current demand. Thus, the observable pieces of migration, those that most theories are based upon, are often context-bound. This context is continually shifting as new policies are passed, and it takes time to see the impact of former policies. Such shifts are not limited solely to policies for highly-skilled workers, but apply to policies for immigrant classifications in general.

Migration theory has thus far excluded the analysis of temporary workers, an important category for highly skilled labour migration. For example, Malmberg (1997: 23) argues, 'Migration is often defined as a permanent and long-distance change of place of residence, as a short-distance move is regarded as local mobility, and moves of short-term residents are regarded as temporary mobility'. As discussed in the introductory sections, skilled migration has largely occurred, at least initially, through the mechanism of temporary visas such as the H1B visa in the US. Thus, the analysis of skilled migration theoretically presents a few challenges to existing migration theory.

theoretical frameworks

While this first section outlines problems with defining skilled migration, the limits of temporality and longer-term effects beyond the immigrant himself, the next section will place skilled migration within theoretical frameworks. Migration theory as it relates to labour migration has occurred within various disciplines. The most frequently applied theoretical frameworks build on concepts related to economic restructuring or individual determinants for migration. This next section primarily outlines economic theory as it applies to labour migration in general, and skilled migration in particular. It focuses on theories that look at macro-level effects, including neo-classical economics arguments on wage effects and job displacement, dual labour markets and globalisation theories, as well as micro-level (individual) determinants of migration and social networks.

Neo-classical economics and skilled migration

macro-economic context

Given that skilled migration is a form of labour migration, it is important to place it within the macro-economic theoretical context. Economic theories, and especially neo-classical economics, have been central to much migration theory. Neo-classical economic theory is based on the assumption that free competition leads to the greatest market efficiency and that individuals will move to areas where they can maximise their own well-being. Within the neo-classical framework, protectionist legislation for both capital and labour is viewed as impeding competitiveness (Rodrik 2001). Additionally, neo-classical economics assumes that a general equilibrium can be reached. In terms of immigration, if full mobility were possible, then markets would become more balanced and wage disparity between regions would diminish. More than just a theoretical notion, the idea is applied in practice, for instance through the 'common' or 'single' market in the European Union, whereby the benefits of the EU are seen to stem from the free mobility of capital, goods, services and persons across the EU member states.

push-pull models

Neo-classical economics has been broadly applied to migration, and remains the core of much migration theory and policy (even though there is much criticism that it is too rational and individualistic), both on the micro and macro levels. It has been applied on an individual level via push-pull models (to answer the micro question of why people stay or go), with economic concerns often considered to be one of the primary root causes 'pushing' people to migrate to destinations with better opportunities or higher wages. Push-pull models were later modified to include non-rational personal factors and intervening obstacles (Lee 1966). Using the definition of Dorigo and Tobler (1983: 1), 'The push factors are those life situations that give one reason to be dissatisfied with one's present locale; the pull factors are those attributes of distant places that make them appear appealing'. This formulation of the push-pull model is often used on the national or regional level, although it implies an understanding of individual motives and assumes a rational approach. More recently, it has further been applied to advocate and understand global economic integration. As Zolberg (1989: 406-407) notes:

> One of the sharpest contrasts between the old and new literatures is the conceptual shift from a view of 'ordinary' international migration as the aggregate of movements of individuals in response to different opportunities, to a view of this process as a movement of workers propelled by the dynamics of the transnational capitalist economy, which simultaneously determines both the 'push' and the 'pull'.

In this formulation, supply is the push factor, while demand is the pull. Push-pull models can be applied on a variety of levels to understand migration flows. However, in general, push-pull models still give the feeling that we can predict migration flows based on a variety of primarily economic factors. This in turn may lead to the assumption that migration may be predictable, a viewpoint that is debated.

The equating of push-pull models with the concepts of supply and demand has interesting policy implications for highly skilled migration. Policies in OECD nations often seem to assume that the supply is greater than the demand. The emphasis is typically on quotas to limit the supply allowed to enter, rather than on countries seeking out hot job candidates to fuel their demand. For example, in Canada, quotas are set each year to determine the number of highly skilled migrants who will be allowed to enter, and criteria are set. DeVoretz (2003: 12) notes that the Canadian government policies toward the highly skilled 'amount to a "tap on, tap off" approach: allow the target to fluctuate widely while officials imaginatively search out new source countries. When Canada was unable to meet its yearly target for skilled workers, it widened the entry gate for family-class entrants. Such imaginative tactics fail to obscure the fact that the supply of skilled immigrants to Canada is not infinitely elastic'. Similarly, studies from Australia have found that skilled migrants often have a list of places they would be interested in, and only come to Australia after the doors to their top choices, the US and Canada, have been closed, often due to restrictive policies (Cobb-Clark and Connolly 1997). Therefore, while neo-classical theory may imply the availability of labour as needed, the reality may not hold up to this assumption.

Third, wages are often viewed as the critical element in understanding labour migration and in applying neo-classical economic theory, with the work of Borjas as particularly influential. Borjas (1994) found that there is little impact from skilled migration on the wages of American natives. However, other findings on the effect of skilled migration on wages, as well as on job displacement, are inconclusive. Saiz (2003) notes that the impact of immigration is dependent on the skill characteristics of the immigrant versus the native population. Saiz then feels it is critical to include highly skilled labour in order to understand the impact of immigration on wages. He explains: *wages*

> [I]f the composition of skilled and unskilled workers is different in the immigrant and native populations, relative wages will change. For example, if immigrants tended to be more highly skilled, this would increase the relative supply of highly skilled individuals, reducing wages for the highly skilled and increasing wages for low-skilled workers. In reality, economists have worried about the potential impact of immigration on *low-skilled* natives (Saiz 2003: 16-17, emphasis in original).

In other words, knowing the immigrant qualifications compared to the native population is necessary to understand the impact of migration (for a more detailed discussion, see also Borjas 1989a; Ghosh 2005: 166-167), particularly as related to wages, and how migration is interpreted and theorised.

The dual labour market, world systems, immigration and global cities

dual labour market theory

Apart from globalisation and mobility, national economic restructuring has also become part of immigration theory through the dual labour market theory and the global cities thesis. The dual labour market theory (Piore 1979) states that the division of labour is based on shortages, with the current economic environment consisting of a primary sector of highly-skilled jobs and a secondary sector of low-skilled, labour-intensive jobs. The dual labour market theory is considered to be non-neoclassical in that it assumes that institutions and discrimination keep people from moving out of the low-waged, secondary sector, and thus the market will not necessarily reach equilibrium and equality. World systems analysis (Wallerstein 1974) also contributes to debates on immigration, as it posits that skilled labour will move from the periphery (developing countries) into the core (developed economies).

In Sassen's global cities thesis these elements of the dual labour market theory and global systems theory are also applied to immigration and concerns about internationalisation and globalisation. Sassen (1991) looks at the increasing communications interconnectivity of cities, and notes that industries in cities have shifted from Fordist factory production to a more globally interconnected knowledge society. Sassen sees this as creating a divided economy that creates similar divides within the population of cities. In this view, the city is marked by an increasing gap between the highly skilled knowledge workers, and low-skilled workers who provide services to cater to their needs, often through the informal economy, in which immigrants play a large role.

Individual-level: Determinants of migration and migration decision-making

determinants of migration

Discussions of the individual determinants of migration are important, particularly with the growing focus on the need for countries to attract skilled migrants. Such discussions assume a 'global competition for talent' as well as the view that skilled migration can lead to human capital development by offering new skills and knowledge and improving international contacts; these two aspects are discussed in more detail later in this chapter. While push-pull models have contributed to this discussion, there are also other important theoretical developments. Chiswick (1978) first discussed the motivations of highly-skilled immigrants to the US, showing a 'self-selection' that is beneficial for the receiving economy. Although there has been a sense of self-selection leading to higher qualifications of migrants compared to their native population (see also Borjas 1989b; Carrington and Detragiache 1998), the skilled migration literature tends to present individuals as 'talent' to be lured to various countries. In this light, models of migration decision-making are important in anthropological and sociological discussions, as well as for the purpose of policymaking.

The literature on the determinants of migration is quite fragmented, and new determinants emerge in the various case studies. In general, it has been argued that not only wages impact migration decisions among the highly skilled, but also career considerations, including the reputation of the firm or where the individual is employed. The development of skills is also crucial, with the ability to gain competency in English or other languages one of the incentives for educated individuals to move abroad. Beyond career considerations, other authors have argued for the importance of places as magnets, building again on the theoretical premises of the global cities theory as well as the lifestyle preferences of individuals (Florida 2002, 2005; Ewers 2007). Family considerations should also be examined, as pioneered by the new economics of labour migration (Stark and Bloom 1985).

Network theories: Migration systems and the role of social networks

Network theories have also been applied to skilled migration. Meyer (2001: 94-95) looks theoretically at the role of networks for highly-skilled migrants in particular. He argues that a focus on 'brain drain' has led to an economic focus in the study of skilled migration. Meyer stresses the importance of analysing knowledge networks to understand skilled migration beyond the notions of supply and demand. In addition, he says that the focus on networks shows more interconnectivity between these two aspects and allows for a balanced discussion of not only brain drain, but also brain gain. Similarly, Saxenian (2002) highlights the role and development of diaspora and transnational networks among Indians and Chinese working in Silicon Valley. As noted earlier, this example has become influential in the discussions of the benefits of skilled migration. Kuznetsov and Sabel (2008) argue that networks are important in migration chains for low-skilled workers, as highlighted by Piore (1979: 89), and that for highly-skilled migrants as well, 'migration chains become open mobility networks – means for discovering where to go to learn how to prosper in the reorganizing economy'. According to these authors, the networks are useful for sharing information for skills development, recruitment and to

networks

facilitate contributions to the home country in the form of remittances and other forms of development. Beyond the role of social networks, Kuznetsov and Sabel (2008) also discuss changing economic structures and networks of firms in the global knowledge economy.

Discussions of 'networks' in migration theory encompass several different phenomena – including recruitment practices and systems, chain migration, international economic systems for production and division of labour and transnational social connections among immigrants.[7] However, the skilled migration literature has thus far predominantly focused on the social and professional networks aspect of skilled migration. For example, the OECD (2008) particularly focuses on policies that support 'scientific diasporas' through websites and organisations as one of the main ways to promote links among scientists abroad to support scientific development in the home country.

New paradigms in skilled migration: Skilled migration, globalisation and competitiveness as win-win situations

new paradigms

As discussed earlier, skilled migration research borrows from other existing migration theories. Nonetheless, new paradigms are developing that seem to draw on economic geography, particularly given the increasing attention to the knowledge economy. Theoretically, the relationships are discussed in new growth theory (Romer 1990) as an alternative to neo-classical economic explanations. However, the ideas are typically used more implicitly, and few analyses of skilled migration have cited this theory directly. Immigration policy towards the highly skilled was largely focused on filling the shortage of IT workers in the mid-1990s and early 2000s, and thus was intertwined with other national policies for boosting technology and international competitiveness (Mahroum 2001: 27). These perspectives can be summarised as discussing relationships between skilled migration, globalisation and competitiveness. Within this discussion, there are two main ideas that hold importance in current skilled migration literature:

1. Skilled migration is presented as a 'race' or 'competition' for global talent or a 'battle for the brains', with the goal of attracting skilled migrants to Europe, particularly for the knowledge economy.
2. Skilled migration is seen as a contributor to economic and human capital development, promoting circular migration to mitigate the brain drain in developing (sending) countries, especially in healthcare and education sectors. For example, knowledge transfer for the scientific and technological sectors is a benefit of skilled migration.

brain drain

The increasing attention to skilled migration for the knowledge economy, and particularly for the IT and software industries, has shifted the paradigm on the need for skilled migration as an economic benefit, and has also tilted the scales in the debate on the effects of skilled migration on developing countries (as sending countries). In the 1960s and 1970s, 'brain drain' became a concern. This debate was linked with the loss to the US of scientists from Europe and Canada, and later also to the healthcare sector, as countries such as the UK and US hired doctors and nurses from developing countries. The loss of these individuals then aggravated strained health services and other public services – especially in the case of developing countries – and limited scientific development. 'Brain drain' of scientists to the US has long been considered to be a barrier to the scientific advancement of countries in the European Union. However, different employment patterns and immigration flows, including return migration, gained attention in the IT and other knowledge-based sectors in the 1990s and 2000s. As a result, skilled migration is now seen as offering potential advantages for developing economies. Table 9.4, from Guellec and Cervantes (2001), highlights these effects. As mentioned earlier, Silicon Valley became recognised as having a significant portion of skilled Indians and Chinese from mainland China and Taiwan who were contributing to its workforce. In addition, Silicon Valley contributed to positive 'knowledge spillover' when these individuals returned to their countries of origin and contributed to the growth of the knowledge economy there, as individuals with personal networks in the US or other countries, thus contributing to the expansion of markets in one or both locations (Kuptsch and Pang 2006; OECD 2002). In this way, the IT industry provides a sort of gold standard for the positive impact of skilled migration, and adds fuel to the concept of global competition for talent.

circular migration

Given that much skilled migration is temporary, there is a likelihood of return migration, and discussions of 'circular migration' have emerged as a core part of the skilled migration literature as well as in policy discussions. This literature emerged in light of the contributions of Chinese and Indian high-tech workers to new business and sectoral development in their countries of origin. The concept of circular migration focuses on skilled migration as a way of advancing human capital and knowledge transfer. The paradigm of 'circular' migration also debates perspectives on the emigration of skilled individuals as causing a permanent loss of qualified labour in the form of a 'brain drain', with the receiving society – which is often already privileged – experiencing a 'brain gain'. However, implicit in discussions of circular migration is an expectation that skilled migration *should* encompass temporary labour movements. Circular migration is often used to

Table 9.4 *Economic effects of skilled migration*

Sending Countries: Possible Positive Effects	*Receiving Countries: Possible Positive Effects*
Science and technology • Knowledge flows and collaboration, return of natives with foreign education and human capital, increased ties to foreign research institutions • Export opportunities for technology • Remittances and venture capital from diaspora networks • Successful overseas entrepreneurs bring valuable management experiences and access to global markets Human capital effects • Increased incentive for natives to seek higher skills • Possibility of exporting skills reduces risk/raises expected return from personal education investments • May increase domestic economic return to skills	Science and technology • Increased R&D and economic activity due to availability of additional highly skilled workers • Entrepreneurship in high growth areas • Knowledge flows and collaboration with sending countries • Immigrants can foster diversity and creativity • Export opportunities for technology Higher education systems • Increased enrolment in graduate programmes and keeping smaller programmes alive • Offset ageing of university professors and researchers Labour market • Wage moderation in high growth sectors with labour shortages • Immigrant entrepreneurship fosters firm and job creation • Immigrants can act as magnets for accessing other immigrant labour (network hiring effects)
Sending Countries: Possible Negative Effects	*Receiving Countries: Possible Negative Effects*
Human capital effects • 'Brain drain' and lost productive capacity due to (at least temporary) absence of higher skilled workers and students • Lower returns from public investment in tertiary education (waste of national public resources)	Higher education systems • Decreased incentive of natives to seek higher skills in certain fields, may crowd out native students from best schools Science and technology • Technology transfer to foreign competitors and possible hostile countries

Possible Global Effects

- Better international flows of knowledge, formation of international research and technology clusters (Silicon Valley, CERN)
- Better job matches, including: greater employment options for workers, researchers' ability to seek work most interesting to them and greater ability of employers to find rare and unique skill sets
- International competition for scarce human capital may have net positive effect on incentives for individual human capital investments.

Source: Guellec and Cervantes (2001: 86, which cites OECD), expanded on the basis of Regets (2000)

argue for 'improved' or 'win-win' outcomes, although it should be noted that the benefits might be overstated, because results depend on both personal and structural factors in the destination countries. There must be sufficient development of the sector in question and of the general infrastructure for skills to be utilised upon the migrants' return.

Conclusion

theories still being developed

This chapter argued that theories explaining skilled migration are still under development. Standard definitions, similarly, have yet to emerge. Although policies on skilled migration have undergone major change in recent decades, empirical evidence on their outcomes is still scant. Skilled migration research currently draws on other theories of labour migration, particularly push-pull models of individual movement and theories related to economic restructuring. However, new paradigms are emerging, such as the 'global competition for talent' notion and the idea of skilled migration as a contributor to human capital development and knowledge transfer. These elements have not yet been placed into a complete theoretical framework, but they have become guiding concepts in the literature of skilled migration.

The skilled migration landscape in Europe will continue to evolve as countries seek their place in the 'global competition for talent'. The individual countries and the EU as a whole are expected to further adjust their policies on skilled labour migration. Changes on both the national and EU fronts will affect skilled migration processes in Europe as well as global comparisons.

EU Directives

Three areas of research are of particular interest related to the paradigm of the global competition for talent. The first one, which has received little research attention up to now, involves the EU's directives to further harmonise European migration policy. Some measures have already been approved, such as the Researchers' Directive and the Blue Card, although some countries have placed specific stipulations on their implementation. This raises questions about the extent to which European countries can and will increase their numbers of skilled migrants. A closely associated issue is how national and supranational policies interact or contradict one another. In terms of migration theory, the addition of this regional perspective is novel, because migration has been seen as a sovereign, national affair in the past. Where policy has been included in models of migration, the political-economic focus has tended to be on national policies and politics. Furthermore, there are questions about whether the EU will exercise a preference for labour from its own member states – particularly skilled labour from Central and Eastern European countries in the Western and Northern European labour markets – versus attracting labour from outside the EU, including from developing countries such as India and China.

focus on integration

Another aspect of skilled labour migration that will likely receive greater research emphasis is migrant nationalities and gender,[8] as well as integration issues. Until now, most integration research has focused on low-skilled migrants. However, skilled migrants also require access to social institutions and services (particularly pensions, education systems for their children and medical care). They may face language barriers as well. Are European countries with relatively little experience with foreign skilled migrants equipped to meet the needs of this population? Furthermore, skilled migrants in Europe come primarily from developed countries at present, but if more effort is made to propel the 'global competition for talent', then new groups will likely also become noticeable – groups that may face discrimination or be seen as 'different' by the local population despite being highly skilled. There is a trend in Europe to emphasise 'integration' courses and language acquisition. Skilled migrants may not wish to meet such demands. Additionally, skilled migrants in Europe are now generally assumed to be temporary residents. The trend of temporary residence may change if policies move towards a long-term human capital form of recruitment, such as a points system.

new determinants

A third emerging research issue involves the 'new' determinants of migration, particularly among groups with the training and skills to fill labour market demands. In recent decades, the US has been the clear leader in attracting skilled migrants, but the UK has also emerged as a 'magnet' economy. There is now talk of the US losing its edge in the global competition for talent (e.g. Florida 2005), and questions are being raised about the situation in European countries. As more countries adopt skilled migration policies, what will determine who goes where? Is current migration theory sufficient to predict or at least to understand the drivers of these new flows and the impact of changing policies?

This chapter described the study of skilled migration as developing. Because much current knowledge borrows from general migration theories, there is reason to question how well the phenomenon of skilled migration is understood in the European context. New research could fill these knowledge gaps.

MAIN IDEAS

Definitions of 'skilled' migration change across *time* and *place*. 'Skilled' is a relative term, dependent on demographics and qualifications of the larger society, and on the skills currently in demand.

New paradigms are emerging, such as the 'global competition for talent' and the idea of skilled migration as a contributor to human capital development and knowledge transfer.

Skilled migration is often associated with short-term movements, which may include a series of destinations, circular migration or both.

Where policy is included in models of migration, the political-economic focus tends to be on national policies and politics.

As more countries adopt skilled migration policies, what will determine who goes where?

Is current migration theory sufficient to predict or at least to understand the drivers of these new flows and the impact of changing policies?

Notes

1 See EMN (2007: 27) for an overview of the policy categories for skilled migration in Europe.

2 For a discussion of statistics, see Dumont and Lemaitre (2004). Though more recent comparative data are available for international student migration, this topic is outside of the scope of this chapter. Recent publications on skilled migration utilising internationally comparative data, such as the OECD (2008), still make conclusions on the basis of the 2001 data or the more general 2000 OECD data on immigrants in OECD countries (DIOC). Similarly, other publications with a broad internationally comparative perspective, such as the International Organization for Migration's (IOM) World Migration Report, have not contained comparative statistics on skilled migration in recent years. The European Labour Force Survey also offers statistics based on survey methodology among recent migrants, which may differ from statistics related to either flows or the work permits issued. Therefore, updating statistics on skilled migration in Europe generally will require the study of national data sources, which may not be comparable.

3 For discussion of the impact of GATS on the global governance of skilled migration see Lavenex (2007).

4 For the law itself, see http://history.nih.gov/01docs/historical/documents/PL106-313.pdf.

5 For instance, Switzerland became more internationalised and had policy reforms to allow for EU workers and more highly skilled professionals in 1991, Ireland

revised its work permits in 2001 and the UK started a skilled migration programme in 2002. In addition, the UK, Ireland and Sweden opened their labour markets to citizens of the Central and Eastern European countries joining the EU in 2004.

6 The UK policy towards skilled migration is relatively recent, although there have been previous skilled flows such as that for doctors and also (given the diversity of the UK population) the post-colonial Indian migration. Until 2002, when the UK implemented the High Skilled Migration Programme, there was nearly a void of policies to attract or even allow skilled migrants to come to Europe, outside of the internal mechanisms of multinational corporations and other businesses (and various bilateral agreements, for instance for health care workers). Iredale (2005: 160-161) explains that the UK's policy then allowed 'individuals with special skills and experience to immigrate, initially for a year but with the opportunity to renew. [...] This is the first time in nearly three decades that foreign workers, other than EU member nationals, have been able to enter the UK without guaranteed employment'.

7 See Rindoks, Penninx and Rath (2006) for a discussion of the economic implications of networks for migration to Europe.

8 For an earlier discussion of gender and skilled migration in Europe see Kofman (2000).

References

Abella, M. (2006), 'Global competition for skilled workers and consequences', in: C. Kuptsch and E. F. Pang (eds), *Competing for Global Talent*, 11-32. Geneva: International Labour Organization (ILO), International Institute for Labour Studies (IILS).

Ackers, H.L. (2005), 'Moving people and knowledge: Scientific mobility in the EU', *International Migration* 43 (5): 99-131.

Bauder, H. (2008), 'Neoliberalism and the economic utility of immigration: Media perspectives of Germany's immigration law', *Antipode* 40 (1): 55-78.

Beaverstock, J. (2005), 'Transnational elites in the city: British highly-skilled inter-company transferees in New York City's financial district', *Journal of Ethnic and Migration Studies* 31 (2): 245-268.

Beaverstock, J. (1991), 'Skilled international migration: An analysis of the geography of international secondments within large accountancy firms', *Environment and Planning A* 23: 1133-1146.

Beaverstock, J. (1990), 'New international labour markets: The case of professional and managerial labour migration within large chartered accountancy firms', *Area* 22: 151-158

Beaverstock, J. and J. Smith (1996), 'Lending jobs to global cities: Skilled international labour migration, investment banking and the city of London', *Urban Studies 33* (8): 1377-1394.

Borjas, G.J. (1994), 'The economics of migration', *Journal of Economic Literature* 32 (4): 1167-1717.

Borjas, G.J. (1989a), 'Economic theory and international migration', *International Migration Review* 23 (3): 457-485.

Borjas, G.J. (1989b), 'Self selection and earnings of immigrants', *American Economic Review* 77: 531-553.

Carrington, W. and E. Detragiache (1998), *How Big is the Brain Drain?* IMF Working Paper. Washington, DC: IMF Research Department.

Cerna, L. (2010), 'Policies and practices of highly skilled migration in times of the economic crisis', *ILO International Migration Papers No. 99*. Geneva: International Labour Office.

Cervantes, M. and A. Goldstein (2008), 'Talent mobility in the global economy: Europe as a destination', in: A. Solimano (ed.), *The International Mobility of Talent: Types, Causes, and Development Impact*, 298-337. Oxford/New York: Oxford University Press.

Chaloff, J. and G. Lemaître (2009), 'Managing highly skilled labour migration: A comparative analysis of migration policies and challenges in OECD countries', OECD Social Employment and Migration Working Papers 79. Paris: Organisation for Economic Co-operation and Development.

Chiswick, B.R. (1978), 'The effects of Americanization on the earnings of foreign-born men', *Journal of Political Economy* 86: 897-921.

Cobb-Clark, D.A and M.D. Connolly (1997), 'The worldwide market for skilled migrants: Can Australia compete?' *International Migration Review* 31 (3): 670-693.

Csedo, K. (2008), 'Negotiating skills in the global city: Hungarian and Romanian professionals and graduates in London', *Journal of Ethnic and Migration Studies* 34 (5), 802-823.

DeVoretz, D.J. (2003), *Asian Skilled Immigration Flows to Canada: A Supply-side Analysis.* Vancouver: Asia Pacific Foundation of Canada.

Dumont, J. and G. Lemaître (2004), *Counting Immigrants and Expatriates in OECD Countries: A New Perspective.* Paris: OECD.

Dorigo, G. and W. Tobler (1983), 'Push-pull migration laws', *Annals of the Association of American Geographers* 73 (1): 1-17.

Dumont, J.-C. and P. Zurn (2007), 'Immigrant health workers in OECD countries in the broader context of highly skilled migration', in: *OECD Sopemi 2007 Edition*, 161-228. Paris: Organisation for Economic Co-operation and Development.

European Commission (2008), *The Employment in Europe Report 2008*. Brussels: European Communities.

EMN (2007), *Conditions of Entry and Residence of Third Country Highly-Skilled Workers in the EU.* Synthesis Report. Brussels: European Migration Network.

Ewers, M.C. (2007), 'Migrants, markets and multinationals: Competition among world cities for the highly skilled', *GeoJournal* 68: 119-130.

Ferro, A. (2004), 'Romanians abroad: A snapshot of highly skilled migration', *Higher Education in Europe* 29 (3): 381-392.

Findlay, A.M. (1990), 'A migration channels approach to the study of high level manpower movements: A theoretical perspective' *International Migration* 28: 15-23.

Florida, R. (2005), *The Flight of the Creative Class.* New York: Harper Business.

Florida, R. (2002), *The Rise of the Creative Class.* New York: Basic Books.

Freeman, G.P. and D.K. Hill (2006), 'Disaggregating immigration policy: The politics of skilled labour recruitment in the US', *Knowledge, Technology and Policy* 19 (3): 7-21.

Ghosh, B. (2005), 'Economic effects of international migration: A synoptic overview', in: *World Migration 2005*, 163-182. Geneva: International Organization for International Migration.

Guellec, D. and Cervantes, M. (2001), 'International mobility of highly skilled workers: From statistical analysis to policy formulation', in: OECD (ed.), *International mobility of the highly skilled*, 71-98. Paris: Organisation for Economic Co-operation and Development.

Guth, J. and B. Gill (2008), 'Motivations in East-West doctoral mobility: Revisiting the question of brain drain', *Journal of Ethnic and Migration Studies* 34 (5): 825-841.

Harris, J.R. and M. Todaro (1970), 'Migration, unemployment and development: A two-sector analysis', *American Economic Review* 60: 126-142.

Iredale, R. (2001), 'The migration of professionals: Theories and typologies', *International Migration* 39 (5): 7-26.

Iredale, R. (2005), 'Gender, immigration policies and accreditation: Valuing the skills of professional women migrants', *Geoforum* 36 (2): 155-166.

Kapur, D. and J. McHale (2005), *Give Us Your Best and Brightest: The Global Hunt for Talent and Its Impact on the Developing World.* Washington, DC: Center for Global Development.

Kofman, E. (2000), 'The invisibility of skilled female migrants and gender relations in studies of skilled migration in Europe', *International Journal of Population Geography* 6 (1): 45-59.

Koser, K. and Salt, J. (1997), 'The geography of highly skilled international migration', *International Journal of Population Geography* 3: 285-303.

Kuptsch, C. and Pang, P.F. (eds) (2006), *Competing for Global Talent.* Geneva: International Institute for Labour Studies.

Kuznetsov, Y. and C. Sabel (2008), 'Global mobility of talent from a perspective on new industrial policy: Open migration chains and diaspora networks', in: A. Solimano (ed.) *The International Mobility of Talent: Types, Causes, and Development Impact*, 84-113. Oxford: Oxford University Press.

Lavenex, S. (2007), 'The competition state and highly skilled migration', *Society* 44 (2): 32-41.

Lee, E.S. (1966), 'A theory of migration', *Demography* 3 (1): 47-57.

Leung, M. (2001), 'Get IT going: New ethnic Chinese business. The case of Taiwanese-owned computer firms in Hamburg', *Journal of Ethnic and Migration Studies* 27 (2): 277-294.

Liversage, A. (2009), 'Finding a path: Investigating the labour market trajectories of high-skilled immigrants in Denmark', *Journal of Ethnic and Migration Studies* 35 (2): 203-226.

Mahroum, S. (2001), 'Europe and the immigration of highly skilled labour', *International Migration* 39 (5): 27-43.

Mahroum, S. (1999), 'Competing for the highly skilled: Europe in perspective', *Science and Public Policy* 26 (1): 17-25.

Malmberg, G. (1997), 'Time and space in international migration', in: T. Hammar, G. Brochmann, K. Tamas and T. Faist (eds), *International Migration, Immobility and Development: Multidisciplinary Perspectives*, 21-48. Oxford/New York: Berg.

Meyer, J. (2001), 'Network approach versus brain drain: Lessons from the diaspora', *International Migration* 39 (5): 91-108.

OECD (2009), *International Migration Outlook. SOPEMI 2009. Special Focus: Managing Labour Migration beyond the Crisis.* Paris: Organisation for Economic Co-operation and Development.

OECD (2008), *The Global Competition for Talent: Mobility of the Highly Skilled.* Paris: Organisation for Economic Co-operation and Development.

OECD (2001), *International Mobility of the Highly Skilled.* Paris: Organisation for Economic Co-operation and Development.

Peri, G. (2005), *Skills and Talent of Immigrants: A Comparison between the European Union and the United States.* Paper 050304. Berkeley: Economics Department, University of California, Davis/Los Angeles: International Institute, University of California.

Piore, M.J. (1979), *Birds of Passage: Migrant Labor in Industrial Societies.* Cambridge: Cambridge University Press.

Ravenstein, E.G. (1885 and 1889), 'The laws of migration', *Journal of the Royal Statistical Society* 48: 167-277 and 52: 241-301.

Regets, M.C. (2000), 'Research and policy issues in high-skilled international migration: A perspective with data from the United States', paper prepared for the OECD Focus Group on Mobility of Human Resources, December.

Rindoks, A., R. Penninx and J. Rath (2006), 'Gaining from migration: What works in networks? Examining economically related benefits accrued from greater economic linkages, migration processes, and diasporas', Report prepared for the OECD Development Centre. IMISCOE Working Paper No. 13. Amsterdam: International Migration, Integration and Social Cohesion Network. www.imiscoe.org/publications/workingpapers/documents/Gainingfrommigration-whatworksinnetworks.pdf.

Rodrik, D. (2001), Comments at the conference Immigration Policy and the Welfare State. http://ksghome.harvard.edu/~drodrik/papers.html.

Romer, P.M. (1990), 'Endogenous technological change', *Journal of Political Economy* 98 (5): S71-S102.

Saiz, A. (2003), 'The impact of immigration on American cities: An introduction to the issues', *Business Review, Federal Reserve Bank of Philadelphia*, Q4: 14-23.

Salt, J. (1992), 'Migration processes among the highly skilled in Europe', *International Migration Review* 26: 484-505.

Salt, J. (1983), 'High level manpower movements in Northwest Europe', *International Migration Review* 17: 633-52.

Sassen, S. (1991), *The Global City: New York, London, and Tokyo*. Princeton: Princeton University Press.

Saxenian, A. (2002), *Local and Global Networks of Immigrant Professionals in Silicon Valley*. San Francisco: Public Policy Institute of California.

Saxenian, A. (1999), *Silicon Valley's New Immigrant Entrepreneurs*. San Francisco: Public Policy Institute of California.

Shachar, A. (2006), 'The race for talent: Highly skilled migrants and competitive immigration regimes', *New York University Law Review* 81 (April): 148-206.

Solimano, A. (ed.) (2008), *The International Mobility of Talent: Types, Causes, and Development Impact*. Oxford: Oxford University Press.

Stark, O. and D. Bloom. (1985), 'The new economics of labor migration', *American Economic Review* 75 (2): 173-178.

Wallerstein, I. (1974), *The Modern World System*. New York: Academic Press.

Wickramasekara, P. (2003), 'Policy responses to skilled migration: Retention, return and circulation', Perspectives on Labour Migration, Paper 5E. Geneva: International Labour Office. www.ilo.org/public/english/protection/migrant/download/pom/pom5e.pdf.

Williams, A.M. and V. Baláž (2005), 'What human capital, which migrants? Returned skilled migration to Slovakia from the UK', *International Migration Review* 39 (2): 439-468.

Zalatel, P. (2006), 'Competing for the highly skilled migrants: Implications for the EU common approach on temporary economic migration', *European Law Journal* 12 (5): 613-635.

Zolberg, A. (1989), 'The next waves: Migration theory for a changing world', *International Migration Review* 23 (3): 403-430.

Zimmermann, K.F. (2005), 'European labour mobility: Challenges and potentials', *De Economist* 153 (4): 425-450.

10 Environmental Migration[1]

François Gemenne

Introduction

Environmental migration has received increased scholarly and policy attention in the last decade. Though environmental drivers have always played a role in migration movements, the number of natural disasters has seemed to be on the rise, and their severity appears to be worsening, possibly due to the first impacts of climate change. Research on environment-related migration flows in recent times has shed new light on the linkages between environmental changes and migration.

history of environmental migration

History shows numerous examples of migrations associated with environmental changes and disasters. In 1755, an earthquake destroyed most of Lisbon, inducing mass population displacements towards other parts of Portugal, with some of those displaced returning to the city later (Dynes 1997). The Dust Bowl migration in the US is another classic example of mass migration associated with environmental disaster. In that case, severe drought and soil-depleting agricultural techniques resulted in dust storms that pushed populations westward. Thousands of farmers from Oklahoma, Texas and Arkansas had no choice other than to sell their farms and move in the 1930s. The environmental 'push' factors are obvious in this migration decision, but it should be stressed that other socio-economic factors were at work as well. The migration took place within the context of the Great Depression (Hansen and Libecap 2004). Furthermore, the prospect of a better life in California played a crucial role as a 'pull' factor (Gregory 1991).

More recently, massive population displacements were triggered by catastrophes such as the Sumatran tsunami in 2004, hurricane Katrina in 2005 and cyclone Nargis, which ravaged Burma in 2008. These disasters raised public awareness about the fate of a new kind of 'refugee'. In addition to those displaced by sudden events, many more are also displacements by slow-onset events. Most of these are related to climate change: villages resettled in the South Pacific islands to escape the rise in sea-level, farmers and pastoralists moving to cities because desertification threatens their livelihoods in sub-Saharan

Africa and Northern China, and Inuit communities displaced by the melting of the permafrost in Alaska. These population movements are not alike, but all can be presented as 'environmental migration' and envisioned through this lens.

consequences of climate change

Environmental migration is widely viewed as one of the most dramatic consequences of climate change. As early as 1990, the Intergovernmental Panel on Climate Change (IPCC)[2] warned that 'the gravest effects of climate change may be those on human migration as millions are displaced by shoreline erosion, coastal flooding and severe drought' (McTegart et al. 1990). Similarly, UN High Commissioner for Refugees, Antonio Guterres, stressed the importance of climate change as a driver of forced migration. In *The Guardian* of 17 June 2008 Guterres underlined the multi-causality of such displacements. 'Climate change is today one of the main drivers of forced migration', he said, 'both directly through impact on environment – not allowing people to live any more in the areas where they were traditionally living – and as a trigger of extreme poverty and conflict' (Borger 2008).

The nexus between environment and migration, however, remains highly controversial in academic circles. This controversy reaches to the very conceptualisation of the topic, and is fuelled, to a large extent, by a lack of empirical research. While the scientific basis of climate change is now well established, research on its impacts on populations, in particular, population movements, has lagged behind (Brown 2008). As a result, definitions, typologies and estimates of environmental migrants remain highly contested, and no real comprehensive policy response has emerged.

new field in migration studies

This chapter addresses the main theoretical debates surrounding the concept of environmental migration. Its aim is to assess the state of research on the subject at the time of writing (2010). The first section describes the studies that have been conducted on environmental migration, most of them recent. The emergence of the topic as a new field in migration research is traced, as well as the various directions in which scholarship has evolved. The second section addresses the key controversies of current debates, summed up here under the headings 'definitions', 'estimates' and 'models'. Previous research on migration – and most crucially, theoretical research – has been 'environmentally-blind' to a large extent (Koser 1996). This has contributed to myths, misconceptions and a powerful discourse by non-governmental organisations (NGOs) and advocacy groups. Finally, the third section assesses what we know of the environment-migration nexus, especially major areas of progress and research challenges. It presents the elements of the complex and intertwining relationship between environment and migration, distinguishing between different environmental causes for migration and different migration patterns.

The emergence of a new concept

Though environmental migration is an ancient phenomenon, as can be attested from many historical documents, the concern for this type of displacement is relatively new, and research on the issue has experienced rapid and increasingly numerous developments in recent years. This section aims to show how the concept was born out of environmental concerns, and how literature on the topic has developed.

Since the 1970s, environmental matters have gained considerable currency, but they were not really linked with migration issues until recently. Since the creation of the Intergovernmental Panel on Climate Change (IPCC) in 1988, climate change has received increased attention from policymakers, researchers and the media, and has since largely overshadowed other forms of environmental disruption. Mass migration movements are now widely presented as an inevitable consequence of climate change, and dramatic estimates of future flows of 'climate refugees' are being circulated.

two major disasters

Two major disasters have served to stress the impact that environmental changes have on migration. On 26 December 2004, a major tsunami hit Southeast Asia, resulting in a mass displacement of over two million people. The scale of the disaster also prompted an intervention by the UN High Commissioner for Refugees (UNHCR), even though the organisation's mandate does not include an operational response to natural disasters (Lambert and Pougin de la Maisonneuve 2007). Eight months later hurricane Katrina devastated the US Gulf Coast, triggering yet another massive population displacement, which lasted for months and evolved into permanent relocation for a third of New Orleans' displacees. These two disasters showed empirical evidence of massive displacements linked to environmental changes; from that time, studies, reports, conferences and workshops on environmental migration would flourish.

Conflicting perspectives

'environmental refugees'

The first mention of the term 'environmental refugee' dates back to 1948 (Vogt 1948), but the concept only gained currency in 1970s, through the speeches of the famous environmentalist Lester Brown. It wasn't really popularised, however, until a 1985 report by El-Hinnawi of the UN Environment Programme provided the very first definition of the concept. 'Environmental refugees' were then defined as 'people who have been forced to leave their traditional habitat, temporarily or permanently, because of a marked environmental disruption (natural and/or triggered by people) that jeopardised their existence and/or seriously affected the quality of their life'. This definition was quickly criticised by many authors, who contended it was so wide and vague 'as to render the concept practically meaningless' (Suhrke and Visentin 1991). Three years later, a working paper by Jacobson (1988) from the environmental think-tank WorldWatch Institute attempted to systematise the study of this new category of forced migrants. Both reports were received with great interest in the field of environmental studies and harsh criticism in the field of refugee studies; they had a 'short-lived shock-effect on the public debate but were rejected as unserious by scholars' (Suhrke 1993). The reports were also perceived as an attempt to use forced migration to draw attention to environmental problems. In particular, the use of the word 'refugee' was criticised, regardless of its legal meaning. Many insisted that the concept had to be better defined, and that a 'doom-and-gloom' scenario was overly deterministic and unrealistic.

An alarmist perspective

alarmist perspective

These early works had paved the way for an alarmist perspective, which would soon forecast massive migration flows related to a wide variety of environmental changes. Many scholars who adopted this perspective were initially interested in the environment-security nexus (Westing 1989; Homer-Dixon 1991; Swain 1996). The linkage between environmental disruption and conflicts was the core concern of this perspective, and soon enough refugee flows were mobilised as an explanatory variable to justify a causal relationship between environmental change and conflicts. Migration was viewed both as a consequence of environmentally-induced conflicts and a trigger of future conflicts over natural resources. Such theories were deeply rooted in a neo-Malthusian perspective,[3] and gained new strength with the commonly held perception that climate change was a threat to the world's security. Alarmist theories were soon to make their way into the policy realm.

Building upon this initial approach, some scholars tried to forecast future migration flows induced by environmental change. The main concern of their research was no longer the threat to security, but the environmental risks and consequences of environmental disruption. Those scholars were led by the environmentalist Norman Myers, who was undoubtedly the most prominent whistleblower in the field. Myers wrote extensively on the topic and dared to forecast precise estimates, which echoed loudly in the media (1997, 2002, 1993). In 1995, Myers published a book jointly with Kent entitled *Environmental Exodus,* and its impact has been considerable; it is still one of the most frequently-cited sources on the subject. The reason for this is simple: the study was the first to offer a forecast of future flows, as well as hotspots at the country-level. Myers and Kent fed the well-known media appetite for numbers, sometimes at the risk of oversimplifying a complex situation.

A sceptical perspective

sceptical approach

Migration scholars adopted a much more cautious and sceptical approach to the issue, and first contended that the concept of environmental migration made little sense, while studies forecasting massive migration flows were grossly overestimated. Kibreab (1997, 1994) vehemently criticised the alarmist approach of environmental scholars, which was increasingly accepted as 'scientific truth'. According to him, the main rationale behind the concept of environmental migration was to depoliticise the causes of displacement, allowing states to derogate their obligations to provide asylum, since 'environmental conditions (did) not constitute a basis for international protection' (1997). He perceived the concept as a threat to refugee protection, and an excuse for governments to justify restrictive asylum policies. Black (1998) refutes the argument that the concept is just an excuse for Northern governments to enforce tighter asylum policies, but he agrees with Kibreab that most of the 'alarmist' literature 'serves only to differentiate a single cause of migration'. He further questions the very concept of 'environmental refugee', and asserts that it would be more useful to consider environmental drivers as part of a complex and multidimensional reality, rather than isolate them as a single, direct causes of migration. Castles agrees that 'the notion of the "environmental refugee" is misleading and does little to help us understand the complex processes at work in specific situations of impoverishment, conflict and displacement'. However, he also acknowledges that environmental factors are not unimportant in these situations, but are rather part of 'complex patterns of multiple causality, in which natural and environmental factors are closely linked to economic, social and political ones'. He therefore calls for 'much more research and better understanding' (2002).

Towards a synthesis?

more collaboration

Scholars such as Castles (2002), Hugo (1996) and Suhrke (1994) had noted that the conflicting perspectives between the alarmist and sceptical approaches stemmed from a disciplinary divide, and had called for more collaboration and empirical research. From the mid-2000s onward, the positions of the alarmist and sceptical perspectives drew somewhat closer to each other. Several factors can account for this rapprochement: the increasing number of multi-disciplinary collaborations; a number of major disasters that struck different parts of the world in 2004 and 2005; and the increased attention given to climate change. These three sets of factors drove a significant evolution in both perspectives.

First, an increasing number of conferences, workshops and publications addressed the topic, bringing together environmental and migration scholars. These collaborative publications, events and projects greatly contributed to the reconciliation of both approaches, which until then lacked forums in which to exchange ideas and findings.

The second factor was that the debate was influenced to a great extent by current events, and in particular the major natural disasters that struck in the mid-2000s. Empirical evidence of environmentally-induced mass displacements was then obvious, and the lack of empirical findings on the issue could no longer be a credible claim for sceptical scholars. As empirical evidence was mounting – at least in the media, if not in academic works – it was increasingly difficult to downplay the role of environmental drivers in forced migration.

media attention

Third, climate change received increased and sustained attention from the media, policymakers and public opinion, following the almost simultaneous release of the IPCC Fourth Assessment Report and Al Gore's film *An Inconvenient Truth*. Large migration flows were presented as one of the most dramatic consequences of climate change, which prompted a renewed interest in the topic in academic spheres, from both environmental and migration studies. As a matter of fact, most publications on the issue from the mid-2000s onward focused only on climate change-induced migration, largely ignoring other environmental causes for migration (Biermann and Boas 2007; Brown 2008; Kniveton et al. 2008; Piguet 2008).

At the same time, empirical studies were making headway. The Environmental Change and Forced Migration Scenarios (EACH-FOR) project, conducted between 2007 and 2009, was one of the most significant initiatives at the time. It was launched in order to fill in the gap in empirical studies on environmental migration. The project selected 23 case studies that were experiencing environmental change, and researched the migration behaviours of the affected populations. It was the first-ever endeavour of its kind, aimed at providing a global picture of environmental migration in a comparative perspective.

This project, however, which was of an exploratory nature, has yet to be followed by other similar projects, and academic debates remain greatly impeded by the lack of empirical studies. Though literature on the topic has significantly evolved over time, the very concept of environmental migration remains vividly debated, in many aspects that will now be discussed.

Definitions, predictions, models

Early works presented the relationship between environmental change and migration flows as being simple and direct. Over time, the academic community acknowledged the complexity of this relationship, and it is now the dominant view that environmental factors are part of a vast ensemble of migration drivers. The obstacles to an agreed upon definition or consensual estimates denote the complexity of the relationship, which has been insufficiently accounted for by migration theories and models.

The definitional issue

lack of a definition

In the absence of any legal definition, a scientific consensus on the definition of environmental migration has yet to be reached. Different reasons account for this difficulty: the problem is partly rooted in the debates over the conceptualisation of environmental migration, but the lack of a definition also feeds, in a 'catch-22'-type situation, the controversies over the concept.

One of the main reasons explaining the lack of consensual definition is linked to the difficulty in isolating environmental factors from other drivers of migration. Most authors stress the multi-causality of migration and the intermingling of factors (Black 2001; Castles 2002; Brown 2008; Boano et al. 2007). Therefore, one can legitimately ask whether isolating environmental drivers is possible, or even makes much sense conceptually. Sceptics tend to argue that it does not, and that doing so would be a distraction from other, more pressing issues (Castles 2004; Kibreab 1997). Alarmists, on the contrary, see urgency in acknowledging and defining environmental migration. Do environmental migrants make up an additional category of forced migrants, or are they better understood within existing conceptual categories?

The question relates to the importance given to environmental factors amongst other drivers: they are deeply rooted in socio-economic, cultural and political contexts, and not easy to disentangle. Even though the importance of environmental drivers is widely acknowledged in the literature, debate remains vivid regarding the need to conceptualise these drivers separately from other drivers of migration.

forced and voluntary migration

This intermingling of migration drivers, however, is far from being the sole obstacle to defining environmental migration. Another major hindrance lies in the confusion between forced and voluntary migration. A common assumption is that environmental disruptions induce only forced – and often brutal – displacements, an assumption emphasised in the term 'environmental refugees'. Suhrke (1994) wonders whether there is 'something about the nature of environmental degradation that tends to produce refugee-like movement rather than migration'. However, many authors stress that environmental factors induce not only forced displacement, but also voluntary migration (Renaud et al. 2007; Suhrke 1994; Hugo 1996). The distinction between forced and voluntary migrants is difficult to make in the case of environmental migration; yet the distinction is a fundamental one to migration studies and policies.

Finally, a further difficulty arises from the absence of any legal definition of the concept. Unlike refugees or internally-displaced persons, no specific legal framework addresses environmental migration. Once again, this can be seen as another 'catch-22' situation: the development of a legal definition is impeded by the conceptual lack of clarity that prevails.

The definitional issue is not just a scholarly matter: environmental migration as a social phenomenon is apprehended through its definition, which is important for the development of normative frameworks and policy responses. Without a clear definition, one cannot identify which populations are of concern and require assistance, nor can one accurately estimate the number of people displaced or prompted to migrate due to environmental factors. Words and typologies also matter for the populations themselves, because of the images and meanings they carry: people displaced by hurricane Katrina angrily resented the use of the term 'refugees', for example.

As stated above, the first definition provided by El-Hinnawi (1985) was met with widespread criticism, with most authors asserting that the definition was too wide and had little practical relevance (Suhrke and Visentin 1991). In subsequent years, many other attempts to define environmental migration were made by a wide range of authors (Myers 1997; Renaud et al. 2007; Cooper 1997). Most of them still revolve around some key elements that were already present in El-Hinnawi's definition:

- With few exceptions, most definitions address only forced displacement, leaving out voluntary migration;
- A strong emphasis is put on the destruction of people's habitat or livelihoods;
- Environmental changes are loosely defined, and can include man-made or natural disasters[4] and sudden or slow-onset changes.

IOM definition

More recently, a definition proposed by the IOM has garnered increased consensus, and has been used as a working definition by a number of scholars (Kniveton et al. 2008; Brown 2008):

> Environmental migrants are persons or groups of persons who, for compelling reasons of sudden or progressive changes in the

> environment that adversely affect their lives or living conditions, are obliged or have to leave their habitual homes, or choose to do so, either temporarily or permanently, and who move either within their country or abroad (International Organization for Migration 2007).

The three features observed in El-Hinnawi's definition are present here as well, and the IOM definition is not significantly different. The IOM definition is equally broad, and therefore also invites alarmist forecasts and does not distinguish between different types of migration: voluntary or forced, temporary or permanent, and internal or international. Furthermore, it does not acknowledge the multi-causality of migration, and does not elaborate on the characteristics of environmental drivers.

The EACH-FOR project proposed how to distinguish between environmental migrants and environmental displacees:

> Environmental migrants are people who chose to move voluntarily from their usual place of residence primarily due to environmental concerns or reasons. [...] Environmental displacees are people who are forced to leave their usual place of residence, because their lives, livelihoods and welfare have been placed at serious risk as a result of *adverse environmental processes and events*[5] (natural and/or triggered by people) (Dun et al. 2007).

Of paramount importance to this definition is the distinction between forced and voluntary migration, a distinction that should 'infuse some realism in the projection of future flows' (Suhrke 1993), since the confusion between different types of migratory movements was a major reason for the lack of clarity that still surrounds estimates and predictions.

Estimates and predictions

difficult to calculate

Estimates and predictions are among the most contentious issues in the conceptualisation of the relationship between environmental change and migration. For the same reasons that explain the absence of a consensual definition, it is difficult to calculate a precise and rigorous number of environmentally displaced persons. Given the lack of comprehensive methodology and empirical studies, the field was wide open for guesses and pessimistic estimates rather than actual numbers. Boano et al. cite no fewer than ten different estimates, from various scholars and organisations (2007).

With regard to actual displacement, the most frequently cited figure comes from the Norwegian Refugee Council, which publishes an annual report on the number of people displaced by disasters – but not accounting for slow-onset events. As for future flows, a figure frequently cited is derived from Norman Myers (2002), who forecast that there could be up to 200 million people displaced by 2050. The figure gained even wider currency after it was endorsed by Stern (2007), in his highly-publicised report on the economics of climate change. Some estimates were even more pessimistic, predicting that up to one billion people could be displaced by 2050 (Christian Aid 2007). This figure, however, included all types of displacement, and not only those induced by environmental changes,[6] contrary to what has often been reported.

Different factors impede upon the collection and development of accurate data and forecasts. Some of these factors are common to all displacement-related issues; others are specific to environmental migration. Crisp (1999) notes that 'while all of the standard works on refugees are replete with numbers, few even begin to question the source or accuracy of those statistics'. A similar statement can be applied to works on environmental migration: most of them reproduce previous statistics, without critically assessing them. Figures provided by Myers are often quoted as scientific truth, without questioning his methodology.

accurate data difficult

The quest for numbers is also hampered by the debates and controversies over the concept and definition of environmental migration. Without a clear definition, providing accurate data seems a daunting task. It is worth noting, however, that a similar problem is encountered when calculating the number of refugees, even though a legal definition exists. In the words of Crisp (1999), '[A]ny form of enumeration exercise must be based upon a clearly defined unit of measurement if it is to produce reliable, usable and comparable data. In the case of refugee statistics, however, such clarity does not always exist.'

Most displacements that are driven by environmental factors are internal, not international. This poses a further statistical problem, since calculating cross-border movements is much easier than calculating internal movements: 'the machinery to collect data on these movements simply does not yet exist' (Brown 2008). Crisp (1999) provides a list of questions that are left unanswered when one is attempting to calculate the number of internally displaced people (IDPs):

> In the absence of a clear criterion such as the crossing of an international border, how far does a person have to move to be considered 'internally displaced'? When do internally (displaced) people cease to warrant that status: when they return to

> their original place of residence, or when they have achieved a certain degree of physical and socio-economic security in the place to which they have fled? Given that a large proportion of the world's IDPs are thought to live in towns and cities, how can they be differentiated from other rural-to-urban migrants?

Some further problems are specific to the nature of environmental migration. When it comes to predictions, figures are usually based on the number of people living in regions at risk, and not on the number of people actually expected to migrate. Estimates do not account for adaptation strategies, different levels of vulnerability to change, or simply – though it might sound harsh – disaster-related casualties.

Predictions also need to take into account demographic changes that are expected to occur over future decades. Whereas global population growth can be predicted to a certain extent, its geographic distribution remains uncertain. In recent years, migration to urban areas has accelerated. An increasing number of people live in regions highly exposed to natural risks and hazards, resulting in an increased number of disasters. These evolutions are particularly significant in developing countries, making estimates of the number of potential migrants a challenging task.

Finally, the impacts of climate change are expected to spur a large number of future displacements. Though it is possible to mitigate these impacts through adaptation strategies and to mitigate climate change itself by reducing greenhouse gas emissions, the future impacts of climate change on societies will greatly depend on future levels of greenhouse gas emissions, and on the amount of funding allocated for the development of adaptation strategies in vulnerable regions. In a nutshell, future displacements depend to a large extent upon what is done today. Because of the inertia of the climate system, the impacts of global warming until 2050 have been largely pre-determined by past emissions (Hansen et al. 2006). Impacts beyond 2050 depend on current emissions, which is why predictions generally do not go beyond that year. Though the impacts of climate change until 2050 are largely known thanks to the IPCC reports, adaptation strategies can minimise how these impacts affect societies. Hence, future displacements will also be contingent upon the adaptation strategies that are implemented today – and migration might be a part of these strategies, as will be shown later in this chapter.

Despite these difficulties, getting the numbers right is an important step for developing adequate policies. The programming of assistance and mobilisation of resources, including funding, depend on accurate numbers (Crisp 1999). In the absence of reliable statistics, numbers can be easily inflated and manipulated, in order to attract attention to some populations, sometimes at the expense of other populations in dire need of assistance.

The insufficiencies of migration theories and models

Traditionally, models of migration have been predicated on economic disparities between countries, and most of them stress the economic motives of migrants, paying little attention to environmental factors. Piguet notes, however, that such factors were present in early models of migration, and have since disappeared (Hietanen 2009). Traditional models generally assume that migration is driven by wage and employment differentials, or political persecution or turmoil in the case of forced migration.

models for internal and forced migration

Models and theories aimed at explaining internal and forced migration, however, tend to give greater importance to environmental drivers. With regard to internal migration, the most classical model is the Harris-Todaro model, which initially focused on labour markets, with unemployment rate and wage differentials as the main drivers of internal migration (Harris and Todaro 1970). Over time, the Harris-Todaro model was adapted in order to include human capital variables such as age, family ties, social networks and so forth. At the macro-level, this resulted in the development of a gravity model, in which these different variables were aggregated in order to provide a explanatory framework for empirical research (Alonso 1986; Greenwood 1997). In its standard format, the gravity model aggregates population size and distance (gravity variables), and economic, labour market and environmental variables. Overall, the literature on internal displacement is more recent, since the plight of peoples uprooted and dispersed within the borders of their country was only recognised as a matter of concern beginning in the 1990s (Mooney 2005). The definition of IDPs approved by the UN General Assembly in 1998 encompasses migrants who have been forced to leave their homes because of an armed conflict, generalised violence, human rights violations or natural and man-made disasters, but have not crossed an international border (United Nations Commission on Human Rights 1998).

With regard to forced migration, even though it has recently been argued that it is increasingly difficult for states to distinguish between migrants and refugees (Crisp 2007), most theories insist on the specificities of refugee (and IDP) movements. Like theories of voluntary migration, models of forced migration pay little attention to environmental factors and constraints. One of the most famous models of forced migration, developed by Gordenker (1989), lists four reasons that can induce forced migration, none of them having anything to do with environmental factors: international war, internal disturbances, changes in the social structure due to political perturbations and international political tensions. Kunz (1973), however, argues that 'it is the reluctance to uproot oneself, and the absence of positive original motivations to settle elsewhere, which characterizes all refugee decisions and distinguishes the refugee from the voluntary migrants', a statement that bears high significance for environmental migration. He recognizes two 'kinetic' types of refugee movements: anticipatory movements involving people before the deterioration of the situation, and acute movements that are unplanned and *en masse*, where the objective is to reach a safe haven. Richmond (1994) applies a similar distinction to environmental migration, and considers that the difference between proactive and reactive migration is more significant than the distinction between forced and voluntary migration.

ignored by classical theories

Though environmental migration drivers have been given slightly more attention in models of internal and forced migration, classical theories have not really accounted for environmental factors. To a certain extent, they can apply to environmental migration and provide an explanatory value, but it is fair to say that the matter has been mostly ignored by classical migration theories. As a result, these theories remain grossly insufficient, and much of the academic discourse on environmental migration has developed within environmental studies, leaving ample room for NGOs, advocacy groups and international agencies to develop their own specific discourse on the topic.

The environment-migration nexus

Beyond these academic debates, what do we know today about the way environmental changes induce migration movements? Surprisingly little. In many ways, the very term 'environmental migration' is deceptive in that it implies a uniform type of migration. It can also refer to a wide range of migration patterns, induced by an equally wide array of environmental changes.

Environmental causes of migration

The environmental causes of migration are usually vaguely described, as if all types of environmental disruption result in similar flows of migration. As a matter of fact, research shows that this is far from the case; not all environmental changes induce similar movements, and some of them do not induce movements at all (Kniveton et al. 2008). Furthermore, similar movements can be induced by different kinds of disruption, while the same disruption can result in very different movements.

environmental causes

Environmental causes of migration can be extremely diverse; some changes are brutal and unexpected, like earthquakes, and others have a slow onset, such as sea-level rise; some are directly man-made, as in the case of industrial accidents, while others stem from a natural hazard, such as volcanic eruptions.

The biggest problem when analysing environmental changes, however, might not be their categorisation, but their relative importance compared to other migration drivers. Literature has repeatedly emphasised the complexity of the relationship between environmental factors and migration. This view has since prevailed in the literature, and has been part of a wider movement stressing the importance of environmental factors in social transformations (Diamond 2005).

Hugo (1996) asserts that there can be no doubt that 'the incidence of disasters has [...] increased as have the associated population displacements', but identifies several other factors that exacerbated the predisposing conditions for environmental migration, thus increasing the incidence of precipitating, migration-inducing events. Such factors include population growth, poverty, intensive agriculture, weak environmental regulations and corruption.

Environmental changes are increasingly perceived as key drivers of migration, if combined with predisposing conditions. These proximate predispositions have to do with social vulnerability; poverty, population density, public policies and so forth. Therefore, environmental changes as a cause of population movements are best understood as precipitating events and processes, which can induce migration when they match predisposing factors. The fact that such changes are becoming more numerous and increasingly associated with population movements is not contested. The underlying causes of these movements, however, remain a highly debated topic. Sceptics argue that these causes lie in social, economic and political processes, while alarmists contend that they are to be found directly in environmental changes.

Migration patterns

migration patterns

Environmental changes can be very diverse, but so can the migration flows induced by these changes. Though they are often gathered under the label of environmental migration, they actually represent a wide spectrum of migration patterns, trajectories and behaviours. Many attempts have been made to classify and categorise them – Black (2001) rightly points out that 'there are perhaps as many typologies as there are papers on the subject'. A common shortcoming of many typologies is that they try to combine a classification of environmental changes with a classification of migration patterns (Jacobson

1988; Piguet 2008; Masters 2000). Such a combination is rooted in a deterministic perspective that assumes specific migration patterns to correspond to specific types of environmental change. Both classifications need to be separated, as migration patterns depend not only upon the type of environmental disruption, but also upon other social, economic and political factors, as well as individual characteristics. Yet a number of distinctions need to be made, since not all migration flows are similar, nor do they require the same policy responses.

International and internal migration

international and internal migration

Amongst the different distinctions that can be made, the easiest is certainly the distinction between international and internal migration. This is also probably the only one for which it is possible to establish clear-cut categories, at least from a formal point of view. This distinction naturally bears an essential meaning for normative frameworks and policies: the fundamental element of international law remains states' sovereignty. Thus, any international agreement on environmental migration would leave out those displaced within their country.

Yet research shows that most people who move due to environmental reasons tend to stay close to their former place of habitat, and travel relatively short distances within their country (Hugo 1996). When international migration occurs, it is usually due to pre-existing patterns of migration that occurred between two or more countries prior to the environmental disruption.

Voluntary and forced migration

Making the distinction between voluntary and forced migration is often presented as paramount for the implementation of assistance and protection policies, but is not an easy distinction to make in the case of environmental migration. Environmentally-displaced persons are often labelled as refugees, though they do not fit the legal definition as contained in the 1951 Geneva Convention, whether or not their movement is compelled.

Though this distinction is essential, it is also highly controversial, and not as clear-cut as it might seem. Migration, even though it is perceived as being voluntary movement, often implies a certain level of constraint, where migrants have little choice on the conditions of their migration. On the other hand, some cases of forced migration, such as some resettlement schemes, might leave some choice to the displacees as to the time and place of their relocation. For these reasons, Hugo (1996) argues that 'population mobility is probably best viewed as being arranged along a continuum ranging from totally voluntary migration [...] to totally forced migration', rather than being separated into clear-cut categories.

line blurred

Such observations are particularly valid when applied to environmental migration: whereas some people must flee for their life – when faced with a brutal disaster, for example – most will simply experience a progressive degradation of their habitat, and might decide to leave once a certain threshold has been reached, or once migration facilitators make it possible. Though their migration is compelled, those who migrate under these conditions retain the possibility to choose when and where they go. Most often, the line between forced and voluntary migration is blurred, and the distinction between 'environmental migrants' and 'environmental displacees' is also best understood as a continuum, where amenity migrants[7] represent one end, and people fleeing for their life in a disaster situation the other. The extent to which migration is compelled largely depends upon the time when migration occurs, an aspect that shall now be developed.

Proactive and reactive migration

Richmond (1994) argues that this distinction is more essential than the distinction between forced and voluntary migration, and reflects the degree of autonomy of the actors involved regarding their migration decision. With regard to environmental migration, he differentiates between 'proactive migration' and 'reactive migration', and states that:

> Gradual environmental degradation, soil erosion, etc., may initially lead to proactive migration, but eventually result in reactive movements as the process of degradation accelerates. Reactive migration that combines environmental and social determinants occurs when whole communities are forced to move as a consequence of environmental degradation or disaster and re-establish in a new location.

proactive and reactive migration

The time when people move reflects their degree of autonomy in regard to their migration, and is often related to its degree of constraint. The threshold at which an environmental degradation becomes no longer sustainable, however, might vary greatly from one migrant to another, as does the degree of proactivity. Therefore, the distinction between proactive and reactive migration should not be viewed as being in discrete categories equivalent to 'before' and 'after'.

Short-term and long-term migration

The question of the duration of the movement bears great importance in regard to environmental migration. Some kinds of environmental changes, such as floods and other extreme weather events, are sometimes assumed to induce only temporary movements, allowing people to return to their homes after a short period of time (Piguet 2008). Empirical evidence, such as the displacements induced by hurricane Katrina, has proven otherwise. Though voluntary migration is often perceived as a long-term move, if not a permanent one, studies suggest that seasonal – hence temporary – movement can be an effective adaptation strategy for coping with environmental change (McLeman and Smit 2006). The duration of the move is not only dependent on the nature of the triggering environmental change, but also, more importantly, on the social and economic characteristics of the migrant, as well as on the policies implemented to address the movement and return of those displaced.

Conclusion

towards consensus

Environmental drivers are hardly addressed in classical migration theories. Nonetheless, migration studies are quickly evolving to rectify the matter, catching up with environmental studies. Scholarly debate is moving towards a consensual approach, away from the previous radical opposition between an alarmist view and a sceptical perspective. Academic discussions today acknowledge the multiplicity and intertwining nature of migration's drivers, including environmental disruptions. Questions remain, however, regarding definitions and predictions of future flows. Policy responses and appropriate normative frameworks are also still at issue, due in part to the remnants of the fundamental divide between alarmists and sceptics.

Do environmental migrants in fact constitute a particular category of migrant? Setting environmental causes apart from other migration drivers makes little sense. Environmental migration is best understood as a dimension of migration's complex dynamics. Use of the concept, however, draws attention to the interactions between environmental changes and migration. Scholars and policymakers have long grossly neglected these interactions. Current concerns over the consequences of climate change shed new light on the environment-migration nexus. Environmental drivers of migration are expected to play an even more prominent role as the impacts of climate change emerge, leading to new policy challenges.

Environmental migration encompasses different types of migration. This calls into question established categories, as well as current frameworks of governance and protection. Until now, the scholarly debate has mostly focused on the conceptualisation of the issue. To make headway, that debate will need to be fuelled by cross-disciplinary empirical studies and re-embedded into migration theories.

MAIN IDEAS

Setting environmental causes apart from other migration drivers makes little sense, as environmental migration is best understood as a dimension of migration's complex dynamics.

Widespread concerns over the consequences of climate change shed new light on the environment-migration nexus.

Drivers of environmental migration are expected to play an even more prominent role as the impacts of climate change become evident and present new policy challenges.

Environmental migration encompasses different types of migration, calling into question established categories as well as current frameworks of governance and protection.

Notes

1 This chapter reflects the state of research at the time of writing, in 2010.
2 The IPCC is a scientific body jointly set up in 1988 by the World Meteorological Organisation (WMO) and the United Nations Environment Programme (UNEP), in order to assess and evaluate the risks posed by human-induced climate change. It is comprised of more than 2,000 scientists and is widely considered as the most authoritative body on climate change.
3 Neo-Malthusian perspectives insist on the concept of a 'carrying capacity' of ecosystems and the need to limit demographic growth in order to achieve sustainability.
4 Even though this distinction itself is questionable.
5 Emphasis in the original text.
6 The people displaced by climate change-related events accounted for 250 million, and those displaced by natural disasters accounted for 50 million, whereas people displaced by development projects, such as dams, accounted for 645 million.
7 Amenity migrants are migrants attracted to a destination by the perception of a more favourable environment. 'Pull' environmental factors are the determinants in their migration choice.

References

Alonso, W. (1986), 'A theory of movements', in: N. Hansen (ed.) *Systems Approach to Human Settlements*. Cambridge: Ballinger.

Biermann, F. and I. Boas (2007), 'Preparing for a warmer world: Towards a global governance system to protect climate refugees'. Global Governance Working Paper. Amsterdam et al.: The Global Governance Project.

Black, R. (2001), 'Environmental refugees: myth or reality?' New Issues in Refugee Research. Geneva: United Nations High Commissioner for Refugees.

Black, R. (1998), *Refugees, Environment and Development*. Harlow, UK: Addison Wesley Longman.

Boano, C., R. Zetter and T. Morris (2007), *Environmentally Displaced People: Understanding the Linkages between Environmental Change, Livelihoods and Forced Migration*. Oxford: Refugee Studies Centre.

Borger, J. (2008), 'Conflicts fuelled by climate change causing new refugee crisis, warns UN', *The Guardian* 17 June.

Brown, O. (2008), 'Migration and climate change'. IOM Migration Research Series. Geneva: International Organization for Migration.

Castles, S. (2007), *Confronting the Realities of Forced Migration*. Migration Policy Institute 2004 (18 March). www.migrationinformation.org/Feature/display.cfm?ID=222.

Castles, S. (2002), 'Environmental change and forced migration: making sense of the debate.' New Issues in Refugee Research. Geneva: United Nations High Commissioner for Refugees.

Christian Aid (2007), *Human Tide: The Real Migration Crisis*. London: Christian Aid.

Cooper, J.B. (1997), 'Environmental refugees: Meeting the requirements of the refugee definition', *New York University Environmental Law Journal* 6 (2): 480-503.

Crisp, J. (1999), '"Who has counted the refugees?" UNHCR and the politics of numbers.' New Issues in Refugee Research. Geneva: United Nations High Commissioner for Refugees.

Crisp, J. (2007), 'Vital distinction: States are having increasing difficulty distinguishing between refugees and migrants', *Refugees* 148: 4-12.

Diamond, J. (2005), *Collapse: How Societies Choose to Fail or Succeed*. New York: Penguin.

Dun, O., F. Gemenne and R. Stojanov (2007), *Environmentally Displaced Persons: Working Definitions for the EACH-FOR Project*. EACH-FOR 2007 (17 November). www.each-for.eu.

Dynes, R.R. (1997), 'The Lisbon Earthquake in 1755: Contested Meanings in the First Modern Disaster'. Preliminary Paper 255. Newark (DE): Disaster Research Center, University of Delaware.

El-Hinnawi, E. (1985), *Environmental Refugees*. Nairobi: United Nations Environment Programme.

Gordenker, L. (1989), 'Early warning of refugee incidents', in: G. Loescher and L. Monahan (eds), *Refugees and International Relations*. Oxford: Oxford University Press.

Greenwood, M.J. (1997), 'Internal migration in developed countries', in: M.R. Rosenzweig and O. Stark (eds), *Handbook of Population and Family Economics*. Amsterdam: Elsevier.

Gregory, J. (1991), *American Exodus: The Dust Bowl Migration and the Okie Culture in California*. New York: Oxford University Press.

Hansen, J., M. Sato, R. Ruedy, K. Lo, D.W. Lea and M. Medina-Elizade (2006), 'Global temperature change', *Proceedings of the National Academy of Sciences* 103 (39): 14,288-14,293.

Hansen, Z. and G. Libecap (2004), 'Small farms, externalities, and the Dust Bowl of the 1930s', *Journal of Political Economy* 112 (3): 665-694.

Harris, J.R. and M.P. Todaro (1970), 'Migration, unemployment and development: A two sector analysis', *American Economic Review* 60: 126-142.

Hietanen, M. (2009), 'Environmental change and displacement: Assessing the evidence and developing norms for response', report of a workshop held by the Refugee Studies Centre and the International Migration Institute, University of Oxford, 8-9 January. Oxford: Refugee Studies Centre.

Homer-Dixon, T. (1991), 'On the threshold: Environmental changes as causes of acute conflict', *International Security* 16 (2): 76-116.

Hugo, G. (1996), 'Environmental concerns and international migration', *International Migration Review* 30 (1): 105-131.

IOM (2007), 'Migration and the environment', Discussion Note MC/INF/288. Geneva: International Organization for Migration.

Jacobson, J. (1988), 'Environmental refugees: A yardstick of habitability'. WorldWatch Paper. Washington, DC: WorldWatch Institute.

Kibreab, G. (1997), 'Environmental causes and impact of refugee movements: A critique of the current debate', *Disasters* 21 (1): 20-38.

Kibreab, G. (1994), 'Migration, environment and refugeehood', in: B. Zaba and J. Clarke (eds), *Environment and Population Change*. Liège: International Union for the Scientific Study of Population.

Kniveton, D., K. Schmidt-Verkerk, C. Smith, and R. Black. 2008. 'Climate Change and Migration: Improving Methodologies to Estimate Flows.' In *IOM Migration Research Series*. Geneva: IOM.

Koser, K. (1996), 'Changing agendas in the study of forced migration: A report on the Fifth International Research and Advisory Panel Meeting, April 1996', *Journal of Refugee Studies* 9 (4): 353-366.

Kunz, E. (1973), 'The refugee in flight: Kinetic models and forms of displacement', *International Migration Review* 7 (2): 125-146.

Lambert, B., and C. Pougin de la Maisonneuve (2007), *UNHCR's Response to the Tsunami Emergency in Indonesia and Sri Lanka, December 2004-November 2006: An Independent Evaluation*. Geneva: United Nations High Commissioner for Refugees.

Masters, S.B. (2000), 'Environmentally induced migration: Beyond a culture of reaction', *Georgetown Immigration Law Journal* 14: 855-866.

McTegart, W.J., G.W. Sheldon and D.C. Griffiths (eds) (1990), *Impacts Assessment of Climate Change. Report of Working Group II*. Canberra: Australian Government Publishing Service.

McLeman, R., and B. Smit (2006), 'Migration as an adaptation to climate change', *Climatic Change* 76 (1-2): 31-53.

Mooney, E. (2005), 'The concept of internal displacement and the case for internally displaced persons as a category of concern', *Refugee Survey Quarterly* 24 (3): 9-26.

Myers, N. (2002), 'Environmental refugees: A growing phenomenon of the 21st century', *Philosophical Transactions of the Royal Society B* 357 (1420): 609-613.

Myers, N. (1997), 'Environmental refugees', *Population and Environment* 19 (2): 167-182.

Myers, N. (1993), 'Environmental refugees in a globally warmed world', *BioScience* 43 (11): 752-761.

Piguet, E. (2008), 'Climate change and forced migration'. New Issues in Refugee Research. Geneva: United Nations High Commissioner for Refugees.

Renaud, F., J.J. Bogardi, O. Dun and K. Warner (2007), 'Control, adapt or flee: How to face environmental migration?' InterSecTions. Bonn: United Nations University Institute for Environment and Human Security.

Richmond, A. (1994), *Global Apartheid. Refugees, Racism, and the New World Order*. Toronto: Oxford University Press.

Stern, N. (2007), *The Economics of Climate Change. The Stern Review.* Cambridge: Cambridge University Press.

Suhrke, A. (1993), *Pressure Points: Environmental Degradation, Migration and Conflict.* Cambridge (MA): American Academy of Art and Science.

Suhrke, A. (1994), 'Environmental degradation and population flows', *Journal of International Affairs* 47 (2): 473-496.

Suhrke, Astri and A. Visentin (1991), 'The environmental refugee: A new approach', *Ecodecision* 2: 73-84.

Swain, A. (1996), 'Environmental migration and conflict dynamics: Focus on developing regions', *Third World Quarterly* 17 (5): 959-973.

UNHCR (Office of the United Nations High Commissioner for Refugees) (2006), *The State of the World's Refugees: Human Displacement in the New Millennium.* Oxford: Oxford University Press.

United Nations Commission on Human Rights (1998), 'Report of the Representative of the Secretary-General on Internally Displaced Persons: Guiding principles on internal displacement'. *E/CN.4/1998/53/Add.2.* New York: United Nations General Assembly.

Vogt, W. (1948), *Road to Survival.* New York: William Sloane Associates.

Westing, A.H. (1989), 'The environmental component of comprehensive security', *Bulletin of Peace Proposals* 20: 129-134.

11 Student Migration

Russell King and Allan Findlay

Introduction

Are students who study abroad migrants? Ask them and they will probably say 'no'. (Unless, perhaps, they are students of migration!) They see themselves as 'international' or 'visiting' students. Their own migratory experiences are far removed from the general perception of migrants as poor and marginalised workers. And yet, by the conventional definitions and statistical criteria of migration, such students *are* migrants. They have crossed an international frontier and are living in another country, often with a different culture and language, for a significant period of time – perhaps six months, one year, three years or more. Their different lengths of stay reflect the various schemes and regimes of student mobility, such as a semester or year abroad, an entire degree programme, a work placement or a 'gap year'.

importance of student migration

Migration researchers often overlook student migration, viewing it as transient and insignificant.[1] The OECD (2006) estimates that there are 2.7 million international students worldwide. This is a very small fraction of the total stock of migrants, which was 200 million in 2008 (IOM 2008: 2). However, three things enhance the importance of student migration beyond its minimal share in the global total. First, student migration is increasing four times faster than total world migration – by 52 per cent compared to 13 per cent from 1998 to 2004.[2] Second, student migration, like highly skilled migration in general, has important economic, social and cultural effects, given the elite background of most internationally mobile students. Third, experiencing migration as a student has a powerful influence on subsequent propensities for migration throughout the rest of life.

On another analytical scale, deeper structural forces power international student migration. One of these is the accelerating internationalisation of higher education. The formerly elite world of universities has been caught up in globalisation, spurred by the revolutionary advances in communication technology of the last two to three decades. On the economic front, university education has become a multibillion dollar global business. Advanced nations now compete to attract talent for the future. International student mobility is stimulated by political and cultural factors as well. The European Union's student exchange programmes, for example, emphasise the cultural benefits of study abroad. Among their objectives is to foster a 'European' identity and create a cadre of multilingual 'Eurocrats' loyal to the project of a united Europe (King and Ruiz-Gelices 2003).

terminology, theory and patterns

This chapter examines the subject of student migration in three sections. The first discusses terminology, addressing in particular the vexing question of whether to call the phenomenon under study 'student migration' or 'student mobility'. The second section explores how student migration can be theorised. Existing migration theory helps, but only up to a point; other important perspectives are derived from changing models of society, the rise of youth mobility cultures and the globalisation of higher education. The third part of the chapter looks at the spatial patterns of student migration, both globally and within Europe, setting out possible explanations for the patterns observed. This section draws on some of our own research on UK students' outward international mobility, in which the constraints of language and socio-economic background loom large. The conclusion reaffirms the strategic and increasing importance of students in the European and global maps of migration and identifies some areas for future research.

Student migration or student mobility?

migration or mobility

The first point of discussion concerns the variable use of the terms 'migration' and 'mobility' in referring to the international moves of students. We see the following distinction implicit in the literature:

- *Student migration* is used where the moves are long-distance – i.e. intercontinental and often between countries at different levels of development – and where the students are moving for a longer period of study, such as an entire degree course, leading to the issues of non-return and potential brain drain.
- *Student mobility* is generally used where moves are shorter-distance – e.g. intra-European – and of shorter duration, such as those embedded within a degree programme (the well-known 'year abroad'), whereby the student returns to his or her home country to complete their qualification. 'Mobility' is often used by researchers in a conceptual way by those wishing to link work on student mobility to the literature on the so-called 'mobility turn' (Urry 2000) that highlights movement as the norm of contemporary social life in contrast with the assumed fixities of the past.

Reflecting this distinction, *migration* is the term used by Skeldon (1997: 108-112) in his discussion of the role of students' international moves in the context of migration and development, by Li et al. (1996) in their study of Hong Kong students in the UK, by King and Shuttleworth (1995) in their analysis of Irish graduate emigration in the 1980s and by Hazen and Alberts (2006), who examine international students in the USA. Academic research on European students' international moves generally employs the term *mobility*, which also reflects the wider EU discourse about encouraging student mobility within a space of free movement and the harmonisation of higher education via the Bologna process (see e.g. Jallade and Gordon 1996; Teichler 1996; Murphy-Lejeune 2002; Findlay et al. 2006; Byram and Dervin 2008). However, migration vs. mobility does not exhaust the range of terminological alternatives. De Wit et al. (2008), in an important collection of essays, prefer the term 'international student circulation', while other studies see international students as visitors, sojourners or even tourists (Battisti and Portelli 1994; Hazen and Alberts 2006; Huang 2008).

In this chapter both *migration* and *mobility* are used, adhering broadly to the contextual differentiation made above. Whenever appropriate, we use the term migration, partly because most students who move internationally for at least a year fulfil the standard United Nations definition of migration; and partly because we wish to challenge the value-laden conception of a migrant as a person seen automatically as a poor, marginalised worker or a refugee.

credit and programme mobility

From an educational curriculum point of view, an important distinction is drawn between credit and programme mobility. *Credit mobility* is where the student moves abroad for just part of their programme of study – typically for a semester or year abroad at another university, or on a work placement – and then returns to their home university to complete their degree or other qualification, bringing the 'credit' from their study or work abroad into their overall degree profile in their home institution. This is a common pattern within European student mobility – notably that sponsored by the Erasmus-Socrates initiative – but also exists in other parts of the world, notably as in the North American 'junior year abroad'. *Programme* or *degree mobility* refers to students who migrate to take their entire qualification abroad – such as a bachelor's, master's or doctoral degree, or some other higher education qualification. If the course is a one-year master's, the length of time may be no longer than the undergraduate year abroad. Otherwise it is likely to be three, four or (in the case of 'professional' degrees like medicine or architecture) five years or longer.

This difference just noted may have a more lasting significance than whether the final qualification is awarded by the 'home' university or the university abroad. Consider, for example, the obvious difference between an Erasmus student who comes to Amsterdam for a semester of classes, and an African student who uses the student status as a way of migrating to Europe. In many countries – especially those outside of Europe, such as the United States and Australia – good students from abroad, including many from developing countries, are first recruited and trained, and then used to fill key skill shortages in national labour markets. Relatively little is known about these 'students who become immigrants' or 'student switchers' as they are sometimes known (Gribble 2008). In some cases their actions reflect a long-term strategy of clever calculation, in others the status adjustment occurs due to a variety of personal, professional and socio-economic factors that come into play only once the student has begun studying in the destination country (Hazen and Alberts 2006).

special nature

Finally, in this definitional clearing of the ground, we want to stress the intrinsically special nature of student migration. Baláž and Williams (2004) point out that students are the only group who primarily migrate to acquire human capital. Student migration has some parallels with other specialised migratory flows, such as scientific and academic staff, experts and functionaries of international organisations, members of religious orders, sports and artistic performers and military personnel (Todisco 2002). Like international retirement migration (see King, this book), it is very much demographically defined by age and life-stage. Students are generally seen as *desirable* migrants and their mobility is encouraged; in fact, those who are in receipt of scholarships and bursaries are paid to move. Some of these features are elaborated further in the next section of the chapter, which addresses theory.

How can student migration be theorised?

multiple perspectives

Located at the intersection of many fields of study – migration, education, human capital, youth studies and so forth – student migration has been looked at from multiple perspectives; but also, in many ways, it has been overlooked precisely because it is not seen as part of 'mainstream' migration. Conventional rational-choice models of migration, which favour economic criteria over others, have only partial relevance, because in reality student migration is about life experience, quality of education and building up human capital for their long-term future rather than immediate work and income. Nevertheless, it is easy to see how pull and push factors operate, and how the individual decision to move (which may be very much influenced by parents and other family members) is made by an evaluation of the balance between these factors. In general, pull factors are dominant. These include the attraction of a country's higher education system or of a particular prestigious university; the desire to acquire a specific qualification not available in the student's home country; access to scholarships; the possibilities to improve one's understanding of another language and culture; and perhaps too, as noted above, opportunities to work, either combined with study, or by staying on after graduation and entering the labour market of the host country. Beyond these standard links to migration theory, we see four other conceptual frameworks as relevant to an analysis of student migration: skilled migration, globalisation, youth culture and social class (King and Ruiz-Gelices 2003: 231-232; Findlay et al. 2006: 293-294).

Students as highly skilled migrants

highly skilled migration

A first, obvious perspective sees internationally mobile students as a subset of highly skilled migration and as part of human capital thinking. The literature on human capital largely neglects to mention student migration (Baláž and Williams 2004: 217), while that on skilled migration often makes only passing reference to students (e.g. Salt 1988, 1997; Koser and Salt 1997). More recently, student migration has been framed within interesting debates about the mobility of talent and knowledge (Williams 2006; Solimano 2008) and about academic and scientific mobility (Ackers and Gill 2008; Byram and Dervin 2008).

The consideration of student migration as part of skilled, academic and scientific mobility leads, in turn, to two different global settings. The first is 'brain exchange' among the highly developed countries of the world, notably Europe, where there is a geographical concentration of advanced countries packed tightly together, but also between Europe and other academically powerful nations such as the US, Canada, Australia and New Zealand, and also among these latter nations. Student circulation among wealthy nations can be seen as training for future managers and professionals destined for careers in global businesses and transnational organisations. The second global scenario is the flow of students and trainee professionals from the developing to the developed world. Even within the advanced countries there are often signs of structural imbalance in student flows, for instance from academically weak or overcrowded university systems to those that are regarded as higher quality and more meritocratic, such as those in the USA, UK, the Netherlands and Germany. Very few students move from developed to less-developed countries for their university education, or even for a short-term mobility experience.

Globalisation and the internationalisation of higher education

internationalisation of higher education

The second broad conceptual framework for student migration is globalisation, both generally – as flows of people accelerate between integrating economies – and with specific reference to the internationalisation of higher education, which is both a context for, and is also shaped by, student mobility (Brooks and Waters 2011). But what is meant by the internationalisation of higher education? Following de Wit (2008a), we can distinguish three levels or components:

- modification of the curriculum by introducing international or global studies, intercultural learning, etc;
- mobility-related initiatives such as study abroad, student exchanges, academic staff mobility, etc; and
- the more direct impact of globalisation and its attendant technologies and market forces, leading to notions of 'borderless education', 'offshore education', e-learning and 'international trade in higher education services', etc.

This last element is especially important in the internationalisation of higher education in the last two decades. While there is still a strong ethos of cooperation in the way universities collaborate for the purposes of joint research and student exchange schemes, a keen competitive edge has also been introduced, leading to a revolution in the way universities sell themselves to aspiring international students. Privatisation, the franchising of new institutions and branch campuses in student-supply hot-spots such as the Persian Gulf, China and Malaysia are all part of the business environment in which student migration now takes place.

transnational political agendas

Transnational political agendas also play a role, the best example being the European Commission's promotion of mobility through a dual discourse of economics and cultural identity, both of which are narrated at both an aggregate and an individual level (King 2003). At the macro level the concept relates to shared European cultural values in order to override the old national rivalries en route to European integration, and the creation of an integrated European labour market enriched by highly educated, multilingual, multiculturally aware young people, enabling Europe to compete with other global economic powers. At the individual level, the rhetoric of student mobility revolves around attending a world-class university, increasing intercultural awareness, having a wonderful personal experience and preparing for a successful career.

Youth culture, mobility and individualisation

A third theoretical framework places international student mobility within research on youth culture and on the role of travel abroad as a rite of passage for young persons. Much more than was the case in earlier generations, students' geographical horizons presently extend beyond their own national frontiers; even before they move into higher education, the experience of travel – either during family holidays or on independent trips such as during a gap year – has given them a taste of living abroad and experience of other cultures. The notion of a youth culture of high mobility can be spun into two well-known theoretical domains associated with the work of John Urry and Ulrich Beck. Urry (2000) has proposed a reading of contemporary Western society that focuses on mobility as its defining characteristic; yet, curiously, the 'mobilities turn' in sociology and in migration studies has so far said little about students as exemplars of this new trend (see e.g. Sheller and Urry 2006), even though they are certainly 'mobility pioneers' (see Kesselring 2006). *youth culture*

A more productive link is with Beck's thesis of 'individualisation', although, like Urry, Beck does not specifically address his analysis to students, despite their ubiquity in contemporary advanced societies. According to Beck, the contemporary young individual faces a variety of choices and incentives unavailable to prior generations, thereby becoming disembedded from traditional social roles and constraints such as social class, family and hometown. Student travel grants, such as Erasmus bursaries, can be seen as one example of 'incentives to action' through which an individual student's 'normal' biography can be enhanced by geographical mobility into becoming an 'elective' or 'do-it-yourself' biography (Beck and Beck-Gernsheim 2002: 3). The mobile student thus stands out from the routine modernities of student life by constructing 'mobility capital' (see Murphy-Lejeune 2002: 51-52) which can be deployed over his or her subsequent lifetime for personal, social or career development. This enables internationally mobile students to present themselves as a 'migratory elite', using their mobility capital (along with the social and cultural capital that this also embodies; see Bourdieu 1986) to create an 'intercultural lifeworld' to differentiate themselves from traditional, non-mobile students (Beck and Beck-Gernsheim 2002: 93; Murphy-Lejeune 2002: 5).

Social class

The notion of internationally mobile students as a privileged migratory elite introduces our final conceptual framework, the relationship between student migration and class. Do those who move abroad for *migratory elite* some or all of their university education represent a cross-section of all students? If not, what are the distinguishing characteristics of the internationally mobile? We will provide some specific answers to these questions from our UK case study later in this chapter. For now, we briefly present some broader evidence, and then return to theoretical perspectives on student mobility and social class.

The *Euro Student* report, commissioned by the German Ministry of Education, surveyed students in eight EU countries (Austria, Belgium, Finland, France, Germany, Ireland, Italy and the Netherlands) and found that international mobility during the degree programme (i.e. credit mobility, as defined above) was significantly associated with two factors, 'pre-university international experience' and 'better knowledge of foreign languages'. Students already in possession of this linguistic and mobility capital were – depending on the country – two to three times more likely to study abroad than those without. The report concluded: 'Regardless of the general degree of international mobility [in the individual countries surveyed], students from low-income families make substantially less use of the opportunities for studying abroad than do those from families with higher income' (Schnitzer and Zempel-Gino 2002: 115).

class-specific phenomenon

In an era of expanding higher education (in many European countries, age-related participation rates in higher education range from 30 per cent to 60 per cent), international student mobility may be regarded as a class-specific phenomenon, allowing the middle and upper classes to sustain and reproduce themselves in a socially and culturally constructed fashion, legitimised by the institutions favouring and marketing student mobility. The self-perpetuating nature of class reproduction has both traditional Marxist echoes and operates through a reworking of the Bourdieuan notion of *habitus*. As Bourdieu (1977: 86-87) observes, 'the habitus acquired by schooling, itself diversified, in turn underlies the structuring of our subsequent experiences'.

In addition to the generalised results of the *Euro Student* survey reported above, other more focused empirical studies, for instance on Hong Kong students studying in Canada (Waters 2006) and on French students studying abroad (Garneau 2007), confirm the close association between social-class dynamics and the ability to access pathways to study abroad. Waters demonstrates how middle-class families' social reproduction is increasingly tied to their offspring's acquisition of high-quality educational credentials from top 'Western' universities. Growing working-class access to local higher education in Hong Kong pushes middle-class parents and students to maintain the relative scarcity value of their qualifications by studying abroad (2006: 188-189). Likewise, Garneau shows how students' initial personal and family resources combine with institutional opportunities (e.g. quality of the home university, existence of exchange programmes with high-prestige partners) to produce a differentiation of returns on the subsequent job market. Study abroad transforms students' 'professional socialisation' and facilitates their access to posts for highly skilled workers in competitive sectors of the new globalised economy (2007: 145-146).

Geographies of student migration

no standardised criteria

As with most migration statistics, internationally comparable data on student migration are impossible to assemble because standardised measurement criteria do not exist. The OECD's *Education at a Glance* is the most accessible and authoritative source, but its dataset is limited by the three major ways in which different countries collect statistics on international students – by citizenship, by place of normal domicile and by place of prior education. In countries like Germany and Switzerland, with large numbers of residents holding foreign citizenship due to restrictions on naturalisation, many students are recorded as 'foreign' even though they were born in the host country. Two further data issues arise. One is whether 'students' are restricted to those studying for a degree in a third-level institution, or whether a wider definition is adopted. The second is the length of time the student has to spend abroad in order to be classified as a 'migrant' as opposed to a 'visiting student'. Although it is not always made explicit, some countries include, and others exclude, short-term visiting students. On this last point, returns from individual institutions within the same country may not be standardised. These problems should be kept in mind when reviewing the following data.

Europe in the global scenario

In 2004, there were 2.7 million students studying abroad worldwide, almost three times the number in 1985; however, this may be an overestimate due to 'resident foreign' students such as those of second-generation migrant origin. The high rate of increase in foreign student stock was noted earlier: one estimate suggests that the number will rise to 7 million by 2025, with half coming from China and India (Böhm et al. 2002). This prediction is based on an annual compound growth rate of 6.2 per cent for student migration, perhaps unrealistic in the current global economic scenario.

OECD

OECD countries host 85 per cent of all foreign students, two-thirds of whom are from non-OECD countries, so there is a marked South–North orientation in the global pattern. Table 11.1 breaks down this global picture by continental region, and reveals some broad macro-regional transfers. Taking destinations first, over half of all foreign students are in Europe, and nearly a third in North America. Regarding origins, African migrating students go mainly to Europe (55 per cent to France alone) and South Americans mainly to North America, while students of Asian origin are more evenly spread. Finally, we note how more than four-fifths of European students who move abroad do so within their own continent.[3]

Table 11.1 *Origins and destinations of foreign students studying in OECD countries, 2004 (%)*

Origin	*Destination*			
	North America	*Europe*	*Asia-Pacific*	*OECD*
North America	44	43	13	100
South America	56	41	2	100
Europe	16	81	3	100
Africa	20	77	3	100
Asia	40	32	28	100
Oceania	27	19	54	100
World	31	52	17	100

Source: OECD data in IOM (2008: 109)

global inequalities

Taking these intra-European movements out of the picture for a moment, it is clear that global inequalities in supply and demand for higher education strongly shape student migration. The broad flow is from areas of high demand caused by high economic and demographic growth (e.g. India, China, Nigeria) to economies seeking to expand their international student populations and that have elastic capacity in their higher education systems and a strong strategy to market the opportunities to live, study and often work in their economies (e.g. North America, North-Western Europe, Australia). Countries in these destination regions have pursued increasingly active recruitment drives for foreign students in recent years, recognising higher education as one of their most important potential exports. Three economic motives lie behind this (although not all factors are present in all recipient countries). These are first, the desire to attract the brightest students globally, thereby helping to bolster the claims to the international excellence of their 'world-leading' institutions; second, there is the anticipation that some international students will stay on after graduating to boost the quality of the nation's talent pool; and third, there is the potential for foreign students to contribute to funding the higher education sector without the need to raise domestic taxes as a result of the higher fees charged to 'overseas' as opposed to 'home' students. However, other factors dictate which precise country students will select – e.g. geographical distance, language of instruction, quality assurance and recognition of qualifications, tuition fees, living costs, immigration rules and visa requirements (Tremblay 2006).

This leads to the country-specific data on origins and destinations in Tables 11.2 and 11.3, which follow. The detailed data largely speak for themselves, so just a few general comments will be made. The outbound migration pattern (Table 11.2) shows some consistent trends across the four dates – a progressive rise in both absolute and relative terms of student migrants from China and India, the constant presence of students from Greece, South Korea and Malaysia (except in 2005, when it was 11th) and the gradual decline of students from the USA until 2005. For the future, the role of countries like Morocco and Turkey in the geography of supply looks interesting: these are two large, modernising countries of intermediate development, located close to Europe. The final general statistical trend to be noted from Table 2 is the increasing dominance of the top two countries: from 8 per cent of the total out-movement in 1975 and 1985 to 18 per cent in 2005.[4]

country-specific data

Table 11.2 *Top ten countries of origin of foreign students, 1975-2005*

1975		*1985*		*1995*		*2005*	
Country	*No.*	*Country*	*No.*	*Country*	*No.*	*Country*	*No.*
Iran	33,021	China	42,481	China	115,871	China	343,126
USA	29,414	Iran	41,083	S. Korea	69,736	India	123,559
Greece	23,363	Malaysia	40,493	Japan	62,324	S. Korea	95,885
Hong Kong	21,059	Greece	34,086	Germany	45,432	Japan	60,424
China	17,201	Morocco	33,094	Greece	43,941	Germany	56,410
UK	16,866	Jordan	24,285	Malaysia	41,159	France	53,350
Nigeria	16,348	Hong Kong	23,657	India	39,626	Turkey	52,048
Malaysia	16,162	South Korea	22,468	Turkey	37,629	Morocco	51,503
India	14,805	Germany	22,424	Italy	36,515	Greece	49,631
Canada	12,664	USA	19,707	Hong Kong	35,141	USA	41,181

Source: OECD and UNESCO data compiled in de Wit (2008b: 33-34)

For destination countries (Table 11.3), the USA has long retained its premier position and looks likely to continue to do so, despite some slight erosion of its dominance (dropping from 28 per cent to 23 per cent of all foreign students over the last ten years). The UK, France and Germany have consistently occupied the next three places since 1990 (since 1985, in fact). Meanwhile, Australia and Canada have moved up the table. Within Europe, 40 per cent of incoming foreign students worldwide and nearly three-quarters of those entering Europe study in the UK, Germany and France; the other demographically

Table 11.3 *Top ten host countries for foreign students, 1980-2004*

1980		*1990*		*2000*		*2004*	
Country	*No.*	*Country*	*No.*	*Country*	*No.*	*Country*	*No.*
USA	311,882	USA	407,529	USA	475,169	USA	572,509
France	110,763	France	136,015	UK	222,936	UK	300,056
USSR	62,942	Germany	105,269	Germany	187,033	Germany	260, 314
Germany	61,841	UK	70,717	France	137,085	France	237,587
UK	56,003	Ex-USSR	66,806	Canada	114,641	Australia	166,955
Lebanon	31,018	Canada	35,187	Australia	105,764	Canada	132,982
Canada	28,443	Belgium	33,335	Japan	66,607	Japan	117,903
Italy	27,784	Australia	28,993	Russia	66,500	Russia	75,786
Egypt	21,751	Japan	23,816	Belgium	38,799	New Zealand	68,904
Romania	15,888	Switzerland	22,621	Austria	30,382	Belgium	44,304

Source: Suter and Jandl (2006: 95); de Wit (2008b: 35-36); based in turn on various sources
Note: China does not publish reliable data on incoming students.

large European countries (Italy, Spain, Poland) have much weaker attractive powers.

It should be noted that the discussion above describes trends relative to absolute numbers. A different picture emerges when the number of international students is standardised relative to the size of the host countries' own student populations. When this is done, the countries with the most 'successful' (some would argue, 'aggressive') international student marketing strategies are picked out. Australia, followed by the UK, has by far the highest ratio of international to locally domiciled students while, by the same measure, the USA drops to fifth position behind Germany and France.

The geography of Erasmus

Erasmus programme

Since the launch of the EU-sponsored Erasmus programme in 1987, 1.7 million third-level students have spent a period of 3-12 months studying abroad. Beneficiaries of the scheme have grown steadily, rising from fewer than 20,000 annually during the late 1980s to 100,000 per year in the late 1990s and nearly 160,000 in 2006-2007. Considering the entire twenty-year period, only five countries account for two-thirds of the out-moving students: Germany and France (15.6 per cent each), Spain (14.0 per cent), Italy (11.3 per cent) and the UK (9.3 per cent). Naturally the geographical range of mobility in the Erasmus programme has expanded, along with recent EU enlargements. Moreover, in recent years a few non-EU countries have also become involved – Norway, Iceland and Turkey – and the recently launched Erasmus Mundus scheme further enlarges the field.

Although Erasmus does not represent, by any means, the sum-total of intra-European student mobility, it has undoubtedly transformed the European student migratory landscape (Garneau 2007). Moreover, Erasmus statistics provide a uniquely standardised dataset on intra-European student moves. As far as we are aware, no migration scholar has yet tried to interpret or model the spatial patterns of Erasmus exchanges. Here, we present a small selection of the available statistics and highlight some of the key patterns observed; our 'explanations' for the patterns are, however, hypothetical.[5]

Table 11.4 shows the inflows, outflows, and net balance for the EU15 for two academic years, 1999-2000 and 2006-2007. Most countries saw consistent growth in both in- and out-movers, reflecting the overall increase in mobility over the period in question (from 107,666 in 1999-2000 to 159,324 in 2006-2007, or 48 per cent). The main country to buck the trend has been the UK, which registered a 28 per cent decrease in outgoing students and a 20 per cent drop in incomers. Review of the detailed time-series data shows that, for out-movers, the UK peaked as early as 1994-1995 (11,988), after which the decline has been continuous. A group of other countries – Ireland, the Netherlands, Denmark and Sweden – appears to be following the UK, with out-movers (but not incomers) declining, albeit to a lesser extent and from a later peak. It is probably not coincidental that all these countries are in Northern Europe and offer all or some of their teaching in English.

Table 11.4 *Erasmus student flows, 1999-2000 and 2006-2007 (EU 15)*

Host Country	*1990-2000*			*2006-2007*		
	In	*Out*	*Net*	*In*	*Out*	*Net*
Austria	2,499	2,952	-453	3,735	3,971	-236
Belgium	3,765	4,404	-729	5,087	4,971	+116
Denmark	2,311	1,764	+547	4,356	1,682	+2,674
Finland	3,020	3,486	-466	5,763	3,851	+1,912
France	17,890	16,824	+1,066	20,673	22,981	-2,308
Germany	14,691	15,715	-1,024	17,878	23,884	-6,006
Greece	1,285	1,910	-625	1,899	2,714	-815
Ireland	3,075	1,689	+1,386	3,870	1,567	+2,303
Italy	8,029	12,421	-4,392	14,779	17,195	-2,416
Luxembourg	18	87	-69	15	146	-131
Netherlands	5,896	4,418	+1,478	6,965	4,491	+2,474
Portugal	2,236	2,472	-236	4,542	4,312	+230
Spain	15,197	16,297	-1,100	27,464	22,322	+5,142
Sweden	4,207	3,087	+3,087	7,048	2,530	+4,518
UK	20,705	10,056	10,056	16,508	7,235	+9,273

Source: European Commission (2008)

imbalances

The other feature clearly evident from Table 11.4 is the pattern of imbalances – the 'net' column. Although the principle of Erasmus is reciprocity in terms of the number of students moving each way, in practice this has not worked out. Some countries, notably Germany, Italy and Greece, export many more students than they attract, whereas the UK and Ireland have a negative 'Erasmus balance of trade', imports being roughly twice exports. The Netherlands, Denmark, and Sweden are also net importers, as is Spain. Although not shown in Table 11.4, it is worth noting that all of the A8 countries, which joined the EU in 2004, as well as Bulgaria and Romania, which joined subsequently, are net exporters to a very marked degree. Of the 2004 accession countries, only Malta and Cyprus have net positive inflows, but the absolute numbers are very small.

How can these patterns be interpreted? The following suggestions are speculative rather than firm explanations (King 2003: 159-161). First, we observe a three-way correlation between those countries where the out-mover trend is static or declining, those that have an imbalance of incoming over outgoing students and those that teach wholly or partly in English. How might these variables be interrelated? Countries that teach their students through the medium of English are attractive to all those students in the rest of Europe who want to improve their mastery of this prime global language. These countries are also attractive to students whose mother tongue is English and who can thus enjoy Erasmus mobility without having to acquire expertise in another language. By the same token, students from English-speaking countries seem to have a reduced incentive to learn and develop other languages through outward mobility. Another factor contributing to the magnetism of this group of countries is the highly regarded quality of their universities and academic programmes, their superior facilities for students and their efficient organisation. In contrast, countries such as Italy and Greece (which have large net outflows of students) are not regarded as attractive because of the language barrier, doubts over academic standards and a reputation for poor administration – perceptual obstacles that also hold for the new EU member-states in Eastern Europe.

spatial dichotomy

If many of the trends and contrasts reflect a spatial dichotomy between a northern 'core' and a southern and eastern 'periphery', and perhaps therefore a kind of internal European brain-drain model, then Spain breaks the mould. This can be arguably explained by the rising popularity of Spanish as a second global language in Europe after English, the increasingly positive image of Spain in Europe, students' prior experiences of holidays there and the climate.

However, despite the principle of free movement enshrined in Erasmus, the market for Erasmus mobility is not free. Because of the norm of reciprocity, popular countries (and their university administrators) put caps on the number of students allowed 'in' so that they do not deviate too much from the smaller numbers who apply to go 'out'. In other words, if left to market forces, the imbalances for the UK and Ireland would be even greater (although still subject to the quota allocations of Erasmus grants). It should be noted that Erasmus flows did not simply evolve according to some abstract principle of spatial organisation. Personal and institutional factors have been crucial, setting up partnerships and networks on the basis of pre-existing academic friendships and research contacts (Collins 2008).

For a more detailed geography of origins and destinations we turn to Table 11.5, which sets out the percentage distribution of outgoing students from ten selected countries across destinations for Erasmus students in the 2006-2007 programme. At the bottom of the table we see the relative importance of each destination country for all Erasmus flows. While some origin countries' flows broadly match global distribution (for instance, Austria, Belgium and the Netherlands), others show particular preferences for certain favoured destinations. The French, for example, are particularly attracted to Spain and the UK, the Germans to France and Spain, the Italians especially to Spain (and the Spanish to Italy), and UK students are drawn disproportionately to France, Germany and Spain.

Table 11.5 *Erasmus flows by destination, selected countries, 2006-2007 (%)*

Origin	*AT*	*BE*	*FI*	*FR*	*GE*	*IT*	*NL*	*PO*	*SP*	*UK*
Austria		2.0	6.4	12.5	6.3	10.8	5.3	2.1	17.8	8.7
Belgium	2.1		4.5	14.0	6.5	9.5	6.5	4.4	25.3	6.4
Finland	6.8	3.5		11.5	15.7	4.2	8.1	2.1	13.1	12.4
France	1.7	1.8	3.8		12.2	7.1	3.6	1.1	23.7	20.3
Germany	1.8	1.4	4.6	18.1		7.6	3.2	1.5	21.4	12.6
Italy	1.6	3.5	2.3	15.6	9.9		3.7	4.6	36.9	7.7
Netherlands	2.6	4.3	6.4	10.4	8.3	6.0		2.2	18.1	12.3
Portugal	1.2	4.9	2.7	5.2	4.2	17.0	4.7		28.0	3.3
Spain	1.6	5.6	3.1	14.4	10.8	23.0	5.0	5.4		12.4
UK	1.9	1.7	2.8	29.8	14.0	9.0	4.5	1.2	22.6	
All EU	2.3	3.3	3.8	13.1	10.9	9.3	4.2	3.0	17.6	10.5

Source: European Commission (2008)

A UK case study: The constraints of language and social class

UK student mobility

Research by the authors (King et al. 2004; Findlay et al. 2005, 2006) helps to understand the dynamics of international student mobility from the UK, and in particular the circumstances surrounding the declining participation in Erasmus mobility noted above. Existing datasets were re-analysed, surveys were carried out (questionnaires were given to registrars in all UK universities and 1,200 undergraduate students in a sample of ten UK universities), and interviews were done (with 46 'mobility managers' and 180 students), in order to answer questions about mobility trends, barriers to mobility, the role of languages and institutional and social-class factors.

The first key finding is that Erasmus is far from the whole story. The steady decline in Erasmus mobility to Europe since the mid-1990s is more than compensated for by increasing mobility to other parts of the world, especially Anglophone destinations such as the US, Canada and Australia, which account for 60 per cent of all outflows.[6] This pattern reflects not only the limited language abilities of UK students compared to their European peers, and their resistance to studying in countries where courses are not given in English, but also other factors such as the demand for study and work opportunities in locations that are perceived to add value to their CV. Survey and interview data indicated a strong desire to engage in paid work placements or to combine study with work abroad, preferably in globally renowned universities or in global companies such as those in Silicon Valley. The questionnaire to institutions of higher education also revealed that *non-Erasmus* mobility to Europe (especially to France and Spain) had increased strongly over the years of the survey (2000 to 2003), although overall numbers remained quite low.

language constraining mobility

Second, languages are an important background factor in constraining mobility. We used HESA (Higher Education Statistics Authority) and Erasmus data to show that the decline in UK Erasmus movers of 32 per cent over the period 1995-1996 to 2002-2003 was closely matched by a 28 per cent decline in students enrolled in language degrees at UK universities (King et al. 2004: 83; Findlay et al. 2006: 310-311). Hence, one of the main traditional supply chains for the Erasmus year abroad is declining. For those not pursuing language degrees, interview and questionnaire data revealed concerns about poor language skills as a major barrier (along with financial considerations) to considering the study-abroad option (Findlay et al. 2006: 304-306).

Third, there is an important institutional dimension to student mobility. While virtually all UK universities make references to internationalisation and student mobility in their mission statements, in practice they are not as committed to encouraging their own students to go 'out' as they are to attracting foreign students 'in', especially non-EU overseas students, for whom much higher fees are charged. Trend data show that student mobility, both Erasmus and non-Erasmus, is becoming increasingly concentrated in the hands of the so-called 'old' universities, as distinct from the 'new' universities which were only given university status after 1992, and which were formerly polytechnics and colleges (see King et al. 2004: 21-26; Findlay et al. 2006:

307-308 for details). The older universities have been able to hold on to their language departments better than the new universities, where language teaching has rapidly contracted. Older universities have better research reputations (and hence funds), enabling them to maintain links to foreign universities and support mobility schemes. Their entry qualifications are higher, and their students tend to come from higher-status socio-economic backgrounds, including a greater proportion of students who have been privately educated.

role of social class

This last feature leads to the fourth and final point about the UK situation – the role of social class. By linking the UK national Erasmus dataset on mobile students with the national HESA register, which records some key socio-demographic data on all students in UK universities, we were able to demonstrate that, compared to the national student population, Erasmus movers were disproportionately white, female, and of higher social class. While these characteristics also define those students pursuing language degrees (the classic supply route for the Erasmus scheme in the UK), the same patterns hold when language students are removed (King et al. 2004: 81-90). Our own survey research, based on questionnaires with final-year students in ten universities, found the same pattern: males, working-class students and students from minority ethnic backgrounds were less likely to have spent a period abroad as part of their degree. Interestingly, we found that there was a stronger association between mobility abroad and mother's education (whether or not in possession of a degree) and professional status than there was when using comparable characteristics from the father (Findlay et al. 2006: 303-304).

Conclusion

This chapter argued that students' international moves are an important but under-researched component of the new map of European migration – and global migration as well. We suggested that student migration is a unique migratory type in terms of its life-stage and motivational characteristics (to accrue human capital). However, it is important to appreciate that it can also evolve into hybrid migratory forms, such as the student-worker, the student-tourist and the student-refugee (King 2002: 99).

shadows other forms of migration

European patterns of student mobility to some degree shadow labour migration and other migration forms. They may also reflect other intra-European exchanges, flows between Europe and other economically advanced parts of the world (especially North America), and incoming flows from poorer countries (perhaps leading to concerns about brain drain). In this chapter, we speculatively 'explained' such macro-flows in terms of language, geographical and cultural proximity, quality and cost of education, and uneven patterns of supply and demand for higher education across the world. We also argued that students' rising international mobility is embedded both within the much wider mobility culture found in contemporary societies, and within students' attempts to create for themselves a distinctive individual biography based on the accumulation of 'mobility capital', which will let them stand out from the crowd in terms of their personal and class habitus.

study of tertiary education

An individualised, behavioural approach to study the meaning of student migration and mobility can yield rich insights. However, we must also appreciate that tertiary education across the world, and within countries, is structured in a highly uneven and hierarchical way by the state, global capital, and the wish of the privileged classes to retain and reproduce their dominant position. The National Academies explains the logic underpinning the United States' strong global competition to recruit international students in the following way: 'To maintain excellence in science and engineering research, which fuels technological innovation, the United States must be able to recruit talented people. A substantial proportion of those people – students, postdoctoral scholars, and researchers – must come from other countries' (The National Academies 2005: 5). A major recommendation of this powerful group is that the United States must strengthen its university and national policies on student recruitment to compete with other advanced economies and attract the best students. Evidence suggests that several European countries, too, have more aggressively targeted overseas recruitment in recent years. Thus, the patterns described in this chapter are not static but dynamic and ever changing to reflect the uneven power of national and international capital in this arena.

MAIN IDEAS

Students' international moves are an important but under-researched component of the new map of European and global migration.

Student migration can evolve into hybrid migratory forms, such as the student-worker, the student-tourist and the student-refugee.

European patterns of student mobility shadow labour migration and other migration forms.

Evidence suggests that several European countries and universities have more aggressively targeted overseas recruitment in recent years.

Notes

1 Standard texts on migration such as Boyle et al. (1998), Cohen (1995), Brettell and Hollifield (2008) and Castles and Miller (2009) say little or nothing about student migration. Only Skeldon (1997: 108-112) presents a more extended discussion, but this is mainly cast within the brain-drain debate and says little about Europe. A recent IOM World Migration Report (IOM 2008: 105-125) has a useful overview with comparative statistics.

2 See IOM (2008: 105) for student migration data; global migration figures are interpolated from IOM (2005: 396, Table 23.1).

3 What Table 11.1 does not show is student mobility *within* the non-OECD areas. There are few statistics on this, but it is known that considerable student mobility takes place within Africa, within Latin America and within Arab countries, and is increasing (IOM 2008: 108).

4 Of course, it must be borne in mind that the totals of migrating students are increasing all the time – by tenfold over the long period 1965-2005, and by two and a half times between 1985 and 2005. Yet, at times, these rates of increase have been no faster than the general growth in student enrolment in tertiary education. For instance, during 1999-2005 there was a 40 per cent increase in total enrolment and 41 per cent growth in international mobility (de Wit 2008b: 33). Other statistical insights not evident from Table 11.2 involve student outmovement indexed against the country's student population. Some small countries, such as Luxembourg, Guinea-Bissau, Cape Verde and Cyprus, have more third-level students abroad than at home. In the US, however, only 0.4 per cent, or 1 in 250 students, are abroad (de Wit 2008b: 33–4; IOM 2008: 109). Yet another statistical consideration is the distinction between one-way and net flows. Most sending countries receive relatively few incoming student migrants, but some of the major receiving countries also 'export' their own migrant students, nearly all of whom go to other advanced countries. However some countries, like Japan, have a near-zero net student migration, since the incomers and out-movers cancel each other out (for more detail, including net flow statistics, see de Wit 2008b: 41-42).

5 Thanks to Laura Killick, holder of a Junior Research Bursary in the Department of Geography at the University of Sussex, for sourcing and doing preliminary analysis of the Erasmus data.

6 The data come from the questionnaire sent to all universities in the UK, of which half (n = 80) responded. For survey details see King et al. (2004: 18-19, 54-57); Findlay et al. (2006: 298-300).

Recommended literature

Ackers, L. and Gill, B. (2008), *Moving People and Knowledge: Scientific Mobility in an Enlarging European Union*. Cheltenham: Edward Elgar.

Brooks, R. and Waters, J. L. (2011), *Student Mobilities: Migration and the Internationalization of Higher Education*. Basingstoke: Palgrave Macmillan.

Byram, M. and Dervin, F. (eds) (2008), *Students, Staff and Academic Mobility in Higher Education*. Newcastle: Cambridge Scholars Publishing.

Dervin, F. and Byram, M. (eds) (2008), *Echanges et Mobilités Académiques: Quel Bilan?* Paris: L'Harmattan.

De Wit, H., Agarwal, P., Said, M.E., Sehoole, M.T. and Sirozi, M. (eds) (2008), *The Dynamics of International Student Circulation in a Global Context*. Rotterdam: Sense Publishers.

Murphy-Lejeune, E. (2002), *Student Mobility and Narrative in Europe: The New Strangers*. London: Routledge.

References

Ackers, L. and B. Gill (2008), *Moving People and Knowledge: Scientific Mobility in an Enlarging European Union*. Cheltenham: Edward Elgar.

Baláž, V. and A.M. Williams (2004), '"Been there, done that": International student migration and human capital transfers from the UK to Slovakia', *Population, Space and Place* 10: 217-237.

Battisti, F. and A. Portelli (1994), 'The apple and the olive tree: Exiles, sojourners, and tourism in the university', in: R. Benmayor and A. Skotnes (eds), *Migration and Identity*, 35-51. Oxford: Oxford University Press.

Beck, U. and E. Beck-Gernsheim (2002), *Individualization*. London: Sage.

Böhm, A., D. Davis, D. Meares, and D. Pearce (2002), *Global Student Mobility 2025: Forecasts of the Global Demand for International Higher Education*. Sydney: IDP Education.

Bourdieu, P. (1986), 'The forms of capital', in: J.G. Richardson (ed.), *Handbook of Theory and Research for the Sociology of Education*, 241-258. New York: Greenwood.

Bourdieu. P. (1977), *Outline of a Theory of Practice*. Cambridge: Cambridge University Press.

Boyle, P., K. Halfacree and V. Robinson (1998), *Exploring Contemporary Migration*. London: Longman.

Brettell, C.B. and J.F. Hollifield (eds) (2008), *Migration Theory: Talking Across Disciplines*. London: Routledge.

Byram, M. and F. Dervin (eds) (2008), *Students, Staff and Academic Mobility in Higher Education*. Newcastle: Cambridge Scholars Publishing.

Castles, S. and M.J. Miller (2009), *The Age of Migration: International Population Movements in the Modern World*. Basingstoke: Palgrave Macmillan.

Cohen, R. (ed.) (1995), *The Cambridge Survey of World Migration*. Cambridge: Cambridge University Press.

Collins, F.L. (2008), 'Bridges to learning: International student mobilities, education agencies and inter-personal networks', *Global Networks*, 8: 398-417.

De Wit, H. (2008a), 'The internationalization of higher education in a global context', in: H. de Wit, P. Agarwal, M.E. Said, M.T. Sehoole and M. Sirozi (eds), *The Dynamics of International Student Circulation in a Global Context*, 1-14. Rotterdam: Sense Publishers.

De Wit, H. (2008b), 'Changing dynamics in international student circulation: Meanings, push and pull factors, trends and data', in: H. de Wit, P. Agarwal, M.E. Said, M.T. Sehoole and M. Sirozi (eds), *The Dynamics of International Student Circulation in a Global Context*, 15-45. Rotterdam: Sense Publishers.

De Wit, H., P. Agarwal, M.E. Said, M.T. Sehoole and M. Sirozi (eds) (2008), *The Dynamics of International Student Circulation in a Global Context*. Rotterdam: Sense Publishers.

European Commission (2008), *Erasmus Statistics*. Brussels: European Commission, Education and Training. (http://ec.europa.eu/education/erasmus/doc920_en.htm. Accessed 1 July 2009.

Findlay, A.M., R. King, A. Stam and E. Ruiz-Gelices (2006), 'Ever-reluctant Europeans: The changing geographies of UK students studying and working abroad', *European Urban and Regional Studies* 13: 291-318.

Findlay, A.M., A. Stam, R. King and E. Ruiz-Gelices (2005), 'International opportunities: Searching for the meaning of student migration', *Geographica Helvetica* 60: 192-200.

Garneau, S. (2007), 'Les expériences migratoires différenciées d'étudiants français : De l'institutionnalisation des mobilités étudiantes à la circulation des élites professionnelles?' *Revue Européenne des Migrations Internationales* 23: 139-161.

Gribble, C. (2008), 'Policy options for managing international student migration: The sending country's perspective', *Journal of Higher Education Policy and Management* 30: 25-39.

Hazen, H.D. and H. C. Alberts (2006), 'Visitors or immigrants? International students in the United States', *Population, Space and Place* 12: 201-216.

Huang, R. (2008), 'Mapping educational tourists' experience in the UK: Understanding international students', *Third World Quarterly* 29: 1003-1020.

IOM (2008), *World Migration 2008: Managing Labour Mobility in the Evolving Global Economy.* Geneva: International Organization for Migration.

IOM (2005), *World Migration 2005: Costs and Benefits of International Migration.* Geneva: International Organization for Migration.

Jallade, J.-P. and J. Gordon (1996), *Student Mobility within the European Union: A Statistical Analysis.* Brussels: Commission of the European Communities.

Kesselring, S. (2006), 'Pioneering mobilities: New patterns of movement and mobility in a mobile world', *Environment and Planning A* 38: 269-279.

King, R. (2003), 'International student migration in Europe and the institutionalisation of identity as "young Europeans"', in: J. Doomernik and H. Knippenberg (eds), *Migration and Immigrants: Between Policy and Reality,* 155-179. Amsterdam: Aksant Academic Publishers.

King, R. (2002), 'Towards a new map of European migration', *International Journal of Population Geography* 8: 89-106.

King, R. and E. Ruiz-Gelices (2003), 'International student migration and the European "year abroad": Effects on European identity and subsequent migration behaviour', *International Journal of Population Geography* 9: 229-252.

King, R. and I. Shuttleworth (1995), 'The emigration and employment of Irish graduates: The export of high-quality labour from the periphery of Europe', *European Urban and Regional Studies* 2: 21-40.

King, R., A.M. Findlay, E. Ruiz-Gelices and A. Stam (2004), *International Student Mobility.* London: HEFCE Issues Paper 30.

Koser, K. and J. Salt (1997), 'The geography of highly skilled international migration', *International Journal of Population Geography* 3: 285-303.

Li, F.L.N., A.M. Findlay, A.J. Jowett and R. Skeldon (1996), 'Migrating to learn and learning to migrate: A study of the experiences and intentions of international student migrants', *International Journal of Population Geography* 2: 51-67.

Murphy-Lejeune, E. (2002), *Student Mobility and Narrative in Europe: The New Strangers.* London: Routledge.

National Academies (2005), *Policy Implications of International Graduate Students and Postdoctoral Scholars in the United States.* Washington, DC: National Academies.

OECD (2006), *Education at a Glance.* Paris: Organisation for Economic Co-operation and Development.

Robertson, S. (2011), 'Student switchers and the regulation of residency: The interface of the individual and Australia's immigration regime', *Population, Space and Place* 17: 103-115.

Salt, J. (1997), *International Movements of the Highly Skilled.* Occasional Paper 30. Paris: Organisation for Economic Co-operation and Development.

Salt, J. (1988), 'Highly skilled international migrants, careers and internal labour markets', *Geoforum* 19: 387-399.

Schnitzer, K. and M. Zempel-Gino (2002), *Euro Student: Social and Economic Conditions of Student Life in Europe 2000.* Hannover: Hochschul-Informations-System.

Sheller, M. and J. Urry (2006), 'The new mobilities paradigm', *Environment and Planning A* 38: 207-226.

Skeldon, R. (1997), *Migration and Development: A Global Perspective.* London: Longman.

Solimano, A. (ed.) (2008), *The International Mobility of Talent.* Oxford: Oxford University Press.

Suter, B. and M. Jandl (2006), *Comparative Study on Policies towards Foreign Graduates.* Vienna: ICMPD.

Teichler, U. (1996), 'Student mobility in the framework of Erasmus: Findings of an evaluation study', *European Journal of Education* 31: 153-179.

Todisco, E. (2002), 'Mondialisation et migration qualifiée', *Migrations Société* 14: 195-220.

Tremblay, K. (2006), 'International student mobility in non-EU OECD countries', in: B. Khem and H. de Wit (eds), *Internationalization in Higher Education: European Responses to the Global Perspective,* 26-53. Amsterdam: EAIE/EAIR.

Urry, J. (2000), *Sociology Beyond Society: Mobilities for the Twenty-First Century.* London: Routledge.

Waters, J.L. (2006), 'Geographies of cultural capital: Education, international migration and family strategies between Hong Kong and Canada', *Transactions of the Institute of British Geographers* 31: 179-182.

Williams, A.M. (2006), 'Lost in translation? International migration, learning and knowledge', *Progress in Human Geography* 30: 588-607.

12 Sunset Migration

Russell King

Well, one of the reasons we moved down here is the fact that Britain has so many immigrants – we no longer feel at home there.
Arthur and Jean, retired British couple, interviewed in Southern Spain, 1996

Introduction

The irony of the above quote should not pass unnoticed. The couple interviewed had migrated to the Costa del Sol in order to 'escape' multicultural Britain. Yet their own immigration to Spain contributed to the transformation of the landscape and society there by mass tourism and retirement migration. Arthur and Jean felt unhappy about the way immigrants in Britain kept to their own customs and apparently renounced the 'British way of life'. However, they seemed oblivious to the fact that they themselves had not 'integrated' – they spoke little Spanish, and all their friends were other British retirees.

international retirement migration

Like hundreds of thousands of Britons and other Northern Europeans, Arthur and Jean are part of a migration that does not feature prominently on the European migration map, with its focus on labour migrants and refugees. 'Sunset migration', generally referred to in the literature as 'international retirement migration' (e.g. King et al. 1998), is very different from earlier intra-European migrations. During the 1950s, 1960s and 1970s, millions of poor and unemployed migrants from Southern Europe moved to industrial North-Western Europe, facilitated by the nascent common market for labour and bilateral recruitment agreements. Sunset migrants go in the reverse direction. They are manifestly not economic migrants, although economic considerations are not absent from their reasoning. As Benson and O'Reilly (2009) have stressed, their migration is driven by the search for a particular lifestyle built around certain environmental preferences (e.g. climate, scenery, location), and marked by a particular life-stage – retirement.

This chapter first defines the notion of sunset migration. It then presents two scenarios – one positive and one negative – for its evaluation as 'rational-choice' behaviour. The chapter then proceeds to examine reasons and motivations, spatial distributions and settlement types, patterns of integration and non-integration, impacts on the local environment and issues for the future. The account draws on a wide range of literature from many disciplines, as well as media reports. Throughout the chapter reference is made to a research project on British retirees in the Mediterranean coordinated by the author in the late 1990s.[1] The quote at the beginning of this chapter is from that project.

Defining the phenomenon and exploring its diversity

two defining features

Sunset migration embodies a process characterised by two defining features: a quest for the sun and a later-life migration, often configured around retirement. Moving to a warmer, sunnier climate can sometimes involve a choice between internal and international migration. Countries such as France and the UK range across wide latitudes, so that the south coast of each in itself offers significant climatic advantages over the rest of the country, even before the added attraction of being near the sea. For international retirement migration within Europe, the key flows are out from the UK, Germany, the Benelux countries, the Nordic countries, Switzerland and Austria; and into Spain, Portugal, southern France, Italy, Greece, Malta and Cyprus. The European case parallels mobilities in other parts of the rich world – for instance from the northern United States and Canada to the sunshine states of Florida, California and Arizona.

Sunset migration has been growing for several decades now, partly on the heels of the boom in international tourism, which started in the 1960s. As an elite phenomenon, however, it had earlier origins, traceable to the settlement of artists and writers in places like the South of France, Tuscany and the isle of Capri. At the turn of the twentieth century the British Consul in Florence estimated that there were already 35,000 British residing in Tuscany. He went on to describe the 'seductive charms' of this region in the following bygone terms:

> It is surprising what number of English people live permanently in Tuscany, not quitting it even for an annual holiday, but going instead, like any good Florentine, to the Tuscan mountains or the Tuscan seaside. An Englishman, say a retired civil servant, comes with his family for a stay of six months to

> 'see' Florence. He arrives charged to the brim with captiousness, prepared not to submit to six months of dirt, and discomfort, and impossible fare, and wholesale robbery, without constant, aggressive, and loud-voiced protest. He finds instead, although the fact is slow to penetrate his intelligence, willing service, cheap living, wholesome food, sound wine, scrupulous cleanliness, a cheery welcome, and honesty closely allied to honour. His doom is sealed, and although he does not yield without a struggle, his native land knows him no more (Carmichael 1901: 10-11).

not a simple process

Despite its beguiling title, sunset migration is by no means a simple or uniform process; it involves complex spatialities and temporalities. In its 'ideal-type' form it runs as follows. The migrating unit is usually a married couple with grown, independent children – often referred to as 'empty nesters'. They move at or soon after retirement, typically aged 60-65, and relocate to an area of Southern Europe they have often visited on holiday where they might have bought a second home at an earlier stage, possibly with retirement in mind. Their socio-economic background can generally be described as 'comfortable'; they often have professional or business backgrounds, with some accumulated savings and an occupational pension.

However, questionnaires and interviews made of North European retired migrants in various destinations reveal substantial variations. First, the retiree may have been resident in the destination country prior to retirement, which would decouple migration from retirement. Research on the retired British in Tuscany found that many had already been living and working in Italy as language teachers, businesspeople or in professions connected to art or music (King and Patterson 1998; King and Scarpa 2001). The Tuscan research also challenged fixed notions of retirement, since many 'retirees' continued to be economically active in various ways – as writers and artists, renters of holiday homes or part-time olive farmers.

Second, many international retirement migrants have been 'career expats', choosing to retire to a warm climate and attractive location after having been overseas for much of their lives. Some may have been born overseas, for instance as British, Dutch or Belgian nationals in India, Indonesia and the Congo, respectively, having had little direct experience of the colonial mother country. Others will have spent long periods abroad in the oil industry, or as consultant engineers, teachers and academics, or as business or marketing professionals. Such individuals may have been geographically mobile during their expat careers; common postings are likely to have been to the Persian Gulf, Singapore, other parts of the Middle or Far East and Southern Africa.

homeland return

A third type of international retirement migration is entirely different. This concerns the return of Southern European international migrants to their native home after their working lives as labour migrants in Northern Europe (or North America, Australia, etc.) have ended. Given the marked cohort characteristic of these labour migrations – the protagonists left as young men and women during the 1950s and 1960s – many have been approaching retirement age since the 1990s (White 2006). The decision to return to their native towns and villages rests on many factors: family circumstances (most have children and grandchildren in the host countries), concerns over healthcare and welfare provision and worries about reintegration into their homeland societies. Some may resolve these dilemmas by adopting a transnational (or 'translocal') retirement lifestyle, dividing their time between the two places. Others return definitively, a 'return of retirement' that has been the subject of a small but evolving body of literature, starting with Cerase's (1974) study on Italians returning from their (mostly pre-war) emigration to the United States, and continuing with research on Ireland (Malcolm 1996), Spain (Rodríguez and Egea 2006), and Switzerland (Bolzman et al. 2006).

Retirement return is fundamentally driven by nostalgia and ties to one's roots; it is therefore quite different from the sunset migration described earlier, and therefore will not be considered further.

Two scenarios

old age a social construct

Older people have traditionally not been a major focus of attention in migration studies, reflecting the view that 'the elderly' are not economically active and are not therefore part of economic migration. If they migrated, it was seen as part of a wider 'family migration' of which they were not the main protagonists; or they were pictured as refugees fleeing from war, ethnic cleansing or natural disasters. More likely they were the family members 'left behind' by young migrating adults. It is now widely acknowledged that 'old age' is a social construct. No longer confined to a few short inactive years between the statutory retirement age and the demographically allotted 'three score years and ten' of average life expectancy several decades ago, the later stages of life are now seen in more positive terms, particularly for the 'baby-boomer' generation. This demographic is currently at or approaching retirement age, possessing a combination of factors giving them greatly enhanced self-confidence: better education than their predecessors, inherited and accumulated wealth, high incomes and pensions, a wider experience of travel and increasing longevity. Warnes (1996: 101) has written that elderly people have been pioneers of social change and new forms of mobility, and can now count retirement abroad as one of their migration options. Opinions are divided, however, over the wisdom of this strategy. Two scenarios compete for our attention: the positive and the negative.

positive scenario

The *positive scenario* sees people's lives enriched and prolonged by a move to a warmer climate, with a more relaxed and hedonistic sociability and plenty of opportunities for year-round outdoor exercise – such as swimming, walking and golf. Sporting deep suntans burnished over many years, sunset migrants look and feel healthier than they would have been in the cold, rainy 'North' with its long winters. Respiratory problems and arthritic joints may improve in the southern warmth. The lower cost of living – such as cheaper housing, lower heating bills, and local food – enables a material improvement in quality of life. Depending on location, low-cost flights allow for frequent trips 'home' or regular visits from children and grandchildren, who can combine family visits with a holiday by the sea. Retirees appreciate living in a social environment where the elderly are respected and crime is lower. They are also able to enjoy new cultural experiences, both through their interaction with the host population and by socialising with retirees of other nationalities, in certain areas creating a new multi-ethnic Europe of the elderly. This last remark may sound rather utopian, but King et al. (2000: 165-198) reported that the great majority of their 1,000 questionnaire respondents and 160 interviewees found more advantages than disadvantages to residing abroad after retirement – 'an impressively positive audit of the decision to move abroad' (2000: 197).[2]

negative scenario

The opposite interpretation sees inherent risks in migrating later in life to a different cultural and linguistic environment with a different welfare system. According to this *negative scenario*, sunset migrants become an isolated and vulnerable group, cut off by language and cultural barriers from the host society whose rules and behaviours they do not understand. Further problems arise when illness strikes or a partner dies; family support is far away, and the hospitals and medical services may be seen and experienced as very different in quality and style from those available in the home country (Hardill et al. 2005). Retirees face 'structured disadvantage' if their provisional residential status and lack of social insurance payments fail to yield the entitlements that their condition requires (Warnes 2002: 143-144; see also Ackers and Dwyer 2002). Retirees may be forced to abandon their dream and return home, but in the meantime they may have lost many of their social contacts and it may be difficult to sell their retirement property abroad. Other problems may arise if fixed pensions fail to keep pace with cost-of-living increases in the country of retirement. Migrants may be financially exposed to property price swings, as under the current financial crisis where the property bubble has burst. Media reports claim that retirees in Spain faced a loss of 40 per cent of the value of their properties between mid-2008 and mid-2009.[3]

three-stage model

The balance between positive and negative outcomes of sunset migration is not clear-cut, and individuals' experience will likely change over time as they age. Gerontologists frequently draw a distinction between the 'young old', typically in their 60s and 70s, and the 'old old', aged 80 and over. The transition from one state to another involves increasing frailty and loss of mobility and independence. Strokes, heart attacks, breathing difficulties and stiffening joints mean a loss of corporeal mobility and perhaps also the ability to drive a vehicle; diminishing mental capacity may be an added factor. Relevant to this discussion is the three-stage model of later-life mobility proposed by Litwak and Longino (1987): first, the early post-retirement years when positive health and unimpaired mobility prevail; second, the onset of frailty and ill-health, whereby mobility is curtailed and proximity to services and support becomes important; and finally chronic infirmity and dependency, which herald the need for regular, close care or a move into an institutional setting. Of course, not every older person proceeds through these stages, and some stages may be temporary, followed by an improvement. However, it is not difficult to appreciate that these later-life changes, which are difficult enough to manage in a familiar home-country setting, are even more challenging, sometimes disastrously so, in a foreign country.

Reasons and motivations

The continuous growth of sunset migration over the past four decades, and particularly since the 1980s, has been driven by a combination of demographic, economic, societal and geographical factors. These, in turn, can be analysed at three levels: the macro-scale processes, which structure the evolution of the phenomenon; individual push and pull forces, which stimulate a personal decision to move abroad; and meso-scale network and institutional factors. We will look at the 'big picture' first, drawing mainly on Williams et al. (1997) and King et al. (2000: 1-36).

demographics

Demography is mainly about the ageing of the European population, and especially the increased numbers of active 'young old' people. This has particular salience in Northern Europe, where the social model of successful ageing is based on individual self-reliance rather than on multi-generational family care. Particularly significant in framing the potential for retirement migration are later-age survival rates (as opposed to life expectancy at birth). Survival rates at age 65 grew by 27 per cent between the 1950s and the 1990s in England and Wales. Perhaps even more significant has been the sharp increase in the *joint* survival rate of couples – the retired couple being the most typical sunset migration unit. When these demographic trends are combined with increasing numbers of people taking early retirement at some point in their 50s, it can be seen that the post-retirement life-span widens considerably – for many people up to thirty years or more.[4]

Although sunset migrants are not economic migrants, there are powerful economic factors shaping the ability of increasing numbers of older people to consider retirement abroad. Key here have been rising incomes since the 1950s and increased lifetime savings among an enlarging middle class created by the shift from blue- to white-collar employment in post-industrial Europe. Financial well-being has been boosted by two further factors: the growth in occupational pensions, especially for professional and public-sector staff; and the windfall of inherited wealth from parents, often coming as potential retirement migrants approach the end of their working lives. Underlying the progressive *embourgeoisement* of the European population over the last half-century has been the increasing participation in upper-secondary and tertiary education.

changing patterns of mobility

Longer periods spent in education, including some knowledge of foreign languages, create the conditions for a third general factor shaping sunset migration: changing patterns of lifetime spatial mobility, in particular the diffusion of mass tourism, which has increased the experience and knowledge of other countries, albeit often 'packaged' in a superficial manner. Virtually all of the researchers who have written on international retirement migration have identified the connection between tourism and retirement migration. They observe that most sunset migrants move to a place they are familiar with from past visits as a tourist (Williams et al. 2000). O'Reilly (2000) goes one stage further and interprets retirement migration as essentially a prolongation of the holiday as a permanent lifestyle.

Fourth, there is the EU context to sunset migration. The hypothesis here is that the enlargement of the EU in the 1980s that incorporated much of Southern Europe (adding Greece, Spain and Portugal to France and Italy) facilitated retirement migration to these countries. The logic behind this argument is that the Single European Act (1986) removed obstacles to freedom of residence and movement, such as property rights, while the Treaty of European Union (1994) brought electoral rights to EU citizens living outside their home country (Ackers and Dwyer 2002: 1-5). However, it would be a mistake to place too much emphasis on this factor, since retirement migration, especially to Spain, had started before that country's accession to the EU in 1986. Retirees have also settled in countries such as Malta and Cyprus (both of which only joined the EU in 2004), as well as in 'new countries' for retirement migration such as Croatia and Turkey, which are not EU member-states.

geography

Finally, underpinning all else, there is geography. Weather is the most obvious attraction of Mediterranean Europe: hot, dry, sunshine-filled summers and mild, not-too-rainy winters. This classic Mediterranean climate finds optimal expression around the Mediterranean coasts of Spain, from Valencia down to Gibraltar, including the Balearic Islands. These coastal regions, with their airports connected directly to many cities in Northern Europe, are also optimally located in terms of access-time: only two to three hours of flight time to be in a warmer latitude. Further discussion is made about the geographical patterns of retiree settlement in the next section of this chapter.

Now we explore micro-scale decision-making and examine individuals' responses to the various migration factors discussed above, as well as other factors. A range of interviews, questionnaires and ethnographic studies are drawn upon that have been carried out over the past decade or so. There is now quite a plethora of such studies,[5] the results of which have been helpfully synthesised by Casado-Díaz et al. (2004). The published literature tends to concentrate on Britons and Germans in Spain, but other national groups (e.g. French, Swiss, Nordic countries) and other destinations (e.g. Portugal, France, Italy, Malta, Corfu) are also represented.

field surveys

Casado-Díaz et al. summarise findings from nine field surveys in different parts of Spain (Costa Blanca, Costa del Sol, Mallorca, Canary Islands) and from the Algarve, Tuscany and Malta. Across all studies (except Tuscany), the most commonly expressed reason for the move was 'climate', nominated as the main reason by between 62 per cent (in Malta) and 92 per cent (the Canaries) of the various surveys' respondents (Tuscany was only 26 per cent – here 'the Italian way of life' was the prime factor, scoring 42 per cent). However, it becomes clear from closer scrutiny of the results, including interview narratives, that references to climate often morph into comments and discourses about better health, outdoor living and even financial elements (e.g. lower heating costs). Moreover, climate is articulated as both a pull and a push factor, with references to factors such as cold northern winters, high or frequent rainfall and grey skies, linked to low morale and being forced to stay indoors. Yet some respondents find disadvantages to the Mediterranean climate: in the south of Spain, summers can be overbearingly hot, whereas in hilly Tuscany winters bring cold and snow.

financial reasons

The second most important cluster of reasons distilled from the survey evidence is financial. Three elements stand out: house prices, heating costs, and the lower cost of food, drink and restaurant meals. These differentials have narrowed appreciably since the first wave of retirees settled thirty or more years ago; but the gap remains for those relocating from Northern European cities where housing and living costs are very high.[6] A third set of reasons focuses around the Mediterranean way of life, which is usually taken to refer to the food, wine-drinking culture, slower pace of life, outdoor lifestyle and general friendliness of the local population. Finally, some of the surveys report a tendency for people on their second or subsequent marriages or partnerships, or who have recently divorced or become widowed, to locate to Southern Europe as part of a 'fresh start'.

meso-scale perspective

A final group of reasons for migration refers to family, work and social connections. This brings in the meso-scale perspective. Some retirees moved to join their adult children who had already migrated – particularly to Spain. These younger-generation migrants had often moved to set up a business in the tourist areas. In other cases the retiree had a spouse or partner who had originated from the country of settlement. This happened quite often in Malta as a result of military and colonial links (Warnes and Patterson 1998). Social networks of earlier-migrated friends are also a factor of encouragement for some individuals and couples to follow suit. Other, more institutional, networks are created by property developers and estate agents who market particular types of property in particular locations to different types of clients, distinguished by wealth, nationality or retirement lifestyle.

Geographical patterns and settlement types

amenity-seeking migrants

Mediterranean Europe functions as a *sunbelt* for retired North Europeans. In contrast to economic migrants, whose lifestyles are linked to work and production, and who are generally found crowded into the poorer niches of metropolitan and industrial areas, Northern European retirees are amenity-seeking migrants who see the European South as a consumption space, which they colonise with their villas, condominiums, swimming pools and golf courses. Here we will discuss the difficulty of statistically measuring retirement migration, then explore the associated settlement forms and landscape transformations.

Sketchy statistics

Assembling comparative statistics on migration is notoriously difficult, and there is no dataset that gives an overall picture of the geography of international retirement migration in Europe. Eurostat has data on foreigners residing in different countries in Europe, including Northern Europeans in Southern Europe, but they are not disaggregated by age, economic activity or subnational region. These data show that, during the 1990s, Britons and Germans made up more than 40 per cent of all Europeans resident in Spain, Portugal, Italy and Greece. Germans led the field in Italy (representing a quarter of all Europeans there, while 17 per cent were British), whereas in Spain, Portugal and Greece, Britons were more numerous (27, 27 and 20 per cent, respectively), with Germans second (15, 16 and 13 per cent, respectively).[7]

A more detailed picture is necessarily a fragmented one, built from individual-country sources. Following are two examples: the most important source country for sunset migration, the UK, and the main destination country, Spain.

UK pensioner data

Useful insights into the UK's retired population living abroad are given by the Department of Work and Pensions database on pensions paid abroad. From 253,000 in 1981, the figure more than doubled to 594,000 in 1991 and in 2005 passed 1 million (Sriskandarajah and Drew 2006: 28). What is also significant is the steady rise in overseas pensioners as a proportion of all UK state pensioners: 6 per cent in the early 1990s, and 9 per cent today. Regarding specific destinations, Table 12.1 shows data for November 2008, with trends over the previous decade. It should be borne in mind that these data do not necessarily refer to UK nationals, but to individuals who have accumulated state pension rights by work and residence in the UK and payment of National Insurance. The table contains some surprises. Nearly seven out of ten pensions are paid to people resident in North America, Australia, New Zealand and Ireland. France, Spain and Italy, the classic sunbelt countries of Southern Europe, feature in the top half of the table, with smaller sunbelt countries lower down – Cyprus, Portugal, Malta and Greece. Notable is the much stronger decade-long increase in the Mediterranean retirement countries, including an approximate doubling of pension recipients in Spain, Portugal, Greece, Cyprus and Malta, and a nearly threefold increase in France. Switzerland also experienced strong growth, possibly linked to its tax-exile attractions for wealthy retirees, as well as to its scenery, climate and high quality of life.

complex patterns

Following Warnes (2001; 2003), the data in Table 12.1 indicate complex patterns of later-life migration from the UK, involving several different migration and retirement processes; these are distilled in Table 12.2, which recalculates some of the data for Table 12.1 into four sets of pension-receiving countries:

- First, there are the countries of long-term British settlement over the post-war period: the former 'White Commonwealth'. If migrants had UK pension entitlements before they left, they were

Table 12.1 *Recipients of UK retirement pensions living abroad, 1999 and 2008*

Country of residence	*1999 (thousands)*	*2008 (thousands)*	*2008/1999 × 100*
Australia	196.8	247.6	125.9
Canada	134.2	158.2	117.9
USA	111.5	134.4	120.5
Ireland	87.2	110.7	127.0
Spain	39.3	92.5	235.6
New Zealand	31.7	47.7	150.7
France	16.3	47.0	288.7
South Africa	33.3	38.3	115.0
Italy	27.6	35.9	130.3
Germany	25.2	34.7	137.8
Jamaica	23.9	20.9	87.3
Cyprus	6.7	15.7	233.4
Netherlands	5.8	8.7	149.2
Portugal	4.3	7.7	181.7
Switzerland	3.4	7.5	220.0
Barbados	3.7	5.2	140.6
Austria	4.4	5.1	114.4
Pakistan	6.2	4.8	77.7
India	4.0	4.8	119.5
Belgium	4.4	4.6	105.2
Malta	2.5	4.4	173.4
Greece	1.9	4.4	235.8
Israel	3.6	4.2	118.5

Source: UK Department for Work and Pensions Information Directorate: Work and Pensions Longitudinal Study
Notes: Only countries with at least 4,000 cases in 2008 are listed. The index figure (third column) is calculated on the basis of the full figures, not the abbreviated totals recorded here.

paid in the destination country on retirement. Another migration channel to these countries involves retired UK residents who joined adult children who had emigrated earlier, often as part of sponsored migration schemes. Finally there is conventional sunset migration, which has taken UK retirees primarily to Florida.

- The second set represents the main sources of post-war labour migration to Britain – Ireland, the Caribbean and Southern Asia. In these cases, pensions are paid to those who have returned home, although some amenity-seeking British pensioners have been retiring to favoured Caribbean islands such as Barbados. Both Group 1 and Group 2 countries had rather low rates of pension growth over the period 1999-2008, 23 and 17 per cent, respectively.
- The third group is the European sunbelt. Here pension recipients have more than doubled since 1999, continuing and accelerating a

trend that became evident in the prior decade (see the 1988-1999 data in Warnes 2001: 380).

- The fourth group is more heterogeneous and difficult to explain in terms of concrete migration processes, except in reference to the growing trend in intra-European migration and international marriages – which are products of European integration, globalisation and more frequent international travel. The large-scale presence of British service personnel in Germany, and the attractions of Switzerland noted above, help to push this group's rate of increase to 40 per cent, higher than Groups 1 and 2, but lower than Group 3.

Table 12.2 *Recipients of UK retirement pensions, by group of country*

	Country group	$\frac{2008}{1999} \times 100$
1	Settlement (Australia, Canada, USA, NZ, South Africa)	123.4
2	Labour migration (Ireland, Jamaica, Barbados, Pakistan, India)	117.1
3	Retirement migration (Spain, France, Italy, Greece, Cyprus, Malta)	212.0
4	Northern Europe (Germany, Netherlands, Belgium, Austria, Switz.)	140.3

Source: UK Department for Work and Pensions Information Directorate: Work and Pensions Longitudinal Study

UK retiree population measures inexact

The payment of UK pensions does not reflect the exact measure of the UK retiree population abroad. Quite apart from the nationality issue of returning labour migrants, there may be UK retirement-age nationals living abroad who do not receive a state pension. Many more may be living abroad but are not registered as resident there, and so are recorded as receiving their pensions in the UK. This leads us to next consider the case of Spain, where some detailed statistics are available, but interrogating the data reveals the complexity of registration systems and of the concept of residence.

Along the continuum between a short-stay tourist and a permanently resident expat are many hybrid types. O'Reilly (1995; 2000: 52-58) has proposed a five-fold typology (see also Williams et al. 2000):

- *tourists* identify Spain purely as a holiday destination;
- *occasional visitors* often own second homes in Spain and visit occasionally, or perhaps quite frequently, but without any obvious pattern;
- *seasonal visitors* divide their time on a more regular and equal basis; typically they over-winter in Spain and spend summer 'at home' in Britain, Germany, Sweden, etc;
- *residents* are those whose primary residence is in Spain, which they regard as their home; however, unlike the final group below, they make rather regular return visits to their country of origin, to see

family and friends, often timed to avoid the heat of high summer and the holiday crowds; and
- *expatriates*, or 'full residents', have moved to Spain permanently and live there all year round.

ambiguity

It is clear that there can be ambiguity about the 'resident' and 'immigrant' status of some of these categories and how they should be recorded by the Spanish authorities. The situation is not helped by the fact that many foreign retirees who have a meaningful relationship with Spain, either owning or renting property on a long-term basis and living there for part or most of the year, have not taken out *residencìa* status, out of ignorance, fear of the bureaucracy or strategic decision-making (for instance to preserve full health-service entitlements in their home country). Rodríguez et al. (2001: 180-181) have highlighted this problem with reference to foreigners (not just retirees) in the Balearic Islands (Table 12.3). Based on local police data, they demonstrate that only a quarter of the Germans living in the islands are classed as permanently resident; the figure for the British, the second largest group of foreigners, is 45 per cent. Other Europeans living in the archipelago (French, Swedes, Dutch, Swiss, etc.) constituted a much higher share of those with permanent residence.

Table 12.3 *Foreigners by residence type in the Balearic Islands, 1995*

Country of origin	*Permanent*	*Temporary*	*Total*	*% permanent*
Germany	7,667	21,873	29,540	26.0
UK	8,347	10,010	18,352	45.5
Other Europeans	11,684	2,054	13,738	85.0

Source: Rodríguez et al. (2001: 180)

Spanish data

The Spanish census enumerates foreign residents by nationality, age and province of Spain. For the same reasons noted above, though the census significantly underestimates the foreign 'presence' in Spain, the broad distributional pattern is probably representative. Table 12.4 presents a selection of data from the 2001 census. The table lists the Mediterranean coastal provinces in north-south geographical order, plus the Balearic and Canarian provinces. The figures are for foreigners over 65, for the four main nationality groups, and for all Northern Europeans. Several features stand out. A notable one concerns the percentage figures in the bottom-right corner of the table: the Mediterranean and island provinces contain 39 per cent of all those over age 65 in Spain, but 94 per cent of North Europeans; and the four main provinces of retired-foreigner concentration (Alicante,

Málaga, Baleares and Santa Cruz de Tenerife) account for three-quarters of North Europeans aged 65 and over, yet less than one-tenth of all those over that age in the 50 provinces of Spain. The bottom two rows of the table show that the degree of concentration in the Mediterranean and island provinces, and in the four key provinces named above, is greatest for the UK and the Nordic countries (Denmark, Finland, Norway and Sweden), slightly less so for Germany, and considerably less so for France, whose older population is relatively more concentrated in the northern provinces. Looking at the penultimate column (Northern Europeans over age 65 as a percentage of all those over age 65 enumerated in each province), we find that the province of Alicante, which contains the Costa Blanca, has the greatest concentration of foreigners over age 65 – one in ten – followed by Málaga, Santa Cruz de Tenerife and Baleares. Of the Northern European nationalities not identified in the table but included in that total (Austrians, Belgians, Dutch, Irish and Swiss), all have distributions that broadly match the Northern European total.

Table 12.4 *North Europeans over age 65 in Spain, 2001*

Mediterranean and Island provinces	*UK*	*Germany*	*Nordic countries*	*France*	*All North Europeans*	*North Europeans as % all >65s*	*All >65s*
Girona	264	385	28	437	1,727	1.7	101,137
Barcelona	252	626	74	665	2,034	0.3	816,762
Tarragona	99	246	9	238	988	0.9	108,357
Castellón	132	149	6	200	625	0.7	85,627
Valencia	378	202	25	414	1,190	0.3	361,654
Alicante	8,849	4,673	2,277	1,322	23,095	9.8	235,215
Murcia	386	166	82	176	955	0.6	171,214
Almería	838	245	19	115	1,362	1.9	72,573
Granada	202	115	151	78	753	0.6	133,453
Málaga	6,521	1,814	3,095	463	13,573	7.5	180,013
Cádiz	346	85	24	42	544	0.4	137,828
Baleares	1,526	1,682	208	476	4,462	3.6	123,576
Las Palmas	363	683	304	86	1,664	1.7	96,406
Santa Cruz	1,896	2,191	185	195	5,075	4.7	107,245
All M and I provinces	22,052	13,262	6,487	4,907	58,047	2.1	2,731,060
Rest of Spain	570	923	129	1,376	3,617	0.1	4,227,456
Total	22,622	14,185	6,616	6,283	61,664	0.9	6,958,516
% in M and I provinces	97.5	93.5	98.1	78.1	94.1		39.2
% in top four provinces	83.1	73.0	87.1	39.1	74.9		9.3

Source: Censo de Población 2001; www.ine.es/censo/en/listatablas.jsp

Settlements and landscapes of retirement abroad

urbanizaciones

There are essentially two destination settings that are valued by sunset migrants moving within Europe. The first is a location on or very close to the coast: most popular here are the Spanish *costas* and islands, and the Portuguese Algarve. This type of retirement migration is driven by climate, sea views, beachfront life and other leisure amenities. The typical residential setting is a villa, detached or semi-detached, which is part of a residential complex. In Spain these take the form of *urbanizaciones*: often quite extensive residential or holiday estates, close to supermarkets and other service and leisure facilities, including golf courses.[8] Where such estates are built *ex-novo*, as most have been, swimming pools, palm trees and extensive private terraces are part of a fabricated landscape designed to evoke a subtropical ambience of leisure and relaxation. For those on tighter budgets, villas give way to blocks of flats with more limited outdoor private and pubic open space.

The second type of destination is the attractive rural setting – often in a separate, independent dwelling such as a restored cottage or farmhouse – where the emphasis is on peace and good views. According to Williams et al. (1997: 129) such retirees seek to recapture 'middle-class myths of a lost rurality in Northern Europe'. Hence, the quality of the rural landscape and the charm of the vernacular architecture are key location factors, found in their most sylvan form in the Italian region of Tuscany. For this form of retirement migration, climate and sunshine are not so overriding as location factors, and so we find 'rural-idyll' retirees locating in cooler areas such as central and south-west France, or eastern Tuscany and Umbria (Hoggart and Buller 1995; King and Patterson 1998).

social class differences

There are clear social class differences between these two retirement migration types (King et al. 2000: 75-80). Those heading for rural environments put special value on culture, the aesthetics of landscape and the local lifestyle; hence they are likely to belong to the professional and middle classes, having had extensive education. Less educated Britons and others moving to Spain are not as interested in culture as in the cost of living and climate. Rodríguez et al. (1998) and Casado-Díaz et al. (2004) find that Britons in Spain are less educated than other Northern European nationalities settling in the same areas. Particularly in the years since 2000, the mass building of inexpensive properties marketed to foreigners in hitherto relatively 'empty' coastal stretches in the provinces of Almería and Murcia in south-eastern Spain has brought significant numbers of lower-middle- and working-class Britons to these areas.

If the Costa del Sol and Tuscany are the archetypes of these two destination settings, there are many intermediate forms. For instance in the south of Spain, some retirees have settled in 'back-from-coast' locations, either in isolated farmstead buildings (*fincas*) or in interior villages such as the famous *pueblos blancos* (white villages) of Andalusia. Around the hilly Riviera coasts of the Côte d'Azur and the adjacent Italian region of Liguria, it is possible to combine the rural idyll (a cottage or village house with scenic views) with nearness to the sea, a short drive away. Buying a property for retirement in rural Southern Europe involves a choice between a house in open countryside, and one in a hamlet, a larger village or a provincial town. For retirees with limited finances and/or limited mobility, buying or renting a small house or flat in a town with services nearby is a more rational choice than potential isolation in a country village or cottage. Others may move and downshift into town as mobility and independence are lost.

coastal and rural environments

Finally, the two destination environments – the coastal and the rural – are correlated with different temporal mobility regimes. Breuer (2005), who conducted a survey of 300 retired Germans in the Canaries, found that 71 per cent of those who lived in *fincas* or in traditional villages stayed 'on site' for at least nine months of the year, whereas 62 per cent of those who lived in coastal *urbanizaciones* were resident for less than three months per year. Overall, there was a strong seasonal contrast: 90 per cent of survey respondents were in the Canaries during November-March, and only 30 per cent during June-August. Germans in the Canary Islands are thus comparable to the retired 'snowbirds' of North America (Warnes 2001). It also seems that the harsher the winter climate in the Northern European country of origin, the more likely retirees are to engage in snowbird seasonal migration with southern Spain and the Canaries, as studies of Norwegians, Swedes and Finns have shown (Myklebost 1989; Gustafson 2002; Karisto 2005).

Paradoxes of integration and non-integration

integration paradoxes

The evidence from many case studies is that sunset migrants, especially those who have settled along the Spanish coasts and on Gran Canaria and Tenerife, tend to cluster together geographically and socially. Friendship networks, social activities, associations and services all tend to be nationality-based, for reasons of language, cultural familiarity and national identity. The most detailed study of integration and non-integration is possibly Karen O'Reilly's (2000) ethnography of the British in Fuengirola. Several ironies are apparent from her study and from others on the same topic (e.g. King et al. 2000: 127-164). The first is that the British tend to associate almost exclusively with each other while abroad, thereby confirming their 'Britishness', while at the same time fashioning a narrative of 'bad Britain' – such as the weather, the nanny state, the crumbling national health service and excessive immigration. Another paradox is that retirees often claim to have adopted the 'Spanish way of life', referring to the laid-back lifestyle, spending a lot of time outdoors and taking an afternoon siesta, for instance, while at the same time speaking very little Spanish, having no meaningful social contact with local Spaniards, and complaining about the *mañana* syndrome and the length of time it takes to get things done! Yet another irony in the discussion over integration is the question: Integrate into what? Along the coasts of Spain, a new society has been 'created' by mass tourism, local immigration, recent immigration from nearby North Africa and rapid building developments, many created specifically for tourists and foreign residents from Northern Europe. Hence, an 'authentic' Spanish society hardly exists. What exists instead is a set of settlements, the sprawling *urbanizaciones* above all, which are almost the antithesis of a community, with owners and renters who constantly come and go, an emphasis on privatised space and social encounters that are dominated by the fleeting yet power-laden economic relationships inherent to tourism.

The situation is rather different in the rural areas favoured, on the whole, by educated migrants with a professional background. Here there is a greater desire to integrate more meaningfully with local people (retirees to rural destinations usually have a better command of the local language), and the local setting facilitates such integration.

Conclusion

impacts

The effects of sunset migration on host-country settings are manifold, and are felt particularly at the local and regional levels. Quite apart from the societal question of non-integration, there are key impacts on demography, the housing and building environment, and local services, especially health care. At the municipality level, sunset migration turns population pyramids upside down.[9] Issues of welfare and pension transferability also loom large. Complications may arise in the domain of health and welfare rights, if returnees choose to live transnationally, dividing their time between two (or possibly more) residences.

Let us draw up the socio-economic balance sheet in more systematic detail. On the positive side, there is an influx of pension income and savings, which can be likened to labour migrants' savings and remittances. Retirees use this financial inflow to buy food, goods and services, thereby supporting the local economy. Shops, bars, restaurants, hairdressers and maintenance services (e.g. plumbers, gardeners, car mechanics, swimming-pool engineers) are all helped by this exogenously financed demand. This money does not circulate only among the 'native' population. One of the effects of international retirement migration, especially where it occurs on a large scale and is allied with tourism, has been to stimulate same-nationality migration in order to service the tourist economy and the foreign resident community. Casado-Díaz et al. (2004: 373) call this phenomenon 'derivative' migration. The interactions between these 'service' migrants and the retired foreign residents have been well documented by O'Reilly (2000).

housing

Housing is another arena where the arrival of retired foreigners has powerful effects on the local economy as well as an obvious visible impact on the built landscape. Although international and national developers and land speculators appropriate some of the larger profits, local building-supplies industries and contractors have been boosted by new housing developments. The demand for construction labour generates flows of internal migrants, for example, from other parts of Spain and Portugal with higher unemployment rates. Migrant workers may come from as far as North Africa and even sub-Saharan Africa and, latterly, from Eastern Europe. Not all building is done to a high professional standard, however, and the aesthetics and architectural style of such developments are an issue of debate. Moreover, some developments have gone ahead without planning permission and land titles, a problem that, to their cost, foreign buyers have discovered only later when they have moved in and been told that their properties are somehow 'illegal'.

The aesthetic impact is rather more positive in rural regions where foreign purchasers have made a significant contribution to restoring and modernising derelict and deteriorating properties. Two groups of local people have benefited from this activity. First, the original owners of the properties have been happy to sell off cottages and farm buildings that previously had little market value (what was 'fashionable' for North Europeans was deeply unfashionable for local rural residents, who were interested in moving to modern houses and flats). Second, craftsmen and builders have benefitted, as their skills became much in demand for restoration projects. However, the influx of wealthy retired foreigners into prized rural regions such as Tuscany, Provence and Dordogne has bid up the prices of rural and village housing. Access for local buyers has often become very difficult – a classic problem in gentrified rural areas throughout Europe.

health and welfare services

Beyond the economics of housing, the other key impact is on health and welfare services – part of the 'structured disadvantage' noted earlier. Detailed survey evidence compiled by Warnes et al. (1999), King et al. (2000: 165-198) and Ackers and Dwyer (2002: 77-106) reveals a diverse picture in this respect. Despite frequent claims by retirees in interviews that they 'feel healthier' in the warmer climate, there is little solid evidence that their health is actually improved or that they live longer. Maybe their more relaxed mental state and their enjoyment of good weather and pleasant surroundings inure them to the minor complaints that come with increasing age. When it comes to chronic illness and significant health deterioration – the onset of Alzheimer's, cancer or a stroke, for example – the choice and the evidence are stark. Should they stay on or return? Clinically, the standard of hospital treatment and health care is now good throughout Southern Europe. However, two problems highlighted by the survey research stand out: the language barrier (though medical staff operating in areas of high retiree density may speak one or more of the relevant languages) and the different culture of hospital aftercare (Southern European hospitals expect the patient's family to provide much of the non-medical support such as meals and washing and clothing the patient). Retirees seldom have this wider family support, although self-help groups can sometimes compensate for this lack. A frequently cited example is the CUDECA network of support for cancer sufferers in Spain, founded by an English woman in 1991 (King et al. 2000: 191-192).

deteriorating health

Another area of concern relates to deteriorating health and housing. In Northern Europe, residential adjustment to failing health and restricted mobility involves state-provided modifications to the dwelling or a move to sheltered housing or care home. Such options barely exist in Southern Europe, except perhaps where they are run by religious charities for the destitute elderly (Williams et al. 1997: 131).

Fading health among sunset migrants provokes other forms of derivative migration, such as the follow-on migration of relatives and friends as carers and the possibility of following the 'Southern European care model' of employing immigrant live-in carers from countries such as the Philippines and Ukraine (see King and Zontini 2000). Or the frail older person may choose return migration to the home country. These are obvious avenues for further research, although they are beset by ethical concerns of researching vulnerable populations. Yet another under-researched topic is the way that death and burial abroad are negotiated by older migrants and their families (Oliver 2004).

future of sunset migration

What might be the future of sunset migration? Until 2008 all forecasts pointed towards a steady (if not sharp) upward trend in international retirement migration. As retirement age nears for the baby-boomer generation – the most privileged birth cohort ever in terms of education, wealth and independence – the stage seems set for continued growth in seeking a retirement space abroad. Sriskandarajah and Drew (2006: 70) boldly estimated, based on the upward trend in pensions paid abroad, that by 2025, 1.8 million Britons or 13.2 per cent of the UK's retired population would 'spend their twilight years abroad', rising to 3.3 million by 2050. New retirement destinations might be expected to emerge. If current tourism trends are an indication, these may include Turkey, the Caribbean, the Red Sea and Thailand. New European source countries can also be envisaged to join the range of suppliers of sunset migrants. Russia looms large here, together with the other 'cold' countries of Eastern Europe such as Poland, Ukraine, and the Baltic republics.

However, the recent global financial crisis casts a new light on all of these predictions. The question now is not so much how many will retire abroad in the future; but how many will return to their home country, cash-strapped by the recession, the collapsing housing markets and the falling value of their pensions and investments.[10]

MAIN IDEAS

The effects of sunset migration are felt particularly at the local and regional levels in the host country.

Complications may arise in the domains of health and welfare rights if retirees choose to live transnationally, dividing their time between two (or possibly more) residences.

The influx of wealthy retired foreigners into prized rural regions such as Tuscany, Provence and Dordogne has bid up the prices of rural and village housing, making access for local buyers difficult.

Despite retirees' claims that they 'feel healthier' in the warmer climate, there is little solid evidence that their health is actually improved or that they live longer.

Based on the upward trend in pensions paid abroad, by 2025, 1.8 million Britons or 13.2 per cent of the UK's retired population might be expected to spend their twilight years abroad. However, changing economic conditions may affect these estimates.

Notes

1 Project entitled 'International Retirement Migration from the United Kingdom to Southern Europe' funded by the ESRC 1995-1998. Co-investigators were Tony Warnes, Allan Williams and Guy Patterson. The main output from this project was the book *Sunset Lives* (King et al. 2000).
2 It must be acknowledged that there is an element of bias in the above result, since those who were in grave difficulty, or who had returned to the UK, would not have completed the questionnaire or offered themselves for interview: an example of sampling on the dependent variable.
3 According to a television documentary 'Spain: Paradise Lost', ITV, 17 June 2009.
4 There are clear signs now that the trend towards earlier retirement has reversed in light of the fiscal crisis over pension funds; this may affect future retiree cohorts.
5 This swelling volume of research on international retirement migration owes much to two networking initiatives supported by the European Science Foundation and coordinated by Tony Warnes from 1998 to 2004. Key outputs from this ESF workshop activity were four edited collections: Friedrich et al. (2004); Warnes (2004); Rodríguez et al. (2005); and Warnes et al. (2006). Among other studies not contained in the above collections see King and Patterson (1998); King et al. (1998, 2000); Rodríguez et al. (1998); Warnes and Patterson (1998); Williams and Patterson (1998); Huber (1999, 2003); Lazaridis et al. (1999); Warnes et al. (1999); O'Reilly (2000); Breuer (2001, 2004, 2005); Casado-Díaz (2001); Friedrich and Kaiser (2002); Gustafson (2002); Oliver (2007).
6 Evidence for this comes from the perusal of estate agents' lists and websites and from the many TV programmes about searching for 'a place in the sun'. An illuminating perspective comes from the British Channel 4 weekly series 'Home and Away' where couples seeking to relocate (including many who are retired or looking to retire) are offered, for their nominated budget, a selection of properties in their favoured location in Britain (the preference of one half of the couple) or in a targeted location abroad, usually in Southern Europe (the other's choice). I have watched at least 20 of these programmes (for research purposes only, of course!), and the 'value for money' (size, location, amenities etc.) is nearly always higher in the 'away' location.
7 These figures exclude Eastern Europeans who, since the 1990s, have built up major immigrant communities in Southern European countries, arriving as labour migrants from countries such as Albania, Romania and the Ukraine. The data are from King et al. (2000: 38), quoting Eurostat 1996 data.
8 According to Rodríguez et al. (2001: 181), golf has been instrumental in encouraging retired foreigners to relocate to southern Spain and to become permanent rather than seasonal residents. Golf is not subject to the seasonal nature of mass tourist demand, and many property developers use the lure of golf courses to sell high-priced housing.
9 For a graphic illustration, see the contrasting population pyramids for Spaniards and foreigners in Mijas municipality (Costa del Sol) in Montanari and King (1994: 28).
10 Recent private survey research claims that seven out of ten British people living in mainland Europe are thinking of moving back. Reasons given are mainly financial, related to the 30 per cent fall of sterling against the euro. Foreign exchange specialists and removal firms date the beginning of the 'return boom' to early 2009 and say that it is still ongoing (Fotheringham 2010).

Recommended literature

Ackers, L. and Dwyer, P. (2002), *Senior Citizenship? Retirement, Migration and Welfare in the European Union*. Bristol: Policy Press.

Friedrich, K., Kellaher, L. and Torres, S. (eds) (2004), 'Older migrants in Europe', Special issue, *Ageing and Society* 24 (3).

Huber, A. (2003), *Sog des Südens: Altersmigration von der Schweiz am Beispiel Costa Blanca*. Zurich: Seismo.

King, R., Warnes, A.M. and Williams, A.M. (2000), *Sunset Lives: British Retirement Migration to the Mediterranean*. Oxford: Berg.

O'Reilly, K. (2000), *The British on the Costa del Sol: Transnational Identities and Local Communities*. London: Routledge.

Rodríguez, V., Casado-Díaz, M.A. and Huber, A. (eds) (2005), *La Migración de Europeos Retirados en España*. Madrid: Consejo Superior de Investigaciones Científicas, Colección Politeya 23.

Warnes, A.M., Williams, A.M., Kellaher, L. and Rodríguez, V. (eds) (2006), 'Older migrants in Europe: Experiences, exclusion and constructive accommodation', Special issue, *Journal of Ethnic and Migration Studies*, 32 (8).

References

Ackers, L. and P. Dwyer (2002), *Senior Citizenship? Retirement, Migration and Welfare in the European Union*. Bristol: Policy Press.

Benson, M. and K. O'Reilly (2009), 'Migration and the search for a better way of life: A critical exploration of lifestyle migration', *Sociological Review* 57: 608-625.

Bolzman, C., R. Fibbi, R. and M. Vial (2006), 'What to do after retirement? Elderly migrants and the question of return', *Journal of Ethnic and Migration Studies* 32: 1359-1375.

Breuer, T. (2005), 'Retirement migration or second-home tourism? German senior citizens on the Canary Islands', *Die Erde* 136: 313-333.

Breuer, T. (2004), 'Deutsche Rentnerresidenten auf den Kanarischen Inseln', *Geographische Rundschau* 55: 44-51.

Breuer, T. (2001), 'Altersruhesitze auf den Kanarischen Inseln: Das Beispiel der deutschen Rentner-Residenten', in B. Freund and H. Jahake (eds), *Der Mediterrane Raum an der Schwelle des 21 Jahrhunderts*. 9-24 Berlin: Humboldt-Universität zu Berlin, Berliner Geographische Arbeiten 91.

Carmichael, M. (1901), *In Tuscany*. London: John Murray.

Casado-Díaz, M.A. (2001), 'De turistas à residentes: La migración de retirados en España'. Alicante: Universidad de Alicante, doctoral thesis.

Casado-Díaz, M.A., C. Kaiser and A.M. Warnes (2004), 'Northern European retired residents in nine southern European areas: Characteristics, motivations and adjustment', *Ageing and Society* 24: 353-381.

Cerase, F.P. (1974), 'Expectations and reality: A study of return migration from the United States to Italy', *International Migration Review* 8: 245-262.

Fotheringham, A. (2010), 'Expats' exodus as Brits give up on *la dolce vita*', *Independent on Sunday*, 14 February: 33-34.

Friedrich, K. and C. Kaiser (2002), 'Rentnersiedlungen auf Mallorca? Möglichkeiten und Grenzen der Übertragbarkeit des nordamerikanischen Konzepts auf den Europäischen Sunbelt'. *Europa Regional* 9: 204-211.

Friedrick, K., L. Kellaher and S. Torres (eds) (2004), 'Older migrants in Europe', Special issue, *Ageing and Society* 24: 307-475.

Gustafson, P. (2002), 'Tourism and seasonal retirement migration', *Annals of Tourism Research* 29: 899-918.

Hardill, I., J. Spradbery, J. Arnold-Boakes and M.L. Marrugat (2005), 'Severe health and social care issues among British migrants who retire to Spain', *Ageing and Society* 25: 769-783.

Hoggart, K. and H. Buller (1995), 'Retired British home owners in rural France', *Ageing and Society* 15: 325-353.

Huber, A. (2003), *Sog des Südens: Altersmigration von der Schweiz am Beispiel Costa Blanca*. Zurich: Seismo.

Huber, A. (1999), *Ferne Heimat – zweites Glück? Sechs Porträts von Schweizer Rentnerinnen und Rentnern an der Costa Blanca.* Zürich: Seismo.

Karisto, A. (2005), 'Residentes finlandeses de invierno en España', in V. Rodríguez, M.A. Casado-Díaz and A. Huber (eds), *La Migración de Europeos Retirados en España*, 195-220. Madrid: Consejo Superior de Investigaciones Científicas, Colección Politeya 23.

King, R. and G. Patterson (1998), 'Diverse paths: The elderly British in Tuscany', *International Journal of Population Geography* 4: 157-182.

King, R. and F. Scarpa, F. (2001), '"Exiles in paradise": l'insediamento di pensionati britannici nella Toscana rurale', in *Studi in Onore di Guido Barbina*, 289-310. Udine: Forum.

King, R., A.M. Warnes and A.M. Williams (2000), *Sunset Lives: British Retirement Migration to the Mediterranean.* Oxford: Berg.

King, R., A.M. Warnes and A.M. Williams (1998), 'International retirement migration in Europe', *International Journal of Population Geography* 4: 91-111.

King, R. and E. Zontini (2000), 'The role of gender in the South European immigration model', *Papers: Revista de Sociología* 60: 35-52.

Lazaridis, G., J. Poyago-Theotoky and R. King (1999), 'Islands as havens for retirement migration: Finding a place in sunny Corfu', in R. King and J. Connell (eds) *Small Worlds, Global Lives: Islands and Migration.* 297-320 London: Pinter.

Litwak, E. and C.F. Longino (1987), 'Migration patterns among the elderly: A developmental perspective', *The Gerontologist* 27: 266-272.

Malcolm, E. (1996), *Elderly Return Migration from Britain to Ireland: A Preliminary Report.* Dublin: National Council for the Elderly, Report 44.

Montanari, A. and R. King (1994), 'Le migrazioni nell'Europa contemporanea', *Le Scienze: Edizione Italiana di Scientific American* 314: 18-28.

Myklebost, H. (1989), 'Migration of elderly Norwegians', *Norsk Geografisk Tidsskrift* 43: 191-213.

O'Reilly, K. (2000), *The British on the Costa del Sol: Transnational Identities and Local Communities.* London: Routledge.

Oliver, C. (2004), 'Cultural influence in migrants' negotiation of death: The case of retired migrants in Spain', *Mortality* 9: 235-254.

Oliver, C. (2007), *Retirement Migration: Paradoxes of Ageing.* London: Routledge.

Rodríguez, V. and C. Egea (2006), 'Return and the social environment of Andalusian emigrants in Europe', *Journal of Ethnic and Migration Studies* 32: 1377-1393.

Rodríguez, V., M.A. Casado-Díaz and A. Huber (eds) (2005), *La Migración de Europeos Retirados en España.* Madrid: Consejo Superior de Investigaciones Científicas, Colección Politeya 23.

Rodríguez, V., G. Fernandez-Mayorales and F. Rojo (1998), 'European retirees on the Costa del Sol: A cross-national comparison', *International Journal of Population Geography* 4: 183-200.

Rodríguez, V., P. Salvà Tomàs and A.M. Williams (2001), 'Northern Europeans and the Mediterranean: A new California or a new Florida?' in R. King, P. De Mas and J. Mansvelt Beck (eds), *Geography, Environment and Development in the Mediterranean*, 176-195. Brighton: Sussex Academic Press.

Sriskandarajah, D. and C. Drew (2006), *Brits Abroad: Mapping the Scale and Nature of British Emigration.* London: Institute for Public Policy Research.

Warnes, A.M. (2002), 'The challenge of intra-Union and in-migration to "social Europe"', *Journal of Ethnic and Migration Studies* 28: 135-152.

Warnes, A.M. (2001), 'The international dispersal of pensioners from affluent countries', *International Journal of Population Geography* 7: 373-388.

Warnes, A.M. (1996), 'Migrations among older people', *Reviews in Clinical Gerontology* 6: 101-114.

Warnes, A.M. (ed.) (2004), *Older Migrants in Europe: Essays, Projects and Sources.* Sheffield: Sheffield Institute for Studies on Ageing.

Warnes, A.M., R. King, A.M. Williams and G. Patterson (1999), 'The well-being of British expatriate retirees in southern Europe', *Ageing and Society* 19: 717-740.

Warnes, A.M. and G. Patterson (1998), 'British retirees in Malta: Components of the cross-national relationship', *International Journal of Population Geography* 4: 113-133.

Warnes, A.M., A.M. Williams, L. Kellaher and V. Rodríguez (eds) (2006), 'Older migrants in Europe: Experiences, exclusion and constructive accommodation'. Special issue, *Journal of Ethnic and Migration Studies* 32: 1257-1427.

White, P. (2006), 'Migrant populations approaching old age: Prospects in Europe', *Journal of Ethnic and Migration Studies* 32: 1283-1300.

Williams, A.M., R. King and A.M. Warnes (1997), 'A place in the sun: International retirement migration from Northern to Southern Europe', *European Urban and Regional Studies* 4: 115-134.

Williams, A.M., R. King, A.M. Warnes and G. Patterson (2000), 'Tourism and international retirement migration: New forms of an old relationship in southern Europe', *Tourism Geographies* 2: 28-49.

Williams, A.M. and G. Patterson (1998), 'An empire lost but a province gained: A cohort analysis of British international retirement migrants in the Algarve', *International Journal of Population Geography* 4: 135-155.

13 Undocumented Migration: An Explanatory Framework

Joanne van der Leun and Maria Ilies

Introduction

Irregular immigration in Europe comes in many shapes and forms. It includes, for example, an international student who did not apply for an extension of his or her residence permit, an Australian backpacker working a temporary job to earn some money before travelling on, and an Eastern European domestic servant in a neighbour's home. Irregular migrants are a mostly invisible group in our society, and it is safe to say that each European country has its share. Beyond the national implications, there is a pan-European dimension to irregular immigration due to the process of European integration, which has rendered European Union member states dependent on one another. In both national and European politics, how member states and the EU respond to this phenomenon, or better yet, how they should respond, represents one of the most contentious political debates today.

Even if irregular migrants are forced by virtue of their status to lead a 'hidden' existence, the discussions they generate rank high and take place openly in local, national and international fora. They are never far from the public eye – though they are usually cast in extremes. Irregular immigrants may be held accountable for an array of social ills, while individual cases of tragedy and lost lives provoke compassion.

migrant population

There is a growing empirical literature on irregular migrants in Europe (Alt 2003; Düvell 2006a; Van Nieuwenhuyze 2008; Van Meeteren et al. 2008; Schrover et al. 2008). Form this we learn that irregular immigrants are primarily men (though the proportion of women is increasing), between 20 and 40 years of age, and they migrate from relatively poor areas to more affluent regions. They are prepared to do jobs that natives shun, often under poor conditions, for wages that are usually lower than those acceptable to legal residents. Contrary to conventional views, most irregular immigrants do not enter the country of destination by crossing a border undocumented. More often, they enter with legal permission (a visa) and overstay, or otherwise violate the terms of their admission. Though all European countries face irregular migration, the 'contexts of reception' (Portes and Rumbaut 1990) and opportunity structures differ highly across time and space.

variables

Four major factors explain contemporary irregular migration flows to Europe (see also Fasani 2008: 15-16):

- *Globalisation of communication means and transport routes.* Countries that were once remote are gradually becoming part of a global market and infrastructure. The wealth gap between developed and developing countries acts as a 'push' factor for those living in the latter, with information as the link connecting them. This brings societies closer. Those living in the developing world know where they could be better off. For the southern EU member states, geographical proximity to unstable, lesser developed areas (e.g. former Yugoslavia and North-West Africa) makes these countries especially susceptible to border flows of undocumented migrants.
- *The underground economy.* All European countries have bottlenecks in the supply of skilled and unskilled labour. Demand is thus generated for workers who are willing to accept uncertain conditions and, usually, a fraction of the official minimum salary, without the social and welfare protections enjoyed by legal residents.
- *Restrictive migration and asylum policy.* There are few possibilities for legal access to Europe, especially for economic migrants. Restrictive policies towards immigration may be a large part of the reason why irregular populations exist (Düvell 2009).
- *Welfare state regimes.* Particularly in Italy, Spain, Portugal and Greece, welfare state regimes rely on informal foreign workers to provide care services (e.g. for the elderly or children). These affordable domestic workers compensate for services that would otherwise be provided by the state (which is the case in Scandinavian countries).

This chapter draws upon the fast-growing literature on irregular immigration. Its aim is to provide readers with the necessary tools to understand the elusive concept of irregular immigration. The following issues are touched upon: the construction of irregular immigration and paths into irregularity, the regulation of irregular immigrants throughout Europe, estimations of immigrant stocks and flows, integration modes for irregular migrants and theoretical frameworks.

The construction of irregular migration: Paths into irregularity

The term 'irregular immigration' is modern, as are national laws on entry, exit and residence. Yet restrictions on movement are not; before strong nation states, cities used to decide who were the wanted and the unwanted. These decisions were often related to issues such as employment, poverty and public disorder (Lucassen 1996; Schrover et al. 2008).

right to free movement

In Europe today, the right to free movement and residence is one of the most visible rights conferred upon EU citizens (European Commission 2008a). European citizens enjoy the right to move across the Union to pursue opportunities such as work, relationships and education. It might be argued that this is only natural, as people have been moving from one place to another for various reasons since the dawn of mankind. Citizens of the Union and their families can move and reside freely within the territory of the member states because this right is enshrined within the body of EU law; however, third-country nationals without proper documentation have no legal standing in the community and therefore cannot claim such rights. The construction of irregularity is directly related to state control and state sovereignty (Abraham and Van Schendel 2005; Schrover et al. 2008: 2), yet what states consider as legitimate or legal might not fully coincide with what individuals consider as such (Abraham and Van Schendel 2005). Transnational movements of people are irregular because they defy norms and formal authority, while in the participants' view they can be acceptable, even licit.

Thus, the irregularity of residence comes into effect when a person interacts with the authorities of the host state, which categorises him or her as sojourning 'irregularly' (Guild 2004: 16). From the perspective of the state, people categorised as irregular are 'offenders of immigration laws' and do not have the right to reside in the host state's territory (Kostakopoulou 2004: 42). Irregularity (much like citizenship) is a political identity, a juridical status that entails a social relation to the state (De Genova 2002: 422; see also Engbersen 2001). This means that a distinction between the study of 'undocumented people' and that of 'irregularity' and 'deportability' is required (ibid.). The term deportability has been coined by the sociologist De Genova (2002) and refers to the way that irregularity is lived, namely in permanent fear of the possibility of being removed from the space of the nation-state; and this renders irregular migrants vulnerable. It should be noted that it is not deportation *per se*, but the possibility that this may occur, 'that has rendered the undocumented (labour) a distinctly disposable commodity'. The essential differentiation between the undocumented immigrants and legal residents is the former's fundamentally different position within national legal systems; they always face the risk of expulsion and temporary imprisonment (van der Leun and Kloosterman 2006: 60).

pathways into irregularity

The pathways into irregularity can be summed up according to the following (see also Vogel and Jandl 2008: 9-10):

- *Geographic flows* consist of movements of persons over a border in breach of immigration law. These are illegal movements over a green or blue border, when the traveller crosses such a border by avoiding controls (sometimes with the help of human smugglers) or by using false documents or false identities. Within the Schengen area of the EU there are no border inspections between the member states; therefore an illegal border crossing takes place when performed without the required travel documents.
- *Status flows* include flows into irregular residence from a legal status. Persons can enter into a country legally with a temporary visa and overstay the allowed period of residence. Asylum applicants who do not leave after their application is rejected and who have exhausted the appeal procedures also add to the pool of irregular residents of a country. Immigrants can repeatedly switch between a regular and an irregular residence status if, for instance, changes in the immigration laws of a country create new legal statuses or rescind previously established ones.
- *Demographic flows* concern births into irregularity. A baby is without status in a country when born to a mother without status. In general, European countries do not grant citizenship to newborns based on the sole fact that these births occurred on national soil. Citizenship is thus transmitted through an ancestor being a national of that particular state. This is a *jus sanguinis* policy, and is in contrast to the *jus soli* principle in citizenship law, which allows persons born in the territory to immediately obtain nationality. The latter is the case in the US, where all babies born in the territory are recognised as US citizens.[1]

irregular labour migration

These irregular migrant inflows accumulate and contribute to the stock of irregular migrants in a given country. In addition to entry and residence, work is another source of migrant illegality, and employment is the backbone of many of the theories of irregular immigration (van der Leun 2003: 35). Irregular labour migration dominates most discourses on irregular immigration throughout Europe and in many cases it overlaps with other forms of migration (i.e. asylum seeking and family reunification and formation). Irregular employment exists not just because poor and desperate people wish to improve their living conditions; businesses need cheap labour input while private homeowners welcome the domestic workers that they might otherwise not be able to afford. The most important asset of undocumented migrants – perhaps even the only one – is their cheap, exploitable labour (Calavita 2005: 15). In general, when thinking of 'irregular migrants', the first and the simplest explanation that comes to mind is of people leaving their countries of origin with the intention to work irregularly in the destination country. De Genova (2002: 422) says that 'undocumented migrations are, indeed, pre-eminently labour migrations'. Furthermore, 'undocumented migrants would be inconceivable if not for the value they produce through the diverse services they supply to citizens' (ibid.). Because irregular migrants have almost no other long-term survival strategy than irregular employment, their role in Europe's informal sectors has been thoroughly assessed by scholars and policy-makers. For instance, estimates place the average of undeclared work at between 11 per cent and 16 per cent of the EU's GDP, with Bulgaria, Greece, Hungary and Slovenia registering the highest rates, at 25 per cent to 40 per cent of GDP (EIRO 2005). It is a well-documented fact that irregular migrants sustain certain economic sectors in various member states. In Italy, for instance, undocumented workers are a substantial labour source for the industrial sector, while in the Netherlands, irregular labour is what makes horticulture a competitive sector (van der Leun and Kloosterman 2006: 59). Estimates show that one-third of the motorways of France were built by irregular workers and approximately one-third of all automobile production in France has been done by irregular workers (Bade 2003: 22).

defining irregular migration

Defining irregular migration is subject to ambiguity and relativity. Would-be irregular immigrants employ an array of side doors and back doors to reach their destination. This leads to an interconnection of the legal and irregular entry modes and flows of people. There are economic migrants who are asylum claimants (mostly in Northern Europe where immigrants are trying to squeeze in through channels created for genuine refugees); asylum seekers who take up irregular employment; economic migrants who use family reunification and formation as an entry option; and genuine refugees who resort to human smugglers and are deemed irregular economic migrants by the host authorities. There is no such thing as a separate, undocumented flow of trans-border movers. However, we can clearly state that irregular immigration is theoretically unwanted by the destination and transit societies – no government would publicly state whether irregular migrants might be somehow economically beneficial, or that they should be granted a set of rights. Thus, even if, 'most irregular immigration is, from the economic point of view, simply a labour migration not approved by the government' (House of Lords 2002), at least certain types of irregular labour are in many cases silently accepted.

no common EU definition

The concept of irregular immigration is even more difficult to grasp because immigration laws do not directly define who is an irregular immigrant; there is no common definition accepted at the EU level. The concept is implicit, rather than explicitly coined by legislators (Guild 2004: 4, 15). For instance, the 2000 Dutch Aliens Act lists twelve cases that fall under the *rechtmatig verblijf* (legitimate residence) category. This means that the rest of the foreigners present on Dutch soil are implicitly irregular residents (Pluymen 2008). There are also different kinds of grey areas and shadowy forms of existence that lie somewhere between legality and irregularity (Groenendijk 2004: 18). This is the case, for instance, with the German *Duldung* (literally 'toleration'), which grants temporary suspension of a deportation order, yet it is not a residence permit (Bade 2003: 21). The status of those possessing a *Duldung* is somewhere between legal and irregular, which could lead to *de facto* uncertain permanent stays (ibid.). Thus, due to complex national legislation, irregular immigration cases range from a relatively simple situation to more sophisticated ones, where the legal-irregular dichotomy is not the most suitable one to describe often complex cases (Düvell 2006b).

A certain linearity is assumed when referring to migrants: the legal becomes irregular, and vice versa. In fact, irregularity is not a 'static' condition. An irregular migrant can move in and out of irregularity over time and space. Certain conditions might not be met over time, and what is legal in one country may be irregular in another. For instance, if an irregular migrant is legalised by the host society, he or she becomes a legal resident. If, however, this newly regularised migrant moves to another EU country to work, he or she falls into irregularity. If the condition upon which an amnesty was offered expires (such as a labour contract), he or she may become irregular yet again. Also, if involved in serious criminal activities or if considered a threat to public order, legal immigrants can lose their residence permit and thus become irregular residents. Irregular migration is thus an analytical immigration category, strongly linked to immigration and citizenship policies.

The regulation of undocumented immigration in Europe

regulating irregular immigration

The regulation of irregular immigration is not a policy domain per se but rather an endeavour to control unauthorised migration in areas such as asylum, trafficking, smuggling, security and family reunification and formation. This is why regulating irregular immigration is a multi-level effort, with measures being taken in the sending, transit and receiving countries and into an array of settings: border-crossing, transport (for instance, carrier sanctions), welfare policies, employment, labour markets, security, external relations and humanitarian and development aid. Moreover, the regulation of the undocumented foreigners takes place both preventively through policies and laws aimed at deterring irregular migration flows from entering a member state, and after the fact, through discouragement policies aimed at irregular residents.

There are essentially three choices that national governments have when dealing with the presence of irregular migrant stocks: unwanted migrants can be expelled, regularised, or the authorities can ignore their presence and accept the status quo. To what extent these policies succeed at curbing and controlling the entry and settlement of irregular migrants, is debatable. Cornelius et al. (1994) say that there is a gap between the goals of national immigration policies and the actual result of the policies in this area. Despite significant increases in the restrictiveness of immigration policies thorough operational means such as increased border controls, and also the tailoring of immigration and asylum policies, governments have not been able to effectively regulate immigration flows and to control the settlement and employment of undocumented migrants.

four levels

The regulation of undocumented immigration in Europe takes place at four levels: the local, regional, national and supranational (European). Cornelius et al. (2004: 15) argue that there is a conversion at the national level, namely a growing similarity among regional countries in terms of the policy instruments they choose to control immigration, in particular the undocumented kind. Moreover, the inability of states to manage immigration unilaterally and effectively has led to an increasing number of multilateral efforts to restrict the movement of persons across national borders, particularly asylum-seekers and irregular migrants. The EU has gained expanding competences in the policy areas of immigration, asylum and border security, as part of an accelerating trend towards the communitarisation of immigration policies. The EU Immigration Pact, which was agreed upon by the member states in the second half of 2008, is regarded as a roadmap for future European immigration policies. In particular, it aims at ending the practice of mass amnesties for irregular immigrants in the EU. General regularisation programmes,[2] as were offered in the past principally by Spain, Italy and Belgium, are viewed as a *pull factor* for fresh migration flows. The Immigration Pact also aims at joint action to strengthen the EU's external borders, as well as to facilitate cooperation with the sending countries. The return policy on irregular aliens from the territory of a state is also a critical element of European immigration policies, as it is regarded as the cornerstone of any successful strategy to prevent or deter irregular migrants from taking up residence in the member states (IOM 2004).

national prerogative

However, even as there is an increased supranationalisation of immigration policies, national governments are reluctant to delegate policy-making authority to the EU in this sensitive area of public policy. Because irregular immigrants are regarded as undermining national sovereignty, the great majority of decision-making in this area remains a national prerogative.

Figure 13.1 summarises the paths in and out of irregularity.

Figure 13.1 *Paths in and out of irregularity*

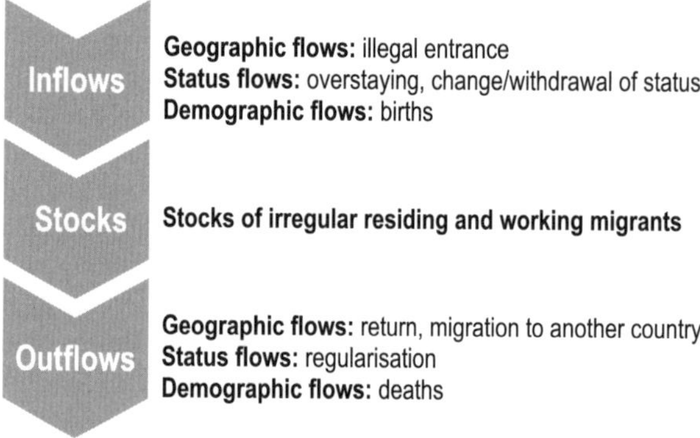

Source: Adapted from Vogel and Jandl (2008: 11)

The size and estimation of irregular populations in Europe

fast growing form of migration

Over ten years ago, the United Nations Commission on Population and Development (1997) described irregular migration as 'one of the fastest growing forms of migration in the world today'. The European Commission says that given differences in demographic developments, living conditions and political stability in Europe – compared to a number of other regions of the world – the current pressure of irregular immigration at the external borders of the EU is likely to continue in the future.[3] Given the extent and ramifications of irregular migrations, quantitative data regarding the stocks and flows of irregular migrants is an important tool for the regulation and management of this phenomenon. However, irregular immigration is a non-registered phenomenon, thus any attempt to quantify it has to employ methods that rely heavily on assumptions, making use of often unreliable and indirect data. Sometimes estimations also serve political purposes, in which case they are purposely tailored to fit certain policy guidelines.

number of irregular migrants

Estimates on the number of irregular migrants refer to either irregular migrant stocks or flows (Jandl 2008). The only explicitly used methodology for estimating border flows of irregular migrants to

Europe is the extrapolation of border apprehensions with a simple multiplier (ibid.). This is a rather simple methodology, based on a commonly assumed ratio of 1:2, namely that for each apprehended irregular migrant, there are two irregular entries. However, there are several problems associated with this method (see also Jandl 2004 and 2008). First, there is the availability and quality of border-apprehension data. This information is generally kept secret by national border enforcement authorities, so estimations in this regard are based on information obtained through informal channels. Second, there is the problem of using the right multiplier. The multiplier that is used needs to be adjusted to the fact that migrant populations are unstable, with peaks during periods of seasonal work availability or during periods of humanitarian crisis (for instance, the high flow of Iraqis due to the ongoing Iraqi war). Also, sophisticated technology and more border enforcement increase the apprehension capacities of border authorities over time. There is also the matter of who exactly to count. Highly mobile populations might move in and out of a country as part of a circular migration process, while border apprehension cases refer to cases, not individuals, so there is the risk that an individual might be counted several times. In sum, although the estimation of irregular migrant flows presents downsides, there are no viable alternatives that can be applied to the European context.

net of cumulative flows

The net of cumulative irregular flows (the difference between immigration and emigration) and visa overstayers determines the size of the irregular migrant stock. Data from regularisation programmes are regarded as a feasible indicator for the extent of the phenomenon for countries that have undertaken such programmes regularly (notably Southern Europe). However, as not all irregular migrants meet the regularisation criteria, such data is a minimum threshold that needs to be amended upwards. For instance, the 2002 regularisation programme in Italy legalised 702,156 foreigners (Fasani 2008), while 2006 estimations placed the number of irregular migrants at 650,000. Not all irregular residents present in Italy at the time applied for legalisation in 2002, and a number of those legalised later lost this status.

capture-recapture method

In the Netherlands, Van der Leun et al. (1998), by analysing apprehension data from the police and with the help of the 'capture-recapture method',[4] estimated the proportion of irregular residents out of the total number of legal immigrants in the four most populous cities of the Netherlands (Amsterdam, Rotterdam, The Hague and Utrecht). This resulted in a total of 7.3 per cent of 545,152 legally residing migrants, which represents a minimum of 40,047 irregular immigrants. Using the same capture-recapture method, Cruyff and van der Heijden (2004) estimated that between 1997 and 2003, between

125,000 and 230,000 irregular foreigners had been residing annually in the Netherlands. Assuming that the truth is somewhere in between, 150,000 is an acceptable 'guesstimation'. The capture-recapture method also has its shortcomings. Though the following three assumptions do not represent the actual situation of irregulars, they are assumptions upon which this estimation method builds in order to generate data regarding illegal residence:

1. The irregular population is *homogeneous*.
2. The observations of the population are *time-independent*, namely that the possibility of getting caught is constant in time.
3. The population is closed in the sense that new entries and exits are not accounted for.

However, irregular residents do not automatically fulfil these conditions. Because of this, the researchers adjust the outline form for continuous registrations, which results in population deviations.

highly subjective surveys

Surveys that focus directly on the clandestine population and assume to identify people in an irregular situation are also highly subjective (Tapinos 1999). For instance, through the so-called 'Delphi' method, a group of immigration experts (e.g. government officials, members of the civil society, employers) are questioned on the presumed size of the irregular population within a country. Their answers are then compared with those of another expert group and the numbers are adjusted accordingly. The final result, a range of estimates (with a minimum and a maximum value), is thus based on the consensus reached among the interviewees. Although useful in generating some ideas about the size of the irregular resident population, the answers of these 'experts' may be biased or one-sided. Piguet and Losa (2002) implemented this method in a Swiss study. They approached 5,500 employers (the response rate was 15 per cent, and approximately 800 co-operated), asking them to estimate the percentage of irregular workers in their particular business domains. Based on the answers, the authors were able to evaluate the number of irregular foreign workers in Switzerland. However, depending on whether they considered the median value or the mean value, their estimates ranged between 70,000 and 180,000 irregularly employed residents. In addition, the high non-response rate suggests a highly selective sample of employers.

information scarce

Both administrative data-recording and estimation methods differ among European countries. Thus, in addition to the fact that information regarding the scale of irregular migrations is scarce, there is little room for cross-country comparisons. This hinders both the development of coherent national immigration policies, as well as the establishment of a common approach to irregular immigration at the European level. Moreover, the least is known about irregular immigrants who leave European countries to return to their homelands. It is often assumed by public authorities that the aim of irregulars is to settle permanently in the host society. Fieldwork shows much more variety. Research conducted among Turkish irregular migrants in the Netherlands shows that many of them decided to go back after a certain time, and others migrated further (Staring 2001). Another Dutch study found that only 19 per cent of rejected asylum seekers (who lost their residence rights) were still in the country ten years later (De Boom et al. 2008: 19). The mobility of irregular immigrants often seems to be underestimated.

A recent attempt to quantify the size of the irregular populations in the EU produced a dynamic aggregate-country estimate of irregular foreign residents in the EU 25 countries in 2005.[5] According to this estimate, there were 2.8 to 6 million irregular residents in the EU at that time. This includes foreign nationals without any valid residence permit as well as working tourists, but it excludes asylum seekers and officially tolerated persons. Table 13.1 presents estimates of irregular migrant numbers (minimums and maximums and the proportion of each in the population) in selected EU member states.

Table 13.1 *Stock estimation of irregular foreign residents in selected EU countries*

Country	*Year*	*Population*	*Estimates of Irregular Foreign Residents*		
			Min.	*Central*	*Max.*
Italy	2007	59,131,287	-	349,000 (0.6%)	-
Spain	2007	44,474,631	280,000 (0.6%)	-	376,000 (0.8%)
Greece	2007	11,171,740	172,000 (1.5%)	-	209,000 (1.9%)
Hungary	2007	10,066,158	30,000 (0.3%)	-	50,000 (0.5%)
Slovakia	2007	5,393,637	15,000 (0.3%)	-	20,000 (0.4%)

Source: CLANDESTINO Undocumented Migration. Data and Trends Across Europe, www.irregular-migration.hwwi.net/Home.2560.0.html

The integration of irregular migrants in European societies

integration

The integration of irregular immigrants appears as a contradiction in terms; preventing the integration of irregular migrants is one of the main objectives of internal migration control (Van der Leun 2003). Yet, it is obvious that when irregular immigrants reside in a territory for an extended period of time, they develop ties to their new environment and incorporate into the host society (Chavez 1994). Jacobson (1996) speaks of quasi-legal ties because these develop in spite of the existence of policies and regulations. In this respect, we can make a distinction between European countries with traditionally weak internal immigration controls, such as Italy, Spain and the UK, and those with dense controls, such as Germany, Sweden and the Netherlands (Düvell 2006a: 179). The devolution of mandates to local governmental actors involved with monitoring immigrants is a strategy employed when nations want to impose stringent migration controls (Guiraudon and Lahav 2000: 182). For example, a disposition of the law of 30 December 1993 in France allows mayors to suspend a marriage procedure between a national and a foreigner, and to ask for an inquiry into the status of the latter (ibid.). In the Netherlands, the 'Linking Act', which came into force in July 1998, aims to partly shift the responsibilities towards internal mechanisms of migration control (Pluymen 2004: 75; van der Leun 2007: 403). The Linking Act makes the entitlement and access of immigrants to secondary or higher education, housing, rent subsidy, facilities for handicapped persons, health care and all social security benefits dependent on their legal residence (Pluymen 2004: 76). Thus, the control and enforcement of immigration policies is delegated to public-services providers such as health institutions, schools and housing corporations. The increased fine-tuning of immigration control in the implementation of this law is dependent precisely on the availability of information regarding the irregular status of the immigrant.

fight against illegal immigration undermined

Empirical studies in various countries (in Belgium by van Meeteren et al. 2008 and in the Netherlands as seen below) demonstrate how the fight against irregular immigration pursued by governments is often undermined by an array of actors, both governmental (e.g. social workers, teachers) and nongovernmental (e.g. members of civil society, families and friends of the irregular migrants). These agencies and individuals help immigrants integrate into the host society by providing them with information and various commodities and services, as well as with jobs (Mahler 1995, Staring 2001, Jordan and Düvell 2002). For instance, in The Hague, there are more than 40 private and semipublic organisations that provide assistance to irregular immigrants (Engbersen et al. 2006), some of which are financed by the municipality (Rusinovic et al. 2002). Irregular Turkish immigrants in The Hague live in the areas inhabited by regular Turkish immigrants – meaning that the former group follows the traces of the latter for incorporation into the society (Engbersen et al. 2006). We can thus speak of more or less informal mechanisms, or as Mahler (1995) calls them, 'parallel institutions' that account for the integration of those who reside without the appropriate documents on national territories. These irregular migrant agencies fill the gap in need that has been created by an irregular status. In countries with strong internal immigration and welfare controls, such agencies are essential means of entry and incorporation into the host society (Düvell 2006a: 182).

As European societies create laws that determine the conditions for irregularity, migrants develop their own subsistence strategies to assimilate into the host society (Erdemir and Vasta 2007). Immigrant networks and communities (the so-called 'ethnic enclaves' in global cities) have the functional role of mediating between the irregular migrant and the broader social context (ibid.). More importantly, these communities act as a bulwark against state control (Vuddamalay 2007). Because of the high level of trust generated, irregular migrants are strongly dependent on these networks, particularly for finding a job within the migrant community. This dependency, however, is double-edged, as it goes hand in hand with 'exploitative forms of solidarity' such as long working hours and no time off from work (Erdemir and Vasta 2007). In sum, although speaking of irregular migrant incorporation into the host society seems a contradiction, relying on communities and on informal channels has made at least some form of integration possible.

subsistence strategies

Theoretical approaches to irregular migration

One of the obstacles to understanding irregular migration is that we do not have one, coherent, universally accepted theory of international migration (Massey et al. 1993: 432; Bretell and Hollifield 2000). Rather, we have a diversity of theoretical frameworks that explain why people decide to move across borders. Even if these theories represent different means to the same end, they provide different bases and approaches for social scientists to understand irregular immigration, and they focus on different levels of explanation.

Neoclassical economics[6] provides the oldest and most popular approach to why people choose to migrate. According to the macro theory in neoclassical economics, international migration is the outcome of wage differences in the country of origin and in the country of settlement. Thus labour markets are the main mechanisms that induce international flows of people. The micro theory in neoclassical economics assumes that individuals decide to migrate based on a cost-benefit calculation. The expected net return fuels international movements. These two theories assume that there is heterogeneity of immigrants along skill lines, and thus the flow of labour (workers) is to be kept separate from that of human capital (skilled and highly skilled workers). As irregular migrants are primarily regarded as workers, we may conclude that the neoclassical economics theory is a feasible explanation for the international flow of irregular immigrants.

why people migrate

A challenge to the neoclassical theory is posed by the *new economics of migration,* which assumes that migration decisions are not made by

new economics of migration

individual actors, but rather by larger units of decision-making – such as family and households. In this case, people act in concert not just to maximise the income of the household, but also to lessen the risks associated with market failures in the countries of origin, through remittances – payments to the household in the country of origin. Some researchers, on the other hand, challenge the role of the family as the main emigration decision-making factor, as well as the rationality of those who migrate, as are assumed by this theory. Ahmad (2008), for instance, explores the 'importance of selfhood' and the 'search for adventure' as propellers that determine young Pakistanis to resort to irregular means of emigration to Europe (in this case human smuggling). Heering et al. (2004) (see also Black et al. 2006), discuss the 'culture of migration' in some countries, in which migrating abroad becomes the default option and those who stay are seen as losers.

However, as we have already mentioned, immigration in general – but irregular immigration in particular – can be a costly affair. Vast empirical research shows that the household and the family of a potential irregular migrant often pool their resources to come up with the necessary sum of money to secure the arrival of the emigrant in the destination country. This involves paying various smugglers for passage, the acquisition of forged travel documents and expensive long-distance air flights. Thus, as far as irregular immigration is concerned, the household's decision to 'invest' in the immigration of one or more of its members is seen against the backdrop of the expected returns – remittances that are expected to benefit the whole family, which is a cost-benefit analysis involving more actors.

dual labour market theory

As opposed to the above-mentioned theories that focus on the 'push' factors in sending countries, the *dual labour market theory* or segmented labour market theory developed in the 1970s assumes that immigration is caused by pull factors in the receiving societies. Bifurcated labour markets in capital-intensive primary sectors and labour-intensive secondary sectors create a segmented labour market structure, which distinguishes among workers (Piore 1979). In many respects, this still holds true. The need for highly-skilled labour also creates the need for a labour force in sectors that sustain the service economy; high-skilled jobs create low-skilled ones such as cleaning, catering, transport, leisure, construction and agriculture (Sassen 1999). The native population has little incentive to accept low-paid jobs, which are unstable, dangerous and with few perspectives of hierarchical mobility, so employers turn to irregular low-skilled immigrants to satisfy these needs (Baganha et al. 2006: 25). However, sociologists argue that due to the structure of the world market, migration is a natural, non-rational outgrowth. The penetration of capitalist economic relations into *peripheral*[7] (former colonial), non-capitalist societies creates the dislocation of populations, so people are inevitably prone to migrate (Massey et al. 1993: 444-445). This is the so-called *world systems theory,* which regards international migration as a natural consequence of capitalist market formation in the developing world. The movements of people from these regions follow the opposite direction of the expansion of the global market, namely towards the core countries. This means that labour recruitment becomes less important over time (Massey 2003). This is the case because the processes of economic globalisation also create links of transportation, communication and information that facilitate the formation of irregular migration flows of people from the developing to the developed countries, where their services and labour are required.

If the immigration process may begin for a multitude of reasons, the determinants of its perpetuation differ across time and space. The *network theory* emphasises how networks are a determinant of international movements as they disseminate information about labour opportunities, reduce costs of movement and increase expected profits for migrants. In the case of irregular flows of people, immigration networks become even more relevant, as these fill the gap created by the irregular status.

institutional theory

Beyond the importance of networks, the *institutional theory* more thoroughly explains the creation of a black market niche for irregular migration. Because there is a numerical imbalance between those who seek to enter developed countries and the legal entry channels created by the receiving societies, private entities offer a variety of alternative services to would-be irregular migrants, such as border smuggling, counterfeit visas, identity and travel documents, black market labour contracts and so on. The sociologist Light (2006) argues that at a certain point in time, irregular immigration may become supply- rather than demand-driven. Both networks and institutions lead eventually to the emergence of a self-determined mechanism of *cumulative causation* of migration (Massey 1990). The mechanism underlying this is the accumulation of social capital, by which members of a community gain migration-related knowledge and resources, which acts as feedback, making additional migration possible (Fussell and Massey 2004). These migration-perpetuation theories show that over time, the international flows of people acquire a certain degree of stability and structure, permitting the identification of *international migration systems*. This cumulative and self-sustaining nature of migration flows means that they cannot be curtailed easily by legislative measures (Portes and Rumbaut 1990).

how governments should respond

If researchers investigate why people migrate illegally, the question that arises is how governments should respond to the presence of those who reside without permission in their territories and whether they, too, are entitled to a set of rights. The debates in this respect are polarised. One extreme is made up of those who believe that states are entitled to decide which foreigners are entitled to reside within their borders; irregular migrants have no standing in the community and thus have no legal basis for claims (Carens 2008). At the other extreme, those who argue that *no man can ever be illegal* frame the debate in terms of the exploitation and vulnerability of irregular migrants, which constitutes a moral basis for the extension of such rights. There are a few studies that focus on the rights of irregular migrants under human rights laws; see, for instance, the book edited by Bogusz et al. (2004). Sociological and policy studies based on empirical evidence such as Jordan and Düvell (2002) and Van der Leun (2003) critically analyse the vulnerable position of irregular migrants and their exclusion from the host community. Carens (2008) makes a moral and philosophical inquiry into what legal rights should be given to those who reside and work in a democratic state without the legal authorisation of that particular state, given the background assumption that the state is morally entitled to exclude such migrants. He argues that basic human rights, such as the security of one's property, the right to a fair trial, emergency health care, work-related earnings and free education for migrant children ought to be conferred to people simply by virtue of their presence within a certain jurisdiction. Moreover, states should build a 'firewall' between immigration law enforcement and the protection of basic human rights, so that irregular immigrants can pursue their basic human rights without exposing themselves to apprehension and deportation (Carens 2008: 167).

Conclusion

sensitive issue

Immigration in general and irregular immigration in particular is a sensitive issue in European societies and politics. This is somewhat understandable. Unlike the 'settler societies', such as the United States, Australia, Canada, the EU member states do not regard themselves as societies of immigration. Today, we speak of immigration in terms of 'post-Second World War migration flows' to the so-called 'old' immigrant-receiving states (such as the Netherlands, France and the UK). While the settler societies offered permanent or long-term residence permits, European countries have chosen to offer more temporary residence and labour permits. Legal migration routes for economic migrants are scarce. But irregular immigration persists in Europe, despite – or perhaps because of – the restrictive character of national policies on legal immigration throughout the European Union. Among others, this reflects the existing economic need for this particular kind of trans-border mover. Contemporary debate around irregular immigration is similarly polarised. Those who call for more restrictions and controls, such as national governments, are positioned against those who advocate admission for workers to meet the economic need.

costs and benefits

To fully assess the influences and consequences of undocumented immigration on European societies, one needs to look at both the winners and the losers of this process, and at both its costs and benefits (Freeman 2000: 2). The costs of irregular immigration for a host society are generated by the fact that irregular migrants make use of public goods without paying into the welfare system (through taxes). Irregular migrants compete with legal migrants and with natives for unskilled jobs and cheap housing. Because they usually work for less money and for longer hours, they reduce the opportunity for those residing legally to find certain types of jobs. Irregular migrants have also been argued to raise levels of criminality within the host society. If they are out of work, they are more likely to commit 'subsistence' crimes, as they have no other way to provide for themselves. On a philosophical level, the presence of irregular migrants represents a challenge to the legitimacy of governments to enforce laws. Yet, one could also view irregular migration as a response to costly market regulations and the lack of availability of local labour for certain types of jobs (usually dangerous, dirty and demeaning work that natives shy away from). It seems logical that in order to have a *supply* of irregular workers, there also has to be a *demand* for such workers. Economists argue that the economically optimal level of irregular immigration for a state is greater than zero (Boswell and Straubhaar 2003: 1). Beyond a certain level, the costs of control to avoid irregular immigration are greater than the damage caused by the irregular migrants. Therefore, it is less expensive for a society to accept some irregular migrants in order to save on the costs of border and immigration control.

unequal benefits

Governments, institutions, civil society and the general public assess the costs and benefits of irregular immigration in different ways. These benefits are not distributed equally within a society. Immigration politics and policies are therefore always the result of bargaining about how many we should let in and how deep the controls and punishments should go. Those who stand to gain from irregular immigration are skilled workers and capital owners; conversely, the losers are native unskilled workers and legal labour migrants. In the great majority of cases, the debate surrounding irregular immigration is about how it affects host societies, and not about the vulnerability and the precarious state of those who live their lives without the appropriate documents.

MAIN IDEAS

The 'settler societies' offered permanent or long-term residence permits, but European countries have chosen to offer more temporary residence and labour permits.

Legal migration routes for economic migrants are scarce.

Irregular immigration generates costs in a host society because some irregular migrants make use of public goods without paying into the welfare system.

Irregular migration could be viewed as a response to costly market regulations and the lack of local labour for certain types of jobs.

It is less expensive for a society to accept some irregular migrants than to erect and maintain elaborate border and immigration control systems.

Notes

1 Some EU member states, such as Germany and Portugal, apply variations of the *jus soli* principle in the case of long-term legal residents.
2 Regularisations or legalisations are general amnesty periods during which irregular migrants are given legal status by the authorities of the country in which they are residing.
3 Communication from the Commission to the Council and the European Parliament Examining the creation of a European Border Surveillance System (EUROSUR), EC (2008b).
4 This method can be exemplified by counting the fish in a pond. We catch 1,000 fish, mark them and set them free. Then we catch another 1,000 fish and examine them; if 100 of them are marked (10 per cent), this means that 10 per cent corresponds to 1,000, so presumably there are 10,000 fish in the pond (Jandl 2004: 5).
5 CLANDESTINO Undocumented Migration. Data and Trends Across Europe, available at http://www.irregular-migration.hwwi.net/Home.2560.0.html.
6 Unless otherwise mentioned, the migration theories have been developed based upon Massey et al. (1993).
7 As opposed to powerful, developed nations, which are known as 'core' countries.

References

Abraham, I. and W. van Schendel (2005), 'Introduction: The making of illicitness', in: W. Van Schendel and I. Abraham (eds), *Illicit Flows and Criminal Things: States, Borders and the Other Side of Globalization*, 1-37. Bloomington: Indiana University Press.

Ahmad, A.-N. (2008), 'The romantic appeal of illegal migration: Gender, masculinity and human smuggling from Pakistan', in: M. Schrover, J. Van der Leun, L. Lucassen L. and C. Quispel (eds), *Illegal Migration and Gender in a Global and Historical Perspective*, 127-150. IMISCOE Research. Amsterdam: Amsterdam University Press.

Alt, J. (2003), *Leben in der Schattenwelt: Problemkomplex 'Illegale' Migration*. Karlsruhe: Von Loeper Literaturverlag.

Bade, J.-K. (2003), *Legal and Illegal Immigration into Europe: Experiences and Challenges*. Ortelius Lecture. Wassenaar: Netherlands Institute for Advanced Study in the Humanities and Social Sciences.

Baganha, M., J. Doomernik, H., Fassmann, S. Gsir, M. Hofman, M. Jandl, A. Kraler, M. Neske and U. Reeger (2006), 'International migration and its regulation' in: R. Penninx, M. Berger and K. Kraal (eds), *The Dynamics of International Migration and Settlement in Europe*, 19-40. Amsterdam: Amsterdam University Press.

Black, R., X. Biao, M. Collyer, G. Engbersen, L. Heering and E. Markova (2006), 'Migration and development: Causes and consequences', in: R. Penninx, M. Berger and K. Kraal (eds), *The Dynamics of International Migration and Settlement in Europe*, 41-63. Amsterdam: Amsterdam University Press.

Bogusz, B., R. Cholewinski, A. Cygan and E. Szyszczak (eds) (2004), *Irregular Migration and Human Rights: Theoretical, European and International Perspectives*. Leiden: Martinus Nijhoff Publishers.

Boswell, C. and T. Straubhaar (2003), 'The Back Door: Temporary Migration and Illegal Employment of Workers'. www.ilo.org/public/english/bureau/inst/ download/boswell.pdf.

Bretell, C. and J. Hollifield (2000), *Migration Theory: Talking Across Disciplines*. New York/London Routledge.

Calavita, K. (2005), *Immigrants at the Margins: Law, Race and Exclusion in Southern Europe*. Cambridge: Cambridge University Press.

Carens, J.-H. (2008), 'The rights of irregular migrants', *Ethics and International Affairs* 22 (2): 163-186.

Chavez, L. (1994), 'The power of imagined community: The settlement of undocumented Mexicans and Central Americans in the United States', *American Anthropologist* 96 (1): 52-73.

CLANDESTINO (nd), *Undocumented Migration. Data and Trends Across Europe*. www.irregular-migration.hwwi.net/Home.2560.0.html.

Cornelius, W., P. Martin and J. Hollifield (eds) (1994), *Controlling Immigration: A Global Perspective*. Stanford: Stanford University Press.

Cornelius, W., T. Tsuda, P. Martin and J. Hollifield (eds) (2004), *Controlling Immigration: A Global Perspective*. Stanford: Stanford University Press.

Cruyff, M. and P. van der Heijden (2004), 'Een raming van het aantal illegalen in Nederland', in: A. Leerkes et al. (eds), *Wijken voor Illegalen: Over Ruimtelijke Spreiding, Huisvesting en Leefbaarheid*. The Hague: Sdu.

De Boom, J., E. Snel and G. Engbersen (2008), 'Asielmigratie en Criminaliteit', paper presented at the 'Dag van de Sociologie', Leuven, Belgium.

De Genova, N.-P. (2002), 'Migrant illegality and deportability in everyday life', *Annual Review of Anthropology* 31: 419-447.

Düvell, F. (2009), 'Paths into irregularity: Policies, politics and laws that contribute to irregular migration in the EU', CLANDESTINO project workshop, 28 April.

Düvell, F. (2006a), *Illegal Immigration in Europe: Beyond Control?* London: Palgrave Macmillan.

Düvell, F. (2006b), 'Illegal migration in Europe: Patterns, causes and consequences', presentation at Stockholm University seminar Irregulars, Sans Papier, Hidden, Illegal and Black Labour, 29 November.

EC (2008a), 'The Directive on the right of EU citizens to move and reside freely in the European Union: The Commission issues report on the application of the Directive', Memo/08/778. Brussels: European Commission.

EC (2008b), 'Communication from the Commission to the Council and the European Parliament Examining the creation of a European Border Surveillance System (EUROSUR)', COM 68 final. Brussels: European Commission.

EIRO (2005), 'Industrial relations and undeclared work', EIRO thematic feature. European Industrial Relations Observatory. www.eurofound.europa.eu/pubdocs/2005/135/en/1/ef05135en.pdf

Engbersen, G. (2001), 'The unanticipated consequences of panopticon Europe: Residence strategies of illegal immigrants', in: V. Guiraudon and C. Joppke (eds), *Controlling a New Migration World*, 222-246. Routledge: London.

Engbersen, G., M. van San and A. Leerkes (2006), 'A room with a view: Irregular immigrants in the legal capital of the world', *Ethnography* 7: 209-242.

Erdemir, A. and E. Vasta (2007), 'Work strategies among Turkish immigrants in London: Differentiating irregularity and solidarity', in: E. Berggren, B. Likic-Brboric, G. Toksöz and N. Trimikliniotis (eds), *Irregular Migration, Informal Labour and Community in Europe*, 294-313. Maastricht: Shaker Verlag.

Fasani, F. (2008), 'Country report Italy', in: Clandestino Undocumented Migration, *Counting the Uncountable: Data and Trends Across Europe*. www.irregular-migration.hwwi.net/Home.2560.0.html.

Freeman, G. (2000), 'Political science and comparative immigration politics', Austin: University of Texas. www.tulane.edu/~dnelson/PEMigConf/Freeman.pdf.

Fussell, E. and D.-S. Massey (2004), 'The limits to cumulative causation: International migration from Mexican urban areas', *Demography* 41 (1): 151-171.

Groenendijk, K. (2004), 'Introduction' in: B. Bogusz, R. Cholewinski, A. Cygan and E. Szyszcak (eds), *Irregular Migration and Human Rights: Theoretical, European and International Perspectives*. Leiden: Martinus Nijhoff.

Guild, E. (2004), 'Who is an irregular migrant?' in: B. Bogusz, R. Cholewinski, A. Cygan and E. Szyszcak (eds), *Irregular Migration and Human Rights: Theoretical, European and International Perspectives*, 3-28. Leiden: Martinus Nijhoff.

Guiraudon, V. and G. Lahav (2000), 'A reappraisal of the state sovereignty debate: The case of migration control', *Comparative Policy Studies* 33 (2), 163-195.

Heering, L., R. van der Erf and L. van Wissen (2004), 'The role of family networks and migration culture in the continuation of Moroccan emigration: A gender perspective', *Journal of Ethnic and Migration Studies* 30 (2): 323-338.

House of Lords (2002), *Select Committee on European Union Thirty-Seventh Report*. www.publications.parliament.uk/pa/ld200102/ldselect/ldeucom/187/18704.htm#a5

IOM (2004), *Return Migration: Policies and Practices in Europe*. Geneva: International Organization for Migration. www.ch.iom.int/fileadmin/media/pdf/publikationen/return_migration.pdf.

Jacobson, D. (1996), *Rights Across Borders: Immigration and the Decline of Citizenship*. Baltimore/London: The John Hopkins University Press.

Jandl, M. (2004), *The Estimation of Illegal Immigration in Europe*. Vienna: International Centre for Migration Policy Development. www.net4you.com/jandl/Estimation-2004.pdf.

Jandl, M. (2008), 'Methods for estimating stocks and flows of irregular migrants', in: A. Kraler, A. and D. Vogel (eds), *Report on Methodological Issues*, Clandestino Undocumented Migration.

Jordan, B. and F. Düvell (2002), *Irregular Migration: The Dilemmas of Transnational Mobility*. Cheltenham: Edward Elgar.

Kostakopoulou, D. (2004), 'Irregular migration and migration theory: Making state authorisation less relevant', in: B. Bogusz, R. Cholewinski, A. Cygan and E. Szyszcak (eds), *Irregular Migration and Human Rights: Theoretical, European and International Perspectives*, 41-57. Leiden: Martinus Nijhoff.

Light, I. (2006), *Deflecting Immigration: Networks, Markets, and Regulation in Los Angeles*. New York: Russell Sage.

Lucassen, L. (1996), *Zigeuner: Die Geschichte eines polizeilichen Ordnungsbegriffes in Deutschland 1700-1945*. Koln: Böhlau Verlag.

Mahler, S.J. (1995), *American Dreaming: Immigrant Life on the Margins*. Princeton: Princeton University Press.

Massey, D.-S. (2003), 'Patterns and processes of international migration in the 21st century', paper prepared for Conference on African Migration in Comparative Perspective, Johannesburg, South Africa, 4-7 June.

Massey, D.-S. (1990), 'Social structure, household strategies, and the cumulative causation of migration', *Population Index* 56 (1): 3-26.

Massey, D.-S., J. Arango, G. Hugo, A. Kouaouci, A. Pelegrino, J.-E. Taylor (1993), 'Theories of international migration: A review and appraisal', *Population and Development Review* 19 (3): 431-463.

Piguet, E. and S. Losa (2002), *Travailleurs de l'ombre? Demande de main-d'oeuvre du domaine de l'asile et ampleur de l'emploi d'étrangers non déclarés en Suisse*. Zurich: Seismo.

Piore, M. (1979), *Birds of Passage: Migrant Labor and Industrial Societies*. Cambridge (MA): Cambridge University Press.

Pluymen, M.H. (2008), *Niet Toelaten Betekent Uitsluiten: Een Rechtssociologisch Onderzoek naar de Rechtvaardiging en Praktijk van Uitsluiting van Vreemdelingen van Voorzieningen*. The Hague: Boom.

Pluymen, M. (2004), 'Exclusion from social benefits as an instrument in the Netherlands', *IMIS-Beiträge* 24: 75-87.

Portes, A. and R.-G. Rumbaut (1990), *Immigrant America: A Portrait*. Berkeley: University of California Press.

Rusinovic, K., J.P. van der Leun, T. Chessa, A. Weltevrede, G. Engbersen and J. Vos (2002), *Nieuwe Vangnetten in de Samenleving: Over Problemen en Dilemma's in de Opvang van Kwetsbare Groepen*. Rotterdam: RISBO.

Sassen, S. (1999), *Guests and Aliens*. New York: The New Press.

Schrover, M., J.-P. van der Leun, L. Lucassen and C. Quispel (2008), *Illegal Migration and Gender in a Global and Historical Perspective*. IMISCOE Research. Amsterdam: Amsterdam University Press.

Staring, R. (2001), *Reizen Onder Regie: Het Migratieproces van Illegale Turken in Nederland*. Amsterdam: Het Spinhuis.

Tapinos, G. (1999), 'Clandestine immigration: Economic and political issues'. Trends in International Migration: Continuous Reporting System on Migration. Paris: Organisation for Economic Co-operation and Development.

United Nations Commission on Population and Development (1997), Activities of Intergovernmental and Non-governmental Organizations in the Area of International Migration. Report of the Secretary General. New York: United Nations.

Van der Leun, J., G. Engbersen and P. van der Heijden (1998), *Illegaliteit en Criminaliteit: Schattingen, Aanhoudingen en Uitzettingen*. Rotterdam: Faculty of Social Sciences, Erasmus University Rotterdam.

Van der Leun, J. (2003), *Looking for Loopholes: Processes of Incorporation of Illegal Immigrants in the Netherlands*. Amsterdam: Amsterdam University Press.

Van der Leun, J. (2007), 'The Dutch "discouragement" policy towards undocumented immigrants: Implementation and outcomes', in: E. Berggren, B. Likic-Brboric, G.

Toksöz, N. Trimikliniotis (eds), *Irregular Migration, Informal Labour and Community: A Challenge for Europe*, 401-412. Maastricht: Shaker Verlag.

Van der Leun, J. and R. Kloosterman (2006), 'Going underground: Immigration policy changes and shifts in modes of provision of undocumented immigrants in the Netherlands', *Tijdschrift voor Economische en Sociale Geografie* 97 (1): 59-68.

Van Meeteren, M., M. van San and G. Engbersen (2008), *Zonder Papieren: Over de Positie van Irreguliere Migranten en de Rol van het Vreemdelingenbeleid in België*. Leuven: ACCO.

Van Nieuwenhuyze, I. (2008), *Getting by in Europe's Urban Labour Markets: Senegambian Migrants' Strategies for Survival, Documentation and Mobility*. IMISCOE Dissertations. Amsterdam: Amsterdam University Press.

Vogel, D. and Jandl, M. (2008), 'Introduction to the methodological problem', in: A. Kraler and D. Vogel (eds), *Report on Methodological Issues*. Clandestino Undocumented Migration.

Vuddamaly, V. (2007), 'Inner-city ethnic enclaves and irregular immigrant networks as new social spaces in global cities: A case study of the "Little India" of Paris', in: E. Berggren, B. Likic-Brboric, G. Toksöz, N. Trimikliniotis (eds), *Irregular Migration, Informal Labour and Community: A Challenge for Europe*, 283-293. Maastricht, Shaker Publishing.

Part III

Regulation of Migration

14 Whither EU Immigration After the Lisbon Treaty?

Elspeth Guild

Introduction

The European Union's new constitutional framework, the 'Treaty of Lisbon', entered into force on 1 December 2009 after ten frustrating years of negotiation and debate. The Treaty makes deep and lasting changes to the way the EU operates and its approach to fundamental rights. Among the modifications introduced, the new legal framework has major consequences for immigration and asylum law and policy.

Lisbon Treaty

Fast on the heels of the Lisbon Treaty came the Stockholm Programme, which sets out medium-term priorities for the EU in the area of freedom, security and justice. This is the policy field where immigration lies as well. The current chapter examines the significance of the Lisbon Treaty for EU immigration law and policy. In short, it makes two observations regarding the Treaty's impact:

- The Lisbon Treaty lifts the limitation on access to the European Court of Justice by all levels of national courts for disputes related to borders, immigration and asylum. This will dramatically accelerate the harmonising effect of EU law in this field.
- The Treaty gives legal force to the Charter on Fundamental Rights. This will be felt quickly in the area of immigration if the experience of the European Court of Human Rights is any indication. Already, human and fundamental rights have become a source of friction between member states and third-country nationals (i.e. nationals of states outside the EU) in conflicts extending beyond the national courts of member states.

The Lisbon Treaty's impact on immigration policy is likely to be greatest in areas that are sensitive in member states due to sovereignty concerns. This means that the 'front-page' effect of EU immigration law is not likely to diminish in the coming years.

The Lisbon Treaty and powers in respect to immigration

TEU and TFEU

The Lisbon Treaty is composed of two treaties (and their protocols and declarations). The first is the new Treaty on the European Union (TEU), which establishes the central provisions for the structure of the European Union and contains the rules about how the EU operates. The TEU will be important when the position of the Charter of Fundamental Rights in EU immigration is discussed. The other treaty that is part of the package is the Treaty on the Functioning of the European Union (TFEU). The first step towards examining the Lisbon Treaty and immigration is to compare the previous powers with the new ones and ask the question: what has changed?

Title V, Chapter 2 TFEU establishes the competences the Union has on border checks, asylum and immigration, which remain fairly similar to their earlier (pre-2009) version. The TFEU now charges the Union with developing a common immigration policy aimed at ensuring, at all stages, the efficient management of migration flows, fair treatment of third-country nationals residing legally in the member states and the prevention of, and enhanced measures to combat, illegal immigration and trafficking in human beings (Article 79 TFEU).

TEC

In the Treaty on the European Community (TEC),[1] which was replaced by the TFEU and TEU, the competence was slightly more limited to measures on conditions of entry and residence and standards on procedures for the issue of long term visas and residence permits, including that for family reunification. The EU had competence to control illegal immigration and illegal residence, including repatriation of illegal residents and measures defining the rights and conditions under which nationals of third countries who were legally resident in a member state may reside in other member states (Article 63 TEC).

What is new?

There are two differences that may be significant between the old and new treaties. In the TEC there is not specific reference to fair treatment for third-country nationals legally residing in the EU, whereas this is now present in the TFEU. This wording comes from the first five-year plan for the implementation of the immigration powers of the EU that was adopted in Tampere, Finland, in 1999. In the Tampere Milestones, the EU promoted the objective of fair treatment of third-country nationals resident in the EU for the first time.[2] This objective has been widely repeated in much of the secondary legislation that the EU has adopted in the field of immigration, such as the Long Term Residents' Directive (Directive 2003: 109) and the Family Reunification Directive (Directive 2003: 86). The inclusion of this reference in the Treaty will have the effect of strengthening the importance of fair treatment, which may become the subject of judicial scrutiny in due course.

human trafficking

The second notable change relates to trafficking in human beings. Until the Lisbon Treaty collapsed the pillars of the EU, this competence had remained in the somewhat more intergovernmental third pillar of the EU.[3] Article 29 of the TEU provided that a high level of safety within the area of freedom, security and justice (the objective of the section) would be achieved by preventing and combating crime, including trafficking in persons. This objective has now been subsumed into the TFEU competence, which covers the field.

The focus that the TFEU places on the efficient management of migration flows as an objective of immigration policy may have a further consequence of bringing the EU's policy on integrated border management closer to its rules on immigration (COM 2008/69). The intersection of policies on visas, border control and controls within the territory of the member states is a priority in this field. One of the difficulties, however, is in determining how to align the two – to what extent should policies regarding admission at the EU's external frontier be closely linked with the treatment of third-country nationals once they have joined the labour force or become part of a community in a member state? Before we discuss how the pre-2009 powers have been exercised, it should be noted that Denmark does not participate in any of these measures, in accordance with a protocol to the previous treaty that was renewed with the Lisbon Treaty. Ireland and the UK are entitled to either opt into any measure in the field of immigration or to remain opted out of its effects, by virtue of a protocol in the previous treaty, which has been transferred to the new treaty. For the most part, they have opted out of the legal migration measures but into the asylum ones. The UK has opted into some of the irregular migration measures as well.

What are the existing EU measures for legal immigration?

measures

The power to adopt measures in the field of immigration was a novelty of the Amsterdam Treaty in 1999. Since then, the EU has adopted ten measures in the area of legal migration,[4] four of which regulate the longer-term entry and residence of third-country nationals. Ireland and the UK have opted out of these measures. The first and most important measure is the Directive on Family Reunification. This was adopted in 2003 and had to be implemented by the member states by October 2005. The objective of the Directive is to create a right to family reunification for third-country nationals who reside legally in the

member states. The way this is pursued is by establishing minimum standards for the admission and treatment of third-country national family members. According to the Directive, family reunification is an EU right for spouses and minor children. The conditions for its exercise are:
- Stable and regular resources to support the family;
- Adequate housing;
- Comprehensive health insurance.

Member states are permitted to apply integration measures to family members either before or after their admission to the state, which is a derogation from the right to family reunification (Van Oers et al. 2010).

The European Commission's assessment

problem areas

In October 2008, the European Commission published the first report on the implementation of the Directive in the member states (COM (2008) 610 final). The report reveals a number of weaknesses in the way in which member states have implemented the Directive. Key among the problem areas are:
- Two member states, AT and BE, require evidence of accommodation prior to the entry of family members, which can impose a considerable financial burden on the sponsor.
- Only half the member states require the family to have health insurance.
- All member states require evidence of stable and regular resources except SE. However, the modalities vary substantially. CY provides no precision on the meaning of the term while FR, LU, RO and LT make reference to the minimum wage. The range of specified income is from € 120 in PL to € 1,484 in NL.
- Three member states, NL, DE and FR, apply integration measures before the family may be admitted to the member state, though some categories are exempted (more member states have subsequently added integration measures as a condition of residence).
- Four member states, CZ, HU, LV and PL, do not have a specific procedure for family reunification, but deal with this in the general immigration rules.
- All member states except IT and PT require fees, but these range from € 35 in CZ and EE to € 1,368 in NL.
- There are substantial variations among the member states regarding access to employment. In the Commission's view, the national provisions in DE, HU and SI exceed what is permitted under the Directive.

CJEU

The Commission expressed concern that the Directive, which is aimed at creating a level playing field for the family reunification of third-country nationals, in fact seems to be resulting in very substantial variations in access to this right. The Court of Justice of the European Union (CJEU) has twice been required to consider the Directive; the first time at the request of the European Parliament, which challenged three exceptional provisions in the Directive – one allowing member states to exclude children over 12 years of age (provided that they had adopted legislation by the time of entry into force of the Directive), another allowing member states to exclude children over 15 years of age, and a third allowing member states to delay family reunification for up to three years if existing legislation provided for such at the time of entry into force. In the Parliament's view, these exceptions were of questionable compatibility with human rights. The CJEU did not find any of the Directive's provisions specifically problematic, finding instead that attention needed to be focused upon its implementation by the member states (C-540/03 Parliament v Council (2006) ECR I-5769). In the end, as the Commission's report shows, only two member states, Cyprus and Germany, used the exception to exclude children over 12 years of age (although the documents available in regard to the negotiations indicate that it was the Netherlands that sought the exception). No member states used the exception to exclude children over 15 years of age (which had been championed by Germany). However, the fact that the first challenge to the Directive was on the basis of human rights compatibility highlights the importance that the EU Charter of Fundamental Rights (which incorporates all the rights contained in the European Convention on Human Rights) is likely to have in this field. This point will later be discussed further.

The EU Court of Justice is engaged

Chakroun case

The CJEU was once again troubled by the Directive in respect to a reference from a Dutch court (C-578/08 Chakroun 4 March 2010). Mr Chakroun, a Moroccan national, had been living in the Netherlands since 1970, and held an indefinite residence permit. In 2006, Mrs Chakroun, also a Moroccan national, who was still living in Morocco, applied for a provisional residence permit so she could join her husband, to whom she had been married since 1972. Her application was refused on the grounds that her husband was not receiving sufficient income to be eligible for family formation. Here the key issues were twofold: what income could member states require of a third-country national seeking family reunification with his or her spouse, and what constitutes social assistance for the purposes of the Directive. The relevant Dutch law that implements the Directive requires a sponsor to have an income equivalent to 120 per cent of the minimum wage. However, Dutch law provides two categories of social assistance: a lower level called general assistance, which is the minimum wage, and special assistance, which is the equivalent of 120 per cent of the minimum wage. Which level was then applicable for the application of the Directive? If only the general social assistance level, then Mr Chakroun's income was sufficient; if the special assistance level applied, then it was not.

unlawful discrimination

The problem was compounded by another specificity of Dutch law – when a couple marry before either of them move to the Netherlands, then the applicable rate of income for family reunification is the lower general assistance level; but if the couple marries after one of them has moved to the Netherlands (as the Chakrouns had done) then the higher special assistance level is applicable to the income requirement. The couple complained that this constituted unlawful discrimination in light of the Directive's objectives. The CJEU pointed out that the Directive specifies the right of family reunification, which any legal resident can rely upon. There is no margin of appreciation for the member states, and because the Directive requires this, the conditions for the exercise of the right must be restrictively interpreted. Therefore the CJEU found:

- 'Social assistance' in the Directive relates to its EU meaning, not its national one, and is defined as 'social assistance granted by the public authorities, whether at national, regional or local level' (para 45);
- 'Stable and regular resources' must be determined in reference to social assistance (para 46);
- The assessment of income must not undermine the objective of the Directive to promote family reunification (para 47);
- The actual situation of each applicant must be examined, as well as the threshold that the state has set in its regulations (para 48);
- Social assistance in the Directive is the level of general assistance only, not special assistance (para 52);
- Different income requirements that are dependent exclusively on where and when the family married (or was formed) are by definition problematic and incompatible with the Directive (para 51);
- The Directive does not permit a difference in income levels to be applied on the basis of when and where the marriage took place (i.e. either before or after one party migrated) (para 66).

In other words, the Dutch legislation was found fully incompatible with the Directive. In its finding the CJEU relied not only on the European Convention on Human Rights for guidance, but referred to the EU Charter of Fundamental Rights on numerous occasions as a source of interpretation.

Long Term Residents' Directive

The second substantial measure that the EU has adopted in this field is the Long Term Residents' Directive. Sadly, at the time of writing the Commission had not yet carried out an assessment of member states' implementation of this Directive, or if it has, the Commission has not published it. Thus, it is less clear how the member states have implemented this measure. However, a number of studies have been undertaken by academics that indicate substantial variations across the member states (Halleskov 2005). The principle of the Directive is that any third-country national, not coming within an excluded group (such as students and diplomats), who has resided lawfully in a member state for five years will obtain a long-term residence status in EU law so long as three conditions are fulfilled:

- The individual fulfils the residential requirement;
- The individual has stable and regular resources to support him or herself and dependents;
- The individual has fully comprehensive health insurance.

conditions

However, similar to the Family Reunification Directive, a fourth condition may be applied by the member states – that the individual complies with integration conditions. It is this requirement that has been the source of most concern among academic researchers regarding the implementation of the Directive (Guild et al. 2009; Carrera 2009; Van Oers et al. 2010). Once an individual acquires long-term EU residence status under the Directive, this can only be lost in accordance with the terms of the Directive, which are very limited. Further, the person is entitled to full and equal treatment with fellow nationals within the member state where the status was acquired (with exceptions for political rights and economic activities that are not open to EU nationals). Finally, the status provides the entitlement to move and exercise activities, economic and otherwise, in other member states, subject to a (fairly limited) test of labour market conditions in the second member state and a potential delay of up to 12 months in accessing economic rights. At the time of writing, the CJEU had not handed down judgment regarding the correct interpretation of the Directive. If the cases that go to the ECHR are any indication of what are likely to be the issues of disagreement between state authorities and individual third-country nationals, it is likely to be the protections against expulsion that will need clarification soonest.

The Blue Card: Highly skilled employment

Blue Card Directive

The third measure that has been adopted and provides immigration rights for third-country nationals is Directive 2009/50 on the conditions of entry and residence of third-country nationals for the purposes of highly-qualified employment (the Blue Card Directive). This Directive seeks to regulate highly-qualified migration to the EU in pursuit of the EU's objective of becoming the most competitive and dynamic knowledge-based economy in the world. It only applies to highly-qualified employment, which is defined as that which requires adequate and specific competence, as proven by high professional qualifications. These are attested by means of any diploma, certificate or other evidence of formal qualifications issued by a competent authority attesting to the successful completion of a post-secondary higher education programme, on condition that the studies lasted at least three years. Professional experience of at least five years may be substituted. In order to qualify for a Blue Card, the individual must hold the necessary qualification, and the employment proposed in the member state must pay at least 1.5 times the average gross annual salary in the member state concerned. After 18 months' employment in one member state, the Blue Card holder is privileged in their movement to another member state for highly-qualified employment.

A substantial number of categories of persons are excluded from the scope of this Directive, such as refugees, seasonal workers and posted workers. However, for the rest, the Directive provides the following: the criteria for admission for the purpose of employment, the procedure for the issue of the Blue Card, the grounds for refusal, and the rights that the worker is entitled to enjoy, which include more favourable terms of family reunification than those that are contained in the Directive of that name. The member states had until 19 June 2011 to incorporate the Directive into national law. Although the Directive was intended to prevent member states competing for the best-qualified foreign workers by reducing the standards and criteria for their admission, it does not affect the right of member states to adopt or retain more favourable provisions for third-country national workers in some key areas:

Blue Card benefits

- Salary requirements; when a Blue Card holder moves to another member state after 18 months in the first state, they do not need to meet the 1.5 times gross annual salary level;
- Procedural safeguards may be enhanced;
- A 24-month limitation on equal treatment with fellow nationals may be relaxed regarding access to highly qualified employment;
- A 24-month restriction on changing employer unless permitted to do so by prior authorisation may be dispensed with;

- Withdrawal of the Blue Card after three months' unemployment or repeated periods of unemployment may be abandoned;
- Equal treatment rights set out in the Directive may be provided earlier than required;
- Family reunification (which is more generous than that which applies to other third-country nationals who have to rely on Directive 2003/86) may be further facilitated; and
- Acquisition of long-term resident status may be made available on more favourable grounds than in the Directive of that name.

If there is competition among the member states for highly qualified and thus desirable migrants, then these are the areas in which that competition may be played out.

Researchers

researchers

The fourth measure that the EU has adopted regarding long-stay migration for economic activities regards researchers. In October 2005 the Directive on the admission of third-country nationals for the purpose of scientific research was adopted (Directive 2005/71), and its incorporation into national law was required by 12 October 2007.[5] According to the preamble, it was intended to contribute to achieving the goal of 'opening up the Community to third-country nationals who might be admitted for the purposes of research'; the EU objective of investing 3 per cent of GDP in research and increasing the number of researchers in the EU by 700,000 was set by the Barcelona Council in 2002, to be achieved by 2010.[6] By doing this, the institutions believe that the EU will be more attractive to researchers from around the world, which in turn will boost its position as an international centre for research. Attention is paid in the preamble to the question of brain drain and backup measures to support researchers' reintegration in their countries of origin. In accordance with the Lisbon process, fostering mobility within the EU is also an objective.[7] The preamble calls for member states to permit family unity for researchers, but does not actually deal with the issue, leaving it to the member states to determine where it is appropriate, in accordance with Directive 2003/86.

research definition

The Directive defines research, researcher and research institution in wide terms: research is defined as creative work undertaken on a systematic basis in order to increase the stock of knowledge of humanity, culture and society, and the use of this stock of knowledge to devise new applications; a researcher is someone who holds higher education qualifications that give access to doctoral programmes; and a research organisation must have been approved for the purposes of the Directive by a member state in accordance with legislation or administrative practice. As the Directive is written in terms of a research institution holding the key to mobility, member state control over access to the territory for researchers takes place through the qualification of a research institution. According to the Directive, the research institution must initiate the procedure. In the event that a foreign researcher overstays his or her permitted time in a member state, the state is allowed to require the research organisation to reimburse costs related to the stay and return of the individual. The Directive allows member states to hold the institution responsible for costs for up to six months after the termination of the hosting agreement.

hosting agreement

Under the Directive, a hosting agreement must be signed between an authorised organisation and a researcher. This agreement must include details of the purpose and duration of the research and the availability of financial resources, evidence of the researcher's qualifications, evidence of resources and travel costs for the researcher (beyond the social assistance system), health insurance and working conditions. Member states are to admit a researcher once their authorities have checked that the individual has a valid travel document, a hosting agreement, a statement of financial responsibility from the research organisation and that the individual is not a threat to public policy, security or health. Member states may still require visas for researchers who meet the conditions of the Directive (article 14(4)), though every facility must be provided to obtain one. The member state shall issue a residence permit to the individual for at least one year (unless the research is to have a shorter duration than that period). Researchers are allowed to teach, but only in accordance with national rules. Once admitted as a researcher under the Directive in one member state, he or she can carry out research activities in any other member state, normally not for more than three months without further formality. Member states must make a decision as soon as possible, and if appropriate, have an accelerated procedure. Refusal of an application must be accompanied by an appeal procedure available to the individual or the organisation. A report on the operation of the Directive was due on 12 October 2010.

An assessment

harmonising measures

As set out above regarding legal immigration, before the adoption of the TFEU, a number of key areas have been the subject of harmonising measures that are based on the principle of minimum standards. Specifically, family reunification, long-term resident status, highly qualified migration and admission of researchers have all enjoyed some degree of harmonisation in this way. The Commission has confirmed that in 2010 further proposals will be adopted regarding other areas of first admission for labour market access, specifically, seasonal workers and inter-corporate transferees. On the other hand, the new five-year plan for the development of the Area of Freedom, Security and Justice under the Stockholm Programme[8] calls for another assessment of the Family Reunification Directive. In particular, it calls for an evaluation and, where necessary, review of the Directive, taking into account the importance of integration measures (para 6.1.4). This is unlikely to make family reunification easier for third-country nationals – other than highly qualified migrants coming in under the Blue Card Directive, who are not subject to integration conditions in regard to their family members. Those member states that have opted to use the integration measures option as a requirement for family reunification have done so in a way that makes family reunification more difficult for third-country nationals in their states (Groenendijk et al. 2007).

The TFEU objective of fair treatment for legally resident third-country nationals may well be tested in this area of integration measures and conditions. Some member states, such as the Netherlands and Germany, have introduced integration measures for family reunification that must be fulfilled before the admission of family members (Van Oers 2010). However, nationals of some states, such as the USA and Japan, are excluded from the requirement as regards the Netherlands. Is this fair treatment consistent with the TFEU objective? It will be up to the CJEU to determine the meaning of fair treatment should a national court request a definition.

What are the existing EU measures for irregular immigration?

neutral language

EU institutions prefer to use the term 'illegal' immigration rather than 'irregular' or 'undocumented migration', which is favoured by other international organisations and institutions (Council of Europe 2010). This is notwithstanding the fact that not only has the Council of Europe's Parliamentary Assembly called on EU institutions to use more neutral language, but the European Parliament has similarly done so with little noticeable effect (Carrera and Merlino 2009). In this area EU institutions have been quite active, adopting over twenty measures since acquiring the competence to do so.[9] The most controversial of the measures has been the Returns Directive (2008/115), which has been denounced by the heads of state of all countries in South America (Acosta Arcarazo 2009). What the Directive seeks to do is establish clear, transparent and fair rules for an effective return policy, which the EU considers to be a necessary element of a well-managed migration policy. The ending of an irregular stay by a third-country national is to occur through a fair and transparent procedure culminating in expulsion.

Directive objective

The objective of the Directive is to develop common standards and procedures to be applied by the member states when returning irregular third-country nationals to other countries. It is required to be in compliance with fundamental rights and international law, including refugee protection and human rights obligations. 'Illegal stay', which is a key concept of the Directive, is defined as the presence in the territory of a member state of a third-country national who does not fulfil or no longer fulfils the conditions of entry as set out in Article 5 of the Schengen Borders Code (on short-stay entry for three months or less), or other conditions for entry, stay or residence in that member state. Return is defined as voluntary or enforced compliance with an obligation to return to either his or her country of origin or a country of transit in accordance with Community or bilateral readmission agreements or other arrangements, or another third country to which the third-country national concerned voluntarily decides to return and in which he or she will be accepted.

The first step that the Returns Directive requires a member state to take is to decide whether or not to issue an individual with an autonomous residence permit or other authorisation offering a right to stay for compassionate, humanitarian or other reasons (Article 6(4)). If the member state decides not to issue some sort of authorisation then it is obliged under the Directive to issue a return decision. Return can be voluntary, which the Directive appears to promote, or enforced if the individual does not leave (Article 8). Where a member state enforces a return decision it must also issue an entry ban on the individual, which in principle should be for a five-year period (Article 11). The most controversial part of the Directive is that relating to detention. In Chapter IV of the Directive detention is incorporated as a normal part of the return process, although it is specifically stated to be a final resort where there is a risk of fleeing or the individual is hampering the return procedure. Detention is subject to a series of safeguards regarding the making of the decision, the right to remedies against the decision and judicial supervision of the detention. The initial limit to the length of detention is six months, but this may be extended for a further twelve months (Article 15). Member states were required to implement it into their national law by 24 December 2011.

The Returns Directive before the Court

Kadzoev case

Like the Family Reunification Directive, the Returns Directive has already been the subject of judicial consideration by the CJEU (C-357/

09 PPU Kadzoev (Huchbarov) 30 November 2009). It was one of the last judgments of the CJEU before the enforcement of the Lisbon Treaty, and it was subject to urgent procedure in view of the fact that the individual was in detention. The case revolved around a Mr Kadzoev or Huchbarov, whose identity has never been fully certain. He had been arrested by the Bulgarian authorities near their border with Turkey, was detained from 3 November 2006 and was still in detention when the case was heard by the CJEU in 2009. The man stated that he was a Chechen and that his name was Huchbarov, but he did not wish for assistance from the Russian authorities. The Bulgarian authorities asserted that his name was Kadzoev, and that he was a Chechen with a Georgian mother. The Bulgarian authorities sent the identity documents that they had in respect to Kadzoev to the Russian authorities, but the latter stated that the documents were from persons and authorities unknown to the Russian Federation, and thus there was no proof of Russian nationality. Various applications for the man to be released from detention failed, not least because he had no address in Bulgaria. In 2007 he applied for asylum, though the authorities continued to detain him, and eventually in 2009 they refused his application definitively without any further right to appeal.

In the meantime, the Bulgarian authorities were having no luck in finding a country to which they could send the man. They failed with the Russians, tried and failed with the Georgians and even approached the Austrian authorities to see if they would take him, again without success. Finally, a Bulgarian court, once again faced with an application for the man's release from custody, asked the CJEU whether the 18-month maximum period of detention under the Return Directive applied in this case. The CJEU found that the Directive was applicable in light of the Bulgarian law that implemented it (notwithstanding the fact that the period for implementation had not yet expired). Two central issues arose – first, could the man's detention while he was seeking asylum count towards the 18 month maximum on detention, and second, could periods of detention during judicial review count towards the 18 month maximum?

Asylum Procedures Directive

On the first question the CJEU looked long and hard at the Asylum Procedures Directive (2004/85). It held that if the requirements of the procedures were followed that permit limits to be placed on an individual's freedom of movement (and which provide substantial guarantees and freedoms to the individual), then the time spent under restriction of liberty does not count towards the 18 month maximum under the Return Directive. However, if the detention continued to be on the basis of national rules, which effectively correspond to detention under the Return Directive, then it does count (para 47). On the second question, the CJEU held that 18 months means 18 months, irrespective of whether judicial review or other legal challenges were launched by the individual. After 18 months the state must release the individual. In no case can the maximum period be exceeded, irrespective of whether the individual is aggressive, has no means of supporting himself or has no travel or identity documents (para 68-69). Further the CJEU held that the possibility of detaining a person on grounds of public order and public safety cannot be based on the Return Directive (para 70). The CJEU accomplished this without even once referring to the EU Charter of Fundamental Rights or the European Convention on Human Rights. No other reference was pending before the CJEU by April 2010.

The judicialisation of immigration

courts of first and final instance

When the EU was provided with competences in the field of immigration in 1999, Article 68 TEC provided that only courts against whose decision there was no further appeal could refer questions to the CJEU on measures arising from the new treaty bases. The result was that only courts of final instance could refer questions regarding EU immigration matters. Member states' courts of final instance tend to be conservative in their use of reference powers (De Burca and Weiler 2001), often preferring to deal with the issue themselves under national law. Courts of first instance often ask the CJEU the most challenging questions of EU law, as they are faced with an immediate problem and are often under substantial pressure regarding the preferred outcomes of the parties involved. The consequence of limiting the reference power to courts of final instance was to dramatically slow the oversight that the area might receive from the CJEU. In addition to preferences between courts, it is also an issue of simple arithmetic – there is only one court of final instance in each state, but there are many courts of first instance. Few cases regarding immigration ever get to courts of final instance, whereas many arrive at the doors of courts of first instance, particularly in member states where there are specialised courts for immigration and asylum issues.

Presently, the field of EU asylum measures is giving rise to the largest number of references to the CJEU from courts across the member states. One might well expect, however, that immigration measures will catch up rapidly. After all, the Family Reunification Directive has already given rise to two judgments. The consequences of the arrival of the CJEU as an important actor in this field are very likely to include the following:

- Definitions of terms in the Directives will be given consistent meanings rather than be left to member state national rules;

- Terms that are identical to one another, or very similar to one another or to terms used elsewhere in EU law, are likely to be interpreted consistently; thus grounds for expulsion that use the term 'public policy' are likely to be given the same interpretation as the same phrase that applies to EU citizens (this has been the approach of the CJEU regarding the EC Turkey Association Agreement);
- The relationship of the rule and the exception or derogation from the rule is likely to be clarified, giving priority to the rule and a limited interpretation to the exception;
- The scope for divergent national rules that stray from a common EU interpretation of the Directives will be diminished, unless it is specifically based on the permitted higher standards (i.e. more favourable to the migrant) permitted in the principle of minimum standards.

critical role

The CJEU has a critical role to play in the development of the EU field on immigration, and this role is now coming into its own. The direction that the TFEU provides to the CJEU regarding the importance of the principle of fairness may be critical. From the initial decisions of the CJEU (discussed above) it appears that the CJEU perceives the field of immigration as one that merits interpretation consistent with the usual rules of EU law. There is nothing exceptional or extraordinary about immigration that sets it apart in regard to the judicial consideration of its consistent elements.

The EU Charter of Fundamental Rights and the Lisbon Treaty

EU Charter of Fundamental Rights

Article 6 TEU provides that the EU Charter of Fundamental Rights, which was adopted in 2000, shall have the same legal value as the Treaties. Although the Charter was drafted and adopted in 2000, it was denied legal effect as a result of disagreements among the member states (primarily the UK in disaccord with the others) about the added value of a legally binding Charter. According to its preamble, the Charter sets out the Union's foundation on indivisible, universal values of human dignity, freedom, equality and solidarity. It confirms that the EU is based on the principles of democracy and rule of law. In order to promote the four freedoms of the EU – the free movement of goods, persons, services and capital – the Charter states that it is necessary to strengthen the protection of fundamental rights, and thus recognises the rights, freedoms and principles set out. A protocol to the Lisbon Treaty seeks to limit the legal effect of the Charter in the UK and Poland (and the Czech authorities have requested to be added to this protocol as soon as possible).

As mentioned above, the Charter includes the rights contained in the European Convention on Human Rights (ECHR), and the Charter's Article 52 (3) states that Charter rights which correspond to ECHR rights shall have the same meaning and scope as those in the ECHR. Thus, the way in which the European Court of Human Rights has interpreted the ECHR in immigration matters becomes a subject of substantial importance for the EU. Here is not the place to consider the jurisprudence of the European Court of Human Rights in immigration matters, which has been extensively examined elsewhere (Blake and Husain 2003; Sikuta and Hubalkova 2007). Nor is it the place to examine how the CJEU has incorporated the ECHR into its jurisprudence (Guild and Lesieur 1997), though it is worth noting that both the Lisbon Treaty and the Stockholm Programme mandate the accession of the EU to the ECHR. The point is that immigration measures in the EU are no longer self-referential. All EU immigration measures contain a standard preamble, which confirms their compatibility with the ECHR and EU fundamental rights standards. Most of the measures, when they were proposed, were subject to a fundamental rights impact assessment, which the Commission carried out. However, there was no external assessment of the human rights and fundamental rights consequences of the measures for individuals. Further, within the EU system there was no obvious way, consistent across member states, in which an individual could lay claim to fundamental rights in light of the implementation of EU measures on immigration. Now, with the legal effect of the Charter within the scope of EU law, this ambiguity has been cleared up.

strategy for implementation

In October 2010, the Commission issued a Communication setting out a strategy for the effective implementation of the Charter (COM (2010) 573 final). It confirms that the Charter, while primarily aimed at the EU institutions and bodies and therefore the law making process, also applies to the member states when implementing Union law. Thus, the member states are directly concerned and engaged by the Charter. It is also important to note that the Lisbon Treaty requires the EU to become a party to the European Convention on Human Rights – a negotiating mandate was adopted in June 2010. According to the Communication, the Commission's strategy is to make the fundamental rights provided for in the Charter as effective as possible (ibid.: 3). The Commission insists that 'The Union's action must be above reproach when it comes to fundamental rights' (ibid.: 4). Further, the Charter must serve as a compass for the Union's policies and their implementation by the member states. The Communication sets out a methodology by which it will examine Charter issues against member state implementation of EU measures. However, with an early challenge in the form of the 'voluntary' expulsion of Bulgarian and

Romanian Roma from France, deep questions have been raised about even the most basic implementation of the Charter, let alone its highest standards.

The Roma expulsion from France in August 2010: A challenge to the Charter

expulsion of Roma

On 28 July 2010 the French authorities issued a press release announcing a series of measures against Travellers and, in particular, Roma (European Commission 2010). The announcement stated that Roma camps would be targeted for the dismantling and expulsion of Romanian and Bulgarian nationals, and from October 2010 a database would commence collecting and retaining the fingerprints of such persons expelled where they were recipients of an aid to return. By the end of August 2010, the French authorities had carried out 979 returns of Roma to Romania and Bulgaria.

The targeting of Roma on the basis of their ethnicity is contrary to Article 21 of the Charter, which prohibits discrimination on the basis of sex, race, colour, ethnic or social origin, genetic features, language, religion or belief, political or any other opinion, membership of a national minority, property, birth, disability, age or sexual orientation. While the Commission entered into discussions with the French authorities, which turned fairly contentious in September 2010,[10] in the end only rather weak action in the form of a demand that France implement the procedural provisions of the EU Citizen's Directive was forthcoming.[11] On 30 September 2010, the European Parliament quizzed Commission officials on the adequacy of the EU response to France's actions.[12] At the moment, it seems clear that the very high expectations that the Commission itself has encouraged regarding the protection of fundamental rights contained in the Charter are not being fulfilled.

Conclusion

impact of Lisbon Treaty

This chapter examined the impact of the Lisbon Treaty on immigration law in the EU. It began by looking at some of the changes introduced by the Treaty in EU objectives. The Lisbon Treaty makes immigration an EU competence, for example, and fair treatment for third-country nationals is an explicit EU objective. It then looked at some existing EU measures in the area of immigration, both legal and irregular, and the impact that the Lisbon Treaty will have on these measures, particularly in light of the role given to the CJEU after 1 December 2009. Finally, the EU Charter of Fundamental Rights was discussed in relation to the legal effect of the Charter on EU immigration measures. A first test of the Charter's promise was the targeting of EU citizens on the basis of their ethnicity in the summer of 2010.

Three key conclusions emerge from this analysis:

- The European Court of Justice will engage directly with national courts of any level on interpretation of the EU immigration measures introduced by the Lisbon Treaty. The outcomes of these interactions will be extremely important in the further development of the field. The consistency of interpretation that is likely to emerge will be central in determining the future evolution of European immigration.
- The Charter of Fundamental Rights brings to the EU's table the disputes that the member states have been having with third-country nationals about immigration and rights. Until now, these have been taken to the European Court of Human Rights. Disputes can be expected regarding family reunification, protection of residence rights, equality of treatment and protection from detention and expulsion. The role of fundamental rights in interpretation of EU immigration measures will be central over the next twenty years, made possible by the Lisbon Treaty.
- EU institutions have yet to deliver the rights protections that the Charter of Fundamental Rights requires, even for citizens of the EU, let alone for third-country nationals. If the experience of the Commission's action against France for the expulsion of Bulgarian and Romanian Roma in August and September 2010 is any indication, both the European Court of Justice and the European Court of Human Rights are going to be very busy, as political leadership to enforce protection of fundamental rights does not seem particularly strong.

The main measures of EU immigration policy have now been adopted. While there will be more legislative initiatives, these will probably be in minority interest areas, such as the regulation of seasonal workers and measures for consolidation. The thrust of EU immigration law will move from law-making to the assessment and judicial control of legislation implementation in the member states.

MAIN IDEAS

The Lisbon Treaty's impact on immigration policy is likely to be greatest in areas that are sensitive in member states due to sovereignty concerns.

The European Court of Justice will engage directly with national courts of any level on interpretation of the EU immigration measures introduced by the Lisbon Treaty. The outcomes of these interactions will be extremely important.

Fundamental rights will feature prominently in the interpretation of EU immigration measures over the next twenty years.

EU institutions have yet to deliver the rights protections required by the Charter of Fundamental Rights, even for citizens of the EU, let alone for third-country nationals.

Notes

1 This treaty was adopted in 1957, which established the European Economic Community (the name was changed to the European Community in 1993). The treaty was amended in 1987, 1993 and 1999, and was finally replaced in 2009 by the Treaty on the Function of the European Union.

2 See www.europarl.europa.eu/summits/tam_en.htm

3 For an excellent explanation of how the pillar structure worked in this field, see Peers (2006).

4 1. Regulation 1030/2002 on residence permit format (OJ 2002 L 157/1); amended by Reg. 330/2008 (OJ 2008 L 115/1).
2. Regulation 859/2003 on third-country nationals' social security (OJ 2003 L 124/1).
3. Directive 2003/86 on family reunion (OJ 2003 L 251/12); deadline October 2005.
4. Long-term residents Directive 2003/109 (OJ 2004 L 16/44); deadline January 2006.
5. Directive 2004/114 on migration of third-country students, pupils, trainees and volunteers (OJ 2004 L 375/12); deadline 1 December 2007.
6. Directive 2005/71 on admission of researchers (OJ 2005 L 289/15); deadline 10 December 2007.
7. Recommendation on admission of researchers (OJ 2005 L 289/26).
8. Decision on asylum and immigration information exchange (OJ 2006 L 283/40).
9. Decision establishing European integration Fund (OJ 2007 L 168/18).
10. Directive 2009/50 on the conditions of entry and residence of third-country nationals for the purposes of highly qualified employment ('Blue Card' Directive) (OJ 2009 L 155/17).

5 Denmark, Ireland and the UK do not participate in this Directive either.

6 This goal does not appear to have been reached.

7 The Lisbon Process: http://www.eu2005.lu/en/actualites/documents_travail/2005/03/22lisboa/index.html
8 http://register.consilium.europa.eu/pdf/en/10/st05/st05731.en10.pdf
9 1. Directive 2001/40 on mutual recognition of expulsion decisions (OJ 2001 L 149/34); implemented 12 February 2002.
2. Directive 2001/51 on carrier sanctions (OJ 2001 L 187/45); implemented 2 November 2003.
3. Regulation 2424/2001 on funding SIS II (OJ 2001 L 328/4).
4. Decision 2001/886/JHA on funding SIS II (OJ 2001 L 328/1).
5. Framework Decision on trafficking in persons (OJ 2002 L 203/1).
6. Directive and Framework Decision on facilitation of illegal entry and residence (OJ 2002 L 328).
7. Directive 2003/110 on assistance with transit for expulsion by air (OJ 2003 L 321/26).
8. Conclusions on transit via land for expulsion – adopted by Council 22 December 2003.
9. Regulation 378/2004 on procedure for amendments to Sirene manual (OJ 2004 L 64).
10. Regulation 377/2004 on ILO network (OJ 2004 L 64/1).
11. Decision on costs of expulsion (OJ 2004 L 60/55).
12. Directive 2004/81 on residence permits for trafficking victims (OJ 2004 L 261/19).
13. Regulation 871/2004 on new functionalities for SIS (OJ 2004 L 162/29).
14. Directive 2004/82 on transmission of passenger data (OJ 2004 L 261/64).
15. Decision on joint flights for expulsion (OJ 2004 L 261/28).
16. Decision on early warning system (OJ 2005 L 83/48).
17. Regulation 1987/2006 establishing SIS II (OJ 2006 L 381/4).
18. Regulation 1988/2006 on SIS II, amending Reg. 2424/2001 (OJ 2006 L 411/1).
19. Decision on European return programme (OJ 2007 L 144).
20. Directive 2008/115 (Returns Directive) (OJ 2008 L 348/98) – deadline 24 December 2010.
21. Directive 2009/52 on sanctions for employers of irregular migrants (OJ 2009 L168/24).
UK opted in to all except 7, 12, 13, 17, 20, 21.
10 BBC News 14 September 2010, EU Vice President sees red and attacks France on Roma http://www.bbc.co.uk/news/world-europe-11302013
11 Amnesty International, Amnesty Dismayed at Commission's Response to France's Roma Treatment, 20 September 2010.
12 Press Release 20 September 2010 http://www.europarl.europa.eu/en/pressroom/content/20100927IPR83712

References

Acosta Arcarazo, D. (2009), *Latin American Reactions to the Adoption of the Returns Directive*. Brussels: Centre for European Policy Studies.

Amnesty International (2010), *Amnesty Dismayed at Commission's Response to France's Roma Treatment*. www.amnesty.org.uk/news_details.asp?NewsID=19019.

BBC News (2010), *EU Vice President sees red and attacks France on Roma* http://www.bbc.co.uk/news/world-europe-11302013. Accessed 14 September 2010.

Blake, N. and R. Husain (2003), *Immigration, Asylum and Human Rights*. Oxford: Oxford University Press.

Carrera, S. (2009), *In Search of the Perfect Citizen? The Intersection between Integration, Immigration and Nationality in the EU*. Leiden: Martinus Nijhoff.

Carrera S. and M. Merlino (2009), *Undocumented Immigrants and Rights in the EU: Addressing the Gap between Social Science Research and Policy-Making*. Brussels: Centre for European Policy Studies.

Council of Europe Commissioner for Human Rights (2010), *Criminalisation of Migration in Europe: Human Rights Implications*, CommDH/IssuePaper (2010). www.unhcr.org/refworld/docid/4b790fc02.html.

De Burca, G. and J. Weiler (2001), *The European Court of Justice*. Oxford: Oxford University Press.

Directive (2003), Council Directive Concerning the Status of Third-Country Nationals who are Long-Term Residents. 2003/109/EC. Brussels: Council of Europe.

EC (2010), 'The situation of Roma in France and in Europe: Joint information note', by Vice-President Viviane Reding, Commissioner Laszlo Andor and Commissioner Cecilia Malmstrom, 1 September. Brussels: European Commission.

EC (2008), Preparing the next steps in border management in the European Union. COM (2008) 69 final. Brussels: European Commission.

European Parliament (2010), Press Release 30 September. www.europarl.europa.eu/en/pressroom/content/20100927IPR83712.

Guild E., S. Carrera and K. Groenendijk (2009) *Illiberal Liberal States: Immigration, Citizenship and Integration in the EU*. Farnham: Ashgate.

Guild, E. and G. Lesieur (eds) (1997), *The European Court of Justice on the European Convention on Human Rights: Who Said What When*. The Hague: Kluwer Law International.

Groenendijk, K., R. Fernhout, D. Van Dam, R. Van Oers and T. Strik (2007), *The Family Reunification Directive in EU Member States: The First Year of Implementation*. Nijmegen: Wolf Legal Publishers.

Halleskov, L. (2005), 'The Long Term Residents' Directive: A fulfilment of the Tampere objective of near equality?', *European Journal of Migration and Law* 7 (5): 203-211.

Peers S. (2006), *EU Justice and Home Affairs Law*. Oxford: Oxford University Press.

Sikuta, J. and E. Hubalkova (2007), *The European Court of Human Rights: Case Law of the Grand Chamber*. Amsterdam: TMC Asser Press.

Van Oers, R. (2010),'Integration tests in the Netherlands, Germany and the UK', in: R. Van Oers, E. Ersboll and D. Kostakopoulou, *A Re-definition of Belonging? Language and Integration Tests in Europe*. The Hague: Brill.

Van Oers, R., E. Ersboll and D. Kostakopoulou (2010), *A Re-definition of Belonging? Language and Integration Tests in Europe*. The Hague: Brill.

15 The Regulation of Undocumented Migration

Giuseppe Sciortino

Introduction

Most countries have a sizeable population of undocumented foreign residents. The United States alone harbours some 12 million resident foreigners (Passel 2007; Passel and Cohn 2008; Passel and Cohn 2009). Within Western Europe, an estimated 2.6 to 6 million foreign immigrants reside without legal status.[1] Even developed countries that have long enforced strict anti-immigration policies, such as Japan, increasingly acknowledge the existence of an undocumented population of migrants – and the increase in this population over time (Kadokura 2007). In fact, evidence suggests that the current world migratory situation is characterised by the rising significance of undocumented populations in most regions (Hutton and Williamson 2005).

important questions

The presence of a sizeable number of undocumented migrants raises important questions, both scientific and humanitarian. As far as the former are concerned, the existence of a large undocumented population – able to live and work in a country for years, even decades, without an 'official' identity – triggers questions about the very nature of states and societies. Contemporary nation-states have a right, sanctioned by international law, to determine if and under what conditions foreigners may live in their territory (Plender 1998). Furthermore, part and parcel of the regulation of their economies is the regulation of the labour supply through migration restriction (Zolberg 1999). Capacity to control the number of individuals eligible for welfare provisions has been a key precondition for the operation of welfare programmes since they originated (Lucassen 1997; Bommes 2003). The self-understanding of modern states as tied to specific nations implies a political concern about cultural and ethnic heterogeneity (Castles 2004), and control of the composition of the population is considered crucial for state security, both internal and external. Given these state interests, a growing population of undocumented foreign residents would seem to present a challenge to current notions of political statehood and societal membership.

modern state practices

The issues raised by undocumented immigrants become even more apparent when viewed in the context of modern state practices. The current understanding of sovereignty translates into an extensive and historically unprecedented political regulation of access to labour markets, housing, consumer markets and infrastructure for mobility. States have established a successful monopoly over both the means of mobility as well as institutionalised identities (Torpey 1998; Torpey 2000). Moreover, contemporary state operations, with their complex bureaucratic machinery, embody a generalised assumption of the universal legibility of the composition of their population as well as of the social transactions taking place within their territories (Scott 1998). Given this context, policymakers and public opinion alike are inclined to interpret the existence of an undocumented foreign population as an epochal challenge to state sovereignty, as proof of inadequate governance and as an indicator of institutional crisis (Cornelius et al. 1994; Hollifield 1996). Albeit popular, such interpretations do not satisfactorily account for some well-known facts: immigration controls have actually been fairly effective in regulating international mobility (Zolberg 1999); many structural 'pull' factors are woven into the fabric of the receiving societies (Samers 2003); our capabilities to monitor and prevent unwanted migration have in fact increased substantially in recent years (Engbersen and Broders 2009); and domestic legal provisions often allow a politically unwanted migration flow to continue (Joppke 1998).

hardening of exclusion processes?

Critical theorists and humanitarian activists interpret the existence of an undocumented population as evidence of an (equally epochal) hardening of exclusion processes, as proof of the emergence of a new revolutionary class and as a factual betrayal of the inclusive nature of the liberal creed (Carens 1987; Agamben 1998; Hardt and Negri 2000). Undocumented immigrants are defined as a vulnerable – and consequently easily exploitable – segment of workers, forced through legal action to function as a reserve labour army (Portes 1977; De Genova 2007). Morally and politically compelling analyses bring to light the frequent violations of human rights that stem from the lack of a certified identity. As an analytical framework, however, they are at pains to account for significant features of the current migratory situation: the limits to repressive action resulting from legal norms; frequent individual and collective regularisation; tolerance of an extensive philanthropic infrastructure, in some cases even financed by public authorities; and the relative serenity with which many immigrants are able to live undocumented – although at a significant cost – for long periods of time.

The existence of a sizeable undocumented foreign population is an important, yet poorly understood, feature of contemporary economically developed societies.[2] This chapter reviews the current literature on the regulation of undocumented populations. First, the historical evolution of the concept of 'undocumented migrants' is discussed and shown to be strictly linked to and contingent upon changes in systems of internal control within the territory of modern, liberal nation-states. It then looks at the contribution of key features of the immigration regimes in different countries to the complex stratification of their undocumented populations, differentiated by degrees of protection from detection and 'deportability'. The main strategies for dealing with irregular migration available to Western, liberal democratic states are then examined. In addition to endorsing a (usually selective) benign neglect of undocumented immigrants, states may try to increase the costs and risks of irregular residence by tightening access to housing, the labour market and social services. States may also try to remove undocumented foreigners by coercion or voluntary expulsion; or they may make an adjustment of status possible.

The making of 'irregular residence'

no 'irregular' migrants

Contrary to widespread linguistic usage, there are no 'irregular' migrants. The failure to comply with the established procedure in a given country does not subsume the entire personal or migratory experience of an individual. The adjective 'irregular' or 'undocumented' does not belong to the domain of description of migratory trajectories as such, but only to their interactions within a set of regulations enacted by a state. To be an undocumented resident, of course, it is necessary to be physically present within a certain territory. However, it is equally necessary that the sovereign authority of that territory enacts regulations incompatible with the given migratory processes. As matter of fact, irregular migration is a perfect case exemplifying the words of Paul of Tarsus, '*Where there is no law, neither is there violation* (Romans 4: 15). Sovereign states may, with the single stroke of a pen, turn hundreds of thousands of irregular migrants into legal foreign residents, as has occurred so many times in the recent past with the enactment of amnesties. The Eastern enlargement of the European Union has had, among its consequences, the sudden mass conversion of many irregular immigrants into lawful EU citizens. The opposite also holds true: changes in legislation may turn previously regular foreign residents into undocumented immigrants, and even citizens into aliens. Irregularity is consequently first and foremost a juridical status that entails a social relation to a state (De Genova 2002).

history

It is no surprise then that the history of undocumented migration coincides with the history of attempts by states to gain control over the composition of their populations. The notion of an undocumented foreign population – as a set of individuals present in a territory in violation of a set of generalised rules relative to their physical presence within the boundaries of a territory – is fairly new. The spatial mobility of subordinates has always been a political concern for a variety of ruling elites. The history of political power is replete with cases of unwanted, undesired, unexpected or unaccepted population movements. And a whole range and means of physical and symbolic violence has been used, at one time or another, to police the boundary between insiders and outsiders. At the same time, however, the idea that such spatial movements should be considered primarily in terms of their having complied, or failed to comply, with a certain set of generalised, abstract regulations is definitely new. The very idea would have been unthinkable two centuries ago.

Conceptually, the first traces of the notion of an 'illegal migrant' appear in the early nineteenth century. Such references are ambiguous, however, and they are usually conflated with ethnic, religious and class considerations. Irregularity is mentioned as an administrative concern, a theoretical possibility or a trivial nuisance. In what is likely to be the first mention of irregular migration, the author mentions it only to specify that such a phenomenon is difficult to repress, particularly if newcomers are ethnically similar to subjects and if the borders of the country cannot be completely sealed (Von Bosse 1839).

In many countries in the mid-nineteenth century, the policing of spatial mobility and residence was largely linked to considerations of economic and social standing, rather than abstract, legal membership. However, historians have recently revisited the widespread assumption of a golden, *laissez-faire*, liberal regime for migration before 1914. During the nineteenth century, a variety of political authorities enacted a large, and somewhat effective, set of laws, regulations and administrative practices aimed at the surveillance and control of foreigners living in the territories controlled by Western states (Roche 1969; Zolberg 1987; Bocker et al. 1998; Fahrmeir 2000; Fahrmeir et al. 2003; Reinecke 2009). In many cases, by doing so they could rely on a longer tradition of restrictive regulations for vagrants (Lucassen 1997; Zolberg 2003). Many of these regulations introduced the possibility of deporting the foreigner who did not comply with the established guidelines, thus initiating a process of differentiation between lawful and unlawful foreign residents. Those measures, however, were clearly targeted towards specific segments of the foreign population defined quite explicitly on occupational, political, ethnic, racial and religious grounds, and were often remarkably similar to the measures adopted to police the country-born *classes dangereuses*.

migration changed

These forms of migration control were deeply changed, however, by a complex set of long-term structural processes: industrialisation, the development of contemporary statehood, the nationalisation of the working classes, the build-up of geopolitical pressures, the rising welfare state and the very same dimension of human mobility triggered by economic development. The combination of these processes unleashed the systematic intervention of Western states concerning the composition of their populations. By the 1920s, all Western European states – and most European offshoots – had created a systematic legal and administrative apparatus able to distinguish between citizens and foreigners and, within the latter category, between lawful and unlawful residents. The basic juridical sanctions against migrants today are consequently less than a century old (Plender 1972; Plender 1998; Ngai 2004).[3]

The establishment of a juridical framework does not automatically imply its social significance. Even after the 1920s, many phases of migration have been characterised by limited policy attention to issues of legal status. For example, during the high labour demand linked to European recovery after World War II, irregularity was not a major concern for policymakers. The main goals of immigration policy at that time were to recruit an adequate number of workers while effectively policing the boundaries between citizens and 'guests'. The undocumented population was primarily composed of workers migrating outside the official recruitment channels and through inactive family members engaged in *de facto* family reunification. The regulations against undocumented residence were considered simply a useful tool to police the foreign workforce and assure its subordination. Irregularity was often considered a transitional phase in the path of migrants, who could easily adjust their status when there was an employer willing to hire them. There is even evidence that some irregular flows, such as the Portugese in post-1962 France, were actually welcomed as an alternative to legal – but unwanted – flows from elsewhere (Marie 1988; Hollifield 1992; Tapinos 2000b). Expulsion, albeit a generalised formal sanction for irregularity, was for the most part only used as a selective measure to deal with foreign misfits and troublemakers (Gordon 2003; Diaz 2004). In the post-war period, and well into the late 1960s, Western European states actively promoted a set of binding international agreements restricting the use of collective expulsions (Henckaerts 1995).

roots of current policy

The current configuration of immigration policy has its roots in the adoption of a restrictive attitude toward labour migration in the mid-1970s (Bade 2000).[4] One of the most fateful decisions of the period was to make access to the labour market contingent upon the previous enjoyment of a lawful title of entry and residence. Subsequently, lawful residence has become a legal and factual pre-condition for accessing a wide variety of crucial social institutions.

In a first phase following the adoption of stop policies, European governments were primarily concerned with the prevention of further arrivals, while the undocumented residents already present in the territory could enjoy a certain degree of tolerance (Engbersen and Van der Leun 2001). The existence of many loopholes in the administrative infrastructure created incentives for semi-compliance, with undocumented residents being able to access legal employment or vice-versa. In recent decades, most of these loopholes have progressively closed – largely in order to prevent the use of welfare services – thus reducing the European space for semi-compliance.

closing of loopholes

The current migratory situation is characterised by the mismatch between a small supply of legal entry slots, the relative autonomy of existing migratory networks and a sizeable demand for foreign labour in agriculture, construction and household services. The result has been the emergence of a mosaic of undocumented populations, able to adapt to local conditions through the development of specific survival strategies and reliance on extended informal structures. In the last few decades, undocumented status has shifted from being an initial nuisance to being a long-term stigma. Such developments should not, however, be taken simply as the outcome of some kind of Foucauldian power or knowledge complex. The current significance of an undocumented status is also the consequence of the introduction of largely liberal measures in favour of foreign-born legal residents. Since the mid-1970s, immigrants across Europe (and to a certain degree, in the United States) have been able to acquire a wide set of residence-based rights – ranging from access to welfare to family reunification – often against the will of governments. As a result, the gap in entitlements and provisions between legal and undocumented immigrants today is more pronounced. In many ways, it is wider than the one between citizens and foreigners. In other words, legal status makes a tremendous difference in contemporary immigrant trajectories precisely because legal, documented residents have access to a large set of rights and protections.

The hardening of the distinction between legal and illegal residence is a major trend in the current immigration policies of Western states. At the same time, contemporary systems of immigration control in Western liberal democracies are more pervasive in scope, but less biased in their operations. Earlier forms of monitoring resident foreign-born populations were explicitly designed according to religious, racial or ethnic criteria. In post-war Europe, religious and ethnic criteria were often implicitly designed to shape the settlements of immigrants, often overriding the distinction between regular and irregular (Tapinos 2000a; Ohliger et al. 2003). Today, while xenophobia may still drive the enactment of specific measures against undocumented migration, policies must be formulated in strictly universal and functional terms. Universal criteria are also stable features in the frequent judicial reviews of these measures.[5] While often empirically intertwined with other factors, legal status has become a fully differentiated dimension of inequality in the social stratification of the foreign population.

The social stratification of the undocumented foreign population

binary distinction

As we have seen, the primary basis for regulating foreign populations takes the form of a generalised binary distinction between lawful and unlawful residents. In legal terms, such a binary code is well defined and increasingly similar across liberal democratic countries (Plender 1998). In its everyday workings, however, similar formal policies can produce very different outcomes when applied to different contexts and categories. Even within each country, the purity of a binary code results in a complex stratification of statuses, each having different consequences. To assess the social meaning of similar norms across various contexts, it is important to keep in mind three general factors that sharply differentiate experiences in specific locales.

The first regards the capacity to detect undocumented migrants, which is largely contingent upon the general capacity of individual states to monitor and constrain social transactions within their territories. As a consequence, to be undocumented in a country that has no policy of compulsory identification is different from being undocumented in a country that requires proof of identification for a large variety of transactions; to be undocumented in a country where there are frequent identity checks carried out by state officials differs from being undocumented in places where this is rare.

embedded liberalism

A second general factor is the degree to which states self-constrain in repressing undocumented migration. All democratic states embrace in some fashion what scholars call 'embedded liberalism': a set of norms – both international and domestic – that limits the range of actions they may pursue (Hollifield 2000), even if its strength may vary considerably. The frequency and severity of judicial reviews of governmental decisions may make a large difference for the undocumented population. Moreover, 'embedded liberalism' restrains states not only from assuming certain norms, but also from adopting certain practices. For example, no Western European state has ever created a website through which anybody may anonymously report a foreigner suspected of being undocumented, as has been done in Japan, without significant controversy.

Finally, the analysis of policies designed to regulate the undocumented population must take into account the effective capacity of states to implement their policies. To claim the right to monitor specific social transactions is not equivalent to being able to do so. Modern Western states are characterised by a high variance in the efficiency of their administrative infrastructure, the ability to sustain action over a span of time and their capacity to overcome resistance and inertia. This explains why it is often possible to find large undocumented populations in states where a large number of transactions are supposedly monitored and the sanctions for undocumented residence are, in formal terms, quite high.

The combination of these factors produces a hierarchy of irregularity, with each stratum defined by a different degree of normative or factual protection from the monitoring and repressive capacity of states. At the top of this hierarchy there are those strata of migrants that are protected, partly or totally, from the repressive action of states by the constitutional and international rules that these very same states have introduced or accepted (Joppke 1999; Hollifield 2006). This is the case for asylum seekers that, according to the Geneva Convention, may not be held responsible for a clandestine entry, even by states that consider it a crime. The flows of asylum seekers, who were the primary target of the alleged 'control crisis' of the early 1990s in Europe (Cornelius et al. 1994), were dramatically curtailed by restrictive reforms later in the decade. Still, the number of asylum seekers is sizeable, and many file their applications when already in the territory, after having been in the country for an unknown length of time. As part of a remedial strategy, it is not unusual that the application is filed only after enforcement officers have located the migrant. Similar considerations apply to migrants deserving humanitarian protection or who are shelved from coactive deportation by the *non-refoulement clause* of the Geneva Convention or by other constitutional provisions. All of these norms are often interpreted very restrictively. Yet figures reveal that in Western Europe there are a sizeable number of migrants living under various forms of humanitarian protection who are effectively protected from deportation.

organisational reality

A different, and lower, stratum of irregular migrants relies on the mundane organisational reality of states. As organisations, states have procedural difficulties, pragmatic weaknesses and outright inefficiencies. Some administrative infrastructures are more effective than others, but they all operate through triage, postponement and issue avoidance. Visa overstayers and working tourists continue to operate, thanks to the fact that Western European states are considerably better at monitoring their borders than their labour markets. In this same vein, there is a stratum of migrants that has a legal identity due to the rarity of substantial controls. In this category are migrants married to people they hardly know, workers directly paying retirement contributions for fictional employment contracts, self-employed migrants declaring income higher than actual in order to meet the conditions for family-reunification and newly-arrived migrants using the documentation of legal migrants that have returned home or moved to a third country.[6] Last but not least, there exists a stratum of undocumented residents that is easy to identify but difficult to deport, a well-known situation among Western police forces. As elaborated elsewhere in this chapter, these are irregular migrants whose deportation would involve costs deemed too high in financial, diplomatic or organisational terms.

low capital

At the bottom of the irregular hierarchy, there are those migrants who have low human, social and/or economic capital. These are migrants who move to a country where they cannot rely on kinship members, have little updated information, possess a few weak contacts and cannot afford reliable brokers, relying on philanthropic institutions and random encounters for their survival. It is a comparatively small segment, but a highly visible one (Diminescu 2003). They comprise the bulk of irregular migrants identified during clandestine border crossings, appear frequently in the news and are highly over-represented among the migrants that are deported. Because they depend largely on the philanthropic infrastructure, such migrants are also easier to contact, and thus are over-represented among informants for qualitative research as well as interviewees for social reporting. In sum, the existence of a hierarchy of irregularity represents a primary reason for the complexities and difficulties of any state policy targeted at regulating the undocumented population.

Managing the undocumented population

efforts towards prevention

Since the mid-1970s, Western states have exercised considerable effort to target and prevent new influxes of irregular migrants. The introduction of visa requirements, the strengthening of border controls, the increasing repression of smugglers and the introduction of carriers' sanctions are the most common policies pursued both in Europe and in North America to discourage the inflows of new undocumented immigrants (Andreas and Snyder 2000; Sciortino 2000; Massey et al. 2002). These policies may be analytically distinguished from policies directed against undocumented residence, as the conditions of *migrants* and *immigrants* are quite different. They are also often empirically distinguishable, since states may pursue a strong reform of external controls without paying particular attention to the undocumented population already within their borders. This has been documented, for example, in the Netherlands and the United Kingdom in the decade following the cessation of immigration recruitment (Jordan and Duvell 2002; Van der Leun 2003).[7] The same has been argued in the United States, where the increasingly militaristic tenor of border controls since the 1980s has been matched by the difficulties in implementing any systematic reform of internal controls (Massey et al. 2002).

strengthening of controls

Over the medium term, however, the strengthening of border controls has had an important consequence for those already within the receiving country (or who have at least succeeded in entering it). The strengthening of controls implies more difficulty in crossing the border and a steep increase in the costs of mobility. As a result, it alters the irregular migration process: once entered, migrants tend to avoid making trips back home. The increased cost of entry, moreover, leads to longer stays in the receiving country (to repay a broker or 'coyote', for example), and is a major incentive to stay in the country, even during downturns.[8] States consequently deal with a perhaps smaller, but surely more stable, undocumented population. And its existence mounts in significance, often interpreted as a magnet for prospective migrants willing to challenge the border controls. Further, the strengthening of external controls must be justified by a particular rhetorical emphasis on the dangers of undocumented migration. Even if initially used to support the introduction of tighter border controls, it is easily appropriated by critics of undocumented migration. Thus, strengthening the border fosters an analogous strengthening of the policies against undocumented residence. However, while strengthening border controls is a relatively uncontroversial act, policies against undocumented residence may strike the delicate nerves of contemporary societies. In the framework of liberal democratic states, regulation of the undocumented may be pursued in three ways: states may progressively raise the costs and risks associated with the condition, thus producing an incentive to leave the country, as well as a disincentive to further arrivals; they may employ more directly repressive methods, evicting irregular residents through expulsion; or they may surrender to their presence and promote a change of status.

Policies aimed at making undocumented residence difficult and costly

making life as irregulars more difficult

The fact that irregularity is a juridical status does not imply that the factual consequences of such status may be derived directly from its normative prescriptions. In modern societies, there are structural limits to the possibility of turning specific statuses into total identities; the legal status of the foreigner is usually only one status among many. The state-asserted relevance of such status for all social transactions is often challenged (and more often, quietly defied). An immigrant's legal status is only relevant when and if the legal reality creates a constraint over the relationships and actions of the actor, and affects the degree to which it does so (Coutin 2000). The social significance of a lawful residency status depends on the type of social transaction in question. While it is generally very low in daily interaction and for many types of consumer actions, it is quite significant for accessing many utilities and services, and highly constraining in the case of political rights and access to the means of international movement. In general, it becomes increasingly significant the more a transaction must be institutionally recognised. Being undocumented is nearly always irrelevant for falling in love, but it has many implications for the wedding ceremony.

empirical relevance

In other words, irregular status never produces total exclusion. If state control over social transactions were wholly pervasive, there would be no undocumented migration worth speaking of. Fascinating as it may appear to critical theorists, any attempt to describe irregular migrants in terms of *homo sacer* (Agamben 1998) is utterly void of any empirical relevance. As empirical research has shown, irregular migrants are able, albeit at a high human cost, to generate income through work, find places to sleep, fall in love, reproduce and raise children, establish personal relationships, buy household appliances and even represent themselves in the public space (Cvajner 2008). In some cases, avoiding detection implies a strong dose of intra-mundane asceticism, as when undocumented migrants renounce participating in important life-spheres in order to minimise risks of detection. This is the case, for example, of maids willing to spend their free time in the flat of the employers rather than risking venturing outside. In other cases, it requires participation in informal markets that translate variations in controls into variation of prices. It nearly always fosters a set of personal relationships regulated by social and cultural, rather than juridical, norms. When crises occur, undocumented migrants access services legitimated in terms of values higher than law compliance, such as those provided by churches and philanthropic institutions. In some cases, the survival strategy of undocumented migrants also requires the capacity to access alternative enforcement agencies such as strong men or criminal cliques (Alt 2003; Van der Leun 2003; Sciortino 2004). In short, undocumented populations need to balance the exclusion from state-monitored areas of social life with an intense recourse to social capital.

state policies

Unsurprisingly, a large number of the policies against undocumented residence are designed to increase the likelihood of detection and to make accessing informal institutions difficult. States may increase the quantity and quality of identity controls in public spaces, thus increasing the chances of detecting undocumented residents. In states with compulsory identity papers, such programmes often do not raise critical legal issues. There are, however, limits to the use of identity checks. If applied to the whole population, the intensification of identity checks is highly expensive and disruptive of existing patterns of social organisation. Extensive identity checks create delays and nuisances for a variety of social endeavours (Brochmann and Hammar 1999). If applied selectively, the burden of such controls falls disproportionately on legal foreign residents, thus triggering charges of ethnic or racial profiling. Identity checks also become ineffective over time. Each strengthening decision is quickly followed by processes of social learning by undocumented migrants that reduce the number of undocumented residents identified in the future. Another obstacle to systematic identity checks stems from the fact that once identified, the undocumented resident must be processed for expulsion (par 3.2). A sharp increase in the number of potential deportees can lead quickly to a serious bottleneck in detention and expulsion facilities that are inadequate for processing large volumes of people.

More sophisticated strategies involve the introduction of punitive measures aimed at discouraging undocumented settlement through denial of access to formal services as well as the discouragement of informal service providers. The first approach restricts access to key formal services, building internal walls around the welfare state. The second makes access to alternative service structures more expensive, more risky and filled with unpleasant consequences. For example, over the last few decades, many states have introduced reforms that require proof of lawful residence for accessing a variety of services and/or conducting important transactions.

access to welfare services

There has been a particular emphasis on making undocumented migrants' access to most welfare services either difficult or outright impossible. Procedural and budgetary reforms have contributed in many ways to increasing the monitoring of any claim to welfare resources (Engbersen 2003). A common tendency in the various waves of welfare reform has been the increasingly systematic attention to conditions of eligibility, explicitly linking the need for more formalised processes to the case of undocumented residents (Sainsbury 2006). Other procedural reforms have tied access to the labour market more strictly to lawful residence status, thus reducing the areas of semi-compliance.[9] Changes have also occurred in states that are traditionally suspicious of any large-scale identification system. Administratively, archives have been linked in ways that make inconsistencies in documentation quickly and easily identifiable.[10] Where deemed necessary, important measures have been taken to strengthen the state monopoly over the means of personal identification: although the proposal of a federal *REAL ID Act* has encountered much resistance, many US states have revised their legislation, making it difficult or impossible for undocumented migrants to obtain a driving licence, a document both extremely useful and very often used as a proof of identity (Johnson 2005).

In parallel, many states have enacted legislative reforms that make informal transactions involving undocumented residents more risky for all involved. Penalties for renting flats to undocumented immigrants have been introduced or raised. The severity of employment sanctions has steeply increased, although often more in theory than in practice (Martin and Miller 2000; Batog 2006; International Labour Office 2009). Middlemen brokers face stronger sanctions for the informal mediation of labour. There have also been attempts, albeit unsuccessful, to reduce the autonomy of the philanthropic infrastructure, introducing penalties for those who provide services to undocumented immigrants for moral, rather than profit, reasons (Council of the European Union 2000).

denial of access

As a whole, the increase in identity checks, the denial of access to public services and the creation of disincentives for informal providers are three ways through which states try to make undocumented residence more difficult and less rewarding. Through these measures, the prospect of a protracted spell of undocumented residence is less appealing to prospective immigrants and more threatening to those who have already arrived. In particular, employer sanctions are considered by many analysts as the cornerstone of any effective policy against undocumented residence: without the possibility of earning an income in the receiving society, the whole migratory project of a large majority of undocumented residents would crumble (Baganha 1998; Reyneri 1998).

The actual impacts of policies targeted to raise the costs of undocumented residence have not yet been evaluated in rigorous, comparative ways. When rigorously pursued for a certain period of time, it is likely that they have an impact on reducing the incorporation of undocumented migrants and surely play a role in reducing the volume of the undocumented population, as existing networks become more selective in activating new arrivals (Cvajner and Sciortino 2010). It may also be argued that the development of information technologies leads to a degree of control previously unachievable (Broeders 2009).

social limits

At the same time, however, there is evidence of structural social limits to the intensity of internal controls (Van der Leun 2003). In addition to the fact that the detection of undocumented residents as such is rarely a top priority for enforcement officials, the intensification of internal controls is heavily dependent on the previous history of state-making. For example, in countries where a significant percentage of the GDP is produced by the informal economy, as in Southern and Eastern Europe, an effective programme of employment sanctions implies a considerable, and conflict-ridden, revolution both in attitudes and practices. A strong tradition of concerns regarding privacy may also create a significant limit to the implementation of internal controls. Specific universal professional subcultures within welfare services are also significant limits to the transparency required by control strategies. Eventually, many migratory flows are able to subvert the structure of internal controls as a blueprint and utilise them functionally: where internal controls are strong and centred on identity-checks, irregular circular migration of 'working tourists' may still result in a massive – but largely undetectable – phenomenon (Irek 1994; Morokvasic 1994; Morawska 2001). The main impact of the strengthening of internal controls is thus likely to produce a restrictive management of the undocumented resident population, both in terms of size and degree of incorporation. At the same time, it implies the consolidation of a twilight zone, marked by a more systematic estrangement from the main institutions of the receiving society (Engbersen 2001). The study of the actual impact of internal controls, and of the survival strategies enacted by undocumented residents, is an area where empirical research is particularly needed.

The re-alignment of physical and legal presence

physical and legal alignment

When a modern state deals with undocumented residents, there is a strong assumption that it is best to restore the alignment between physical and legal presence, through the return of the undocumented resident to his or her country of citizenship. The right of a state to expel aliens from its territory has been recognised for centuries (Cockburn 1869), just as it has been the duty of each sending country to re-admit its own citizens (Pastore 1998). Expulsion, moreover, is among the oldest tools of immigration control, used over the last two centuries for a variety of purposes (Caestecker 2003; Reinecke 2009). Since the immigration slowdown of the mid-1970s, both nation-state governments and European institutions have stressed the importance of reforming expulsion legislation and procedures to make them more effective. Such improvements are also the goal of a growing number of international agreements, involving both the sending and the transit countries. Notwithstanding, there is little doubt that expulsion policies are nearly always considered deeply unsatisfactory by both policy-makers and public opinion. After several waves of reforms, European expulsion policies are still characterised by high legal complexity and uncertain implementation (Nascimbene 2002). The difficulty in using expulsion measures to reduce the size of the undocumented population applies to both voluntary and coercive measures.

voluntary or assisted return

One type of expulsion programme that is meant to reduce the size of the undocumented population has been implemented in the last few decades under the term 'voluntary' or 'assisted' return. These programmes are rarely completely voluntary, as the threat of deportation is always present in the background. But they usually underplay the coercive aspects of expulsion, providing instead some kind of incentive – usually a mix of monetary payment and resettlement aid in the home country – to various categories of 'unwanted' migrants in exchange for leaving the country. Programmes of voluntary return usually do not raise the humanitarian concerns endemic in forced repatriation. They do not require strong collaboration between the transit and sending countries, and given the cooperation of the returning foreigners, they rarely present a particular bureaucratic problem. Unsurprisingly, the idea of assisted return has always been popular. The creation of monetary incentives for a foreigner to leave a given country is a solution that had already been used by some European states in the second half of the nineteenth century (Leenders 1995). Programmes of mass 'voluntary' repatriation have also been implemented with some degree of success for certain categories of unwanted migrants, as in some US programmes for Filipinos in the 1920s and 1930s (Ngai 2004). Similar programmes have also been adopted by some European states for former guest-workers in the aftermath of the oil shock in the 1970s (Hollifield 1996) and for refugees of the Balkans wars after their conclusion (Black and Koser 1999). When applied to contemporary undocumented residents, however, these programmes are often ineffective: the amount of the incentive is rarely judged by immigrants as being anywhere close to what they might expect (or hope) to gain by remaining in the country. Very often, the amount doesn't even cover the expenses already incurred from entering the country. In fact, as the tightening of immigration controls implies a steep increase in the cost of migration, the gap between expected and stipulated incentives grows wider,[11] and many assisted return programmes consequently fail to become popular. Others end up being used by immigrants who would have left the country anyway.

forced expulsions

When programmes of assisted return demonstrate their weaknesses, a frequent reaction is to call for a more systematic use of forced repatriation, an option legally available to states under international law (Plender 1998). Even forced expulsions, however, are difficult to implement. As a matter of fact, in all Western countries, the number of aliens actually removed is a tiny fraction of the estimated undocumented population. Even more troubling for policymakers is the fact that a large number of the undocumented that are apprehended do not leave the country – states are remarkably ineffective in making them do so.[12] At the individual level, the threat of being expelled is usually a constant existential stress, shaping a large part of the survival strategies of undocumented residents (De Genova 2002) . At the collective level, however, expulsions do not seem to produce a significant effect as a generalised tool of control over undocumented populations.

One primary factor that contributes to such an outcome is the strength of embedded liberalism present in Western states. Although expulsion is claimed to be an absolute, purely Westphalian, attribute of sovereignty, it is in fact seriously constrained by both international and domestic laws (Plender 1998). In particular, Western states are banned from operating mass expulsions; they are bound to offer individual judicial review of cases. Several other international and constitutional norms closely circumscribe the use of expulsion as a migration control mechanism. While mass expulsion has been used several times as a tool of immigration control in the last fifty years, it has never occurred in Western, democratic countries (Henckaerts 1995). A closely-related reason for this is that carrying out expulsions (within the established liberal regulations) incurs a notable cost in terms of organisational and economic resources. After being detected, the undocumented migrant must be detained, administrative checks must be performed, papers in two (or more) languages must be processed, consular authorities must be contacted, aeroplane tickets must be purchased, and so on. It is often necessary to wait for a judicial review of the case and, in some cases, enforcement officials are required to accompany the deportee to the final destination. In many cases, cooperation from authorities in the sending country cannot be taken for granted; in others, the procedure requires more time than expected; and in still others, key documents are missing. In all these cases, the cost of expulsion skyrockets, the chances of a successful expulsion decrease and the immigrants often end up being released into the state again (Sciortino 2000).

level of resistance

A third factor in explaining the difficulty of carrying out expulsions is the level of resistance by immigrants once they are selected for expulsion. Immigrants who are to be deported have nothing to lose, and they often behave accordingly. In some cases, undocumented migrants may go to court to fight the expulsion or they may apply for political asylum or humanitarian protection. Asylum seeking often begins only after detection, sometimes after a considerable period of illegal residence (Finotelli 2007). Other forms of resistance include the destruction of identity papers or the adoption of false nationalities. As any expulsion requires a certified identity, those who succeed in avoiding identification or are able to muddy the waters with multiple identities have a higher chance of avoiding deportation. In any legal system where there is a limit to the length of detention, unidentifiable residents may avoid repatriation simply by spending enough time in detention. A third category of resistance techniques is rooted in the complexity of the practical transportation of a deportee. Expellees may oppose their removal physically, through rioting, violence or self-destructive behaviour. In certain cases, these techniques may be effective, as documented by the many cases in which aeroplane pilots refused to take off owing to the resistance of one or more deportees. Collectively, the frequency of such acts of resistance precipitates a major increase in surveillance, thus further driving up the cost and difficulty of expulsion.

The above-mentioned difficulties do not necessarily imply that expulsion policies are useless or self-defeating. On the contrary, the evolution of immigration policies over the last decades seems to point to a gradual institutional development as well as a learning process by policymakers and enforcement officials (Nascimbene 2002). At the state level, various reforms have streamlined the expulsion process and reduced the delays implicit in the judicial review of the decision. Many countries have introduced sanctions for undocumented residents who defy expulsion orders, thus making subsequent detections longer and even less appealing. The European Commission has invested significant effort, both in coordinating the existing policies and in designing databases that should be able to provide biometric information useful for identification purposes. Diplomatic cooperation has sometimes been secured through an increasing number of re-admission agreements. While it is true that immigrants have reacted to these changes by developing many counter-strategies, it is also true that in this cat-and-mouse game the costs are suffered disproportionately by undocumented immigrants (Broeders and Engbersen 2007; Broeders 2009).

excessive expectations

The problem here is not so much with the actual effectiveness of expulsion policies, but rather with the exceedingly high expectations projected onto them. While recent reforms may have increased the effectiveness of expulsion as a specific measure targeted to specific cases, actual experiences also reveal that the conception of expulsion as a generalised tool for immigration control remains highly unrealistic.

Regularisations and adjustment of status

Expelling undocumented residents is a way to re-align physical and legal presence materially, through the exclusion of the undocumented resident from the territory of a polity. The same goal, however, may be achieved by transforming an undocumented resident into a lawful one. As irregular or 'illegal' status is the product of an interaction between certain migratory trajectories and the regulations enacted by the state, the latter may re-align or 'adjust' actual and legal populations through a change in regulations. States may introduce new conditions for attaining a legal resident status: a certain term of residency within the country or presence in the country on a certain day. If these are the only conditions, the adjustment of status is produced through a general amnesty, which converts a given fact – actual presence – into grounds for activating a new legal status. In many more cases, being already in the territory is only one among the prerequisites for regularisation, such as the existence of relatives lawfully residing in the country or an employer willing to lawfully hire the irregular resident. Other common grounds for adjustment of status are humanitarian, as when the state considers a severe medical condition or time spent within a previous toleration or temporary protection programme. Such adjustments of status may be acquired in many ways, with the large-scale mass amnesties that were enacted recently by Southern European states being only one of them (De Bruycker 2000; Barbagli et al. 2004; Levinson 2005).

regularisation measures

It is first important to distinguish between *dejure* and *defacto* regularisation measures. In reality, many undocumented migrants adjust their legal status through channels not intended by policymakers to produce such an outcome. For a good deal of the last quarter of the twentieth century, a sizeable number of undocumented migrants succeeded in adjusting their status through asylum procedures or other programmes of humanitarian protection. Some claim that in Germany the asylum process has long been the functional equivalent of the Southern European mass amnesties (Finotelli 2007). Where an active labour immigration policy exists, undocumented residents may try to become regularised by going through the procedure as if they were still abroad (Sciortino 2009). A large number of undocumented migrants in Western Europe have automatically acquired legal status through foreign policy actions linked to the Eastern enlargement of the European Union. Still others acquire legal residence through a variety of informal channels, including bribery, lobbying or administrative loopholes.

As far as *de jure* regularisation programmes are concerned, the main distinction is between programmes that promote either individual or collective regularisation. In many Western states, there are long-term programmes or legislative provisions allowing some undocumented residents to apply individually for an adjustment of status. Before the immigration slowdown of the mid-1970s, a large number of irregular migrants had adjusted their status simply by showing proof of an employer willing to hire them (OECD 1990), and a key immigration reform of that period was intended precisely to stop such practices

(Brochman and Hammar 1999). Even today, however, there are conditions in which states acknowledge the possibility of an individual adjustment of status, such as an extraordinary period of irregular residence (*fait accompli*) or marrying a citizen.[13] These programmes usually deal with a relatively small number of cases and operate in low-visibility conditions.[14] They are designed for cases that, for legal or practical reasons, would raise serious problems if treated otherwise. In other cases, regularisations are defined as a one-time affair: undocumented residents meeting specific conditions must apply for regularisation by a certain deadline. The current research on mass-regularisation programmes has focused primarily on three issues: the diffusion of the practice, the reasons for which states enact regularisation programmes and the consequences of these programmes for the migratory situation of the regularising state.

mass regularisation

For a long time, there has been a tendency to see mass regularisation as a Mediterranean peculiarity, linked both to their inexperience with immigration policy-making and their supposedly 'cultural' tolerance for illegality. More recent research, however, has clearly shown that this practice is hardly a Mediterranean specialty (Baldwin-Edwards and Kraler 2009). Such measures have been enacted in Europe by France, Belgium and the United Kingdom in recent decades, as well as by the United States (in 1986) and other developed countries (Levinson 2005). Other forms of adjustment of status, mostly grounded in humanitarian considerations, also exist in countries that strongly oppose the notion of regularisation for undocumented residents (Blaschke 2008). Adjustment of status is consequently a much more widespread practice than is generally assumed.

Why do governments enact mass regularisation programmes? They are, after all, highly visible and controversial. As undocumented migrants emerge from the shadows and rush out into the open, governments must admit the relative failure of previous immigration controls, and political adversaries claim that the government rewards law-breakers and encourages further unauthorised immigration. As regularised immigrants obtain access to welfare benefits and the right to family reunification, mass regularisations have serious consequences both for the state budget and for the migration regime.[15] Why then do states regularise undocumented migrants? Unfortunately, there are few empirical studies of the political processes through which regularisation programmes are enacted (Zolberg 1990; Colombo and Sciortino 2004). Policymakers usually provide three main categories of justification: humanitarian, economic and functional (for strengthening future controls). Programmes for the adjustment of status are deemed necessary to put an end to the social exclusion and marginality that characterises the undocumented population; they are deemed useful in reducing the negative fiscal and economic consequences of the large presence of workers in the shadow economy who are not paying taxes and making statutory contributions; and they are necessary to wipe the slate clean, so that improved measures of immigration controls may be applied effectively to smaller groups of newcomers. All these reasons are strictly linked to a general structural consideration: the settlement of a sizeable population of undocumented migrants, together with the social infrastructure necessary for their survival as undocumented, represents a major stumbling block for the expectation of 'legibility' that is at the core of everyday activities in contemporary states. A sizeable settled, but undocumented, population implies, moreover, a significant presence in the labour market of the receiving society as well as the establishment of social ties. This means that the undocumented population is both too large and too entrenched within the social fabric to be removed coactively. Regularisation in these cases plays a crucial role in regaining a modicum of transparency in social transactions.

consequences of regularisation

The consequences of regularisation remain inadequately explored. Some argue that regularised immigrants often revert to irregular status, due to the difficulties of maintaining proof of a legitimate income. Italian and Spanish studies, however, have documented convincingly that very few regularised immigrants actually relapse into undocumented status. At least in those countries where regularisation has been a functional equivalent to labour migration policy, the main effect of amnesties has been a stable insertion into the legal workforce (Carfagna 2002). A second claim is that regularisation programmes produce an incentive to further irregular arrivals, in the expectation that further channels of regularisation will follow. The evidence available does not allow for making firm conclusions on this point. On one hand, the strength of irregular migration in certain countries, like the United States, seems to point to the fact that the expectation of a quick regularisation is not necessarily a key factor in triggering large-scale migratory flows (Massey et al. 2002). On the other hand, fieldwork in Southern European countries has documented that recurring regularisations produce a widespread expectation, embedded in many migratory networks, that undocumented residence is a low-cost option, and just a matter of being patient and 'waiting for the papers' (Cvajner and Sciortino 2010). It is likely that the consequences of regularisation programmes are contingent upon factors within the entire migration policy package. To effectively reduce the size of an undocumented population, it is necessary for an amnesty to be accompanied by an effective active labour migration policy or by an equally tight set of measures that sanction informal employment and informal residence (Rijpma and Pastore 2009).

Conclusion

Today, virtually all developed states have undocumented foreign populations living within their territorial boundaries. Such a population is produced by a mismatch between a limited supply of legal entry slots in receiving states and a growing demand for admission, empowered by the relative autonomy of immigrant networks and the demand for foreign labour in the economy of the receiving country. Such populations are increasingly defined in terms of a specific yet broadly conceived legal perspective, and are differentiated not only from the country's citizens but also from legal foreign residents.

For various reasons, contemporary democratic states must tolerate a certain proportion of undocumented residents. Their existence highlights the limits of immigration control measures. It thus raises questions concerning the nature of contemporary states and their relationships with other social spheres. Democratic states today use three main strategies to regulate undocumented migrant populations: they may endeavour to make irregular entry and residence more difficult and less profitable; they may evict irregular residents through expulsion; and they may promote an adjustment of status to bring such a population – or a segment of it – within the bounds of official life. All three strategies speak against the adequacy of the two dominant, polarised interpretations currently available: 'the unredeemable crisis of state power' and the notion of 'Europe as an almighty fortress'. Regulation of undocumented populations shows a trend towards a restrictive stance. At the same time, a variety of structural constraints makes it difficult to conceive of a Western liberal democracy without a sizeable undocumented population. Learning to live with that, and to walk the fine line between unreasonable repression and unreasonable tolerance, is one of the most complex and least studied tasks of immigration policy.

MAIN IDEAS

Virtually all developed states must deal with undocumented foreign populations living within their territorial boundaries.

An undocumented population is the result of a mismatch between a limited supply of legal entry slots in receiving states and a growing demand for admission.

The granting of a wide set of rights to regular foreign residents has implied an increasing significance of legal status in the life of immigrants.

The existence of a sizeable segment of undocumented residents highlights the limits of immigration control measures and raises questions concerning the nature of contemporary states and the state's relationship with other social spheres.

There are two dominant polarised interpretations of the situation regarding undocumented populations: 'the unredeemable crisis of state power' and the notion of 'Europe as an almighty fortress'. Both have proven to be inadequate.

A variety of structural constraints makes it difficult to conceive of a Western liberal democracy without a sizeable undocumented population.

Notes

1 See the results of the clandestino project: http://clandestino.eliamep.gr/.

2 It can also be stressed that undocumented immigration seems to be, from the point of view of states, much more important than undocumented migration. While states usually give high emphasis to border controls, the often-lenient treatment of transit migrants is convincing proof that such emphasis is linked to their role in preventing the settlement of unwanted immigrants. It is consequently unfortunate that most research, owing to the funding opportunity structure, is focused nearly exclusively on irregular migration rather than irregular residency (Black 2003; Sciortino 2004).

3 Among historians, there is still disagreement concerning whether the first systematic use of the concept was made in the Soviet Far East in the 1920s (with reference to Korean and Chinese migrants) or in 1930s Palestine (with reference to Jewish migration). Some even claim that the identification of the first instance of a full-fledged state policy systematically targeted to categorise a large number of residents as 'illegal residents' and to contain and reduce their size did not occur until US policies against Mexican immigration were created in the1950s.

4 At the time, experts estimated the undocumented population in Western Europe to be approximately half a million people (CCMW 1974).

5 Contemporary policies against undocumented migration seem consequently to operate in line with the general de-ethnicisation trend identified in other dimensions of immigration policy (Joppke 2003; Joppke 2005).

6 Many undocumented migrants are in fact not undocumented at all. In many cases, they use forged documents or identity substitution (Vasta 2006). In the United States, many undocumented migrants actually pay income taxes and contribute to social security, through the use of fraudulent social security numbers.

7 Similar claims have been advanced more recently for France (Belorgey 2008).

8 In the United States, it is estimated that policies enacted in the 1980s along the Mexican-US border have effectively halved the number of undocumented migrants returning to Mexico within a year of their entry (Massey et al. 2002). In Western Europe, the development of irregular 'pendel' migration has been registered only in flows that could rely on liberal tourist visa policies, while in all the other cases irregular entry has been followed by a lengthening of the period of residence (Finotelli 2007).

9 All these direct measures were formulated as recommendations by the European Commission as early as 1995-1996. See recommendations of 22/12/95 and 27/09/96.

10 The E-VERIFY system in the US allows, for example, any employer to determine the eligibility of their new employees to work in the United States.

11 The amount of the incentive can hardly be generous. In addition to budgetary constraints, there are political limits. No matter how expensive the alternatives may be, the provision of a substantial incentive would be interpreted by many sectors of the public as an unjust reward for having broken the rules.

12 The available data are far from adequate. For Europe, the main source of data is provided in a report by the Centre d'étude de Gestion Démographique pour les Administrations Publiques and the Berlin Institute for Comparative Social Research (2008), that includes the main control data, including apprehensions and removals, for 2003. More recent data are available on the website of the European Migration Network (http://emn.sarenet.es/). A problem with all these data is that they often conflate irregular migrants (detected while they were crossing the border or in its vicinity) and irregular immigrants (detected in the territory after a certain spell of residence). Even so, the available evidence supports this claim.

13 Rarely, the adjustment of status may also be part of 'rewarding legislation' for irregular immigrants who cooperate with authorities in identifying smugglers or exploiters (Rijpma and Pastore 2009). In some other cases, adjustment of status is a way to deal with the conclusion of previous toleration measures and the legal or practical difficulties in enforcing mandatory return.

14 The exception is the United States, where individual adjustment is the prevailing practice.

15 This is likely to be a main reason why states that provide citizens with universal cash entitlements, such as Germany with the *soziale Hilfe*, are particularly critical of mass regularisations (Finotelli and Sciortino 2006).

References

Agamben, G. (1998), *Homo Sacer: Sovereign Power and Bare Life*. Stanford: Stanford University Press.

Alt, J. (2003), *Leben in der Schattenwelt: Problemkomplex illegale Migration*. Karlsruhe: Ariadne Buchdienst.

Andreas, P. and T. Snyder (eds) (2000), *The Wall around the West*. Lanham: Rowman and Littlefield.

Baganha, M. (1998), 'Immigrant involvement in the informal economy: The Portugese case', *Journal of Ethnic and Migration Studies* 24 (2): 367-386.

Baldwin-Edwards, M. and A. Kraler (2009), *Regine: Regularisation in Europe*. Amsterdam: Amstedam University Press.

Barbagli, M., A. Colombo and G. Sciortino (eds) (2004), *I sommersi e i sanati: Le regolarizzazioni degli immigrati*. Bologna: Il Mulino.

Batog, K. (2006), 'Immigration policy vs. labor policy: An analysis of the application of domestic labor laws to unauthorized foreign workers', *Loyola University Chicago International Law Review* 3: 117-34.

Belorgey, J.-M. (2008), 'Contagions de la clandestinité', *Social Science Information* 47 (4): 499-504.

Black, R. (2003), 'Breaking the convention: Researching the "illegal" migration of refugees to Europe', *Antipode* 35 (1): 34-50.

Black, R. and K. Koser (1999), *The End of the Refugee Circle?* Oxford: Berghahn.

Blaschke, J. (2008), 'Trends on regularisation of third country nationals in irregular situation of stay across the European Union', European Parliament Directorate-General Internal Policies, Policy Department C, Citizens Rights and Constitutional Affairs, PE 393.282.

Bocker, A., K. Groenendijk, T. Havinga and P. Minderhoud (eds) (1998), *Regulation of Migration: International Experiences*. Amsterdam: Het Spinhuis.

Bommes, M. (2003), 'The shrinking inclusive capacity of the national welfare state: International migration and the deregulation of identity formation', *Comparative Social Research* 22: 43-67.

Brochmann, G. and T. Hammar (1999), *Mechanisms of Immigration Control*. Oxford: Berg.

Broeders, D. (2009), *Breaking Down Anonymity: Digital Surveillance of Irregular Migrants in Germany and the Netherlands*. Amsterdam: Amsterdam University Press.

Caestecker, F. (2003), 'The transformation of nineteenth-century West European expulsion policy, 1800-1914', in: A. Fahrmeir, O. Faron and P. Weil (eds), *Migration Control in the North Atlantic World*, 120-137. Oxford: Berghahn.

Carens, J. (1987), 'Aliens and citizens: The case for open borders', *The Review of Politics* 29 (2): 251-273.

Carfagna, M. (2002), 'I sommersi e i sanati: Le regolarizzazioni degli immigrati in Italia', in A. Colombo and G. Sciortino (eds), *Stranieri in Italia: Assimilati ed Esclusi*, 53-91. Bologna: Il Mulino.

Castles, S. (2004), 'The factors that make and unmake migration policies', *International Migration Review* 38 (3): 852-884.

Centre d'étude de Gestion Démographique pour les Administrations Publiques and Berlin Institute for Comparative Social Research (2008), 'Migration and asylum in Europe 2003'. http://ec.europa.eu/justice_home/doc_centre/asylum/statistics/docs/2003/ 2003_annual_statistics_report.pdf. Accessed 20 November 2009.

CCMW (1974), *Illegal Migration*. Geneva: Churches Committee on Migrant Workers.

Cockburn, A. (1869), *Nationality: Or, the Law Relating to Subjects and Aliens*. London: W. Ridgeway.

Colombo, A. and G. Sciortino (2004), 'Semir, il questore e la sardina: Rappresentazioni delle sanatorie sulle pagine de "La Repubblica"', in: M. Barbagli, A. Colombo and G. Sciortino (eds), *I Sommersi e i Sanati: Le Regolarizzazioni degli Immigrati in Italia*, 223-261. Bologna: Il Mulino.

Cornelius, W., P. Martin and J. Hollifield (1994), *Controlling Immigration: A Global Perspective*. Stanford: Stanford University Press.

Council of the European Union (2000), 'Initiative of the French Republic with a view to the adoption of a council directive defining the facilitation of unauthorised entry, movement and residence', *Official Journal of the European Communities* C253: 1-2.

Coutin, S. (2000), *Legalizing Moves: Salvadorean Immigrants' Struggle for US Residency.* Ann Arbor: University of Michigan Press.

Cvajner, M. (2008), *Emigrazione e cambiamenti nella vita sentimentale e sessuale delle donne: Uno studio sulle migranti dall'Europa orientale.* Trento: Universita' di Trento.

Cvajner, M. and G. Sciortino (2010), 'A tale of networks and policies: Varieties of irregular migration careers and their evolutionary paths', *Population, Space and Place* 16 (3): 210-225.

De Bruycker, P. (ed.) (2000), *Regularisations of Illegal Immigrants in the European Union.* Brussels: Bruylant.

De Genova, N. (2007), *Working the Boundaries: Race, Space and 'Illegality' in Mexican Chicago.* Durham: Duke University Press.

De Genova, N. (2002), 'Migrant "illegality" and deportability in everyday life', *Annual Review of Anthropology* 31: 419-447.

Diaz, S. (2004), *"Clandestinos", "Illegales", "Espontaneos"... La Emigracion Irregular de Espanoles a Alemania en el Contexto de las Relaciones Hispano-Alemanas, 1960-1973.* Madrid: Comision Espanola de Historia de las Relaciones Internacionales.

Diminescu, D. (ed.) (2003), *Visible Mais peu Nobreaux: Les Circulations Migratoires Roumaines.* Paris: Editions de la Maison des sciences de l'homme.

Engbersen, G. (2003), 'The wall around the welfare state in Europe: International migration and social exclusion', *Indian Journal of Labour Economics* 46 (3): 479-495.

Engbersen, G. (2001), 'The unanticipated consequences of panopticon Europe: Residence strategies of illegal immigrants', in: V. Guiraudon and C. Joppke (eds), *Controlling a New Migration World,* 222-246. London: Routledge.

Engbersen, G. and D. Broders (2009), 'The state versus the alien: Immigration control and strategies of irregular immigrants', *West European Politics* 32 (5): 867-885.

Engbersen, G. and J. van der Leun (2001), 'The social construction of illegality and criminality', *European Journal of Criminal Policy and Research* 9: 51-70.

Fahrmeir, A. (2000), *Citizens and Aliens: Foreigners and the Law in Britain and the German States, 1789-1870.* Oxford: Berghahn.

Fahrmeir, A., O. Faron and P. Weil (2003), *Migration Control in the North Atlantic World.* Oxford: Berghahn.

Finotelli, C. (2007), *Illegale Einwanderung, Flüchtlingsmigration und das Ende des Nord-Süd-Mythos: Zur funktionalen Äquivalenz des deutschen und des italienischen Einwanderungsregimes.* Münster: LIT.

Finotelli, C. and G. Sciortino (2006), 'Looking for the European soft underbelly: Visa policies and amnesties for irregular migrants in Germany and in Italy', in: S. Baringhorst, F. Hollifield and U. Hunger (eds), *Herausforderung Migration: Perspektiven der vergleichenden Politikwissenschaft.* Berlin: LIT.

Gordon, D.A. (2003), '"Il est recommandé aux étrangers de ne pas participer": Les étrangers expulsés en mai-jun 1968', *Migrations Societé* 15 (87-88): 45-65.

Hardt, M. and A. Negri (2000), *Empire.* Cambridge (MA): Harvard University Press.

Henckaerts, J.-M. (1995), *Mass Expulsion in Modern International Law and Practice.* Leiden: Martinus Nijhoff.

Hollifield, J. (2006), 'The emerging migration state', *International Migration Review* 38 (3): 885-912.

Hollifield, J. (2000), 'The politics of international migration', in: C. Brettell and J. Hollifield (eds), *Migration Theory: Talking Across Disciplines,* 137-186. New York: Routledge.

Hollifield, J. (1996), 'The migration crisis in Western Europe: The search for a national model', in: K. Bade (ed.) *Migration, Ethnizität, Konflikt*, 367-402. Osnabrück: Universitätsverlag Rasch.

Hollifield, J. (1992), *Immigrants, Markets and States: The Political Economy of Postwar Europe*. Cambridge (MA): Harvard University Press.

Hutton, T. and J. Williamson (2005), *Global Migration and the World Economy*. Cambridge (MA): MIT Press.

ILO (2009), *Regularization and Employer Sanctions as Means Towards the Effective Governance of Labour Migration*. Geneva: International Labour Organization.

Irek, M. (1994), *Der Schmugglerzug: Warschau Berlin Warschau – Materialien einer Feldforschung*. Berlin: Das Arabische Buch.

Johnson, K. (2005), 'Driver's licenses and undocumented immigrants: The future of civil rights law', *Nevada Law Journal* 213.

Joppke, C. (2005), *Selecting by Origin: Ethnic Migration in the Liberal State*. Cambridge (MA): Harvard University Press.

Joppke, C. (2003), 'Citizenship between de- and re-ethnicization', *Archives Européennes de Sociologie* 44 (3).

Joppke, C. (1999), 'The domestic legal sources of immigrants rights: The United States, Germany and the European Union'. Working Paper SPS 99/3. Firenze: European University Institute.

Joppke, C. (1998), 'Why liberal states accept unwanted immigration', *World Politics* 50 (2): 266-293.

Jordan, B. and F. Duvell (2002), *Irregular Migration: The Dilemmas of Transnational Mobility*. Cheltenham: Edward Elgar Publishing.

Kadokura, T. (2007), 'Where will the underground economy go from here?' *The Japanese Economy* 34 (2): 111-119.

Leenders, M. (1995), 'From inclusion to exclusion: Refugees and immigrants in Italy between 1861 and 1943', *Immigrants and Minorities* 14: 115-138.

Levinson, A. (2005). *The Regularisation of Unauthorized Migrants: Literature Survey and Country Case Studies*. Oxford: COMPAS.

Lucassen, L. (1997), 'Eternal vagrants? State formation, migration and travelling groups in Western Europe, 1350-1914', in: J. Lucassen and L. Lucassen, *Migration, Migration History, History: Old Paradigms and New Perspectives*, 225-251. Berne: Peter Lang.

Marie, C. (1988), 'Entre économie et politique: le "clandestin" une figure social a geometrie variable', *Pouvoirs* 47: 45-92.

Martin, P. and M. Miller (2000), *Employer Sanctions: French, German and US Experiences*. Geneva: International Labour Organization.

Massey, D., J. Durand and N. Malone (2002), *Beyond Smoke and Mirrors: Mexican Immigration in an Era of Economic Integration*. New York: Russell Sage Foundation.

Morawska, E. (2001), 'Gappy immigration control, resourceful migrants and pendel communities', in: V. Guiraudon and C. Joppke (eds), *Controlling a New Migration World*, 173-199. London: Routledge.

Morokvasic, M. (1994), 'Pendeln statt auswandern: Das Beispiel der Polen', in M. Morokvasic and R. Hedwig (eds), *Wanderungsraum Europa: Menschen und Grenzen in Bewegung*, 166-187. Berlin: Sigma.

Nascimbene, B. (ed.) (2002), *Expulsion and Detention of Aliens in the European Union*. Milan: Giuffrè.

Ngai, M. (2004), *Impossible Subject: Illegal Aliens and the Making of Modern America*. Princeton: Princeton University Press.

OECD (1990), *Comparative Analysis of Regularisation Experience in France, Italy, Spain and the United States*. Paris: Organisation of Economic Co-operation and Development.

Ohliger, R., K. Schonwalder and T. Triadafilopoulos (eds) (2003), *European Encounters: Migrants, Migration and European Societies since 1945*. Aldershot: Ashgate.

Passel, J. (2007), 'Unauthorized migrants in the United States: Estimates, methods and characteristics', OECD Social, Employment and Migration Working Papers 57. Paris: Organisation of Economic Co-operation and Development.

Passel, J. and D. Cohn (2009), *A Portrait of Unauthorized Immigrants in the United States*. Washington, DC: Pew Hispanic Center.

Passel, J. and D. Cohn (2008), *Trends in Unauthorized Immigration: Undocumented Inflow Now Trails Legal Inflow*. Washington, DC: Pew Hispanic Center.

Pastore, F. (1998), 'L'obbligo di riammissione in diritto internazionale: Sviluppi recenti', *Rivista di diritto internazionale* 81 (4): 973-994.

Plender, R. (1998), *International Migration Law*, Revised 2nd ed. Dordrecht: Martinus Nijhoff Publishers.

Plender, R. (1972), *International Migration Law*. Leiden: A.W. Sijthoff.

Portes, A. (1977), 'Labor functions of illegal aliens', *Society* 14: 31-37.

Reinecke, C. (2009), 'Governing aliens in times of upheaval: Immigration control and modern state practice in early twentieth-century Britain, compared with Prussia', *International Review of Social History* 54: 39-65.

Reyneri, E. (1998), 'The role of the underground economy in irregular migration to Italy: Cause or effect?', *Journal of Ethnic and Migration Studies* 24 (2): 313-331.

Rijpma, J. and F. Pastore (2009), *Review of Current International Approaches with Regard to Regularisation and Disincentives for the Employment of Irregular Migrant Workers. Regularisation and Employer Sanctions as Means towards the Effective Governance of Labour Migration*. Geneva: International Labour Organization.

Roche, T. (1969), *The Key in the Lock: Immigration Control in England from 1066 to the Present Day*. London: John Murray.

Sainsbury, D. (2006), 'Immigrants' social rights in comparative perspective: Welfare regimes, forms of immigration and immigration policy regimes', *Journal of Social Policy* 16 (3): 229-244.

Samers, M. (2003), 'Invisible capitalism: Political economy and the regulation of undocumented immigration in France', *Economy and Society* 32 (4): 555-583.

Sciortino, G. (2009), *Fortunes and Miseries of Italian Labour Migration Policy*. Rome: CeSPI.

Sciortino, G. (2000), *L'ambizione della Frontiera: Le Politiche di Controllo Migratorio in Europa*. Milan: FrancoAngeli.

Sciortino, G. (2004), 'Between phantoms and necessary evils: Some critical points in the study of irregular migrations to Western Europe', *IMIS-Beiträge* 24: 17-44.

Scott, J. (1998), *Seeing Like a State*. New Haven: Yale University Press.

Tapinos, G. (2000a), 'Illegal immigrants and the labor market'. February, *OECD Observer*. Paris: Organisation of Economic Co-operation and Development.

Tapinos, G. (2000b), 'Irregular migration: Economic and political issues', in: *Combating the Employment of Illegal Immigrant Workers*. Paris: Organisation of Economic Co-operation and Development.

Torpey, J. (2000), *The Invention of the Passport: Surveillance, Citizenship and the State*. Cambridge: Cambridge University Press.

Torpey, J. (1998), 'Coming and going: On the state monopolization of the legitimate "means of movement"', *Sociological Theory* 18 (3): 239-259.

Van der Leun, J. (2003), *Looking for Loopholes: Processes of Incorporation of Illegal Immigrants in the Netherlands*. Amsterdam: Amsterdam University Press.

Vasta, E. (2006), *The Paper Market: 'Borrowing' and 'Renting' of Identity Documents*. Oxford: COMPAS.

Von Bosse, P. (1839), 'Einwanderung', in: J.S. Ersch and J.G. Gruber (eds), *Allgemeine Encyclopedie der Wissenschaften und Kuenste Vol. 32*, 374-76. Leipzig: Gleditsch.

Zolberg, A. (1987), 'Wanted but not welcome: Alien labor in western development', in: W. Alonso (ed.), *Population in an Interacting World*, 36-73. Cambridge (MA): Harvard University Press.

Zolberg, A. (1990), 'Reforming the back door: The Immigration Reform and Control Act of 1986 in historical perspective', in: Y. McLaughlin (ed.), *Immigration Reconsidered*, 315-339. New York: Oxford University Press.

Zolberg, A. (1999), 'Matters of State: Theorizing Immigration Policy', in C. Hirschman, P. Kasinitz and J. DeWind (eds), *The Handbook of International Migration: The American Experience*, 71-93. New York: Russell Sage Foundation.

Zolberg, A. (2003), 'The archaeology of "Remote Control"', in: A. Fahrmeir, O. Faron and P. Weil (eds), *Migration Control in the North Atlantic World*, 195-222. Oxford: Berghahn.

About the Authors

Ahmet Akgündüz obtained his PhD in social sciences from the University of Amsterdam. From 1993 to 2010, he was affiliated with the Institute for Migration and Ethnic Studies (IMES), University of Amsterdam. Since 2010, he has been a research fellow at IMES and a lecturer at the Faculty of Economics and Administrative Sciences of Izmir University, Turkey. He is author of the book *Labour Migration from Turkey to Western Europe, 1960-1974: A Multidisciplinary Analysis* (2008). Akgündüz is currently working on two projects: The Labour Market, Guest Worker System and Employment of Foreign Workers in Post-War Europe and The Cold War and Immigration: Immigration of Bulgarian Turks to Turkey, 1950-1990.

Monica Boyd is a professor at the University of Toronto and holds the Canada Research Chair in Immigration, Inequality and Public Policy. She has written numerous articles, books and monographs on the changing family, gender inequality, international migration policy, immigrant economic integration, immigrant women and ethnic stratification. Her present research focuses on immigrant offspring, including the 'one-and-a-half' and second generations, immigrant language skills, labour market integration, the migration of highly skilled labour and immigrant re-accreditation difficulties. She currently is associate editor of *International Migration Review* and member of the editorial board of the *American Sociological Review.*

Stephen Castles is Research Professor of Sociology at the University of Sydney and Research Associate of the International Migration Institute (IMI), University of Oxford. He works on international migration dynamics, social transformation and migration and development. His recent books include *The Age of Migration: International Population Movements in the Modern World* (2009); *Migration and Development: Perspectives from the South* (2008); and *Migration, Citizenship and the European Welfare State: A European Dilemma* (2006).

Allan Findlay is Professor of Geography at the University of St Andrews, Scotland. He previously held appointments at the University of Glasgow and the University of Dundee, and was a research associate at the International Labour Office and visiting professor at the University of Umeå in Sweden. He is Chair of the International Geographical Union's Commission on Population Geography and co-editor of the journal *Population, Space and Place*. His main research interest is production migration. Recent projects include international student mobility, the role of 'escalator regions' in shaping internal migration processes and methods of forecasting migration, including environmentally linked movement.

François Gemenne is an FNRS fellow with the Centre for Ethnic and Migration Studies (CEDEM) at the University of Liège and associate fellow with the Institute for Sustainable Development and International Relations (IDDRI) at Sciences Po in Paris. He holds a PhD in political science. Gemenne's research interests include environmental migration, the geopolitics of climate change and the control of migration and the obstacles to free movement. He teaches subjects pertaining to migration and the environment at Sciences Po Paris, the University of Liège and the Free University of Brussels. In 2010, he was awarded the ISDT-Wernaers Prize for achievement in the communication of science to the general public.

Elspeth Guild is Jean Monnet Professor ad personam of European Immigration Law at Radboud University, Nijmegen (Netherlands) and Professor of Law at Queen Mary University of London. She has published widely on the subject of borders, immigration and asylum in Europe. Her most recent monograph is *Security and Migration in the 21st Century* (2009). She is a frequent adviser to EU institutions on free movement of persons.

Maria Ilies is Policy Analyst at the European Commission, DG Employment, Social Affairs and Inclusion, where she works on the development, management, monitoring and evaluation of policies in the field of social inclusion. Prior to joining the Commission in 2011, she worked at Erasmus University Rotterdam and the University of Leiden as a researcher in the field of migration.

Russell King is Professor of Geography at the University of Sussex and Willy Brandt Guest Professor in Migration Studies at Malmö University, Sweden. He is the founding director of the Sussex Centre for Migration Research and, since 2000, editor of the *Journal of Ethnic and Migration Studies*. His interests in the field of migration range from labour migration and return migration to lifestyle migration and international student mobility. He has carried out empirical research on migration processes in various parts of the world, but has a special interest in Europe, especially Southern Europe and the Balkans.

Aimee Kuvik is a PhD candidate at the Amsterdam Institute for Social Science Research (AISSR) and Institute for Migration and Ethnic Studies (IMES) at the University of Amsterdam. Her research explores the concept of the global competition for talent, theoretically and empirically, using as an example the life sciences sector in Europe. She was a Fulbright scholar at Vilnius University in 2008-2009 and the Swedish Institute guest scholar at REMESO in Norrköping in 2009-2010. She is co-editor of the book, *Mobility in Transition: Migration Patterns after EU Enlargement*, which includes analyses of skills and mobility from Central and Eastern European countries.

Marco Martiniello is Research Director at the Belgian National Fund for Scientific Research (FRS-FNRS) and teaches sociology and politics at the University of Liège. He is the Director of the Centre for Ethnic and Migration Studies (CEDEM) at that university. He also teaches at the College of Europe (Natolin, Poland). He is member of the executive board of the IMISCOE Research Network (International Migration and Social Cohesion in Europe) and President of the Research Committee n°31 Sociology of Migration (International Sociological Association). He has authored, edited or co-edited numerous books, chapters, articles and reports on migration, ethnicity, racism, multiculturalism and citizenship in the European Union and in Belgium, with a transatlantic comparative perspective. They include *Citizenship in European Cities* (2004); *Migration between States and Markets* (2004); *The Transnational Political Participation of Immigrants: A Transatlantic Perspective* (2009); *Selected Studies in International Migration and Immigrant Incorporation* (2010); and *La Démocratie Multiculturelle* (2011).

Ewa Morawska is Professor of Sociology at the University of Essex. She specialises in comparative-historical studies of international migration and ethnicity in Europe and the United States. Her recent publications include *Studying International Migration in the Long(er) and Short(er) Duree: Contesting Some and Reconciling Other Disagreements between the Structuration and Morphogenesis Theories* (2011); *'Diaspora' Diasporas' Imaginations of the Homeland: Exploring the Polymorphs* (2011); *Ethnicity as a Primordial-Situational-Constructed Experience: Different Times, Different Places, Different Constellations* (2011); *A Sociology of Immigration: (Re)Making Multifaceted America* (2009); and

[Im]migration and Ethnic Research Agendas in Europe and the United States: A Comparison (2008).

Joanne Nowak is a doctoral candidate in sociology at the University of Toronto, where her research combines network analysis with professions research to illuminate the social context of nurse emigration from Ghana. Her general research interests include the intersection between international migration and development, gender and migration issues and migration and immigration policy, as well as the politics of migration. She is the co-author of several book chapters and articles on migrant women, and has presented at conferences in both Canada and the United States.

Eva Østergaard-Nielsen is Associate Professor of the Department of Political Science at the Autonomous University of Barcelona. She holds degrees in anthropology and political science from Copenhagen University and a PhD in politics from the University of Oxford, St Antony's College. Her research interests include the politics of migration in both the receiving and sending countries, transnational networks and forms of political participation and citizenship by migrants and various types of non-state individuals. She has published widely on these issues in books, edited volumes and journals such as *Global Networks*, the *Journal of Ethnic and Migration Studies*, and *Ethnic and Racial Studies*.

Dragos Radu is a visiting lecturer in economics at King's College, London and a research fellow of the Hamburg Institute of International Economics (HWWI). Before joining King's he was a research fellow at the Policy Studies Institute and a member of the EU Marie Curie Excellence Grant research team for the project, Expanding the Knowledge Base of European Migration Policies (2004-2008) at the University of Edinburgh.

Jan Rath is Professor of Urban Sociology and Head of the Department of Sociology and Anthropology at the University of Amsterdam. At that same university, he is a member of the Institute for Migration and Ethnic Studies (IMES) and the Centre for Urban Studies, as well as European Chair of International Metropolis. An anthropologist and urban studies specialist, Rath has authored, edited or co-edited numerous books, chapters, articles and reports on the sociology, politics and economics of post-migration processes. These include *Immigrant Businesses: The Economic, Political and Social Environment* (2000); *Unravelling the Rag Trade: Immigrant Entrepreneurship in Seven World Cities* (2002); *Immigrant Entrepreneurs: Venturing Abroad in the Age of*

Globalization (2003); *Tourism, Ethnic Diversity, and the City* (2007); *Ethnic Amsterdam* (2009); *Selected Studies in International Migration and Immigrant Incorporation* (2010); and *Selling Ethnic Neighborhoods* (2012).

Giuseppe Sciortino teaches sociology at the Università di Trento, Italy. His main research interests are migration studies, social theory and cultural sociology. Among his recent works are *Great Minds: Encounters with Social Theory* (2011) and *Foggy Social Structures: Irregular Migration, European Labour Markets and the Welfare State* (2011).

Thomas Straubhaar is Director of the Hamburg Institute of International Economics (HWWI) and Professor of Economics at the University of Hamburg. His special area of research is international economic relations. He has published extensively on migration, remittances and migration policymaking, and was a member of the Expert Council of German Foundations on Integration and Migration.

Joanne van der Leun is Professor of Criminology at the University of Leiden Law School, and is programme director and teacher of the criminology bachelor's and master's programme. Her principal areas of research have been in criminology and sociology, covering topics such as crime and migration in the urban context and migration policies in practice. In 2001 she received her PhD from Erasmus University Rotterdam. Her dissertation, *Looking for Loopholes: Processes of Incorporation of Illegal Immigrants in the Netherlands*, was published in 2003 by the Amsterdam University Press. She publishes on migration and crime, international illegal migration, processes of incorporation of migrants, urban problems and crimmigration.

Eftihia Voutira is Professor of Anthropology of Forced Migration at the Department of Balkan, Slavonic and Oriental Studies, University of Macedonia, Thessaloniki, Greece. She received her BA in philosophy at the University of Chicago, her MA and PhD at Harvard University and her MPhil and PhD in social anthropology at the University of Cambridge. Key works include *Conflict Resolution: A Cautionary Tale* (1995); *Anthropology in International Humanitarian Emergencies* (1994); *Anthropology* (1998); *Between Past and Present: Ethnographies of the Postsocialist World* (2007); and *The Right to Return and the Meaning of Home: A Post Soviet Diaspora Becoming European?* (2011).

IMISCOE Research titles

Marek Okólski (ed.)
European Immigrations: Trends, Structures and Policy Implications
2012 ISBN 978 90 8964 457 2

Ulbe Bosma (ed.)
Post-Colonial Immigrants and Identity Formations in the Netherlands
2012 ISBN 978 90 8964 454 1

Christina Boswell and Gianni D'Amato (eds)
Immigration and Social Systems: Collected Essays of Michael Bommes
2012 ISBN 978 90 8964 453 4

Maurice Crul, Jens Schneider and Frans Lelie (eds)
The European Second Generation Compared: Does the Integration Context Matter?
2012 ISBN 978 90 8964 443 5

Bram Lancee
Immigrant Performance in the Labour Market: Bonding and Bridging Social Capital
2012 ISBN 978 90 8964 357 5

Julie Vullnetari
Albania on the Move: Links between Internal and International Migration
2012 ISBN 978 90 8964 355 1

Blanca Garcés-Mascareñas
State Regulation of Labour Migration in Malaysia and Spain: Markets, Citizenship and Rights
2012 ISBN 978 90 8964 286 8

Albert Kraler, Eleonore Kofman, Martin Kohli and Camille Schmoll (eds)
Gender, Generations and the Family in International Migration
2012 ISBN 978 90 8964 285 1

Giovanna Zincone, Rinus Penninx and Maren Borkert (eds)
Migration Policymaking in Europe: The Dynamics of Actors and Contexts in Past and Present
2011 ISBN 978 90 8964 370 4

Michael Bommes and Giuseppe Sciortino (eds)
Foggy Social Structures: Irregular Migration, European Labour Markets and the Welfare State
2011 ISBN 978 90 8964 341 4

Peter Scholten
Framing Immigrant Integration: Dutch Research-Policy Dialogues in Comparative Perspective
2011 ISBN 978 90 8964 284 4

Liza Mügge
Beyond Dutch Borders: Transnational Politics among Colonial Migrants, Guest Workers and the Second Generation
2010 ISBN 978 90 8964 244 8

Rainer Bauböck and Thomas Faist (eds)
Diaspora and Transnationalism: Concepts, Theories and Methods
2010 ISBN 978 90 8964 238 7

Cédric Audebert and Mohamed Kamel Dorai (eds)
Migration in a Globalised World: New Research Issues and Prospects
2010 ISBN 978 90 8964 157 1

Richard Black, Godfried Engbersen, Marek Okólski and Cristina Pantîru (eds)
A Continent Moving West? EU Enlargement and Labour Migration from Central and Eastern Europe
2010 ISBN 978 90 8964 156 4

Charles Westin, José Bastos, Janine Dahinden and Pedro Góis (eds)
Identity Processes and Dynamics in Multi-Ethnic Europe
2010 ISBN 978 90 8964 046 8

Rainer Bauböck, Bernhard Perchinig and Wiebke Sievers (eds)
Citizenship Policies in the New Europe: Expanded and Updated Edition
2009 ISBN 978 90 8964 108 3

Gianluca P. Parolin
Citizenship in the Arab World: Kin, Religion and Nation-State
2009 ISBN 978 90 8964 045 1

Maurice Crul and Liesbeth Heering (eds)
The Position of the Turkish and Moroccan Second Generation in Amsterdam and Rotterdam: The TIES Study in the Netherlands
2008 ISBN 978 90 8964 061 1

Marlou Schrover, Joanne van der Leun, Leo Lucassen and Chris Quispel (eds)
Illegal Migration and Gender in a Global and Historical Perspective
2008 ISBN 978 90 8964 047 5

Corrado Bonifazi, Marek Okólski, Jeannette Schoorl and Patrick Simon (eds)
International Migration in Europe: New Trends and New Methods of Analysis
2008 ISBN 978 90 5356 894 1

Ralph Grillo (ed.)
The Family in Question: Immigrant and Ethnic Minorities in Multicultural Europe
2008 ISBN 978 90 5356 869 9

Holger Kolb and Henrik Egbert (eds)
Migrants and Markets: Perspectives from Economics and the Other Social Sciences
2008 ISBN 978 90 5356 684 8

Veit Bader
Secularism or Democracy? Associational Governance of Religious Diversity
2007 ISBN 978 90 5356 999 3

Rainer Bauböck, Bernhard Perchinig and Wiebke Sievers (eds)
Citizenship Policies in the New Europe
2007 ISBN 978 90 5356 922 1

Rainer Bauböck, Eva Ersbøll, Kees Groenendijk and Harald Waldrauch (eds)
Acquisition and Loss of Nationality: Policies and Trends in 15 European Countries
Volume 1: Comparative Analyses
2006 ISBN 978 90 5356 920 7
Volume 2: Country Analyses
2006 ISBN 978 90 5356 921 4

Leo Lucassen, David Feldman and Jochen Oltmer (eds)
Paths of Integration: Migrants in Western Europe (1880-2004)
2006 ISBN 978 90 5356 883 5

Rinus Penninx, Maria Berger and Karen Kraal (eds)
The Dynamics of International Migration and Settlement in Europe: A State of the Art
2006 ISBN 978 90 5356 866 8

IMISCOE Textbooks

Marco Martiniello and Jan Rath (eds)
Selected Studies in International Migration and Immigrant Incorporation (Vol. 1)
2010 ISBN 978 90 8964 160 1

Marco Martiniello and Jan Rath (eds)
An Introduction to International Migration Studies: European Perspectives (Vol. 2)
2012 ISBN 978 90 8964 456 5